The Overman
in the Marketplace

The Overman
in the Marketplace

Nietzschean Heroism in
Popular Culture

Ishay Landa

LEXINGTON BOOKS
A division of

ROWMAN & LITTLEFIELD PUBLISHERS, INC.
Lanham • Boulder • New York • Toronto • Plymouth, UK

LEXINGTON BOOKS

A division of Rowman & Littlefield Publishers, Inc.
A wholly owned subsidiary of The Rowman & Littlefield Publishing Group, Inc.
4501 Forbes Boulevard, Suite 200
Lanham, MD 20706

Estover Road
Plymouth PL6 7PY
United Kingdom

British Library Cataloguing in Publication Information Available

Library of Congress Cataloging-in-Publication Data

Landa, Ishay, 1969–
  The overman in the marketplace : Nietzschean heroism in popular culture /
Ishay Landa.
      p. cm.
  Includes bibliographical references (p.   ).
  ISBN-13: 978-0-7391-1985-3 (cloth : alk. paper)
  ISBN-10: 0-7391-1985-0 (cloth : alk. paper)
  1. Nietzsche, Friedrich Wilhelm, 1844–1900. 2. Heroes. 3. Hero worship. 4.
Popular culture. I. Title.
  B3317.L2655 2007
  193—dc22   2007017520

Printed in the United States of America

♾™ The paper used in this publication meets the minimum requirements of
American National Standard for Information Sciences—Permanence of Paper for
Printed Library Materials, ANSI/NISO Z39.48–1992.

To the memory of my beloved mother, Beatriz.

When Zarathustra came into the nearest town lying on the edge of the forest, he found many people gathered in the marketplace, since it had been promised that a tightrope walker would perform. And thus spoke Zarathustra to the people: "I teach you the Overman . . ."

—Nietzsche, *Thus Spoke Zarathustra*

Contents

Acknowledgments

In writing this book, I have enjoyed the assistance, encouragement and support of numerous people; the following list is inevitably incomplete.

I am greatly indebted to Adi Parush, from whose erudition, generosity, and unshakable support I have profoundly benefited. I wish to thank Ilana Krausman Ben-Amos, James South and Bernhard Taureck, for their inestimable encouragement. Greatly valuable commentary, suggestions and assistance I have received from my brother Aaron. I also wish to thank, for their love, Oded, Einav, Neta, Gabriel Diego and Amir Yehuda.

I would like to express my gratitude to the Kreitman Foundation for the generous scholarship without which this work could never have been completed.

I wish to thank Lexington Books, in particular Patrick Dillon, for the dedicated work put into the publication of this book.

Very special thanks to Luis, my father. Everything that I may say will fall short of doing justice to the wisdom, inspiration, dedication, constructive criticism and support he has given me. This work is but a modest tribute to the Marxist humanism, the down-to-earth utopianism, and the critical populism, which he, tenderly, instilled in me. *To be radical is to grasp things by the root. But for man the root is man himself.*

Finally, my profound love and gratitude to Maria, whose warm companionship, lucid advice, unwavering faith and abiding affection have sustained me. *Wann, wenn nicht jetzt? Wo, wenn nicht hier? Wie, wenn ohne Liebe? Wer, wenn nicht wir?*

Introduction:
The Hero as Social Metaphor

In the field of popular culture a struggle takes place involving different conceptions of heroism. These representations bear considerable ideological weight, as they regularly imply a hierarchy, a social complex of rights and duties, constructed in accordance with the hero's virtues. The hierarchies that emanate from the heroic narrative may suit the existing social order, thus turning into its ideological vindication, or they may contradict it and entail the need for its amendment, even reversal, until a new order is formed which accommodates the rights of the hero. Hence, however displaced in escapist surroundings, the hero remains a social metaphor.

Two essential propositions stand at the basis of the discussion. The first is that in the transition from the nineteenth century to the twentieth, there emerges a new heroic model in the realm of popular culture, taking its place alongside previous types. The second claim is that a determinant factor in bringing about this model is the root striking of ideas, of a cultural climate, which can be broadly defined as Nietzschean. As a counter-force to the humanistic, realistic and materialistic spirit, which, from about the mid-sixteenth century and the beginning of the ascendance of the bourgeoisie, had fostered a protagonist embedded in society, instructed and limited by it, the twentieth century advances and culminates a new heroic 'challenge' that emphasizes unique individualism, competition and amorality. Taking on the nineteenth-century romantic rebellion against realism, yet transforming the revolutionary character of the early Byronic rebel, the Nietzschean hero becomes a crusader against the perceived leveling down of mass society. Whereas the bourgeoisie in its revolutionary phase, playing its self-ordained role as the 'universal class' that represents the plight of 'the people' against tyranny, had enthusiastically embraced the 'mediocre hero' of Walter Scott,

1

this realistic middleman which served, à la Hegel, to confirm the *greatness of history* rather than that of the individual, the post-revolutionary *hegemonic bourgeoisie* (post 1848, that is) was increasingly seeking to resuscitate-cum-cultivate heroic patterns which will confirm mass inertia vis-à-vis individual genius. Thus the realistic hero—and even Dumas's 'glamorous' musketeers, once revisited, appear as *picaros* and gutsy buffoons rather than superheroes, with their motto of solidarity, *un pour tous, tous pour un,* and taking their clue from the social 'comedies' of Balzac, himself a famous follower of Scott—is ousted in favor of a neo-aristocratic hero who roams beyond good and evil, no longer bound to a universalistic mission, in fact doing all he can to repel the rising tides of egalitarianism.

Western culture in the twentieth century, I maintain, is saturated with Nietzschean motifs which, internalized, have become an immanent component of the system of beliefs, attitudes and ideologies that form this culture. Nietzscheanism, much like social Darwinism, psychoanalytic theory or Marxism, is a comprehensive discourse, ethical, aesthetic and social, with its own distinct terminology and set of ideologemes. In that sense, it would perhaps be correct to claim that the greater part of those who 'think Nietzsche'—that is, take an outlook on the world from an emotional, ethical, aesthetic or social vantage point which is Nietzschean—do so without being aware of the fact. As Stanley Rosen had stated, 'in apparent contradiction to Nietzsche's own assertion that he does not write for the mob, his doctrines have been disseminated throughout the general public, and not the least among people who have never heard of his name or read a page of his voluminous writings.'[1] This is similar to the way in which one needs not be familiar with the writings of Darwin, Marx, or Freud in order to understand society as a permanent struggle whereby the fittest survive, to think 'Marxian,' or to explain people's behavior by referring to repressed sexual energy. Unlikely apostles of a Nietzschean outlook, though highly effective ones in disseminating Nietzschean creeds among the general public, are such heroes of popular culture as Tarzan, Howard Roark, James Bond and Hannibal Lecter.

In his classic study of the archetypal hero in world mythologies, Joseph Campbell provides a useful definition of the hero:

> The composite hero of the monomyth is a personage of exceptional gifts. Frequently he is honored by his society, frequently unrecognized or disdained. He and/or the world in which he finds himself suffers from a symbolic deficiency.[2]

Campbell's apposite characterization captures the sense in which heroic narratives are structurally (and were from times immemorial) stories about society, in which a social conflict, a 'symbolic deficiency,' is being addressed. To be sure, as Fredric Jameson has influentially claimed, literature *as such* is a 'socially symbolic act,' every narrative being informed by what he termed 'the political unconscious.'[3] Yet heroic narratives, revolving around 'a personage of exceptional gifts' who is engaged in fierce struggles *for* or *against* his society, to maintain its structure or to change it, provide a particularly powerful means of dramatizing social problems, a shortcut to the heart of the 'symbolic deficiency' that needs resolving. The perceived hero, whether 'true,' that is historically existing person (examples would be Caesar, Napoleon, 'Che' Guevara), imaginary (Gilgamesh, Hercules, Siegfried or Superman) or *imagined as true* (as in the case of such half-historical, half-mythical figures as Moses, Samson, Jesus or El Cid), is an immensely convenient vehicle for a melodramatic account of a crisis affecting a given society, community, or national collective. The story of the hero often serves to represent, define, and indeed *create* the values and norms of a given collective—as in the case of Jeanne d'Arc for French nationalism, or Robin Hood's role as a locus of Saxon pride and resistance to the Norman elite. He/she can be an hierarchic symbol, vouching for deference and cohesion, as well as an insurrectionary role model, defying the powers that be. The symbolic importance invested in heroes can explain the passionate and ongoing historical debates about the significance of given figures, say Napoleon Bonaparte, who has been a hero for both radicals and conservatives, in and outside France. In cases where the sociopolitical significance as well as national allegiance of the hero is less debatable—William Wallace, Lenin, Mussolini, Ben-Gurion, Nasser—the glorified hero of a given camp will become the villain for the opposing camp, the hero becoming a 'madman,' a 'tyrant,' a 'conqueror' or a 'terrorist.' For that reason, the erection, maintenance as well as *deconstruction* of heroic monuments is an ever prospering business involving such high stakes, politically, historiographically and culturally.

It is possible to interpret all cultural production in terms of clashing visions of heroes and of heroism, since even the *anti*-heroes of modernity are to a significant extent not only a refutation of former heroic ideals but also the formation of an heroic model in its own right, inasmuch as the anti-hero often becomes, precisely by dint of his weakness, mediocrity or even inferiority a vindication of the social values and interests of subaltern groups: a pertinent example would be Jaroslav Hašek's 'good soldier' Švejk, a national hero if ever there was one, who challenges the entire Austro-Hungarian army precisely from a position of smallness, nay idiocy:

> [Behind the table] sat a gentleman with a cold official face and features of such bestial cruelty that he might have just fallen out of Lombroso's book, *Criminal Types*.
> He gave Švejk a bloodthirsty look and said:
> 'Take that idiotic expression off your face.'

'I can't help it,' replied Švejk solemnly. 'I was discharged from the army for idiocy and officially certified by a special commission as an idiot. I'm an official idiot.'[4]

Notwithstanding the undeniable truth contained in the famous remark of Brecht's Galileo, that it is an unhappy land that needs heroes, admiration of heroic figures ought not, in and of itself, be considered a precarious, proto-fascist practice. Heroic narratives can, and often do, galvanize resistance to hegemonic discourses. Take the case of Muhammad Ali—according to the director Spike Lee one of the 'very few true heroes' of his age[5]—who, while an healthy and active prizefighter was reviled by the American establishment, particularly after his refusal to serve in Vietnam, but who has now become, in passivity and disease, something of an all-American hero. Shortly before taking on George Foreman in the celebrated 1974 fight in Zaire where he regained the world title after being politically banned from boxing, Ali has delivered, during one of his characteristically frolicsome press conferences, the following monologue, intriguing in the subversive way it conceives of heroism:

> *[Simulating a fight, Ali is jumping, throwing punches in the air and talking animatedly:]* I just got the power now; I mean I got a power that I've even not realized until after. . . . How did I do that? Allah, God, I'm his tool. For my people. This man looks slow. God has made this man look like a little kid. His so-called 'right hand' ain't nothing now. I don't even feel him. . . . I walk right in and take my shots. Because . . . I think about my people being free . . . Now he looks little in comparison to what I'm getting from it; he ain't nothing now. *[Ali abruptly stops bouncing and punching, takes a step back, assumes a scared, pensive expression, and continues his monologue, now with a lowered voice:]* But if I'm thinking about *me* and George Foreman who knocked out Joe Frazier, like *he* was God. . . . And the white press and the power structure rated me to get tired in 5 or 6. Then I go out like Norton against him and get scared. *[Reassumes his confident posture:]* But I'm not thinking about the world and what they say. My God controls the universe.[6]

The contrast drawn in this soliloquy is between two heroic discourses, collective and individualistic, the former grasped as genuine the latter as empty and futile. The heroic deed is here a function of collective purpose, a power invested in the heroic agent by way of a mystical-ideological union with a community, whose cause he feels himself to be representing. Inverting the notion of the supreme, self-sufficient individual, Ali advances a conception of the heroic individual as a personification of social aspirations, in this case for freedom. Not even a paternal figure protecting the weak and the oppressed from a superior power-position, the hero is here himself defended by 'the weak,' without whose symbolic empowerment he would remain utterly feeble.

The way heroes are defined in a given collective reflects and impinges on the way such a collective arranges its priorities, construes its values and envisions its goals. Švejk, once again, provides an excellent illustration of that point. As the author states programmatically in the preface:

> Great times call for great men. There are unknown heroes who are modest, with none of the historical glamour of a Napoleon. If you analysed their character you would find that it eclipsed even the glory of Alexander the Great . . . I am very fond of the good soldier Švejk . . . Unlike that stupid fellow Herostrates he did not set fire to the temple of the Goddess in Ephesus just to get himself into the newspapers and school books.
>   And that is enough.[7]

Here we have, I think as plainly as could be, a case of the *anti*-heroic *hero* as social metaphor. We have come to regard as self-evident the role that heroes play in sustaining national myths, given the broad attention, scholarly and otherwise, that has been accorded this subject: Wilhelm Tell as linchpin of the Swiss national narrative, Mustafa Kemal 'Atatürk' of the Turkish one, Siegfried of the German, and so on and so forth. The connection between heroic narratives and national identities is all the more easily grasped once the notion of *nationality as a narrative*, of the so-called 'imagined community,' in the wake of Benedict Anderson and Ernest Gellner, has become pivotal in modern theory of nationalism. Thus, few would call into question the claim that no nation can afford to dispense with its heroes.

Things, however, are somewhat more complicated and elusive once we turn our attention to literary (or filmic) heroes and try to figure out their role in sustaining collective identities. Certainly, many of those figures are *also* recognized national heroes, say James Bond as an international icon of Englishness. Yet for the most part, literary heroes (in our case, heroes of popular culture) are not national heroes in any sweeping sense. Although we may strongly identify Howard Roark, Superman or Hannibal Lecter with American culture, this is, at most, only one of the ways in which to understand their symbolic import. Even if the first two are undoubtedly means to promote a certain meaning of 'Americanism'—Roark in the sense of free-enterprise and anti-statism, Superman standing for democracy, decency and 'good citizenship'—the very nature of this ideological cargo already indicates that the issue here cannot be understood merely in terms of 'nationalism': for rather than standing vis-à-vis an external enemy, such heroes are above all facing their own society, the 'symbolic deficiency' *from within*. Thus, for example, Ayn Rand's hero had defended the purity of capitalism first and foremost against those many Americans who have supported Roosevelt's New Deal. The ideal Americanism of Rand is therefore best understood in terms of class ideology, competing for hegemony with other views as to how American society is to be structured. Rand's hero, as a 'social metaphor' for capitalism, can be contrasted with the vision of another émigré to America, Charlie Chaplin, who used his anti-heroic tramp to convey precisely messages of humanism which Rand so detested.[8]

One of the main goals of this study is to illuminate the social metaphor embodied in the diverse Nietzschean heroes in popular culture, of which Howard Roark is one. This is a task that will be undertaken throughout an analysis, first of Nietzsche's theories, then of popular Nietzscheanism, and whose results obviously cannot be anticipated at this introductory phase. Yet from the fact that only few of the figures I discuss are German it could already be concluded that the Nietzschean hero is not primarily a national hero. This has to do with the fact that the 'symbolic deficiency' Nietzsche sought to redress was international in scope rather than German and that, apart from a brief phase of patriotic enthusiasm revolving around Germany's unification, Nietzsche had little or no belief in a particularly 'German' solution to this problem. On the contrary, he generally regarded all nationalisms, including the German one, as part of the problem, a sure symptom of modernity. Since the affliction, according to Nietzsche, was universal, or at least affecting Western, modernized countries (as opposed to countries not yet caught in the sway of 'modern ideas' such as Czarist Russia or Confucian China), the remedies he envisaged were not nationalistic in nature or scope. Democracy, socialism, nationalism, mass culture, indeed *mass society* in its entirety, had to be managed and contained across national boundaries. And Nietzsche's prospect of a unified Europe—Europe as '*mistress [Herrin] of the earth*' as he once proclaimed[9]—was devised specifically for that purpose. The internationalism of the Nietzschean hero—the fact that he could be American or British as well as German—should therefore not surprise us:

> I write for a species of man that does not yet exist: for the 'masters of the earth.'
> . . . In Plato's *Theages* it is written: 'each one of us would like to be master over all men, if possible, and best of all God.' This attitude must exist again.
>   Englishmen, Americans, and Russians—[10]

Nietzsche was little interested in the specific *nascent-tradition* of German heroism, which he came to know, and eventually dislike, especially through Wagner's mediation. His personal 'heroes'—Alcibiades, Cesare Borgia, Napoleon, Emerson, Lord Byron—were mostly *not* Germans (although he strongly admired *some* Germans *as well*, for example Goethe, Heine or, with growing reservations, Schopenhauer). Since the ultimate problem as far as Nietzsche was concerned were the modern masses becoming a sovereign political power, and since this was decidedly an international phenomenon, the Nietzschean hero could make his appearance internationally, wherever there is mass society, that is, in principle, everywhere. This is not to say that the tradition of German heroism heralded by the likes of Paul de Lagarde and Julius Langbehn,[11] is completely different from that of Nietzsche; clearly, the neo-paganism characteristic of much of German romanticism reverberated powerfully throughout Nietzsche's writings and his attack on Christianity should, to an extent, be situated within a general tendency, in Germany, to recast religion in a pagan mould. Yet Nietzsche's aim was not to revert to the mythical glory of the Middle Ages as a means of justifying the anti-Enlightenment brand of German nationalism. His 'paganism,' rather, tended to look back to classical antiquity, and what he imagined to find in the Graeco-Roman world was not some nationalist ethos of mystical tribalism, but rather a robust, illusion-free, basically secular-minded master-morality, the affirmation of slavery and of hierarchy as a universal tonic for a civilization that has been leveled down by Judeo-Christian egalitarianism. In that respect, Nietzsche's heroic recipe was significantly less German than Thomas Carlyle's, whose heroic doctrines reserved a privileged place for German heroes—notably Friedrich 'the Great'—which also explains its incomparably greater historical resilience, as it remains active and influential at a time when Carlyle's exhortations to hero-worship have faded into all but obscurity. Thus, in what remains the classic account of the heroic vision of Carlyle and Nietzsche, termed 'heroic vitalism,' Eric Bentley could have established, as early as 1945, that 'Carlyle is now a nullity. He will probably remain so. The life of his spirit might plausibly be dated 1795–1945.'[12] Nietzschean heroism—secular, cynical, hedonist, predominantly *liberal*—was compatible with modernity well after the decline of fascism whereas Carlyle's one—pathetic, grandiose, theatrical, predominantly *proto-fascist*—was bound irretrievably with the romantic fashions of the nineteenth century. The Scotsman threw in his lot with German nationalism whereas Nietzsche, the German, far more clear-sightedly it has to be said, did not commit himself to any such tribalism. Indeed, Nietzsche's departure from the patterns of romantic heroism may have been the precondition for the abiding success of his heroic model and the reason that Nietzschean heroes are like fish in water in modern culture, appear perfectly at ease in the modernity they hold in contempt—think of the laid-back elegance of a James Bond or of a Hannibal Lecter—whereas the romantic hero proper seems hopelessly encumbered by the heavy and antiquated paraphernalia of spears, helms and robes, his overzealous or over-brooding gestures sorely out of place on the modern stage.

I refer to Northrop Frye's classic typology of the literary hero in order to suggest the genealogy of the Nietzschean hero and the way it relates historically to other forms of literary heroes, from the earliest myths, through medieval romance and on to modern (Western) literature.[13] According to Frye, what characterizes modern literary heroism is the overall rejection of the exceptionally gifted hero, who is increasingly replaced by the mediocre, even inferior, protagonist of realism and of modernism. In that respect, modern literature clearly signifies a moving away from heroic narratives, as classically understood. Hence, the modern 'hero'—the main character of a modern narrative—will only occasionally, in fact exceptionally, be also a 'hero'—in the classical sense of having superior strength, valor, virtue, and so on. In that respect modernity signifies the demise of the age of heroes, whether classical (mythical) heroes or medieval (chivalrous) ones. Yet, while taking on Frye's basic genealogy, I suggest explaining this development in social terms, as reflecting the rise to predominance of the bourgeoisie, to which have corresponded the consolidation of realism and the modern novel as well as of the realistic, mediocre, 'true to life' hero. The Nietzschean hero of twentieth-century popular culture is a social metaphor against democratic values denounced as herd mentality, upholding the grandeur of the competitive individual, glorying in struggle and conquest. In that respect, he signifies a refutation of the bourgeois heritage of realism and mediocrity and a harking back to distinctly pre-bourgeois heroism; yet, as I try to show, this is not a merely nostalgic move, a last, die-hard, almost suicidal battle for the revival of past glories, as in Carlyle. Rather, the Nietzschean heroic model dovetails nicely with the new needs of the bourgeoisie, that has become the dominant class in modern, Western societies.[14]

Anti-realist though he certainly is, the Nietzschean hero is not *un*realistic; rather than swimming hopelessly against the currents of history, the Nietzschean hero draws his strength from the fact that he becomes a champion of decidedly modern values: notably individualism and competition. The revival Nietzschean heroism entails must be understood as taking place not in opposition to bourgeois requirements and sensibilities but in ultimate, if not straightforward and seamless, conformity with them. This I attempt to substantiate by referring to Jerry Palmer's highly valuable theory of the modern hero of the thriller as a 'competitive hero,' who, even as he seems to revive former heroic traditions in fact turns on their heads the ideals of the feudalist socioeconomic order (such as spirituality, charity or self-effacement) in favor of a decidedly modern and pro-capitalist set of values (success, hedonism, gain).[15] The Nietzschean hero becomes the strongest, most symptomatic and militant expression of that modern tendency. The Nietzschean 'great man' is he who breaks apart from communal limits declaring himself self-sufficient, if not, in extreme cases, the very goal of society. As Nietzsche avowed early on:

> [O]ne giant calls to another across the desert intervals of time . . . undisturbed by the excited chattering dwarfs who creep about beneath them. . . . It is the task of history to be the mediator between them and thus again and again to inspire and lend the strength for the production of the great man. No, the goal of humanity cannot lie in its end but in its highest exemplars.[16]

The 'symbolic deficiency' that the Nietzschean hero qua social metaphor attempts to redress is the very elimination of heroism in the classical sense under modern, egalitarian conditions. The refutation of the masses as 'herd' therefore underlies all such narratives of Nietzschean heroism, even if such refutation may take on very different, and apparently little related forms: from the refined hedonism of James Bond, who challenges mass apathy by *savoring danger*, to the cruelty of Hannibal Lecter, who *savors the flesh of mass people*, feeding provocatively on the despicable 'last-man,' whom Nietzsche once decried as a 'diminished, almost ludicrous species, a herd animal, something good-natured, sickly, and mediocre, today's European.'[17]

In disagreement with the governing stance in recent Nietzsche scholarship, I propose to comprehend Nietzsche's philosophy above all as a *political project*, albeit in the broad sense of the term. As I seek to ascertain, Nietzsche's ethics, aesthetics and epistemology do not hold an independent status in his writings, and they certainly do not model and dictate his political line. They rather stem from, reflect and draw upon his fundamental sociopolitical convictions. Nietzscheanism is here seen as an intellectual and emotional response to the far-reaching socioeconomic changes the West underwent, and is still going through. It reinforces a neo-aristocratic stance, militantly reacting against the two principal political vehicles of egalitarianism: democracy and socialism. Although the political interpretation of Nietzsche's thought advanced throughout the following pages is consciously oppositional, it generally aligns itself nonetheless with the important work of a number of scholars, a partial list of which will include Fredrick Appel,[18] Malcolm Bull,[19] Daniel Conway,[20] Robert C. Holub,[21] Domenico Losurdo,[22] Urs Marti,[23] Renate Reschke,[24] Marc Sautet,[25] Bernhard Taureck,[26] Irving Zeitlin,[27] and Geoff Waite[28] (as other important confrontations with Nietzsche from without Nietzsche scholarship could be mentioned Terry Eagleton,[29] Fredric Jameson,[30] and John Carey[31]). For all their multiplicity of viewpoints and emphases, these Nietzsche students (and others, not mentioned here) are united in challenging the long-reigning conception of Nietzsche, querying key aspects of both the liberal interpretation, effectively founded by Walter Kaufmann,[32] and of the poststructuralist, 'new Nietzsche,' emerging in France in the 70s (via the work of such names as Bataille—a harbinger and founder of this approach—Deleuze, Foucault and Derrida), and attaining to immense influence through the so-called deconstructionist school in America.

The book explores a field that remains largely neglected in Nietzsche's-scholarship, as the percolation of the philosopher's doctrines into popular culture was barely touched upon, let alone systematically worked out. The rare attention apportioned to this subject matter usually confined itself to a few remarks, scattered here and there in the works of a few critics, or to vast generalizations about the all-encompassing Nietzschean impact on Western culture, such as can be found in Alan Bloom's *Closing of the American Mind*. The dominant line in present research largely avoids dealing with Nietzsche's linkages to that which stands outside the borders of 'canonical culture,' and the mere popular adoption of the philosopher is normally viewed as a vulgarization and abuse of his ideas. Differing from that, I will attempt to show that Nietzsche's popular versions did not deviate from or perverse the 'source,' not, at any rate, more so than Nietzsche interpretations belonging to 'high culture' or academic circles. Popular culture, far from being essentially alien to Nietzsche's philosophy, is actually a very fitting container—within certain limitations—to the reception and processing of the Nietzschean message. The philosopher's affirmation of the Dionysian life, of danger and struggle, and his concern with removing the partition that separates art and science from life, suits popular culture, and especially its heroic genre. Realism, the dominant literary genre of the nineteenth century, was far less adequate for the expression of the Nietzschean world-view; it corresponded, in fact, precisely to that traditional bourgeois ethos of fraternity, mediocrity, and democracy that Nietzsche sought to implode, realizing that it had outlived its initial, political utility. Realism emphasized the *anti-heroic*, the mundane, the objective social limitations that restrain the self-expression of the individual, hindering any triumph over the dictates of reality. There arose a need to develop, or renew, other narrative modes, more favorable to the demands of the imposing hero. Of course, much of twentieth-century 'high culture' also turned its back on realism, as diverse avant-garde movements took center stage—symbolism, expressionism, surrealism, or the psychologism of the stream-of-consciousness narrative mode; but here the highlighted features were mostly modern humanity's anxieties, failures, loss of values. In other words, its anti-heroic profile was again accentuated, though from other perspectives and in line with different ideological requisitions. These cultural trends were therefore attacked by reactionary circles—most notoriously, the Nazi concept of *entartete Kunst*—precisely on account of exposing the degeneration of the bourgeois soul, not its health and ascendance. It was not in this space that the 'positive,' assertive values of the new hero could be celebrated. By contrast, popular culture served as a much more convenient stage for the presentation of this new, essentially anti-realistic, valor.

Importantly, however, popular culture should not be reduced to a simple means of mass indoctrination, a defenseless domain for Nietzscheanism to victoriously march into and colonize at the expense of the docile, semi-barbaric natives. Modern popular culture, namely that culture which is produced under market conditions for mass consumption, is essentially dialectical, negotiating between competing ideologies, at times constituting a battleground upon which they compete. This book contests some of the standard premises about the supposedly inferior nature of popular culture, recurrently construed as the unavoidable result of mass production and consumption. The 'entertainment industry,' its many foibles not denied, is more than the mechanic output of senseless distractions. Heavily commercialized though it is, popular or mass culture retains a genuine potential for resistance, a permanent option of counteraction and an abiding utopian longing.

In this light, I investigate the fate of the Nietzschean elements once they came under the *collective's treatment*. It is shown how, sometimes inside the boundaries of a single text, motifs from the Nietzschean discourse collide with other, and quite antagonistic, themes. I also look into the apparently paradoxical fact that works of art that represent an aristocratic ethos, managed to gain such a marked popularity among the 'victims' of this value-system. Although I assume that Nietzscheanism is fundamentally elitist, I do not presuppose a strict political uniformity rigidly binding its diverse manifestations. In some cases, the initial philosophic posture underwent extensive transformations and was submerged within radically opposing ideological discourses (Jack London provides a fine case in point; the Tarzan tales, another). Correspondingly, we will register the existence of a current of *anti*-Nietzscheanism in popular culture, of texts in which Nietzschean ideals, metaphors and images are resisted with varying degrees of radicalism. This will help us to perceive popular culture as an arena of ideological struggle, its implications at times far-reaching.

This preliminary layout is worked out through an analysis of a series of works of popular culture, both literary and cinematic. The study consists of two main parts. The first focuses more on Nietzsche's thought than on applications of it, and attempts to lay the methodological foundations for the ensuing discussion. The second part takes Nietzscheanism as its subject matter rather than the philosopher's original thought, although I refer back to the latter wherever needed in order to establish the thematic and ideological connections. Nietzschean elements are traced and evaluated, with the emphasis put on their sociopolitical significance. Several texts are included in the discussion that are difficult to classify, located somewhere between popular and high culture, such as the works of Jack London or Fritz Lang. Occasionally, I consider texts of an unmistakable 'canonical' or 'high' status, such as Peter Handke's *The Hour of True Feeling*. This is done in order to dispel any illusion that the ideological motifs discussed in works of popular culture are mere vulgar appropriations. By the practice of juxtaposing, for example, Joseph Conrad and James Clavell, I hope to show how very similar social concerns are addressed on both sides of the supposedly impassable border between the high and the low and that the differences are ones of style and intended audience, but not necessarily of ideology. In choosing the texts, I applied two main criteria. Firstly, I was interested in those texts most explicitly tangential to the Nietzschean discourse, and providing its strongest expression. Pure Nietzscheanism, of course, cannot be found, but only, as it were, approximations. The question was therefore one of choosing those texts in which Nietzschean motifs are both *clear-cut* and *prevailing* within the story/film's general context, as opposed to mere isolated or ephemeral allusions to Nietzsche (of which, to be sure there are many instances. Thus, to provide just one salient example, in the first Harry Potter film the villain Voldemort tells Harry: 'There is no good and evil. Only power. And those too weak to seek it.'[33] This is a resounding Nietzschean utterance in popular culture, yet one that seemed to me too isolated within its overall context to warrant the film's inclusion in the discussion). In the texts of Ayn Rand, Ian Fleming, James Clavell, or Thomas Harris, Nietzschean themes are consistently foregrounded, pertaining to the very core of the narrative. Secondly, I opted as a rule for texts of enduring popularity and influence, in order to show quite directly the centrality of the Nietzschean heroic model. Hence I have chosen some of the most well-known characters of twentieth-century popular culture, such as Tarzan, James Bond and Hannibal Lecter. In addition, I was interested in representing the variety of the expressions of popular Nietzscheanism and the diversity of its motifs and ideologemes, such as naturalism (Tarzan), hedonism (Bond), individualism (virtually all of the Nietzschean heroes), natural aristocracy (King Rat), or crime-glorification (Lecter). In retrospect, and although this was not intended, I also realized that the texts discussed spread out nicely in chronological order to give something of a panoramic vista of twentieth-century popular culture, beginning with the early expressions of popular Nietzscheanism of the first decade in the work of Jack London, continuing with E. R. Burroughs in the 1920s, Ayn Rand in the 1940s and 1950s, Ian Fleming in the 1950s and 1960s, James Clavell in the 1960s and 1970s, and ending with Thomas Harris in the 1980s and 1990s. I make no claim to have produced a comprehensive catalogue of Nietzscheanism in popular culture, which must in any event remain beyond the reach of a single author. Much work still needs to be done and I have almost completely avoided—mainly for 'logistic' limitations of space, time, and, not least, personal proficiency— venturing into areas where Nietzsche has left a considerable mark, such as popular music, video games or science fiction (where appropriations/confrontations with Nietzscheanism are abundant; the names of Robert A. Heinlein or Alfred Bester spring immediately to mind, and there are many others). I can only hope that the analytical framework here employed and some of the conclusions I have reached would prove useful, if only as a starting point, to future scholars intrigued by the intersection between philosophy and pop culture.

I

A BLUEPRINT FOR THE NIETZSCHEAN HERO

1

Nietzsche, the Popular and the 'Grand Economy'

'Nietzscheanism,' this study assumes, does not begin with Nietzsche. His philosophy was no Big Bang in the world of ideas, which, exploding in an historical vacuum, brings into being an unprecedented world-view. His originality notwithstanding, Nietzsche forms part of a broad cultural tradition, originating in the Platonic philosophy and persisting through the work of such thinkers as Machiavelli, Sade, Emerson, Stirner, Carlyle, J. S. Mill and Spencer to name but a few vital points of reference. Similarly, the Nietzschean popular hero could not be understood apart from the work of such diverse authors as Byron, Lermontov, Stendhal, Balzac, Sue, Verne, Conan Doyle and the even earlier, quasi-'overmanly' villains of Gothic literature, as in the novels of Walpole, Radcliffe or M. G. Lewis. A significant part of the ensuing discussion will accordingly aim at establishing precisely the degree of 'proto-Nietzscheanism' of diverse authors and thinkers who helped to shape a heroic narrative with many affinities to the Nietzschean one. Yet, and for all that continuity, Nietzsche's fundamental significance lies in the fact that he is the quintessential representative and formulator of this 'language,' as regards impetus, pungency and extremity. For it is in Nietzsche's discourse that a number of separate and random motifs in Western culture attain a still unsurpassable cohesion, a keenness of expression, an intensification and exacerbation, as well as broad and intricate influence, which allows us to speak of Nietzschean*ism*, in a way which could hardly be done, for example, in regards to Stirner*ism*, Mill*ism* or Carly*lism*. Even in those cases in which the ideas of an individual thinker did expand into a broader stream of thought or line of creation and were affixed an –ism, as in the case of Machiavellianism or, still more importantly in our context,

Byronism, these cannot replace the distinctiveness of Nietzscheanism nor offer nearly as pertinent a framework in discussing our set of popular texts.

From the preliminary stages of this research, as I was beginning to ponder the essential methodological issues involved in mapping what I felt were ubiquitous manifestations of Nietzscheanism in popular texts, I faced the basic difficulty of applying the term 'Nietzschean' to texts or characters in which direct reference to Nietzsche was, more often than not, absent. The solution that suggested itself was the separation in principle of 'influence' from 'affinity' and the decision that my proper concern will be the latter. The Nietzschean hero, I decided, will not be defined in terms of an explicit influence of Nietzsche, a proven, as it were 'empirical' connection between a given text and Nietzsche's 'source,' which may or may not exist; the decisive question will rather have to be whether it is possible to speak of marked parallels between the Nietzschean discourse and a given text and/or character. Once such a Nietzschean discourse could be defined, the question of demonstrable influence would be transcended. A Nietzschean hero would be that character which displays strong enough similarities with a Nietzschean outlook even where Nietzsche is not mentioned (either in the text itself or externally, as a documented influence on a certain author), and where unmistakable references to Nietzschean terms and mottos such as 'the will to power,' *'ressentiment,'* 'live dangerously!' and so on, are not to be found; conversely, certain texts and characters may refer directly to Nietzsche or Nietzschean terms *without* qualifying as properly 'Nietzschean.' Thus it was clear to me from the start that the figure of James Bond evinces enough Nietzschean traits to be referred to meaningfully as Nietzschean hero, even though (or so I believed at the time) direct reference to Nietzsche was not made in Ian Fleming's stories; while Superman, whose very name is borrowed from Nietzsche, is not, properly speaking, a Nietzschean hero.

While this may sound a little abstract, the problem, as well as the solution, can be rendered more palpable by examining a scene from a recent popular film, *Spider-Man.* In this scene, the eponymous hero is captured by the Green Goblin, the villain. The Goblin then attempts to persuade his captive to join forces with him in his criminal enterprises. He argues that both he and Spider-Man, though superficially situated on opposing sides of the moral divide, are actually 'not so different.' Once Spider-Man declines such likeness, accusing the Goblin of being a murderer, the latter makes the following attempt at revaluating his interlocutor's values:

> Here's the real truth. There are eight million people in this city. And those teeming masses exist for the sole purpose of lifting the few exceptional men onto their shoulders. You, me, we're exceptional.[1]

Now, can the Goblin's argument be approached as 'Nietzschean'? In my mind the answer must be affirmative, to the point that it would be capricious *not* to admit the Goblin's role as an evil Nietzschean. The German philosopher, though, is not named, nor are mentioned any of his trademark, unequivocal terms. Talk of 'masses' and of 'exceptional men' is obviously not by necessity to be associated with Nietzsche. Nor do we have any guarantee that the scriptwriters of *Spider-Man* have ever as much as heard of Nietzsche (let alone read him). Yet the unmistakable thematic affinity of the Goblin's *contrast* of 'the teeming masses' *with the* 'exceptional men,' on the one hand, with Nietzsche's emphasis on 'great men' as standing above the vile rabble, on the other, quite decides the question, irrespective of the authors' knowledge or intentions. Whenever any such dichotomy is drawn between towering, unique individuals and the insignificant multitude whose sole purpose is to supply them with servants, it is a *Nietzschean dichotomy* which is drawn; for Nietzsche is the most radical, consistent and influential proponent of such an outlook. By the same token, whenever one speaks or writes about 'class struggles' or 'corporate exploitation,' we are justified in detecting the basics of a *Marx*ian discourse, even though the speaker/author may rather have another figure in mind, say Lenin or Gramsci, or another school of thought, say anarchism. Similarly, the Green Goblin may have, as it were, Stirner, Carlyle, or Le Bon in mind when arguing the case for mass unworthiness. But Nietzsche, surely, is more fundamental than any of these in that specific discourse, is closer to its core if not constituting it altogether, and hence ought to be given priority. If Superman, by comparison, in both comics and moving pictures, cannot be said to represent a Nietzschean worldview than he is less of a Nietzschean figure than the Green Goblin, although Nietzsche did (virtually) coin the term 'superman' while he spoke nowhere of green goblins. Interestingly, such an emphasis on Nietzscheanism in terms of a distinct, definable discourse was made recently by Robert Hewitt Wolfe, the co-producer and 'head writer' of the science-fiction TV series *Andromeda*. This series features a species which are called 'the Nietzscheans' whose society is said to be founded on the philosophies of Friedrich Nietzsche. In an Internet interview, Hewitt Wolfe was asked to 'talk about the literary background of the Nietzscheans' and, in answering, provided us with his rationale for choosing the term 'Nietzschean' from a number of other possibilities, ultimately discarded as less adequate:

> We were looking for a race that could be both good and bad and have both positive and negative qualities. I was trying to think about a cool approach for that race and 'Darwinists' didn't really sound that good. 'Dawkinite' . . . doesn't work either. 'Machiavellianite' is too long. So it ended up 'Nietzschean.' It's cool, short but tough to spell. There are also other associations with Nietzsche.

. . . Godlessness, rabid self-interest, sometimes even destructive self interest.
Monsters staring at the abyss and having it stare back, ubermenschen [sic].[2]

From within the popular culture 'industry' Hewitt Wolfe thereby asserts,
after his own playful fashion, that Nietzscheanism does have a core to it,
that it is a distinctive discourse revolving around certain identifiable, inter-
related key motifs, and that it is somehow more primordial, significant and
forceful than other, parallel discourses, taking as their center the thought of
Machiavelli, Darwin or Dawkins. Affinity must therefore precede influence
or mere terminological similarity, although these can certainly help to confirm the Nietzscheanism of a given text, make it, so to speak, official (as in
the case of *Andromeda*). In some cases, I have found my initial intuitions
corroborated, as it were, by the emergence of 'stronger' evidence, where
what appeared as 'affinity' turned out, in fact, to be 'influence.' For instance,
as I was reading more of Ian Fleming's James Bond novels, I discovered not
only ever stronger thematic affinity between them and Nietzscheanism but
increasingly more direct references to Nietzschean terminology and at least
one reference to Nietzsche himself. These pieces of 'evidence' collected
along the way have lent an official status to the Nietzschean themes permeating the stories, and were certainly welcomed as such; yet they could
only complement the overwhelming affinity which was evident from the
start, regardless of any direct allusions.

NIETZSCHE'S ESSENCE: INESSENTIALITY?

Certainly, such an insistence on thematic affinity is bound, in turn, to raise
objections of a completely different kind since it implies a definable Nietzschean discourse in the first place, an essence to Nietzsche's thought,
which can be at least roughly outlined, thereafter to serve as a yardstick in
evaluating the relative validity of competing interpretations or applications
of Nietzsche. And yet, much of post/modern Nietzsche-interpretation
anathematizes such an unfashionable view while advocating the opposite
premise that no such essence to Nietzsche can be disclosed at all, that Nietzsche, of all great thinkers, is the least vulnerable to 'the charge' of championing some rigid set of truth-claims. What is characteristic to him and
praiseworthy about him, we are told time and again, is rather contradiction,
playfulness, relativism, the permanent, mischievous construction and deconstruction of mere *appearances of truth*. By constantly changing masks,
bombastically proclaiming eternal doctrines only to topple them over with
gay laughter, Nietzsche teaches us a vital lesson in pluralism, creative tolerance and 'freedom of spirit.' As Derrida, the trailblazer of such a view, has
claimed: '[W]as not Nietzsche one of the few great thinkers who multiplied

his names and played with signatures, identities, and masks? And what if that would be the heart of the matter, the *causa*, the *Streitfall* (point of dispute) of his thinking?'[3] Nietzsche's gist is therefore pluralistic, non-metaphysical, and hostile to any oppressive meta-narratives. Alan White, endorsing Derrida's 'postmodernist,' French Nietzsche, restated the implicit association of Nietzsche with a liberal, flexible and pluralistic political mind-set, fundamentally opposed to the rigidity of totalitarianism:

> Until the 1960's, Nietzsche was generally read as . . . an advocate of power politics, devoted to producing supermen who would rule the world. Since the early 1970's, this reading—which I now christen with the two names 'Germanic' and 'metaphysical' (it might also be called 'modern,' 'positivistic,' 'objectivistic,' 'realistic,' or 'angelic')—has been countered, initially in France, by an impressive array of thinkers who have seen Nietzsche's works as undermining the very possibility of the communication, indeed even of the possession, of unambiguously determinable teachings. The Nietzsche that emerges from these readings—to which I henceforth refer as 'postmetaphysical' and 'French' (options would include 'postmodern,' 'relativistic,' 'idealistic,' and 'diabolical')—is an advocate not of totalitarian cosmos but rather, in extreme cases, of anarchic chaos.[4]

Similarly, Steven Aschheim's impressive study on Nietzsche-reception in Germany accepts as its theoretical premise the assumption that there are as many Nietzsches as there are Nietzsche-interpreters—thus, that there is no essential Nietzsche. As stated programmatically early on: 'This book is animated by the conviction that . . . Nietzsche's work cannot be reduced to an essence nor can it be said to possess a single and authoritative meaning.'[5] Throughout the decades, Aschheim observes, Nietzscheanism was interwoven with 'a broad range of cultural and political postures: anarchist, expressionist, feminist, futurist, nationalist, Nazi, religious, sexual-libertarian, socialist, *völkisch*, and Zionist.'[6] It is this variety, Aschheim argues, which must constitute the historian's object of study, a multiplicity to be recognized and documented, while discarding the outdated attempt to artificially put order into this chaos by imposing one's own, 'correct' interpretation. We are basically made to understand that Nietzsche's philosophy *is* this conflicting chaos, the fusion and conflict between the most diverse and adverse positions, and the Nietzschean legacy could be likened to a peeled onion which does not conceal a core, but is rather the sum of its layers.

The position that will be defended here will take issue with that approach on two principle grounds, epistemological and political. Epistemologically, it will reject the *essential inessentiality* attributed to Nietzsche. Not denying the undeniable, namely, that different interpreters approach Nietzsche differently and make different things of him, I will nonetheless dispute the assumption that all such interpretations are equally Nietzschean or equally non-Nietzschean. To be sure, anyone is entitled to read Nietzsche in his or her own way and be influenced by that aspect of his thought and not by another. There is nothing to be said against creative filtering and selective absorption of ideas, which would be virtually inevitable in the case of a thinker as protean, impish and stimulating as Nietzsche. Yet from this it does not follow that everything that is being made *of* Nietzsche or in Nietzsche's name is indeed *Nietzschean*. This is an epistemological assumption, with which those great many Nietzsche scholars who claim from every platform that Nietzsche was 'abused,' 'distorted,' 'vulgarized,' 'appropriated,' 'perverted,' and, at the very least, 'misunderstood' by the fascists should have no cause to disagree (although it will be argued here from a very different perspective and, correspondingly, carry very different political content). Yet, I feel certain, not even Derrida, White or Aschheim and others on the post-metaphysical camp should find cause to feel epistemologically aggrieved by such a claim. For do they not, too, admit essentialism into their Nietzsche exegesis, if only surreptitiously so, and in a new, anti-essentialist guise? The 'diabolical' argument that is implied by these thinkers, that Nietzsche was pluralist rather than totalitarian, may be more palatable than the 'angelic' contention that Nietzsche was totalitarian rather than pluralist; but I don't see that it is in any way less essentialist. For if it is true that, from an 'angelic' point of view, the notion of Nietzsche as pluralist must be sternly rejected, it is no less true that, from a 'diabolical' point of view, the notion of Nietzsche as totalitarian must be firmly discarded. Thus, it is not really the essence of Nietzsche which the postmodernists question, but 'only' the (totalitarian) essence of this essence. And so, when all is said and done, we must still 'angelically' choose between two metaphysical options, two competing truth-claims, and decide whether Nietzsche was 'pluralist,' 'totalitarian' or something in between these two extremes.

With Derrida, as we have seen, this underlying *anti-essential essentialism* is readily evident in the very installment of perspectivism, of a multiplicity of names, as 'the heart of the matter,' the *'causa,'* and the *'Streitfall'* of Nietzsche's thought. One would be hard pressed indeed to exceed the essentialism of such terminology. The case is not substantially different with Aschheim; if anything, the paradoxes of the paradigm are thrown into an even greater relief in his book since it is written in a decidedly *pre*-post-modernist style, and hence without the combination of mischievousness, opacity and rhetorical density which makes Derrida's precise argument much more difficult to pin down. In the book's first chapter, 'the Historian and the Legacy of Nietzsche,' providing something of a methodological introduction, Aschheim explains the need for a non-essentialist approach to Nietzsche, which alone can accommodate the breathtaking multiplicity of the historical applications of Nietzsche. At the beginning, however, this approach does not suggest itself as another interpretation of Nietzsche, but is advanced under the relatively restricted and specific pretext of defining the proper role of the cultural historian:

> The philosopher is not only free to judge and evaluate—he is obliged to do so. Cultural historians, however, must be exceedingly wary of such exercises. It is the dynamic nature of Nietzsche's influence, the complex diffusion and uses of his ideas, not their inherent truth, falsity, or even plausibility that must lie at the center of historical analysis. *Essentialized* approaches tend to obscure rather than illuminate the historical record by pressing the relevant material into a preconceived mold.[7]

Defending a strict disciplinary separation of aims and methods between philosophy and historiography, Aschheim clarifies that there is nothing wrong with judgment and evaluation of Nietzsche as such, and that they are even to be demanded of a philosopher. His point is only that they should not form part of the cultural historian's work. The latter should simply bracket questions of essence, while focusing on the documentation of Nietzsche's actual legacy. At that introductory stage, Aschheim does not embrace a nonessentialist theory of Nietzsche but only the far more modest, tactical and functional, nonessentialist *historiographic method*: 'Only a *Rezeptionsgeschichte* sensitive to the open-ended, transformational nature of the Nietzsche legacy will be able to appreciate its rich complexity.'[8] Thus, it is *not Nietzsche's thought* itself which is judged 'open-ended' and 'transformational,' but 'the Nietzsche legacy,' that which different individuals and groups have made of him in Germany between 1890 to 1990.

Whether one wishes to subscribe to such a demarcation of the cultural historian's task or not, it is clear that Aschheim *does not abide by it*. For, almost immediately, he begins to advance his own reading of Nietzsche as an *essentially* apolitical, pluralist, anti-systematic and radical thinker. In page 5, for example, in refuting Arno Mayer's claim that Nietzscheanism was a conservative force in pre-1914 Germany, Aschheim claims that conservatives were 'shocked and frightened by [Nietzsche's] radical questioning of authority and tradition.'[9] Nietzsche's thought, that is, is not allowed to remain within brackets but is immediately dragged out to prove another historian's interpretation wrong. Important here is not whether Nietzsche can justifiably be defined as 'a radical questioner of authority and tradition,' but the unmistakable *essentialism* of such 'judgment and evaluation.' In page 6, we are further told that: 'Socialism, anarchism, feminism, the generational revolt of the young—they were all touched by the libertarian magic of Nietzsche.' And shortly ensuing, comes the following, perfectly philosophical, evaluation of Nietzsche's thought: 'Nietzsche's congeniality to so many contrary tendencies and interests and capacity to elicit open-ended responses reflected a central property of his post-Hegelian thought and method: his rejection of systematizers and systems and his determination to attack problems from a plurality of perspectives. . . . His aphoristic style reflected his rejection of fixed systems.'[10] Maybe so; but why is this less a philosophical theory about the meaning of Nietzsche's work than those other theories which insist that Nietzsche's thought was not *all that un*systematic or iconoclastic? In page 9, Aschheim continues to substantiate his theory of Nietzsche as an essentially non-political thinker, at least alien to political systems, whose teachings were taken out of context and politicized by susceptible and less than overmanly, (pseudo-) Nietzscheans: 'The rhetoric may have been scintillating but most Nietzscheans after all were human, all too human. Quite unable to perform acts of this lonely, creative kind they rushed into the consoling arms of protective political and ideological frameworks. Only thus could Nietzsche be made palatable, a fact that also could be rationalized in Nietzschean terms.' In page 11 (note the persistency of the effort at a theoretical construction of Nietzsche's meaning) Aschheim shows his concurrence with Alan White's 'French Nietzsche,' approvingly citing Bataille's statement that 'Nietzsche's thought constituted *"without any hope of appeal*, a *labyrinth*, in other words, the very opposite of the *directives* that current political systems demand from their sources of inspiration."' Bataille, postulating an anti-ideological Nietzsche, does not suffer from the same, skeptical treatment accorded to the other, 'human, all too human,' *political Nietzscheans*. Far from following his own advice of refraining from efforts to get at Nietzsche's authentic meaning, Aschheim joins Bataille and claims that, 'Despite Nietzsche's own repeated warnings —"I want no 'believers'; . . . I never speak to masses. . . ." —the mythicisation and political appropriation of Nietzsche was inevitable.'[11]

In short, a theory of Nietzsche's essence as an anti-political pluralist is smuggled into Aschheim's narrative, indeed will guide it from now on, notwithstanding his own insistence on reserving evaluation to philosophers. And so, although in page 3 Aschheim maintains that 'The cultural historian cannot claim access to a privileged grasp of the unadulterated text by which all subsequent uses should be judged. There should be no set portrait of the "authentic" Nietzsche, nor dogmatic certainty as to his original intent,' he himself does not show great doubt about such original intent. The case appears to rely throughout on the wobbly premise that to *identify a dogma* in Nietzsche must itself be 'dogmatic,' whereas to deny him a system, to claim that Nietzsche was open-ended, is, correspondingly, an open-minded, non-dogmatic claim. All this suppresses the fundamental fact that in order to determine whether Nietzsche was political or not, whether he was proto-fascist, socialist, feminist or whatever else, one has no choice but to refer back to the text and attempt, however 'philosophically,' to decode it that way or another. To be sure, when approaching 'dogmatic thinkers' Aschheim by no means feels obliged to refrain from 'judging' their 'subsequent use,' equipped with a 'privileged grasp of the unadulterated text.'

Thus, for example, when reporting on Lukács' essentialist view of Nietzsche as a proto-fascist, he applies a critical tone throughout, in the obvious reliance on some authentic Nietzsche that evidently, or so he thinks, does not match Lukács's description: 'In order to make Nietzsche constitutive of this new, virulently antisocialist, proto-Nazi ideology, Lukacs had to resort to special explanations.'[12] My immediate point, once again emphasized, is not to argue against Aschheim's critical view of Lukács' interpretation; we are not presently concerned with deciding whether Nietzsche was political or non-political, although we shall address this issue shortly. My aim is only to expose the false pretenses at the heart of the postmodernist line of Nietzsche-interpretation, which disallows anybody else's essentialism while clinging fast to its own. The game of Nietzsche interpretation, for those who wish to partake in it, will have to be played, won or lost, on the field of essentialism.

Furthermore, I would question the idea that the myriad takes on Nietzsche must themselves be understood as providing the incontrovertible proof that there is no essence to Nietzsche, or that, at most, his essence is necessarily pluralistic, accommodating the most diverse and conflicting meanings. Again, I will not be disputing the evidence as such, that Nietzsche was indeed appropriated and admired by many different individuals and groups with no immediately obvious common denominator or shared interest; but the very same evidence can lead to a quite different conclusion. Georg Lukács, no less than Aschheim, White or Derrida, and well preceding them, had recognized Nietzsche's 'pluralism,' i.e. the expansive, flexible, adaptable nature of his largely aphoristic thought, which can be assembled and reassembled in a kaleidoscopic manner to yield the most diverse results. Yet his explanation of such adaptability was very different: 'such myths and aphorisms, depending on the bourgeoisie's immediate interests and their ideologues' endeavors, could be arranged and interpreted in the most diverse, often diametrically opposed ways. But the constant harking back to Nietzsche—in each instance a "new" Nietzsche—shows that there was a definite continuity beneath it all.'[13] This continuity, for Lukács, had to do with an underlying social coordinator secretly conducting the apparently frenzied shifts on the surface of the Nietzschean kaleidoscope. Nietzsche's versatility—so Lukács, writing on the eve of the philosopher's sweeping rehabilitation in the West—is to be understood in the context of the struggles inherent to capitalist society and as abidingly accommodating the interests of the bourgeois class.

Such an analysis also does much to contextualize and destabilize Alan White's confident contention that Nietzsche scholarship has to be divided between a pre-70's, 'Germanic' and 'metaphysical' era, and a post-70's French 'diabolical' one. Lukács, as early as 1953, far from imagining that the only way Nietzsche could be interpreted is as 'an advocate of power politics'

(White), countered what, for him, was the dominant bourgeois reading of Nietzsche, manifesting the greatest outward diversity yet deeply united by vested interests. And, surely, he would hardly have been swept off his feet by the emergence of the French 'new Nietzsche,' in which White identifies so many radical potentialities and a brave new epistemology. Whether one agrees with Lukács or not, there is nothing in the rise of the postmodernist Nietzsche as such that settles the issue. Chronologically, Lukács belongs to what seems a remote past, but his anticipatory critique of all 'new Nietzsches' remains as relevant as ever to our contemporary debate. If it is to be refuted, it will not be, at any rate, on the vacuous ground of 'non-essentialism.'

The case of two early and renowned popularizers of Nietzsche, Jack London and H. G. Wells, can serve as a useful illustration of the tension between essence and application. As is well known, both authors were avowed socialists and admirers of Nietzsche: a fact which, *prima facie*, appears to confirm that Nietzscheanism is compatible with or adaptable to socialism, and consequently to invalidate the essentialist contention that it is inherently anti-socialist. Yet upon closer examination the cases of both these pioneers of popular Nietzscheanism lead to very different conclusions, ultimately *supporting* rather than undermining the particular essentialist reading of Nietzscheanism as a counterforce to socialism. For in fact, both authors were wavering between their leftist political convictions and their Nietzscheanism, struggling to find a coherent and satisfying compromise. Far from presenting us with some harmonious synthesis, many of their works are marked by an irreducible conflict between the two dominant poles of their worldview. To the extent that they veer towards the socialist pole, Nietzscheanism, if not altogether discarded, fades into the background; conversely, inasmuch as Nietzscheanism gains the ascendancy in their discourse, socialist positions are weakened, questioned, sometimes outright abandoned. Much of their prose could be read as a site of intense and agonized ideological contention, albeit seldom a fully conscious one. London was unceasingly trying to mediate between his two great spiritual mentors, Marx and Nietzsche, between the humanist commitment to socialist struggle and the grim, social Darwinist view of nature's ruthlessness and the inescapable culling of the weak. Yet he could never attain a solid and abiding middle ground (I say more on this in chapter 3).

A similar oscillation can be detected throughout Wells' writings, although his socialist convictions, in my view, were never quite as profound and militant as London's. Ultimately, the Nietzschean side would prevail, and the later Wells will scathingly attack the delusions of Marxism. Yet already in his earliest stories the conflict is everywhere manifest. In *When the Sleeper Wakes* (1899), for example, Graham, the reluctant hero who awakes after two hundred years in coma to find himself in 'a nightmare of Capitalism tri-

umphant,'[14] does war, in the name of socialism and 'the pe
cynical Nietzschean despot, Ostrog. Yet Graham himself i,
about the revolution, questioning not merely its chances c
moral and social legitimacy as well. As John Carey observec
evinced a similar, structural indecision:

> The utopias he invents seem to waver and turn into dystopias as we watch, rob-
> bing us of certainty. . . . Wells makes it harder to guess his point by putting
> what seem to be his views about the individual and the mass into the mouth
> of decidedly sinister characters. Ostrog, the bullying dictator . . . , lectures Gra-
> ham about the merits of aristocracy and the necessary extinction of the unfit
> millions: 'the world is no place for the bad, the stupid, the enervated. Their
> duty . . . is to die.' This, after all, is what Wells advocated in *Anticipations*, yet
> Ostrog is evil.[15]

Wells is, therefore, 'nearly always in two minds,'[16] which is another way
of saying that he was torn between Nietzscheanism and socialism. Quite
like London, he did not happily tread the golden road between the two ideological positions, or orchestrate them into a tuneful duet. Instead, he himself and his works became an arena upon which the two were fiercely battling. And it is only in that rather limited sense that Wells, or London, could
be described as socialist Nietzscheans.

LIBERAL NIETZSCHE, NIETZSCHEAN LIBERALISM

The next chapter is dedicated mostly to the unfolding and substantiation of
my understanding of Nietzsche as a thinker in the liberal tradition. Since
the validity of the entire argument hinges on this reading of Nietzsche as a
formulator of a new, *bourgeois ethos*, it presently warrants a separate, if preliminary, exposition. We will return afterwards to interweave the conclusions of this political discussion into a theory of popular Nietzscheanism.

It is not my contention that Nietzsche was an outright liberal thinker and
bourgeois intellectual comparable with Locke, Montesquieu, Constant,
Smith, Bentham or J. S. Mill. No doubt, to the extent that the term 'bourgeois' is understood as designating merely a cultural stance, a way of life and
a state of mind, revolving around efficiency, security, industry, common
sense, moderation and so on Nietzsche was anything but a bourgeois; to that
extent we can unproblematically accept Peter Gay's view of Nietzsche as 'the
hidden father of so much antibourgeois ideology'[17]; similarly, if 'liberalism'
is understood as a social and political doctrine emphasizing human and civil
rights, constitutional government, parliamentary rule, the democratic sovereignty of the people and the optimistic notion of 'progress,' then Nietzsche

would emerge as its staunchest adversary. However, from the perspective which will guide the present study, the bourgeoisie is conceived first and foremost as a *class*, not an *idea*, and liberalism the socioeconomic theory and policy of such class. And as the needs of the class change through evolving historical circumstances, so does liberalism transform itself to address these challenges. Rather than representing fixed entities, platonic ideals beyond material reality, both the bourgeoisie and liberalism must be seen as engulfed in the flux of history, and hence in a permanent state of transformation.

In order to grasp the particular dynamics of modern liberalism it is vital to distinguish between 'political liberalism' as a classical set of ideals and institutions, and 'economic liberalism,' which consists in clearing the ground for the unfettered accumulation of capital. Political liberalism and economic liberalism, which at the onset of the bourgeois revolution went hand in hand and appeared inseparable, subsequently revealed themselves in some fundamental respects as quite incompatible. The same historical proof of the pudding, moreover, has distinctly demonstrated that economic liberalism was more primordial for the bourgeois class than was political liberalim. At some points, the gap between the two turned out so wide that the bourgeoisie, precisely in order to *defend* economic liberalism, was driven to drastically downgrade—if not altogether discard—liberal ideals and institutions at the ideological and political levels. By comparison, tenets of political liberalism were embraced and defended by the sworn enemies of economic liberalism, the socialists. As Albert Lindemann, himself no socialist, asserted: '[B]y the early twentieth century the socialists proved to be more consistent and unshakable defenders than the liberals themselves of many values that have been vaguely termed liberal (free and reasoned discourse, toleration, defense of civil liberties, international harmony).'[18]

Surely, the finest illustration of the discrepancy between liberalism in its political and economic forms is the irresistible rise in the last three decades of what has generally come to be known as 'neoliberalism.' Now, let us assume that no knowledge of actual neoliberalism in its ideological and political manifestations is available to us, and that we are nonetheless asked to derive a general notion of it in consideration of nothing but the naked term; what would we be able to conjecture? Taking as our premise the standard discourse of *political* liberalism, the logical surmise would be that neoliberalism cannot but signify an adamant defense of the parliamentary system, a radical attempt to expand popular representation in politics and revitalize democratic proceedings, promote human and minority rights, etc. Neoliberalism, however, in fact stands for the theoretical demand and the practical policy of *narrowing* democratic intervention in economic matters to the absolute minimum in the name of a return to the putative classicism of laissez-faire and the illegitimacy of any egalitarian intervention in the 'free market.' In the words of Wilhelm Röpke, a classical spokesman, 'constitutional forms' are to be promoted which will 'work against the honestly undeniable dangers of general franchise and permit a true government by responsible people.'[19] An even more eminent representative of neoliberalism, the Nobel laureate Friedrich August von Hayek, has averred that 'liberalism is incompatible with unlimited democracy,' which he additionally referred to as 'the dictatorship of plebiscites.'[20]

It is in that sense, in freeing economic liberalism from the shackles of political liberalism, above all in ensuring that political liberalism shall not destroy the premises of capitalism and unwittingly foster a radical alternative to itself, that Nietzsche, in the following pages, will be considered in some major respects a liberal. For the philosopher's abiding campaign against the sociopolitical enfranchisement of the masses renders important service to the cause of economic liberalism. We shall see how Nietzsche's thought was in some harmony with classical bourgeois and liberal doctrines—for instance in comparing his ideas with those of J. S. Mill. If Nietzsche's utterances differ from the characteristic rhetoric of the more conventional defenders of capitalism such as Hayek, this is due mainly, as far as the sociopolitical content is concerned, to the open endorsement of slavery—the necessity of exploitation—as the inexorable basis of culture, which cuts across the entirety of Nietzsche's corpus, whereas the likes of Hayek as a rule would not admit such 'cruel-sounding truth,'[21] always claiming that capitalist labour arrangements do not result from compulsion but from the freedom to sign a contract and benevolently operate, at least in the final balance, to promote the 'common good.' Nietzsche, furthermore, substantiated the need for slavery not upon mundane, pragmatic grounds, the base pretext of material 'well-being' towards which he evinced aloof contempt, but as serving the noble cause of culture, of great art, which Hayek, Milton Friedman or Alan Greenspan do not, as a rule, concern themselves with. As already the early Nietzsche stated in *The Greek State*:

> In order for there to be a broad, deep, fertile soil for the development of art, the overwhelming majority has to be slavishly subjected to life's necessity in the service of the minority, *beyond* the measure that is necessary for the individual. At their expense, through their extra work, that privileged class is to be removed from the struggle for existence, in order to produce and satisfy a new world of necessities. Accordingly, we must learn to identify as a cruel-sounding truth the fact that *slavery belongs to the essence of culture*. . . . The misery of men living a life of toil has to be increased to make the production of the world of art possible for a small number of Olympian men.[22]

Nietzsche, that is, was a cultural critic, by his own famous definition 'the last anti-political German,' preoccupied with aesthetic matters; yet even if we choose to take the philosopher at his word and believe him that he stood far above any strictly material concerns, the basic fact cannot be ignored that, if his 'aesthetics' necessitate slavery, if his 'world of art' demands that we curb democracy or abolish it altogether, if the production of 'culture' means the ruthless material subjugation of the vast majority of people to the benefit of an elite, than a *socioeconomic theory* of exploitation is inscribed into the very core of his *aesthetic theory* of noble culture. And it is precisely here, I argue, that Nietzsche's pertinence for capitalism lies, in the fact that the dreary fact of exploitation became glamorized in his writings and elevated into a cultural imperative. Nietzsche's ubiquitous critiques of political and ideological liberalism, as well as his no less massive attacks on bourgeois culture and philistinism cannot in the least compromise this harmony with economic liberalism; on the contrary. As Terry Eagleton appositely put it: 'Nietzsche is an astonishingly radical thinker, who hacks his way through the superstructure to leave hardly a strut of it standing. As far as the base goes, his radicalism leaves everything exactly as it was, only a good deal more so.'[23] Nietzsche's cultural critique served to further *cement the base*, the essential pattern of labour arrangements, by combating precisely those aspects of the superstructure—of bourgeois culture and political liberalism—perceived as endangering the essential class hierarchy. Nietzsche's talk about 'a broad, deep, fertile soil for the development of art' seems to confirm his *Marxism in reverse*, the recognition that the contemporary superstructure of culture is only conceivable upon the firm, material base of slave labour.

It is interesting to note how the essential class structure of capitalism was expressed by *both* Marx/Engels *and* Nietzsche in virtually interchangeable terms. In both formulations, the complexity of society is equally abstracted into a fundamental opposition between those few who exploit and those many who do the working. The only difference is that, in the case of Marx and Engels this condition is seen, and criticized, from the point of view of labour: 'All that we want to do away with is the miserable character of this appropriation, under which the labourer lives merely to increase capital, and is allowed to live only in so far as the interest of the ruling class requires it.'[24] And does not Nietzsche see the exact same relation, yet from the vantage point of capital, when he speaks about 'ordinary men, . . . the great majority, who exist for service and general utility and who *may* exist only for that purpose'?[25] Elsewhere, in specifying the destructive effect of the leveling 'nihilistic trait' in the sphere of 'economics,' Nietzsche was quite unambiguous: 'the abolition of slavery.'[26] Besides 'slavery,' the other two essential constituents of the capitalist mode of production, private property and capital accumulation, were firmly established by Nietzsche as representing the rudiments of life itself. Private property, to begin with, was justified in the following terms:

But there will always be too many who have possessions for socialism to signify more than an attack of sickness—and those who have possessions are of
one mind on one article of faith: 'one must possess something in order to *be*
something.'[27]

Hence, when it comes around to the vital social question of 'possessions,'
indeed *the* question, Nietzsche aligned himself squarely with the propertied
classes. Truth may be relative, morality perspective-dependant, but property
is an absolute. Yet he went beyond a mere confirmation of private property,
proceeding immediately to ground the further act of accumulation of possessions in life:

But this is the oldest and healthiest of all instincts: I should add, 'one must
want to have more than one has in order to *become* more.' For this is the doctrine preached by life itself to all that has life: the morality of development. To
have and to want to have more—*growth*, in one word—that is life itself.[28]

Thus, capitalism and life itself are made one and the same, practically interchangeable, and in the absence of capitalism, life—both being (possessing) and becoming (accumulating)—would be but living death. Exploitation, to complete the picture, is no less rooted in life, forming a biological
compulsion beyond the reach of history:

[L]ife itself is *essentially* appropriation, injury, overpowering of the strange and
weaker, suppression, severity, imposition of one's own forms, incorporation
and, at the least and mildest, exploitation . . . 'Exploitation' does not pertain to
a corrupt or imperfect or primitive society: it pertains to the essence of the living thing as a fundamental organic function, it is a consequence of the intrinsic will to power which is precisely the will to life.[29]

To live truly and properly is therefore to Exploit, Possess and Accumulate;
this is the sacred ideological Trinity which Nietzsche's radicalism, far from
putting into question, was meant to put *beyond* any possible questioning.
Under this light, the will to power reveals itself as the metaphysical extension of the *will to money*.[30] Intriguingly, Nietzsche at times specifically theo-
rized about the vital role of the money-making, middling *and liberal* bourgeoisie in forming the basis for a cultural revitalization. Here reveals itself
the surprising advantage of mediocrity over genius in withstanding the egalitarian frenzy of 'the social hodgepodge':

In such circumstances, the center of gravity necessarily shifts to the mediocre:
against the dominion of the mob and of the eccentric (both are usually
united), mediocrity consolidates itself as the guarantee and bearer of the future. Thus emerges a new opponent for exceptional men—or a new seduction.
Provided they do not accommodate themselves to the mob and try to flatter

the instincts of the 'disinherited,' they will have to be 'mediocre' and 'solid.' They know: *mediocritas* is also *aurea* [mediocrity is also gold: Walter Kaufmann's translation]—indeed, it alone disposes of money and *gold*. . . . A high culture can stand only upon a broad base, upon a strong and healthy consolidated mediocrity. . . . The power of the middle is, further, upheld by trade, above all trade in money: the instinct of great financiers goes against everything extreme. . . . The honorable term for *mediocre* is, of course, the word '*liberal*.'[31]

Again, my intention is not simply to equate Nietzsche with the common ideologue of laissez-faire, who upholds the market, the whole market and nothing but the market. No doubt, the wide-ranging, multi-faceted perspective of the philosopher, as compared with the narrow view of the standard market-apologist intent on immediate gains, endowed the former a much more flexible class position. Thus, we can occasionally find him, especially in his so called 'middle period'—centering around *Human, All Too Human* (1878–1880) and expanding into such books as *Daybreak* (1881) and *The Gay Science* (1882)—endorsing a political solution which is the farthest removed from neoliberalism (at least, that is, along the scale of alternatives open *within bourgeois economy*), and foreshadowing, rather, the Keynesian welfare state. Since the preservation of the class hierarchy and the prevention of a comprehensive socialist alternative was the foundation of Nietzsche's social vision, he was at times perfectly willing to criticize naked exploitation of labor when that meant dangerously exacerbating class enmity to the point of imperiling the overall stability of the system. As in the following example:

What we now refer to as justice, is from this point of view a highly refined usefulness, which does not take in consideration only the present moment and exploits the opportunity, but rather reflects with responsibility on the lasting consequences, therefore taking care of the well-being of the worker as well, of his physical and spiritual satisfaction, *in order that* he and his descendants will continue to work for our descendants, and will be available for a longer period of time than a single individual's life. The *exploitation* of the worker was, as one now understands, a stupidity, a ruthless enterprise at the cost of the future, which endangered society. Now we have before us almost a war, and the price for achieving peace, for sealing contracts and wining trust, will at any rate be very high, since the foolishness of the exploiters was great and long-lasting.[32]

Nietzsche appears here to dramatically retract his former statement that the 'misery of men living a life of toil has to be increased' to facilitate great art, advancing in its stead the opposite demand to ensure the worker's 'well-being.' Yet he takes such a stand only under the guidance of the fresh insight—'as one now understands'—that 'foolish' exploitation—rather than 'unjust' or 'cruel'—might viciously turn against the economic liberals themselves. Nietzsche chides economic liberalism on strictly pragmatic grounds and promotes, against the irresponsible zeal to maximize profits at the immediate present, the contraceptive measure of a 'highly refined usefulness' whose purpose is to ensure that the *very principle of profit* will survive on an enduring basis. To the extent that the ruthless practices of economic liberalism, by *over*-exploiting the worker, become themselves a potentially destabilizing factor jeopardizing the future, Nietzsche is willing to show his teeth to the masters as well, and recommend what one commentator readily celebrated as 'an enlightened labour policy.'[33] From *The Greek State* to *Human, All Too Human* (and beyond, certainly) the philosopher's social imperative remains the inevitability of slave labour. Yet, whereas in the earlier instance Nietzsche confidently spurs his Olympian men to unscrupulously milk their slaves of labour for all they are worth, it later dawns on him that the slave's basic needs must also be attended to, if he is to remain a slave at all. A contented slave, obviously, is better than none at all.

Notwithstanding, it is only on very rare occasions that Nietzsche, for whatever reasons, will explicitly censure exploitation in work-relations.[34] Hence, such a passage presents a serious temptation to those many interpreters at pains to present the reader with a view of the German philosopher as a humanitarian of sorts, even as a maverick socialist. The great impediment in appropriating this passage *en bloc* is, of course, that one thorny half-phrase, situated irritatingly exactly in the center of the passage, in which Nietzsche unmistakably clarifies that the whole point of this new-felt solidarity with labour is to ensure, *at the long run*, the interests of the upper classes, and to restrain, *at the long run*, those of the worker: '*in order that* he and his descendants will continue to work for our descendants.' By the use of '*he and his* descendants' to speak of the worker, and of '*our* descendants,' to speak of those enjoying the fruits of labour, Nietzsche states as plainly as possible where *he* socially belongs; he does not even pretend social impartiality in the name of 'culture' (or, alternatively, of 'relativism,' 'skepticism,' 'perspectivism' or 'French diabolism'). Even so, the lines circumscribing this unfortunate aside are so pregnant with 'proletarian potential' that some of the most respected figures within Nietzsche scholarship could not resist the temptation. Thus, and in order to *rehabilitate* such a passage for the purposes of Nietzsche's general rehabilitation, they had to find a way to remove the bothersome core of the passage and preserve its precious peel. Jacob Golomb, for instance, simply extracted from the final part of the passage the very beneficial words 'The *exploitation* of the worker was, as one now understands, a stupidity, a ruthless enterprise at the cost of the future, which endangered society,' and presented this as an 'aphorism with a Marxist tone.'[35] Keith Ansell-Pearson exhibited even greater ingenuity; not willing to let the invaluable words go to waste in which Nietzsche speaks about the 'well-being of the worker' etc., he paraphrased them and then skipped over the tricky little section, to end by a similar quotation to that of Golomb. This he introduced as 'a passage that will surprise many of his readers.'[36] By such inventive maneuvers, the fox managed both to eat the grapes and effortlessly get out of the vineyard. It is illuminating that the only way for those interpreters to accomplish their rehabilitative task is by omitting precisely what Nietzsche himself chose to emphasize: the explanatory remark beginning with an italicized 'in order that.'

Hence, even when Nietzsche occasionally found reason to disagree with the practices of economic liberals (as opposed to his ubiquitous critique of political liberalism, to say nothing of socialism), he did so only on the pretext of representing better and more enduringly than they the long-term interests of the class system. On the exact same ground, of guaranteeing an abiding basis for capital accumulation, Nietzsche, in 1888, advanced a critique of individualism, another key tenet of classical, political liberalism:

> What does the Renaissance prove? That the reign of the individual has to be brief. The squandering is too great; the very possibility of collecting and capitalizing is lacking; and exhaustion follows immediately. These are times when everything is *spent*, when the very strength is spent with which one collects, capitalizes, and piles riches upon riches.[37]

Once again, key elements of the superstructure are sacrificed so as to preserve the base; if unbridled individualism collides with the premises of 'capitalizing,' 'the reign of the individual has to be brief.' This critique of 'undue' individualism has been a constant in Nietzsche's thought once he had grasped that the sanctity of the individual's life, of absolutely *any* individual, cannot be reconciled with the requirements of economic expansion. On that grounds he had refuted Utilitarianism, for failing to consider the durable interests of the species and nearsightedly concentrating on immediately realizable utility: 'The Utilitarians are naive—And in any case we must first *know what* is useful: here too they look only five steps ahead—They have no conception of the grand economy, which cannot do without evil.'[38] Once political liberals have embraced the Christian ideal of individual immortality the vital process of selection is checked; economic liberalism finds its path obstructed by harmful sentimentality:

> Through Christianity, the individual was made so important, so absolute, that he could no longer be sacrificed: but the species endure only through human sacrifice—All 'souls' became equal before God: but this is precisely the most dangerous of all possible evaluations! If one regards individuals as equals one calls the species into question, one encourages a way of life that leads to the ruin of the species: Christianity is the counterprinciple to the principle of *selection*. . . . The species requires that the ill-constituted, weak, degenerate, perish: but it was precisely to them that Christianity turned as a conserving force.

. . . What is 'virtue' and 'charity' in Christianity if not just this . . . hampering of selection?[39]

It is on that account, of refusing to sacrifice men, that the Christian ideal is deemed antithetical to 'education, knowledge, cultivation of good manners, *gain, commerce*.'[40] Its moral obsession is pernicious because 'everything decried as immoral is, *economically considered*, higher and more essential [than the moral: I.L].'[41] The Christian value judgment is to be destroyed since—through its modern incarnations, democracy and socialism—it fetters the workings of *the grand economy*.

Thomas Mann was certainly right to specify as a crucial error of Nietzsche 'the completely false way in which he assesses the relation between morality and life, treating them as if they were opposites.'[42] Yet this was no philosophical 'error' on Nietzsche's part as Mann preferred to believe, but an indispensable element within Nietzsche's ideological scheme. In order to denounce any moral interference with the socioeconomic order as inimical to life he *had to* misrepresent the relation between morality and life and treat them 'as if they were opposites.' Thereon relied the whole weight of his argument: to treat life and morality, both Christian and socialist, as dialectically intertwined, to accept morality as an integral part of The Real, would have meant to renounce the notion that Christian/socialist policy is a priori unnatural, and constitutes a 'world-slandering.' Throughout his writings, with relentless repetitions and in a myriad of slightly altered formulations Nietzsche had advanced the idea that any attempt to challenge the present socioeconomic hierarchy and transcend it would be 'life-denying,' 'unnatural,' 'world-slandering,' etc. 'All ideals are dangerous,' he maintained, 'because they debase and brand the actual.'[43] But what is this 'actual' to start with? And why should it *not* be debased and branded? After all, was not Nietzsche supposed to be committed to an iconoclastic devastation of all systems, lending his irreverent skepticism to a *demolition* of all actualities? The real 'real,' so to speak, the totality of all phenomena, knows no such distinctions between 'the ideal' and 'the actual,' between 'morality' and 'life.' Surely life—understood as biological and material existence—impinges on morality—ideologies, values, theories and so on—and morality on life, without the 'reality' of society, its actuality, thereby either diminishing or increasing. Society is just as real in that basic sense whether socialistic, fascistic, capitalistic, Christian, aristocratic, Hindu or pagan. Therefore, truly to accept the actual and say unconditionally 'yea' to it, could mean little more than to abandon any critical project, to squarely and stoically accept whatever society, morality and economy are given, *as well* as affirming all those social, moral or economic forces which strive to *change* what is given. But since Nietzsche, in fact, was bent on reversing the very *real* and *actual* advance in the power of the masses, he, too, no less than any socialist, had to promote his own 'beyond,' his own 'ideal' of what society must look like and negate that which stood in opposition to it. Hence, to offset the socialist attempt to move 'beyond Capital,' Nietzsche promoted his own *beyond* good and evil, so that, at the same time that 'exploitation' was made 'organic,' inseparable from life, the struggle *against* exploitation was rejected, debased and branded, as inorganic, as life-denying. Nietzsche clearly operated with a certain notion of 'the actual' to which he was firmly committed, and in defense of which he was ready to repel any slandering. This actual was alternatively and interchangeably termed 'the world,' 'life,' 'the real,' 'will to power,' 'nature' and so on. As against the 'self-crucifixion of two millennia' Nietzsche once recommended the 'reverse attempt': 'to conjoin the *unnatural* inclinations, I mean *the inclination for the beyond*, for things contrary to sense, reason, nature, in short all previous ideals, which were all world-slandering ideals, with a bad conscience.'[44]

Whenever humanity was displaying those inclinations and ambitions favorable to the grand economy such as possessiveness or competitiveness, Nietzsche would defend this as stemming from the unalterable core of the human makeup, and heap scorn on the heads of the foolish idealists who fly in the face of nature. As in the following passage from *The Wanderer and his Shadow*, where he dismisses the Platonic/socialist idea of communal ownership, absolutizes private property and grounds it in human nature: 'If, however, one wishes to . . . restore property to the *community*, with the individual as no more than a temporary tenant, then one will destroy the land. . . . Plato's utopian basic tune, continued on in our own day by the socialists, rests upon a defective knowledge of man. . . .'[45] Yet whenever humanity was indulging in 'natural' vices far less compatible with the present system, in fact potentially calling for some alternative order, such as the desire to cruise cozily through life, without pains and hardships, to work as little as possible and enjoy the simple pleasures of communal, strife-free existence, Nietzsche would turn to heap scorn rather *on humanity*. Here he would have no trouble in becoming himself a fuming idealist, sermonizing against the follies and failings that are merely human, all too human. At that point, all affirmation of the actual and the natural ceased, and the reluctant herd was spurred, both kicked and cajoled, towards the promised land of the *Übermensch*. Facing capitalism, Nietzsche was a fatalist; facing socialism, he was a world-reformer. Notwithstanding all avowals of *amor fati*, Nietzsche attempted to go beyond significant parts of the real, notably beyond mass society. Far from unconditionally affirming what *is*, he in fact spearheaded a movement of the most militant reaction against the masses. And he has conducted this anti-mass crusade in the name and service of the hypostatized Real, World, Nature, Life, which were all, at bottom, precisely the sacred Trinity of Exploitation, Possession and Accumulation. To imagine anything beyond *that*, let alone strive in such direction, is what Nietzsche could never accept. He satirized the would-be reformers of this world for refusing to accept the social misery of the present as a natural given, a truth not to be tampered with: 'The *true* life,' Nietzsche ironically represents the position of social reformers, 'is only a faith (i.e., a self-deception, a madness). The whole of struggling, battling, actual existence, full of splendor and darkness, only a bad, false existence: the task is to be redeemed from it.'[46] Against this background, Nietzsche's *counter*-task transpires with great clarity: to refute any such redeeming, to celebrate actual existence, the 'splendor and darkness' of the grand economy; to reject, in short, all systems that reject *The System*.

Thus, in spite of his critique of political liberalism, the essential affinity in social goals which underlies Nietzsche's relationship with economic liberalism is quite profound. Nietzsche's ideal culture shares with the neoliberal ideal economy the primordial class interest, in guaranteeing that the worker 'and his descendants will continue to work for our descendants.' Compare the following passage in which Hayek unfolds his own version of 'beyond good and evil':

> Distributive justice . . . is irreconcilable with a competitive market order . . . Mankind could neither have reached nor could now maintain its present numbers without an inequality that is neither determined by, nor reconcilable with, any deliberate moral judgments.[47]

This reads as Hayek's own banishing of slave morality—unmistakably that of failures driven by *ressentiment* ('The envy of those who have tried just as hard, although fully understandable, works against the common interest')—from the economic sphere, the free market that must further remain free from the baneful intervention of any 'deliberate moral judgments.' And was not capitalism itself historically bound with the ideological vindication of the 'market against the resistance of the "moral economy,"'[48] the unleashing of market forces relying, as it were, on a proto-Nietzschean, extra-moral agenda? That Hayek's economic refutation of equality and of morality is motivated by plain functional considerations, whereas Nietzsche's is based on lofty concern for culture, merely goes to show how Nietzsche's cultural project was tangential to liberal economy, the former constituting something of a philosophical reflection of the latter. And so, to complement Hayek's somewhat Nietzschean statement, we can cite a somewhat Hayekian Nietzsche from *The Gay Science*:

> Hatred, the mischievous delight in the misfortunes of others, the lust to rob and dominate, and whatever else is called evil belongs to the most amazing economy of the preservation of the species. To be sure, this economy is not afraid of high prices, of squandering, and it is on the whole extremely foolish. Still it is *proven* that it has preserved our race so far.[49]

Thus, far from disputing the sanguine and ever more common view of Nietzsche as a liberal of sorts, I simply insist that this be conceived as a double-edged argument: the relationship of Nietzsche and liberalism is a coin with two sides, and if those merchandising Nietzscheanism are all too happy to display the side which shows Nietzsche the good liberal—the free-spirited anti-totalitarian and so on—the coin could just as easily be flipped over to expose the rather more sinister, *Nietzschean kernel* of liberalism, which has slave labour as its unspoken premise.

This struggle against that which threatens class hierarchy is not some isolated facet of Nietzsche's thought, which can be identified and henceforth carefully detoured. It rather expands into an all-pervasive apprehension vitally informing Nietzsche's most diverse concerns and guiding his forays into culture, morality, psychology, aesthetics, religion and so on. One of this work's aims is to show how Nietzsche's apology for capitalism was organic, not confined to this or that aspect of his thought, but rather underpinning the entirety of his project: thus, we shall observe along the way how Nietzsche erected a metaphysical construction in support of market society and in retaliation against antagonistic forces to it, at the levels of ethics, aesthetics, epistemology, theology, criminology, theory of gender roles and—most central to our interest—popular culture. Similarly, it percolated into his discussion of more specific themes, informing, for example, his notions of music, sport and gastronomy. In all these cases, it should be clear, we are not confronted with some narrow party program. For if Nietzsche was indeed 'political' this was not necessarily or strictly in a fascist, Nazi, neoliberal, anti-democratic or anti-feminist variants of politics. Rather, it consisted of a multi-faceted refutation of many alternatives to 'the actual,' a refutation that was devised precisely to be able to fight efficiently on several fronts and in different guises and to recruit as many followers from as many constituencies as possible.

The time is long gone when the extravagant paradoxes of Nietzsche's thought were pedantically dismissed as poor philosophizing. For some time already we are able to recognize Nietzsche's *will to contradiction*, the programmatic nature of his 'incongruities.' But we are wrong in seeing no more to the matter than the mark of a superb free spirit that exceeds the pettiness of mere 'systematizers,' and naïve in failing to sense the coordinating *center* beneath the contradictory surface. Certainly, far from being an assortment of preposterous and self-refuting propositions, the abiding power of Nietzsche's utterances owes much to their undeniable perspicacity. For who is to deny the pertinence of Nietzsche when he points mercilessly to the latent egoism, possessiveness, self-interest and hypocrisy lurking behind bourgeois morality and psychology, behind 'love' and 'altruism' and 'pity'? Yet, far from making us consider that such may be, however partially, the historical products of a competitive age, Nietzsche's ideological purpose reveals itself in the reverse attempt to *ontologize* these vices, to root them in the metaphysical will to power, so as to rule out in advance any effort to transcend them. Perceived from this vantage point, his critique of modernity emerges as its entrenched apologia, taking the form of an assault on modernity's putative benevolence, laxity, mediocrity, humanness. For, as Nietzsche assured us: 'Ours is the most decent and compassionate age.'[50] At the time that the Western rulers of the world were moving apace towards imperialistic expansion and domination, perfecting their war machinery and exploitative apparatus, and preparing the ground for the perpetration of unparalleled brutalities, Nietzsche was lending his faculties to a devastating attack on the age's compassion and pacifism; at the time that the groundwork was being laid for mass killings on unprecedented scale, Nietzsche was philosophically discarding the value of the mass; at the time that the bourgeoisie was struggling to disentangle itself from its own historical commitment to humanism and equality, Nietzsche was launching his own campaign against Judeo-Christianity as the purported vehicle of egalitarianism; and as the possibility of a solidary human community was being thwarted in actual politics, Nietzsche was doing more than any other major thinker to bring the term 'herd' into disrepute.[51] Thus he takes his stand to the right of Bismarck—which he denigrated as a democrat of sorts, catering to the masses[52]—and of Spencer, whose social Darwinism did not quite reach deep enough in uprooting the very idea of the community.[53] It is this fundamental ideological design, as opposed to some disturbing 'excesses' which we must recognize at the very heart of Nietzsche's thought.

Even Nietzsche's occasional 'deviations' from the habitual argumentative line are as a rule means by which the dominant sociopolitical enterprise is being *further advanced*. A couple of brief examples will demonstrate how the philosopher's 'contradictions,' once interrogated for their social content, reveal a rather harmonious pattern. Nietzsche at times slackened his relentless attack on the benevolent degeneracy of the age. Yet he identified redeeming aspects only where modernity appeared to be in some conformity with his venture of reanimating master morality. Thus, though repeatedly decrying the pernicious pacifism of modernity, Nietzsche at one occasion allows himself to note with satisfaction how Europe, in fact, is not all that incorrigibly tamed and insipid: 'I am *glad* about the military development of Europe. . . . The barbarian in each of us is affirmed; also the wild beast.'[54] To be sure, this affirmation of 'the barbarian in each of us' rests on the assumption that *none of us* happen to be revolting slaves, a point which is elsewhere made clear: 'There is nothing more terrible than a class of barbaric slaves who have learned to regard their existence as an injustice, and now prepare to avenge, not only themselves, but all generations.'[55] Still more strikingly, Nietzsche finds cause for optimism even in what concerns the otherwise utterly insufferable specimen—the human 'herd animal.' Yet this is not the result of some diabolical shift of perspective, nor of a newfound sympathy for the defenseless sheep paraded to the slaughterhouse. Far from it, the herd animal is now gratifyingly contemplated as furnishing the perfect toy to great, authoritarian men:

> I have as yet [1884] found *no* reason for discouragement. Whoever has preserved, and bred in himself, a strong will, together with an ample spirit, has more favourable opportunities than ever. For the trainability of men has become very great in this democratic Europe; men who learn easily and adapt themselves easily are the rule: the herd animal, even very intelligent, has been prepared. Whoever can command finds those who *must* obey: I am thinking, e.g., of Napoleon and Bismarck.[56]

Forming rebellious troops, the herd is a phenomenon of dismay, endangering culture; rightly disciplined and coordinated, it proves quite useful. Detestable, evidently, was not the herd as such, but only the shepherd-*less* herd.

The overwhelmingly successful liberal re-appropriation of Nietzsche initiated and championed by Walter Kaufmann in the aftermath of the Second World War ('domesticating the politically suspect philosopher for a liberal postwar Anglophone audience'[57]) was not a mere personal crusade—as such, no doubt, it could never have attained its predominance—but rather owed its triumph to concrete historical and social conditions. As I wish to argue, it profoundly reflected *the need* of the West to reintegrate *the essence* of Nietzscheanism into its post-war ethos, while discarding that which was inessential and unsalvageable. That, according to the mainstream of Nietzsche scholarship, Nietzsche is not to be perceived as partaking in the fascist adventure, contributing to it or sharing with it any significant trends of thought, is symptomatic of the general reluctance of Western elites to acknowledge *their own* significant political and ideological compliance with fascism, and their attempt to shift the blame—quite along Nietzschean lines—onto the irrational, vulgar, ignorant, *resentful* 'masses.' In that sense, the denial of Nietzschean politics is part and parcel of a larger ideological denial of the liberal legacy. The revisionist reversal of historical roles, the fact that the masses—which fascism came on the scene in the first place precisely to incorporate, contain and discipline—were now ascribed the blame for it, is just one of the more striking ironies of such sweeping ideological revision. Thus, a renowned figure in Nietzsche scholarship such as Peter Sloterdijk has recently advanced the claim that 'brother Hitler, reaching his arm to all,'[58] was a mass man representing *egalitarianism* as opposed to elitism, and thus had nothing whatsoever to do with Nietzsche, the noble elitist, the consummate antipode of mass mediocrity. Pursuing the same social logic is Yirmiyahu Yovel's contention that Nietzsche's historical misfortune was the usurpation of his ideas by the vulgar masses and the frustrated slaves:

> Modern politics is, inevitably, mass-politics. He who combines the dream of the exceptional Dionysian hero with the reality of mass society (as Nietzsche is tempted to do in his bad moments), creates an unrealistic mix and necessarily invites distortions. Nietzsche's *'Übermensch'* cannot be generalized—that is, vulgarized . . . Fascism, that Nietzsche would have loathingly rejected, is one of the tragic caricatures of such impossible combination of nobility and commonness. When 'Dionysian' powers are bestowed upon a shopkeeper, a bus-driver or a small intellectual worker, who are placed beyond good and evil, the outcome must take horrible dimensions. Nietzsche himself would have indeed recognized in Nazism everything he abhorred: extreme nationalism and xenophobia, mass culture and state cult, *ressentiment* and other familiar marks of 'slave' culture. . . .[59]

Yovel, quite like Nietzsche, seems to regret the fact that 'modern politics is, inevitably, mass-politics.' Accordingly, far from admitting that Nietzsche wished to control the masses, he makes the opposite claim that the philosopher intended, somehow, in his 'bad moments,' to bestow exceptional powers upon unworthy mass people, like shopkeepers, bus-drivers or small intellectual workers. Just as in Sloterdijk, we are invited to believe that the problem with fascism was not its brutal elitism, the disregard for common people and the methodical cruelty defining its theory and method, but, on the contrary, its *excessive egalitarianism*, the empowering of the vile plebs, the unleashing of barbaric slaves. Proper and benign Nietzscheanism would be, as implied by both Yovel and Sloterdijk, a Nietzscheanism of the worthy elite, exercised responsibly, out of the mob's reach and keeping the envious rag and tag well under control.[60] In view of this it can be appreciated how, by rehabilitating Nietzsche, the elite was, in some fundamental respects, rehabilitating itself. Only this, I maintain, could account for both the zeal invested in this apologetic undertaking and its almost complete success.

NIETZSCHE'S ESSENCE AND POPULAR CULTURE

If much of the 'high' theoretical debate concerning Nietzsche's social significance has been marked by such an apologetic impulse, actively downplaying and mystifying Nietzsche's elitism and enshrouding in hazy and lyrical veils the triadic core of Exploitation, Possession and Accumulation, popular Nietzscheanism, as well as popular anti-Nietzscheanism, has always been characterized by taking on precisely these social implications of Nietzsche's thought. Grasping the bull by the horns, numerous popular texts have dealt with what Nietzsche theoreticians have endeavored to obscure: labour arrangements and social hierarchy, elitism and slavery, which were either embraced, in the case of Nietzschean popular narratives, or resisted, in anti-Nietzschean popular narratives. Yet how is this popular frankness to be approached and accounted for?

To my knowledge, the only attempt ever made to produce a theoretical framework in which these Nietzschean themes could be systematically analyzed was done recently by Thomas Hibbs.[61] Yet his explanatory model, more specifically his evaluation of the social role of Nietzscheanism, is virtually antithetical to mine (as will be further discussed in chapter 2). Paul Zweig, in a relatively early work, has celebrated Nietzsche as something of the philosophic patron of adventure literature, resisting the unnatural elimination of the adventurous quest by weakly bourgeois realism.[62] Yet he neglected to analyze or even mention any concrete manifestations of such Nietzschean adventurousness in popular texts. Moreover, the analytical model he applied was thoroughly depoliticized, not integrating any considerations of the social significance of Nietzscheanism, beyond an aesthetical protest against the tameness of modern, bourgeois culture.[63] Geoff Waite, in a path-breaking work, has highlighted the immanent expansionary and incorporating nature of Nietzsche's teachings, the way they were devised to form a barrier to communist utopia. Nietzscheanism, Waite argues, has permeated Western culture *high and low*, becoming a major influence in subverting the democratic ethos of the masses. Waite speaks about Nietzscheanism in terms of 'the spectacular technoculture of everyday life,' a subtle, omnipresent, subcutaneous force, militating against the masses yet, crucially, involving them actively and directly: 'Nietzsche—who is an "anomaly" no longer but part of our second nature—is also "savage" but against the masses in his willingness to induce some of the multitude to will their own self/destruction.'[64] However, Waite's 'cornucopian' (Malcolm Bull's adjective) effort at fathoming the pervasiveness of Nietzsche's counterrevolutionary thought, concentrated on Nietzsche's 'prophylactic' incorporation of the Left, the way he re-programmed feminist and socialist agendas so as to deprive them of their radical power; the *popular Nietzsche*, incorporating not intellectuals but the broad masses, and thus indeed becoming 'our second nature,' remains largely a supposition, though a vital one, within his work.

Apart from such rare instances, the dominant line in Nietzsche scholarship was conspicuously silent on the matter of the philosopher's linkages to that which stands outside the borders of 'canonical culture.' This curious theoretical myopia may be partly attributable to the association of Nietzsche's popularization with the fascist 'profanation' of his ideas and, since the danger is associated with the impertinent meddling of mass people—shopkeepers, bus drivers and other lowbrows, the seemingly reasonable countermove is to restore Nietzsche to the safe custody of academic protectors. As Yovel claimed, to associate Nietzsche with the masses is a *contradictio in adiecto*, an 'impossible combination of nobility and commonness.' I try to lay bare the inner contradiction, as well as the unspoken rationale, in the effort to isolate the 'authentic' Nietzsche from the damaging effects of 'unwarranted' popularization, and in trying to retreat to the original, 'uncorrupted' text. Nietzsche himself repeatedly stressed the irreducible and beneficial *danger* bound to his philosophy, at one point famously celebrating himself as a dynamite, a harbinger, if not directly an instigator, of 'wars such as there have never yet been on earth.' Surely, speaking of himself as a 'destiny,' a 'man of fatality,' and prophesizing that 'only after me there will be *grand politics* on earth,'[65] he had in mind more than *academia politics* (however ferocious it can undoubtedly be)? As early as *Schopenhauer as Educator*, Nietzsche passionately discarded academic philosophy on the explicit grounds that it is *not dangerous*. He enthusiastically cited Emerson saying that one ought to be careful 'when the great God lets loose a thinker on this planet. Then all things are at risk,'[66] and proceeded to contrast such genuine thinkers with timid, ascetic, professional academicians, who shy away from involving their thought in actual life:

> Now, if such thinkers are dangerous, it is of course clear why our academic thinkers are not dangerous; for . . . they cause no alarm, they remove nothing from its hinges; and of all their art and aims there could be said what Diogenes said when someone praised a philosopher in his presence: 'How can he be considered great, since he has been a philosopher for so long and has never yet *disturbed* anybody?' That, indeed, ought to be the epitaph of university philosophy: 'it disturbed nobody.'

Precisely such a cowardly attempt to elude danger is what makes university philosophers, in Nietzsche's view, as effeminate as they are ineffectual in worldly matters: 'But this, of course, is praise of an old woman rather than of the goddess of truth, and it is not to be wondered at if those who know that goddess as an old woman are themselves very unmanly and thus, as might be expected, completely ignored by the men of power.' To challenge such a deplorable state of things, in which philosophy becomes 'a matter of complete indifference to anyone,' the true friends of philosophy must demonstrate 'by their deeds that love of truth is something fearsome and mighty.'[67] Against such a background the deep irony in the attempt to restore Nietzsche's philosophy, in *Nietzsche's name*, to responsible scholarly patronage, is thrown into vivid relief. For Nietzsche meant, quite programmatically, to *be dangerous*, to disturb, to remove things from their hinges, to become a political and social factor and, last but not least, to attract 'the men of power.'

So do we have a case to proclaim festively that the 'genuine' Nietzsche, finally unearthed, is indeed the 'popular' one? Can we rely on such tropes in

Nietzsche and conclude that he was all about (popular) bravado, assertiveness, militancy, aggression, virility? Surely, we would thereby merely be bending the stick too far the other way, and ignoring the (elitist) Nietzsche that wears masks, that is refined, ironical, gentle and ailing. For, if Nietzsche spoke quite unequivocally—at times—against academic philosophizing, would it not be equally false to assume that he meant to be read popularly? Didn't he elsewhere, as above quoted, insist with equal vigor that he 'never speaks to masses'? And if popularizers of Nietzsche prefer to underline the former position, why should elitist Nietzscheans be deemed any less justified in appealing to the latter stance?

Inexorably, this merely thematic, as opposed to an *ideological* reading of Nietzsche, condemns us to opt with equal arbitrariness for one of these two arch-interpretations, or leaves us with the postmodern 'solution,' hardly more satisfying, of 'unifying' the two into an anti-essential Nietzsche, that undermines the possibility of meaning. Yet what if the antinomy of high and low Nietzscheanism is a merely apparent one? What if, on an ideological level, the high and the low unite precisely *in their difference*, and, rather than two exclusive options, form two complementary departments of a single Nietzschean project, a project for *everyone and no one*, meant to be *both* elitist *and* popular? If Nietzsche's ideas were indeed tailored to fit the benign figure that his high theorists wanted to cut, this was not simply an abuse of his ideas, or a misinterpretation. Nor can it be assumed that, since Nietzsche was selectively read in the academia, 'the real' Nietzsche must be sought after in the popular domain. The high Nietzsche—in terms of implied readership, style and content—is certainly just as real (and just as deceptive) as the low one. If the 'popular Nietzsche' deals much more candidly with the 'grand economy' and its requirements, the 'high Nietzsche' is *just as genuine and relevant* in its concomitant attempt to *put a veil across it*. For Nietzscheanism, I wish to suggest, is nothing if it is not precisely the convergence of blatancy and dissimulation, the vanquishing, *laughing* predator, united with the *weeping*, gentle soul. Or, put in yet another way, the convergence of the *low and the high*. Consequently, Nietzsche's essence can only be approximated by conjoining the popular and the elitist versions, by critically tracing the interconnection between their partial truths and partial lies. The very success of the Nietzschean project in safeguarding the grand economy depends on its uncanny ability to take over the high and the low, reassure the elite as the same time that it entices the masses, to radicalize the Right while incorporating the Left.[68]

Understanding Nietzscheanism as a social project allows us to transcend the narrow horizon of mere thematic quibbling and the immanently futile attempt to decide whether the real Nietzsche was the one reflected in popular culture or that expounded in 'high' scholarship. The high and the low are to be grasped as integral departments of this project, each entrusted with its own task, yet commonly striving—wittingly or not—toward a single, unified goal. Nietzsche's project, by definition and intention, is *both* elitist and popular, encouraging the selective readings of his gospel and reckoning in advance that both will prove of use, even as they compete to exclude each other. Both Nietzsche's elitist custodians and his popularizers are wrong in believing genuine Nietzsche to be squarely in their camp, yet effectively *de-signed* for such error. The irreducible ambivalence of Nietzsche's utterances in the matter, to the point of—apparent—incompatibility, is calculated just so as to enhance this particular dynamics of *popular elitism* and of *elitist pop-ulism*. As a rule, Nietzsche's 'paradoxes' do not resolve themselves logically, but 'only' *ideo*-logically, their rationale being their pragmatic import, not their logical coherence. A position that aims to transcend Nietzscheanism, as opposed to partake in the project, must therefore always keep in mind this pragmatic unity of Nietzsche's contradictions, and only *half*-trust his 'unequivocal' assertions. Nietzsche, Geoff Waite tells us, 'explicitly insults the base-level of society,' and

> also insults the kind of books—indeed popular or mass culture *tout court*—that are aimed at this base-level. 'Books for all the world are always foul-smelling: the stench of small people clings to them.' Most readers undoubtedly assume that *this* book, *Beyond Good and Evil*, at least, is not intended to be a vulgar book. Or is it? Most likely, it is such a book, as the vulgarity of this very pas-sage shows, but among *other* things.[69]

This astute comment on Nietzsche's *anti-vulgar vulgarity*, however, is not to be understood merely as a jab at Nietzsche's 'hypocrisy' and definitely not as a critique of his style. In fact, few readers can claim to have equaled Waite's awareness of Nietzsche's consummate stylistic mastery or to have been more appreciative of his rhetorical virtuosity and subtlety. If Nietzsche is here being vulgar, it is not some stylistic blunder, but, on the contrary, a measure of his rhetorical sophistication. For Nietzsche *means and manages* to be the anti-vulgar vulgarian, for he wishes to be an active agent in both departments, the high and the low. Nietzsche calculated for the popularity of his doctrines, took care to guarantee their universal user-friendliness. As he wrote to his publisher Ernst Schmeitzner in February 1883, announcing the completion of a '*decisive* step,' his book *Thus Spoke Zarathustra*: 'It is a "poetical work" [Dichtung] or a fifth "evangel" or something, for which there is no name as yet. It is by far the most earnest and *also* the merriest of my productions, and accessible to everyone.'[70]

It would be quite unjustified to assume that popular Nietzscheanism is merely and necessarily a vulgar profanation of Nietzsche's elevated ideas, or that it grossly misstates and hopelessly caricaturizes his real political/anti-political ideas, reducing them into so many empty and dangerous clichés. As already argued, Nietzsche's popularizers embarrassingly let the

cat out of the bag, unveiling truths which academic discourses as a rule prefer to keep politely out of sight. It is true that Nietzschean heroism in popular culture does not absorb all or most of the ideas which are central to Nietzsche's philosophy, tapping into certain elements of Nietzsche's thought,
while passing over others. Yet 'selection' only means 'distortion' if the original meaning of the primary utterances or discourse is reversed or at least
dramatically changed so as to warrant contrasting messages, and, moreover,
as is usually implied, such that are generally more ominous, violent, irascible etc. As a rule, this is *not* the case of popular Nietzscheanism, which
grasps in a basically correct way—at least as compared with its higher
counterpart—the essentials of Nietzsche's grand economy. We obviously
cannot know how Nietzsche would have personally reacted to twentieth
century mass culture, to cinema, sport, TV and MTV (just as little, be it said,
as we can be certain as to his reaction to modernism, to communism or to
fascism); similarly, one can only speculate about the way Nietzsche would
have reacted to his own popular versions, say to encountering his ideas and
terminology in the works of H. G. Wells, Ayn Rand, Ian Fleming or Quentin
Tarantino. All we are legitimately allowed to do is to define a Nietzschean
project, outline its main features and then compare it with its popular manifestations (or, perchance, distortions). In that sense, and not that of Nietzsche's personal aesthetic preferences, it will be shown how the popular
Nietzscheans, authors and heroes alike, are, for the most part, rightful followers rather than uncalled-for usurpers.

What vitiates the approach of those many commentators complaining
about the abuse of Nietzsche's 'original text' by the fascists (or, by extension, by Nietzsche's mass culture popularizes)—beyond the fact that they
themselves regularly prove rather unreliable readers of that primary text—
is their systematic failure to consider the possibility that the potential for
the simplification of Nietzsche was not uncalled-for but exactly *called-for*,
consciously built into his utterances from the very start, which were devised
to be simplified, appropriated, used and abused. What if, rather than following the advice of the philosopher's liberal custodians who urge us to see
Nietzsche as a thinker naively neglecting to consider the future impact of
his sometimes inflammatory rhetoric, we need to grasp Nietzsche precisely
as a *rabble-rouser* of sorts, albeit one of aristocratic aims and idiosyncratic
means (indeed, it seems to me that we may do worse than refer to Nietzsche
in order to ponder the symptomatic case, very frequent historically, of the
rabble-*hater* qua rabble-*rouser*)? What if the real Nietzsche was also a calculating disseminator of violence, a copywriter of slogans, catchy and suggestive battle-cries, which were thought of and designed to explode? From that
unorthodox vantage point the simplification of Nietzsche in popular texts
would be understood rather as *a magnification*, the caricaturist accentuating
of *truthful elements* as opposed to dishonest or shallow distortion.

Indeed, if such simplified, extracted versions enhance Nietzscheanism precisely in their distilled form, and are necessary means for attaining its sociopolitical goals, than such 'vulgarization' is what *qualifies*, rather than disqualifies them. If Nietzscheanism in popular culture endorses and facilitates the Nietzschean struggle against democratic and socialist nihilism, and if it carries the campaign for restoring master morality forward onto mass territory, inculcating the revaluation of all values among the multitudes, then it would be the goal which justifies, even necessitates, such means. If we are correct in the conviction that the Nietzschean project aspires to expand, and needs to infiltrate mass culture in order to accomplish its aim, then products of popular Nietzscheanism find their rationale as legitimate descendants rather than unaccounted-for bastards. Such Nietzschean ideals, mottos and imperatives as the *Übermensch*, the blond beast, *amor fati*, eternal recurrence, living dangerously, etc., were all, to a considerable extent, meant precisely as popular—in the broadest sense of the term and including popular culture—banners, to be used *in war*. The criteria, therefore, in deciding whether, for example, a specific use of the notion of the *Übermensch* in a given popular text is a Nietzschean one or not, would not be its absolute, one-to-one correspondence with Nietzsche's original utterances (which, surely by intent, were more evocative than conclusive anyway, leaving the door ajar for interpretation to come in), nor its level of complexity and sophistication; it would rather have to be the degree of compatibility of such popular application with the essentials of the Nietzschean discourse/project of the grand economy and its imperatives. It is on that account that we have judged Superman (the comic-book hero) only a very remote kin of Nietzsche's *Übermensch*. Yet not because he offers a simplified version of the latter, but on account of disagreeing with the original, sociopolitical design of the *Übermensch* as the antithesis of the nihilistic last man of mass society. By the same token, Ernest Everhard, the hero of London's *The Iron Heel*, is unmistakably meant to be a version of the *Übermensch* inasmuch as he possesses super-human force of character and indestructible determination. Yet he engages his powers in a life-and-death struggle against the agents of the grand economy, and heads a slave revolt supporting basic ideals of slave morality such as compassion, solidarity, justice etcetera: 'He was a natural aristocrat—and this in spite of the fact that he was in the camp of the non-aristocrats. He was a superman, a blond beast such as Nietzsche has described, and in addition he was aflame with democracy.'[71] Applying that crucial ideological yardstick, neither Superman nor Everhard are properly Nietzschean, since the former does not take part in the Nietzschean project, while the latter does all he can to undermine it. Having laid the foundations for the research and outlined its main goals, we now need to explore the historical context from which the Nietzschean hero emerges and to illuminate his fundamental social role vis-à-vis the grand economy.

2

How to Tame a Bulldog: The Social Mission of the Nietzschean Hero

The history of Nietzschean heroism runs parallel to the history of the bourgeoisie. *The hero* has accompanied *the class* like a shadow: a spiritual, psychological, aesthetic, ideological projection. He was the outcome of a radical transformation, a 'paradigm shift' in the sphere of ideology, which commenced in the nineteenth century and culminated in the twentieth. Broadly speaking, this break meant a continual withdrawal from the ideals and ethos of the French Revolution. It signified the emergence of a purely bourgeois discourse suited specifically to capitalism. If, before the revolution, the bourgeoisie affirmed its universal nature versus feudal privileges and discrimination, and was thus only too happy to embrace the populace at large—albeit with certain reservations of taste—it now became ever more aware of its particular position and, gradually but securely, established its identity *over and against* the plebeians, against 'the masses.' The pact between bourgeoisie and working class was merely a transitory phase, a practical step. As Karl Marx put it: 'In order to oppose the court, they [the bourgeoisie] had to court the people.'[1] Facing absolutism, the bourgeois individual was content to affirm his partnership in the ultimate brotherhood called 'humanity.' But, after he had attained the desired emancipation, 'humanity' was no longer such a warm, friendly haven. It began to feel somewhat too intimate a gathering, too *crowd*ed. 'Humanity' and 'the people' were therefore rechristened, interchangeably, 'the crowd,' 'the mass,' 'the mob,' 'the multitude,' and so on. Under the shielding umbrella of 'humanity,' the individual could, for the first time in history, assert himself against tradition and find a genuine self-expression. 'The mass,' on the other hand, became the individual's Procrustean bed.

NIETZSCHE IN THE MAZE OF MODERN INDIVIDUALISM

Certainly, there was more to this ideological shift than a cynical breach of the pledges of the past. It stemmed equally from the contradictions immanent in bourgeois ethics and the essential ambivalence of revolutionary Enlightenment terminology, most conspicuously as regards 'liberty' and 'equality'. Before having any sweeping moral content, these notions reflected the need to politically ensure the basis for a market economy. Hence, 'liberty' corresponded to a *free market*, to the abolition of commercial barriers and protective tariffs and to the uninterrupted flow of goods and money, including, evidently, the freedom of signing contract necessary for all economic and labor transactions, and only then *human* freedom in the abstract. Therefore, any attempt to question the integration of the two liberties, market and human, into a consonant whole, any claim that human freedom may actually entail not freedom *of* the market but freedom *from* the market, was, and remains, virtually inconceivable on properly bourgeois-capitalist terms.

Similarly, the bourgeois notion of 'equality', as David Harvey observed, 'does not mean that everyone is or should be considered equal in all respects. It simply means that we would not exchange one use value for another under conditions of free exchange unless we valued the two at least equally well. Or, put in money terms, a dollar equals another dollar in terms of its purchasing power no matter whose pocket it is in.'[2] Under this light, it is clear why these notions could hardly have retained their validity in a broader social context, outside the limited boundaries of the economic sphere. At the onset of the bourgeois revolution, however, they seemed compatible, indeed indistinguishable. In other words, political and economic liberalisms were still considered but one, integral Liberalism. In the course of time, however, the incongruities underlying the liberal ethos became increasingly clear, generating two discourses of equality, two distinct, indeed opposed senses of the term, even if rarely appearing in pure form: the bourgeois which meant equality before the law and the socialist one, which insisted on socioeconomic equality, the very thing which capitalistic exchange rules out. Whereas the middle classes, in Harvey's example, were content to acknowledge the equality between dollars the socialists demanded that the *possessors of the dollars* should also be equal—an admittedly absurd claim within market economy.

As the eminent theoretician of liberalism C. B. Macpherson was able to show, the liberal conception of man and society was from its earliest stages inextricably bound with the perspective of the bourgeois class and conditioned by market society, as could be traced back to the primordial writings of Hobbes and Locke. Hobbes, Macpherson observed, has 'built his whole system on deductions from a model of man and a model of society which were . . . models of bourgeois man and capitalist society.'³ Accordingly, the egalitarian discourse of the bourgeoisie could not be understood unless within this framework of the market: 'Not only was this *equality of right* required for the operation of a market society, but at the same time it was the existence of the market that made the new equality possible. Traditional hierarchical society had required *unequal rights* as between ranks.'⁴ And so, from the very start, the bourgeois notion of equality rested firmly on the basis of market relations, hence comprising a structural indecision: on the one hand, it affirmed the *universal equality* of men once liberated from the artificial restrictions of the feudal caste system; on the other hand, men were liberated only to enter market transactions and be directly made *universally unequal*, each man accorded a different price-tag, registering the fluctuations of supply and demand: 'A man's value . . . was his price, that is, what another would give for the use of his power.'⁵

On a comparable basis, the French philosopher Alain Renaut has identified liberal individualism as a radically egalitarian ideology militating against the divinely ordained hierarchies of the ancien régime: 'the principle of hierarchy is thereby excluded in favor of the principle of equality. Such an individualism is the "cardinal value of modern societies," notably in the economic-political sphere, where the principle of equality takes the form of "liberalism."'⁶ As long as the bourgeoisie remained in opposition to absolutism this emphasis on political equality was of a revolutionary character. The French Revolution appeared to signify a glorious victory for individualism. The Declaration of the Rights of Man of 1789 'finally elevated equality and liberty—the "implications of individualism"—to the rank of supreme values.'⁷ Bourgeois individualism was thus an ideological construction which initially undermined hierarchy, proving extremely productive against the power-structure of the nobility. Elucidating his heliocentric theory, Bertolt Brecht's Galilei provides us with the gist of this bourgeois individualist revolution: 'Space had lost its center overnight, and by morning it had countless centers. From now on, everybody is seen as the center and nobody. For all of a sudden there is a lot of room.'⁸ With the collapse of the old hierarchy, once the earth/monarch are ousted from their illegitimate positions of domination, power is diffused throughout society. Each individual becomes important in itself, becomes, so to speak, the center of the universe, but alongside a myriad of other centers. This Brechtian notion of individualism, whose terms correspond to the early stages of the bourgeois revolution, grants the individual independence yet *not* supremacy. It is individualism fully compatible with the idea of equality, indeed one that makes no sense at all without equality at its basis: everybody can be *a* center only so long as nobody is *the* center.

On the other hand, however, individualism was part and parcel of the crystallizing ideology of free market economy, with its notions of private interests, individual enterprise, and the benefits of unbridled competition, as expounded from Hobbes to Mandeville and beyond. Here, individualism was basically understood as the individual's egoistic impulses, his self-serving activity which was postulated as the motor for economic advancement. *This* individualism was/is not only isolationist—in the sense that the individual is in principle indifferent to society, even if his self-seeking activity is ultimately said to promote general prosperity—but potentially *hostile* to society, inasmuch as it may restrict his personal freedom. It was thus only natural for the first ideological manifestation of individualism, the egalitarian one, to have been more dominant as long as the political struggle with the aristocracy was still going on, and to an early stage of capitalism when the conflict with the proletariat had not yet fully matured. Later on, however, by the same token, it was individualism of the second cast which became more relevant. It is befitting indeed that today, in a fully ripe capitalist society, it is essentially this second meaning of the term which remains dominant, namely individualism *against* the masses, whereas the other historical form of individualism, that which fought *against hierarchy*, remains but a dim echo whose egalitarian impulse is no longer easy to comprehend. The fully modern 'market-individualism' is not only independent from equality, but must forcefully discard it. Human *inequality* is its premise.[9] The two forms of individualism, the *political* and the *economical*, are seen to discard one another, the realization of the one signifying the annulment of the other.

Yet, although the contradiction between 'equality' and 'equality,' namely between the bourgeois-political meaning of the term and the socialist-economic one, was inherent to the liberal discourse, it only began to arouse serious problems and require conceptual clarification once the clash between these two classes was no longer concealed by their mutual effort to overcome absolutism. As the nineteenth century progressed it became increasingly a matter of aligning oneself with one of these mutually exclusive interpretations. From a bourgeois perspective, the pressing task was to articulate an individualistic discourse which will refute all egalitarian notions of the socialist kind, and abolish the dangerous utopia of an *actual*, as opposed to merely *formal* equality between all humans.

This, in a nutshell, is the historical context from which the modern liberal discourse of individualism has emerged. It was not concerned above all with questions of personal ethics but was first and foremost a *sociopolitical means of class-struggle*. Listening attentively to the proclamations of nineteenth-century bourgeois thinkers of individualism, we discover how their individualistic language was embedded in collective discourse and formulated vis-à-vis the working class—advantageously referred to as 'the masses,' 'the crowd,' the 'mob,' the 'multitude,' and so on. Ralph Waldo Emerson, for example, one of the most important thinkers to shape the American liberal ethos, extolled individualism, speaking enthusiastically about the need 'to believe your own thought, to believe that what is true for you in your private heart, is true for all men. . . . A man should learn to detect and watch that gleam of light which flashes across his mind from within, more than the lustre of the firmament of bards and sages.'[10] But it would be a mistake to assume that Emerson's praise of individual freedom was merely such an endorsement of creativity, independent thinking and the rejection of tradition. Clearly anticipating Nietzsche—who was to be a great admirer of his— Emerson affirmed that 'Good and bad are but names very readily transferable to that or this; the only right is what is after my constitution, the only wrong what is against it.'[11] Emerson envisioned a rebellion of the individual against social conventions that involved a proto-Nietzschean 'transvaluation of values.' By this I mean that it was no longer directed against social oppression, inequality, despotism and so on. Instead, it took the distinctive form of a protest against social solidarity, against equality:

> [D]o not tell me, as a good man did to-day, of my obligation to put all poor men in good situations. Are they my poor? I tell thee, thou foolish philanthropist, that I grudge the dollar, the dime, the cent I give to such men as do not belong to me and to whom I do not belong. There is a class of persons to whom by all spiritual affinity I am bought and sold; for them I will go to prison, if need be; but your miscellaneous popular charities; the education at college of fools; the building of meeting houses to the vain end to which may now stand; alms to sots; and the thousand Relief Societies;—though I confess with shame I sometimes succumb and give the dollar, it is a wicked dollar which by-and-by I shall have the manhood to withhold.[12]

Such a passage vividly demonstrates how far has the bourgeois come from those youthful, fraternal days when he still felt obliged to mankind as such. The universal love of the heyday of revolutionary Enlightenment—poetically encapsulated in Schiller's *Ode to Joy*: 'Be embraced, Millions! Take this kiss for all the world!'—was rapidly waning. By and by, such universal commitment transformed itself into an identification with 'a class of persons' and a loathing of other 'classes of persons,' the 'miscellaneous' 'fools' and 'sots.' Likewise, it goes to prove how the newfound *spiritual* authenticity of the enlightened individual had quite tangible, *economic* implications: every coin gone to Relief Societies was heartily 'begrudged.' This can be seen as an early example (1841) of how middle-class opposition to welfare measures and progressive taxation found its philosophical and ideological voice. Ingeniously, Emerson succeeded in making the insistence to hold on to every cent compatible with a superior level of personal ethics. With such encouragement, many a bourgeois individual could thus objectively act like a miser and still regard himself subjectively as a highly spiritual individual, defending his cherished privacy against the vicious assaults of the uncultured mass.

In view of this, we can better understand the social, *collective* logic, of bourgeois individualism.[13]

Precisely on this basis, we should grasp Nietzsche's highly contradicting notion of individualism and his conflicting statements on the matter. Nietzsche struggled to come to terms with this paradoxical nature of modern individualism, and to distinguish between its colliding elements: 'The modern European is characterized by two apparently opposite traits: individualism and the demand for equal rights; that I have at last come to understand.'[14] For Nietzsche, it consequently became a question of encouraging positive individualism, namely the one which affirms inequality between individuals, while refuting the claims of egalitarian individualism, which he abhorred. Thus, on the one hand, Nietzsche advocated an extreme view of the individual as a granite-like unit which rebuffs any attempt at social engineering:

> The individual is, in his future and in his past, a piece of fate, one law more, one necessity more for everything that is and everything that will be. To say to him 'change yourself' means to demand that everything should change, even in the past.[15]

On the other hand, however, he made it quite clear that the individual, a piece of fate or not, ought not become the measure of all things but rather must be integrated within a broader, and thoroughly un-egalitarian, scheme: 'My philosophy aims at an ordering of rank: not at an individualistic morality.'[16] Nietzsche attempted to distill a new, advanced form of individualism, purged of all egalitarian remnants. 'Thus it was,' diagnosed Renaut, 'that Nietzsche's most profound contribution to the history of subjectivity came to situate itself in a conflict between individualisms, in the transition from one model of individualism to another.'[17] Renaut proceeded to offer valuable insights into the precise nature of this new individualistic model. To start with, he tells us, such individualism 'would correspond not to the democratic ideal of equality but to that on an aristocracy which admires distance and hierarchy.[18] Even more important is Renaut's linking of Nietzschean individualism not simply with some abstract aristocratic ideal, but with our own contemporary, capitalist model. Nietzsche remarkably anticipates the individualism of our own days 'down to the tiniest details: narcissism, exclusive concern for oneself, the cult of independence, the sacrifice of the social, even the consumerist ethic.'[19] Thus, Nietzsche has ideologically completed the re-hierarchization of individualism which was initially supposed to tear down hierarchies. He has successfully prefigured, along with the bourgeois class, a brand of individual who mightily resists equality, who fulfils his individual identity precisely in the permanent struggle to overshadow the personalities of others, to assert his uniqueness vis-à-vis the anonymity of 'the majority of men.'

NIETZSCHE AND THE NEW BOURGEOIS ETHOS

Nietzsche lent passionate, philosophic as well as poetic, expression to the fear of the bourgeois individual in face of advancing mass democracy. His philosophy can claim a considerable share in the making of the mythological dichotomy between the talented, unique individual and the mediocre many. That such feeling of superiority was in fact ridden with deep insecurity, with an at least intuitive understanding that so much of this reputed supremacy rests upon social circumstances and may vanish when these alter, is manifested all along the line, from the affirmation of slavery as the basis for culture to the refutation of compulsory education. Nietzsche's free individual, even more than Emerson's, was not the individual as such, in the abstract, but only the individual as member of the ruling-classes: 'I set it down that egoism pertains to the essence of the noble soul, I mean the immovable faith that to a being such as "we are" other beings have to be subordinate by their nature, and sacrifice themselves to us.'[20] Notice the way Nietzsche here seamlessly switches from the singular 'noble soul' to the plural 'we,' quietly turning a personal trait of an individual 'egoist' into a group attribute. When today so many Nietzsche scholars enthusiastically emphasize his commitment to 'individual expression,' to 'free development,' and so on, it is easy to lose sight of the fact that such individualism was reserved to an elect minority, whose free development, moreover, meant the deliberate narrowing and crippling of the individualities of the vast majority. Nietzsche is greatly misconstrued when taken to be the critic of modern mediocrity and instrumentality, an aristocratic outsider, dismayed by the monotony of bourgeois civilization. Rather than wishing to remove mediocrity, Nietzsche declared it indispensable for the existence of the elite: 'Hatred for mediocrity is unworthy of a philosopher: . . . What *I* fight against: that an exceptional type should make war on the rule—instead of grasping that the continued existence of the rule is the precondition for the value of the exception.'[21] Or, interchangeably: '*The dwarfing of man* must for a long time count as the only goal; because a broad foundation has first to be created so that a stronger species of man can stand upon it.'[22] Far from attacking capitalist instrumentality Nietzsche contemplated means of inculcating it as a value, a value for the serving-man:

I attempt an *economic* justification of virtue.—The task is to make man as useful as possible and to approximate him, as far as possible, to an infallible machine: to this end he must be equipped with the values of the machine (—he must learn to experience the states in which he works in a mechanically useful way as the supremely valuable states; hence it is necessary to spoil the other states for him as much as possible, as highly dangerous and disreputable).

The first stumbling block is the boredom, the monotony, that all mechanical activity brings with it. To learn to endure this . . . that is the invaluable task and achievement of higher schooling. . . . Such an existence perhaps requires a philosophical justification and transfiguration more than any other. . . .[23]

Systematic manufacturing of mediocrity and monotony in the laboring masses were hence squarely endorsed by Nietzsche; the problem for him arises only when those who are meant to serve rebel against their condition and insist on sharing the privileges of creativity and luxury reserved for the ruling class. When this collective prerogative was threatened by the rising mobocracy the reaction was unsurprisingly one of vehement repulsion. It is in this context of escalating class struggle that Zarathustra's extreme militancy against 'the rabble' must be understood:

> Life is a fountain of delight; but where the rabble also drinks all wells are poisoned.
>   . . . And many a one who turned away from life, turned away only from the rabble: he did not wish to share the well and the flame and the fruit with the rabble.
>   . . . And like a wind I will one day blow among them and with my spirit take away the breath from their spirit: thus my future will have it.
>   Truly, Zarathustra is a strong wind to all flatlands; and he offers his advice to all that spews and spits: 'Take care not to spit against the wind!'[24]

And is Zarathustra here, in refusing 'to share the fruit' with the horde any less genuine than Emerson, grudging his dimes and cents?

The place where the initial pact between the bourgeoisie and the 'rabble' of the proletariat begins to dissolve is precisely where the Nietzschean hero mounts the stage. Few thinkers have played as substantial a role in the making of this ideological transformation as Nietzsche. He was deeply aware of the need to develop a new ethos, which will correspond to the changes in the historical status of the bourgeoisie and the new challenges it had to confront. These challenges were significantly no longer from *above* but from *below*. Nietzsche realized that there was a 'before' and an 'after' of the French Revolution, and that the Enlightenment project, which the bourgeoisie had defended and which had defended the bourgeoisie, was no longer a reliable weapon. More precisely, the weapon of the Enlightenment has remained, in itself, as effective as ever, but its firepower was now directed against the former revolutionaries. The Enlightenment 'belief in the earthly happiness of all' has expanded dangerously into the 'threatening demand for . . . an Alexandrian earthly happiness.'[25] As Eric Bentley usefully put it, paraphrasing Nietzsche's position: 'The new bourgeois liberalism was not a new system of values . . . but only a complex of ideas instrumental to the overthrow of the old regime. To regard these ideas as ideals would be sheer nihilism.'[26]

Thus, from now on, the efforts of many bourgeois thinkers were concentrated precisely on the attempt to weaken the very claims and beliefs that the bourgeoisie itself has given rise to, to systematically dismantle the universalistic and humanistic motto of 'Liberté, égalité, fraternité.' For Marx, analyzing the bourgeois reaction to the independent stance taken by the proletariat during the 1848 revolutions, 'Fraternity lasted only so long as there was a fraternity of interests between bourgeoisie and proletariat,'[27] and: 'It was now a matter of abolishing this word and the illusions hiding in its ambiguous bosom.'[28] Of course, the old creeds of feudalism were no longer suited for this task. There was no turning back, despite Metternich's obstinacy, to the reign of God and Monarch, as a wave of revolutions and the 'spring of nations' had clearly shown. Nietzsche had accepted as much when he whispered—note the intimacy!—'*In the ear of conservatives*':

> [E]ven today there are parties whose goal is a dream of the crabwise *retrogression* of all things. But no one is free to be a crab. There is nothing for it: one *has* to go forward, which is to say *step by step further into décadence* (—this is my definition of modern 'progress' . . .).[29]

Notwithstanding the apparent capitulation implied in such a passage, Nietzsche rose to meet the challenge of 'decadence' and put forward a comprehensive alternative theory to support hierarchy where religion, the most important Ideological State Apparatus of the nineteenth century, in Althusser's terminology, could no longer play such a vital part.[30] In the rather regrettable absence of God as a social overseer, nature will have to play the patron of hierarchy. This was the pith of social Darwinism, an outlook to which, as regards sociopolitical import, Nietzsche ultimately belonged. I would argue that it is precisely in his *critique* of Darwin, that Nietzsche actually becomes *more* of a *social* Darwinist. Nietzsche believed that the outcome of evolution will not be a higher type of human being but rather a perfect herd animal. The healthy principle of natural selection which under properly ruthless conditions ought to ensure the survival of the strongest, would be reversed by the hordes of mediocre individuals, once they exploit their sheer numerical superiority to sweep aside the extraordinary specimen and create an environment favourable for the weak. Hence, nature could not be entrusted with the creation of the *Übermensch*, unless a way can be found to help it overcome the ruse of weakly egalitarianism.[31] What was needed was therefore a willed, conscious transvaluation of all values. Therein lay the importance of 'the will to power,' that Trojan horse that Nietzsche introduced into the heart of modern culture. With this central notion Nietzsche attempted to escape the dead end of Darwinism; the will to power is at once natural, inasmuch as it is the underlying motivation behind all life, and *anti*-natural, inasmuch as, under 'normal,' natural conditions, the tendency is to repress the will to power, to curb its operations in favor of the safety of morality. Only a cultural revolution refuting the comforts of conventional morality might exert humanity to celebrate its will to power and resist the mellow temptations of democracy and socialism.

The following passage from the *Nachlass* usefully encapsulates the three cardinal aspects of Nietzsche's outlook discussed so far: first, its grounding in the exact historical juncture where bourgeois ideology decisively splits apart; secondly, its justification of the new hegemony; and, finally, the central role of the will to power in underpinning the entire construction:

> N.B.:
>   1. Individuals liberate themselves.
>   2. they enter into struggle with one another, they come to an agreement over 'equality of rights'(—'justice' as the aim—);
>   3. once this is achieved, the actual inequalities of force produce an enhanced effect . . . Now individuals organize themselves in groups; the groups struggle for privileges and predominance. Strife breaks out again in a milder form.
>
>   One desires *freedom* so long as one does not possess power. Once one does possess it, one desires to overpower; if one cannot do that (if one is still too weak to do so), one desires 'justice', i.e., *equal power*.[32]

This chart is of great significance because it epitomizes not merely Nietzsche's personal views, but also the nucleus of middle-class ideology in general. Nietzsche furnished a sketch of the evolution of the bourgeoisie as corresponding to the different historical phases it went through. His outline of the three main phases in the development of the individual's struggle for power, though not providing a reliable account of the historical proceedings, nevertheless reflects the essential ideological shift of the bourgeoisie. Initially a revolutionary class, fighting against feudal restrictions, the aftermath of the French Revolution saw it as the dominant class, seeking to protect and expand its preeminence opposite the proletariat. What Nietzsche registers, in other words, is the increasingly wavering posture of the middle classes vis-à-vis the tenets of the Enlightenment; as long as it needed to brave feudal institutions, the Enlightenment project served the bourgeoisie to perfection: the endorsement of equality and of justice against the ancien régime was extremely useful for its purposes. As Nietzsche put it, they gathered under the banner of 'equality of rights' and 'justice.' Once, however, this goal was finally achieved, these very same claims became a hindrance instead of an aid, for now they were voiced against the hierarchical structure of which the bourgeoisie itself was master. For the purposes of the working class the Enlightenment remained a highly useful ideological complex, as under 'liberty, equality, fraternity,' it could still quite coherently state its case. But those on the opposite side of the social divide appropriately entered a process of gradual ideological transmutation. They banished, to a greater or lesser degree, obsolete egalitarian humanism to extract a much greater value from irrationality, pessimism, vitalism and ultraist individualism.

Nietzsche's contribution was in justifying such *volte-face* and grounding it on the existential struggle for power. In order to do that, to be sure, he had to lay bare this historical turnabout, to show very clearly how the middle classes have disowned their former egalitarian ethos; yet, far from denouncing the bourgeoisie as hypocritical or deceitful, such uncovering was undertaken with the intention of establishing the legitimacy, in fact *inevitability* of such a move. The bourgeoisie may not have been faithful to the people, may have deserted its universal task, yet only on account of *remaining* loyal—on a deeper and more significant level—to the will to power. This was a translation of the actual history of the bourgeoisie to the language of the will to power. For this aim, Nietzsche clearly needed to mythicize history, fundamentally by establishing the individual as the basis of the bourgeois revolution, asserting that 'individuals liberated themselves.' In phase three of his half-historiographical/half-genealogical draft, he argued that 'the individuals organize themselves in groups,' on the basis of their proportionate individual power. Thus he described classes as *defined by individuals*, and not as *defining the individuals*; the entire social stratification of the ancien régime, which largely extended into the bourgeois era, was alleged to be a completely recent product, developing only after the Revolution was completed. This historical 'illusion' was instrumental in 'authenticating' that the new order ensued form a completely fresh start, a social tabula rasa, and was not molded into the social patterns of yore. The class system could therefore have been presented as compatible with the bourgeois ideal of meritocracy, as it was claimed merely to reflect the difference in competence between individuals.

Considered thus, Nietzsche's emancipatory 'exposure' of power, so central to postmodernism and poststructuralism, epitomized in the work of Foucault, was in fact an attempt to *install* power and exploitation as the irrevocable basis of all (healthy) politics, and thereby absolve the bourgeoisie of its betrayal of former egalitarian ideals. Foucault famously celebrated Nietzsche as a 'master of suspicion,' while the latter, on the very contrary, wished to counter the 'suspicion' of those who denounced the cynical power politics of the bourgeoisie. To that accusation Nietzsche ingeniously responded: yes, it is power politics, and there is nothing wrong with that; the real wrongdoers are the social radicals, who desire to ban the use of power. Befittingly, Nietzsche punished the bourgeois conservatives of his day precisely on account of the way they shirked from admitting power as the sound motive for their actions. Lacking such assertiveness, they inevitably yielded ground to the radicals: 'And the party opposed to [the socialists] is just as ludicrous, because it does not admit the element of violence in the law, the severity and egoism in every kind of authority.'[33] Because the conservatives still abide by the principles of morality they must accept the terms dictated by the herd. What is needed is a bold offensive that will change the rules of the game altogether, discard the self-defeating stratagems of parliamentary pseudo rule and proudly announce an old-new, aristocratic morality: "'I and my kind' want to rule and survive; whoever degenerates will be expelled or destroyed'—this is the basic feeling behind every ancient legislation."[34] If the bourgeoisie was ever more aggressive in its actual use of political power, ever more militant in the escalating struggle with the socialist menace, Nietzscheanism can be seen as the philosophical vindication of such a move, of the struggle to banish the *ideological* residues of humanism which the bourgeoisie needed to get rid of in actual *politics*.

FROM NIETZSCHE TO AYN RAND

Apparently, such a reading of Nietzsche as a philosophic protector of bourgeois interests runs stubbornly against his frequent criticisms of the bourgeoisie, its narrow-mindedness, greed, lack of refinement, search for comfort, and so on. For how can someone still be considered a pro-capitalist ideologue who has decreed 'industrial culture' to be 'altogether the most vulgar form of existence that has yet existed. Here one is at the mercy of brute need; one wants to live and has to sell oneself, but one despises those who exploit this need and *buy* the worker'?[35] Here, however, it is vital to refrain from automatically assuming the identity of a cultural critique of capitalism with a political one. For what Nietzsche found reprehensible about 'industrial culture' was precisely what he considered *counterproductive* at the *political* level. Thus, when the former citation is understood in its immediate context, it becomes easy to appreciate how the real effort was to offer a better support to the capitalistic division of labor, not to upset it:

> *On the lack of noble manners.*— Soldiers and leaders still have far better relationships with each other than workers and employers. So far at least, culture that rests on a military basis still towers above all so-called industrial culture . . . What the workers see in the employer is usually only a cunning, blood-sucking dog of a man who speculates on all misery; and the employer's name, shape, manner, and reputation are a matter of complete indifference to them. The manufacturers and entrepreneurs of business probably have been too deficient so far in all those forms and signs of a *higher race* that alone make a *person* interesting. If the nobility of birth showed in their eyes and gestures, there might not be any socialism of the masses . . . But the lack of higher manners and the notorious vulgarity of manufacturers with their ruddy, fat hands, give him [the most common man—I.L.] the idea that it is only accident and luck that have elevated one person above another. Well, then, he reasons: let *us* try accident and luck! Let us throw the dice! And thus socialism is born.[36]

That is, what Nietzsche found disturbing about industrial culture was not that the employer is 'usually only a cunning, bloodsucking dog of a man,' but that the worker is able to recognize him as such. In that respect, Nietzsche's cultural critique was essentially the work of an instructor in manners, tutoring a vulgar entrepreneur in the art of appearing an 'interesting person,' and furnishing the industrialist with fine aristocratic gloves so that he can cover his 'ruddy, fat hands.' His cultural critique was quite prepared to change the 'employer's name, shape, manner, and reputation,' so that the basic nature of his commanding relation with the laborer will persist intact. Nietzsche also exposes the purely symbolic character of nobility, admitting, as it were, that it consists of a set of imposing gestures compelling the deference of the commoners. In this light, the whole idea of the social 'pathos of distance,' so central to Nietzsche's thought, is exposed as playacting, a grand dramatic performance which, if successful, creates an illusion of inner distinction, and arouses the spectator's admiration, recognition and, finally, submission.[37]

In Ayn Rand's showpiece of popular Nietzscheanism, *The Fountainhead*—which the author had initially considered dedicating to Nietzsche—there can be found almost a replica of this image of a noble capitalism, one that is able to command the working class by its immanent charisma, to cast an irresistible spell over the proletariat. This unique gift is embodied in the overmanly architect Howard Roark who alone represents the true essence of capitalism. Roark is truly *a unit*, in Rand's terms, complete in itself, dedicating his life to a celebration of his individualistic pith and impervious to external demands and expectations. Unlike the other architects in the novel, who are merely 'second-handers,' devoid of autonomous substance and thus directed by the dictates of society, by the ignoble mob, Roark is the utterly self-sufficient hero, destined to triumph against all social obstacles.[38] Now let us observe the impact of such nobility as it confronts the working class, represented by the electrician Mike. Mike is a crude individual of limited capacities but, befitting the ideal servant, also an honest, sturdy person. Described as bulldog-like, his nature is fierce and suspicious, but at the same time calling for the taming hand of the ordained master. Their relationship commences with a cold incredulity on Mike's part, as they first meet casually on a construction site. This is the phase of *suspicion*. Mike contemptuously rejects Roark's proposal to show him how to correctly get his pipes around a beam since, at that introductory stage, he believes Roark to be the typical middle-class 'second hander,' the arrogant, inept, college smart aleck, for whom he can feel no respect.[39] In snubbing Roark's advance, Mike is not merely speaking for himself but tacitly expressing the overall contemptuous disposition of all his associates, of the working class in general, toward the incompetent elite.

Then, however, comes a crucial moment, in which Roark energetically grabs the electrician's tools and exquisitely shows the astonished workingman what he is truly made of. This is the second phase in their relationship—*recognition*. The blue flame shining out of Roark's blue-blooded hand, this transmission of his inner value, inspires veneration in the rough, skeptical toiler. Mike concedes defeat, surrenders before such display of immanent nobility.[40] Following his recognition of Roark's magnificent skills comes a phase of warm friendship in which the two, architect and electrician, cohabit harmoniously, on apparently equal terms. But there remains yet another development for the circle to be completed. When Roark wins his first commission as an architect, Mike, his 'bulldog face spreading into a huge grin,' spontaneously presents himself at the construction site, ready to render service: '"Hello, Red," said Mike, much too casually, and added: "Hello, boss."'[41] This is the third phase—*submission*. From the 'much too casual' 'hello, Red,' to the proper, deferential, 'hello, boss.' Just like Nietzsche had predicted, true nobility wins the day and the worker assumes his ineluctable place in the hierarchical order. Suspicion—recognition—submission: the *vini, vidi, vici* of the noble capitalist. The dangerous, bulldog-like worker, could have easily turned into a predatory socialist, but instead, handled by a true nobleman, was tamed into a devoted pet. It required no force, happened quite voluntarily, the natural order of things asserting itself. As Rand makes quite clear, Mike's cheerful compliance is certainly no exceptional reaction, for it merely exemplifies the general impact of Roark's soothing, gubernatorial touch upon all 'the workers in the house'.[42]

CAPITALISM AS ARTIST-GOD

Nietzsche's cultural critique, however, was not restricted to such engineering of social illusions in the service of the class system. In culturally complementing capitalism, it certainly reached deeper than the level of etiquette. Alongside censuring the bourgeoisie's *vulgarity*, Nietzsche was decidedly vitriolic when dealing with its *benevolence*. As is well known, Nietzsche was a vehement detractor of utilitarianism, of the pursuit of material prosperity and comfort, arguing, for example, that the noble man 'leaves happiness to the great majority: happiness as peace of soul, virtue, comfort, Anglo-angelic shopkeeperdom à la Spencer.'[43] In contrast to such English liberalism with its promise of earthly contentment, he extolled the benefits of pain, danger, risk. The standard liberal endorsement of the market economy presented it as a flawless, quasi-ideal system, which creates wealth, rewards economic enterprise and assures general socioeconomic well-being. Such a guileless idealization of capitalism, however, suffered from a massive ideological handicap as it could only account for the positive, productive sides of capitalism, not for its destructive failings. As the nineteenth century progressed and the bourgeois project had become real existing capitalism, controlling both the economy and the state, such failings became increasingly difficult to deny. Presenting the capitalistic society as the best of all possible words, as a utopia of prosperity, welfare and comfort, the standard argument had little explanative power when it came to dealing with a largely anticlimactic reality of abundance for the few amidst poverty for the many, social and psychological alienation, friction and general insecurity. At this precise point, the conventional liberal and utilitarian ideological armor had lent itself vulnerable to radical social critique, which vouched for an alternative of equality, security and harmony.

Here arose the objective need to come about with fresh justifications of the market economy, such that will succeed where the old arguments had considerably lost vigor. That mission was historically fulfilled by social Darwinism, within which Nietzsche, as already suggested, was a key, albeit maverick, player. Whereas the standard argument had dealt only with the capitalistic pledge of happiness but had cast a blind eye over its potential for catastrophe, the social Darwinist argument managed to integrate precisely the catastrophic dimension into its discourse. This it did, of course, by grounding the catastrophe on the 'natural' struggle for survival, and showing the inevitability and eventual usefulness of competition with all its 'cruel' aspects. Social Darwinism was thus able to take the suffering, anxiety and strife of social reality and transform them—at least ideologically—from unbearable curses into precious blessings. [44]

Hence, far from shaking the pillars of the capitalistic mode of production, this cultural critique was vital in furnishing them with theoretical abutment. In one remarkable passage, as I suggest to read it, this inner truth of the Nietzschean project, its hidden material logic of which Nietzsche himself was doubtless only partially aware, emerges with particular force. Approximating the zenith of his philosophical career (1886), Nietzsche is looking back at his first book, *The Birth of Tragedy*, and is struck by the prescience of what he was already then tentatively trying to accomplish. Nietzsche sees already behind this early and embryonic attempt the bold celebration of a new, amoral artist-god. What I find remarkable about this description, however, is that this artist-god, arising to face us from the unfathomable depths of primordial myth, uncannily fits in all his crucial features the classical Marxist description of—capitalism:

> Indeed, the whole book knows only an artistic meaning and crypto-meaning behind all events—a 'god', if you please, but certainly only an entirely reckless and amoral artist-god, who wants to experience, whether he is building or destroying, in the good and in the bad, his own joy and glory—one who, creating worlds, frees himself from the *distress* of fullness and *overfullness* and from

the *affliction* of the contradictions compressed in his soul. The world—at every moment the *attained* salvation of God, as the changing, eternally new vision of the most deeply afflicted, discordant, and contradictory being who can find salvation only in *appearance*: you can call this whole artists' metaphysics arbitrary, idle, fantastic; what matters is that it betrays a spirit who will one day fight at any risk whatever the *moral* interpretation and significance of existence. Here, perhaps for the first time, a pessimism 'beyond good and evil' is suggested.[45]

In *The Birth of Tragedy* Nietzsche discarded historicism and the shallow world of phenomena, society and politics; he delved into the depths of nature, art and the psyche; unraveled the workings of the primordial myth, of existence, of the Kantian noumenon only to return full circle and stare the capitalist mode of production right in the face. For hasn't Nietzsche inadvertently provided us here with a description/celebration of capitalism, with its abounding power to 'build and destroy,' its restless, frenzied 'eternal changing,' its circular crises of 'fullness and overfullness,' and its inner 'contradictions and afflictions' which it is able to solve 'only in appearance' displacing them to a higher level? The pessimistic, mythical view of an aesthetical deity is well-nigh perfectly homologous to the social Darwinist theoretical framework, however far apart from each other they may appear. For, just as the social Darwinists replaced God with nature and its medium of natural selection, so did Nietzsche's artist-god offer himself as an alternative to the antiquated deity. Furthermore, both substitute gods, whether called Evolution or Dionysos, were working on behalf of the material forces of capitalism. What Nietzsche's artist-god was meant to substitute was the old notion of a god concerned with the well-being of each individual.[46] Nietzsche's notion of divinity, by contrast, urged his readers to accept the fact that god is completely indifferent to the fate of humans, who are for him but playing things with which he toys to satisfy his aesthetic impulses. Here, the appropriate metaphor is again a primordial creative-destructive force, a Schopenhauerian Will with a dash of diabolic gaiety, which shapes and dissolves the world without paying the slightest heed to human interests and the moral illusions they apply to justify them. As Raymond Geuss perceptively commented:

> The non-individuated reality behind all appearances, what Nietzsche calls *das Ur-Eine* ('the primordially one') (*passim*), is itself a kind of artist. . . . Nietzsche writes that this primordial unity is like a child playing in the sand on the beach, wantonly and haphazardly creating individuated shapes and then destroying them, taking equal pleasure in both parts of the process, in both creation (Apollo) and destruction (Dionysos). Our world is nothing but a momentary configuration of shapes in the sand. The child's play does not in any significant sense follow 'rational' principles and has no purpose beyond itself. It is innocent and 'beyond good and evil'. . . .[47]

The ideological usefulness of such new 'religion' is indeed vast, for if we come to accept our world as governed by an irrational child, the world of phenomena, Nietzsche's 'actual,' is vindicated metaphysically, with its medley of tensions, contradictions, torment, 'cruelty,' 'injustice' and so on, while any critical or reformative movements are reduced to futile 'optimism,' a jaundiced, aesthetically inferior resistance in the face of the eternal. If, prior to the new Nietzschean 'theodicy,' the individual could substantiate his right to safety and happiness by appealing to a higher benefactor, a merciful anthropomorphic God, now it was precisely this deity that revoked in advance any such expectations. Nietzsche's view was therefore barely atheistic at all. It was not the case that there was no longer a higher authority to which agonizing humanity could turn to in its distress; god was not really dead; it was *god himself,* rather, who lavishly inflicted all sorts of misery on humanity merely to satisfy his artistic whims.

The nature of this artist-god was so conceived that 'worshipping' it entailed an affirmation of even the most acute human suffering, as pertaining to the divine plan of the world as an aesthetic phenomenon. Not only was the 'new' god unjust and amoral, but he deserved to be celebrated as such: 'The world and life may come to *seem* "justified" for us to the extent to which we, through various aesthetic experiences, can come close to identifying ourselves in the primordial child and seeing the beauty of the play.'[48] In this way, the unpleasant vicissitudes of capitalism could be presented to modern man as divine and awe-striking; the working of an artist-god was supposed to be evident precisely in the chaotic arbitrariness of this mode of production, in its uncontrollability, periodic circular crises and disregard for human needs and conventions. Since the artist-god was far from commanding omnipotent abilities, as was clear to Nietzsche, we were prompted to actively assist him in preserving the sand-like precariousness of our social ground: 'If the individuals are to become stronger, society must remain in *a state of emergency,* always in the expectance of great variations: lead a *continually provisional existence.*'[49]

Nietzsche's contempt at utilitarianism as decadent was therefore by no means a critique of capitalism as an economic system, but, on the contrary, an attempt to neutralize what was considered the decaying element in bourgeois culture and politics, which may eventually eat into the foundations of the class system and veer towards democracy and socialism. In other words, Nietzsche rebuked the bourgeoisie for not being capitalistic enough, or, interchangeably, for being capitalistic on account of the wrong, utilitarian, comfort- and safety-seeking reasons. Utilitarianism, according to Nietzsche, was merely a democratic prelude to socialism, as attested to particularly by its emphasis on the 'the happiness of the greatest number.' In that respect Nietzsche's cultural critique of philistine bourgeois complacency was broadly anticipative of, if not emulated directly by such proto-fascist thinkers as Tommaso Marinetti, who protested against the 'timid clerical conservatism symbolized by the bedroom slippers and the hot water bottle,' favoring instead the heroic hygiene of war[50]; or Vilfredo Pareto, who found that the liberal institution of democracy is conducive to the survival of *the weakest*: 'Going along to the polling station to vote is a very easy business, and if by so doing one can procure food and shelter, then everybody— especially the unfit, the incompetent and the idle—will rush to do it.'[51]

MARKET HEROISM

The example of Ayn Rand's aristocratic capitalist demonstrates how, within Nietzscheanism, two apparently incompatible cultural tendencies, namely bourgeois culture and heroism, are brought into harmony. Superficially examined, the notion of heroism which Nietzsche promoted seems to reflect an aristocratic sensitivity *set against* the ascending, materialistic middle-class values and 'bedroom slippers' mentality. For, as one might initially object, who could feel himself further estranged within the confines of bourgeois, profit-oriented culture, than the hero, a knightly figure willing to sacrifice his fortune and his life for the sake of antiquated ideals, obsolete conceptions of boldness, bravery, glory? Is not Nietzsche giving voice to the agonized, diminishing class of the aristocracy, which sees its noble values eroded by the mundane nouveau-riche class for whom nobility is, at best, a charming nostalgia? Nietzschean heroism, however, as the juxtaposing of Nietzsche and Rand helps to illustrate, should not be mistaken for a call to an aristocratic alternative to capitalism, a withdrawal to a preceding social order. As Nietzsche explained with the crab metaphor, a conservative retreat is out of the question. Capitalism is a lasting reality not to be denied but rather to be confronted realistically. And, from a realistic point of view, what an aristocrat should aim for facing the bourgeois social order, is to abet its positive aspects and forestall the negative potentialities. A way should be found through which hierarchy could best be boosted whereas the leveling down, the democratic tendency of the bourgeois revolution, be held in check. Nietzsche was useful to the bourgeoisie not because he was its outright spokesman, a bourgeois ideologue *tout court*. No doubt, his relation to capitalism was an uneasy one, of a cultural aristocrat still struggling to come to terms with the arch cataclysm of 1789 and the post-revolutionary order. But it was specifically his position as a relative *outsider* that rendered his thought so deeply germane to the contemporary needs of the bourgeoisie. Nietzsche's attempt to make the best of the new social order, which, for him, meant to *aristocratize* it to the greatest possible extent, came at a time when the bourgeoisie needed nothing more than just such ennoblement. If the patrician philosopher was keen to interfere in the bourgeois order to interrupt its democratization, the parvenu bourgeois class was no less eager to receive such refined ideological training.

The extent of the compatibility of Nietzsche's adamant denial of equality with bourgeois thought can be gauged by taking a look at one of the quintessential texts of liberalism, John Stuart Mill's classic treatise *On Liberty*. The concise title is something of a misnomer inasmuch as the book deals not only, or even mainly, with liberty but also, or more so, with what is perceived as endangering it: equality. Mill, like so many theorists of the post-revolutionary era (1848 onwards), had to deal with the deep incongruities manifesting themselves at the heart of the classic Enlightenment ethos. The union of equality and liberty turns out to be a mismatch, despite a brief optimistic honeymoon, since unbounded equality means precisely the limitation of economic liberty. Hence, objectively regarded, he set out to develop a theory of liberty tractable to the interests of the propertied classes and against the demands of equality. The book is possibly the strongest ever statement concerning the ostensible conflict between 'liberty' and 'equality,' and the need to choose between them, obviously in favor of the former, which is by now an almost axiomatic bourgeois notion.[52] In liberal discourse, which today more than ever is the consensual one, Mill has been de-historicized almost into a platonic ideal of tolerance and pluralism, representing an idealistic commitment to minority rights, freedom and forbearance, above any fanatic, sectarian interest. Yet underlying Mill's concern for minority rights were his misgivings about majority rule and the unsavory implications of mass democracy for the *wealthy* minority, apprehensions expressed, for example, in *Considerations on Representative Government*:

> In all countries there is a majority of poor, a minority who, in contradistinction, may be called rich. Between these two classes, on many questions, there is complete opposition of apparent interest. . . . [I]s there not a considerable danger lest they [the poor majority] should throw upon the possessors of what is called realized property, and upon the larger incomes, an unfair share, or even the whole, of the burden of taxation . . . in modes supposed to conduce to the profit and advantage of the labouring class? . . . Legislative attempts to raise wages, limitation of competition in the labour market . . . are very natural . . . results of a feeling of class interest in a governing majority of manual labourers.[53]

Mill was anxious about the increasing probability within a parliamentary democracy of a working-class government which might take the drastic, liberty-countering measures of progressively raising the income tax and limiting the pliancy of cheap labour supply (a like-minded sensibility for minority rights was expressed—admittedly in a grotesque manner—by Ayn Rand, in her eloquently titled piece: 'America's Persecuted Minority: Big Business'[54]). As against this peril, Mill recommended the fairly unoriginal remedy of a diluted democracy in which the tiny, rich minority and the massive, poor majority are 'equally balanced, each influencing about an equal number of votes in Parliament.' [55] In this way the balance will effectively be turned in the favor of liberty and against equality. Thus, ironically enough, Mill's concern with tolerance was triggered subliminally/ideologically, by a basic *intolerance*. He was objectively driven to defend persecuted minorities as part of the pressing capitalist need to impose upon the vast majority in society a socioeconomic arrangement favored only by the minority. Hence he became, in effect, the mouthpiece of a *persecuting* minority. For it is one thing do defend, say, Protestant rights in a Catholic country and quite another kettle of fish to enforce Protestantism on the whole population. Mill, to be sure, was no reactionary and that he was profoundly motivated by genuine humanitarian sensitivity, is beyond doubt. But precisely his moderate, mild, middle-of-the-road, in many regards outright progressive position (notably his pioneering support for the emancipation of women), testifies that the anti-democratic position pertains to the very heart of liberalism and is bound with its intrinsic logic, rather than constituting some regrettable, merely 'anti-liberal,' aberration.

Thus, for all Nietzsche's scorn at Mill's benevolent utilitarianism, which was still formally committed to the ignominious 'good of the greatest number,' Mill's ubiquitous lamentations concerning the modern rise of mediocrity evince significant similarities to Nietzsche's analysis of the pernicious leveling of modernity. For instance when Mill speaks on behalf of the genius oppressed by the masses:

> Persons of genius, it is true, are, and are always likely to be, a small minority; but in order to have them, it is necessary to preserve the soil in which they grow. Genius can only breathe freely in an *atmosphere* of freedom. . . . In sober truth . . . the general tendency of things throughout the world is to render mediocrity the ascendant power among mankind. In ancient history, in the middle ages, and in a diminishing degree through the long transition from feudality to the present time, the individual was a power in himself; . . . at present individuals are lost in the crowd. . . . The only power deserving the name is that of masses, and of governments while they make themselves the organ of the tendencies and instincts of the masses.[56]

It can be seen how Mill's utilitarian pledge to the interests of the 'greatest number' is already in the process of being transmuted into a justification of elite rule, playing the individual genius against the inert masses. At the very least, a serious tension manifests itself here between the classic utilitarianism which informs Mill's position at the level of theory and the realities of crystallizing mass democracy at the level of politics. Mill was wavering between his theoretical commitment to the majority and his actual fear of it.

His solution to this problem would seem rather a denial of it: the gifted individual, the benefactor of mankind, must be shielded against the masses *for the good of the masses*. Likewise, the institution of private property and the enormous iniquities it entails (and Mill unswervingly admitted, for instance, that 'the condition of numbers in civilized Europe, and even in England and France, is more wretched than that of most tribes of savages who are known to us'[57]) is ultimately beneficial for the working class itself, since, in the long run, the unbounded prosperity of the rich will trickle down and enrich society at large.

Mill would never abandon, nor even seriously bring into question, his sacred tenet of 'the common good,' just as he would never renounce his belief in rationalistic research in the name of absolute sociopolitical neutrality. But his theories would seem to legitimate rather different conclusions: since the masses of individuals are said to be mediocre, passive and uncreative they need to be stimulated by a handful of active individuals in order for human progress to be achieved. Innovative individuals are 'the salt of the earth; without them, human life would become a stagnant pool. Not only is it they who introduce good things which did not before exist; it is they who keep up life in those which already existed.'[58] In this light, the basic political task would seem to be the identifying and cultivating—if not directly breeding—of such select individuals in order to create an aristocratic vanguard, which will assume leading positions in society and politics—a mission which broadly corresponds to Mill's vision of a 'qualitative' democracy as opposed to the rule of sheer numbers. The affinity, at least a potential one, between this position and Nietzsche's project of the breeding of higher men is conspicuous. It is true that in Mill's version of things the significance of the genius is still formally measured strictly in terms of the utility he/she can bring to the well-being of the community as a whole. Nietzsche, of course, boldly discarded this commitment to the common good. 'We must think of the masses,' he once claimed, 'as unsentimentally as we think of nature: they preserve the species.'[59] But once humanity is cast in the role of the herd it becomes but a question of the shepherd's personal, whimsical inclination, to decide whether the herd should be protected or rather used for his own advantage, like herds, in all truth, are normally being used, to supply their shepherds with warm wool, fresh milk or even tasty meat. Once we accept, as Mill frequently does, the notion of the masses as a conglomerate of indifferent, cattle-like persons, qualitatively inferior to the handful of geniuses supposed to lead them and improve their lives, it does not seem so terribly outrageous to take another step in this direction and suggest that it should be *the masses* who serve the good of their superiors.

Considered thus, from a historical perspective, Mill's thought emerges not so much as opposed to Nietzscheanism, but as a transitional phase in its development.[60] The genius must enjoy special social privileges if he is to thrive, and when Mill spoke of guaranteeing 'an atmosphere of freedom' he clearly had more in mind than mere deference to the genius on part of the masses. The atmosphere of liberty rather entailed, as we have seen, an interdiction of mass intervention in the free market, a banning of the attempt to raise wages and taxes, or modify labour arrangements. If the organized working class sets out to free *its* numerous individuals by reducing their labor hours or raising their salaries this, far from enhancing liberty in Mill's eyes, actually constitutes a heavy violation of the atmosphere of freedom, from which the genius must benefit. The genius would therefore appear to stand ultimately for the bourgeois class in its entirety, small in number and supposedly gifted, while the multitude of indifferent persons rising against him is the hydra of the working class. The conflict between collectivism and individualism was formulated not only in terms of the working class threatening the bourgeoisie; in addition to that, Western, European effervescence was said to be encroached upon by Eastern, Asian stagnancy:

> The modern *régime* of public opinion is, in an unorganized form, what the Chinese educational and political systems are in an organized; and unless individuality shall be able successfully to assert itself against this yoke, Europe, notwithstanding its noble antecedents and its professed Christianity, will tend to become another China.[61]

Whatever 'noble antecedents' Mill had in mind, as he was writing *On Liberty* (1854–1859) European civilization, represented by the spearhead of British imperialism, was not busy in repelling a Chinese offensive, cultural or otherwise; rather it was forcing itself on China, during the second Opium War (1856–1860). It is noteworthy that Nietzsche, as I have discussed elsewhere,[62] was likewise putting this Asia-vs.-Europe cultural metaphor to good use, although on that occasion he rather fantasized about the restless European worker being replaced by a modest, subservient Chinaman:

> Perhaps we shall also bring in numerous *Chinese*: and they will bring with them the modes of life and thought suitable to industrious ants. Indeed, they might as a whole contribute to the blood of restless and fretful Europe something of Asiatic calm and contemplativeness and—what is probably needed most—Asiatic *perseverance*.[63]

Yet such superficial difference, of course, is but another point of profound *agreement*: Nietzsche wanted to bring *the worker* under the very same Confucian control from which Mill wanted to free *the bourgeois*. In *The Gay Science*, for that matter, Nietzsche advanced the exact same point as Mill, when warning against the socialist project of asphyxiating European genius by Chinese inertia:

China, for example, is a country in which large-scale dissatisfaction and the capacity for *change* have become extinct centuries ago; and the socialists and state idolaters of Europe with their measures for making life better and safer might easily establish in Europe, too, Chinese conditions and a Chinese 'happiness,' if only they could first extirpate the sicklier, tenderer, more feminine dissatisfaction and romanticism that at present are still superabundant here. Europe is sick but owes the utmost gratitude to her incurability and to the eternal changes in her affliction: these constantly new conditions . . . have finally generated an intellectual irritability that almost amounts to genius and is in any case the mother of all genius.[64]

Nietzsche's project is thus to a considerable extent the completion of Mill's, and it also discloses the latent truth of liberalism: the bourgeois individual (read: class) frees himself from Chinese discipline, at the same time that the broad masses are subjected to it with a vengeance. 'Individuality,' 'creativity,' 'liberty,' 'genius' etc., are only meritorious when exhibited by the bourgeois but must be denied at all costs when the worker starts to get 'restless.' As John Carey put it with typical lucidity, 'an uneasy situation emerges, in which some human beings are individuals, but most are not.'[65] Although Carey's insight into the liberal/individualist position was not made in reference to Mill it reads, remarkably, as a paraphrase of the latter's categorical dictum that 'Persons of genius are, *ex termini, more* individual than any other people.'[66] Thus, in both Mill and Nietzsche, it is a case of Confucius for the toiling many, the Anti-Christ for the creative elite.

This comparison between Nietzsche and Mill is but one concrete illustration of how Nietzsche was no real adversary to the cause of liberalism (understood historically, as a class ideology rather than as an abstract, timeless set of ideals), not simply some aristocratic outsider, but a thinker whose refutation of the classical liberal tenets of equality and fraternity was, if not wholly integral to liberalism, at least analogous to a predominant vein of thinking shaping within liberal circles proper. Mara and Dovi, though from a perspective generally favorable to *both* liberalism *and* Nietzsche, came to a similar conclusion, observing that in many respects 'Nietzsche provides more a radicalization of than a fundamental opposition to Mill's position,'[67] and that, though Nietzsche's view of Mill was 'contemptuous and dismissive' he was actually 'ignorant of the extent to which he and Mill agree on crucial questions.'[68] That Nietzsche was swiftly rehabilitated in the West from the fifties on, that he was rescued from Nazi 'appropriation' and restored to the ranks of respectable liberal thinking, is therefore not simply the product of a misunderstanding of his views. In some fundamental sense Nietzsche *was* in fact a liberal, and his homecoming is thus rather coherent.[69] What this *re*-appropriation tactically represses, however, is the need for a critical reexamination of *liberalism itself*. It ignores or apologetically disowns the possibility that fascism was a movement incubated in the womb of liberalism, rather than being its stern 'totalitarian' foe.[70] And it takes for granted the democratic credentials of liberalism, indeed assumes the identity of liberalism and democracy, whereas for many a liberal thinker since the nineteenth century—eminent examples would be, besides J. S. Mill, Tocqueville, Spencer, Bagehot, Röpke and Hayek—democracy was ever more a thorn in the side.

Nietzsche's vehemently 'anti-liberal' pronouncements must therefore be understood as a *liberal* denial of liberalism, which, like most rightist radicalism, is at bottom defensive and conservative, a case of 'if we want things to stay as they are, things will have to change.' Indeed, to grasp the gist of Nietzsche's social position, we will do well to keep in mind the clear-sighted prince of Salina, of Lampedusa's *Il Gattopardo*, who realizes all too well that the only future for the Sicilian aristocracy depends on its ability to ally with the rising bourgeoisie in order to check any further advance of Garibaldian radicalism. Given such insight, and for all the aesthetic repugnance at the vulgar, ambitious nouveau-riche Don Calogero, the prince marries the latter's money into the family: 'I fear Tancredi will have to aim higher, by which of course I mean lower.'[71] The new and dazzling couple, Tancredi the prince's nephew and Angelica the plebeian's daughter, signify the future: an aristocracy turned bourgeois, a bourgeoisie turned aristocratic, in a Sicily in which 'all will be the same though all will be changed.'

NIETZSCHE CROSSES THE ATLANTIC

Thus, by fine-tuning our perception of Nietzsche's position, what we find is not an attempt to replace the bourgeoisie with an aristocracy but to 'aristocratize' the bourgeoisie; not to retreat to a pre-capitalist stage in order to regain the heroic qualities predating the imperative of the market, but rather *to invest the market with heroism*. The heroism required must dart over the hurdle formed by the fact that the rule of profit, the crude, materialistic struggle to extract surplus value, writes off heroism, at least as traditionally understood. The solution is a sort of romantic capitalism. With Nietzsche this was arguably a second-best alternative, for he might have preferred the stable, dependable version of hierarchy of the ancien régime, free of the inner dynamics of capitalism and its greater social mobility and agitation. In Ayn Rand, by comparison, this tension between aristocracy and bourgeoisie was already completely transcended: Howard Roark, the true capitalist, is the ultimate, instinctive nobleman. Nietzsche still believed in the need for the capitalist to be transformed into a nobleman or a military leader, while for Rand, taking Nietzsche's position a step further, *the true essence of capitalism is nobility*.

Georg Lukács had consistently contended—for which he was consistently maligned—that romantic anti-capitalism (proposed by the likes of Malthus, Carlyle, Schopenhauer, Nietzsche) was objectively but an essential complement to the classical *defense* of capitalism (Smith, Bentham, the Mills, Bastiat, Say). In Rand, we can add, these parallel lines finally met. Romanticism (which Rand declared her ideal artistic approach[72]) ceases to be the secret mistress of capitalism to become its official, proud spouse. Hence, instead of merely dismissing the crudity of Rand's capitalist apologia,[73] it would be more useful to recognize the real significance of her move, which finally brings a much-embellished truth into the open. If her enthusiastic, boisterous announcement on the rise of the noble, romantic-capitalist is embarrassing to certain ears, this simply reflects her greater candor in comparison with her more refined predecessors who normally took great care to keep the liaison furtive. Of course, for this 'truth' to be convincing Rand had somehow to explain away the apparent reality of capitalism, which, far from giving an impression of 'nobility' is actually, as she herself repeatedly decried, inexorably bound with the ignoble consumerist appetites of the masses. Instead of guaranteeing the autonomy of the heroic individual-capitalist, the logic of selling rather compels the latter to cater to mass taste, dragging him towards the lowest common denominator. The Randian answer was the persona of Howard Roark, impervious to material consideration, the capitalist-artist. Paradoxically, however, he was above all impervious to *capitalism* itself, dismissive of the mundane need to accrue surplus value. Hating the vile mob, Rand was trapped in the contradictions of the capitalist mode of production, squeezed between the political fact of monopoly owning of the means of production and the economic fact of mass consumption. For capitalism shows on the one hand an *exclusive* tendency—namely the tendency to concentrate the means of production in ever fewer hands—and an *inclusive* tendency—namely, the need to expand as far as possible the number of consumers. This perpetuates an uneasy situation in which the masses are welcomed, economically, as consumers, but feared as political contenders. The masses must therefore not mistake *buying* power for *political* power.

Instead of conceding abhorrent 'mass society' to be the necessary consequence of commodity production, Rand denounced it as some moral degeneration, a flirtation with socialism; only fake capitalists court the masses, whereas true, noble ones, who understand the secret dimension of capitalism as an 'unknown ideal,' shun such compromises with disgust. Whereas capitalism rests absolutely on the production of exchange values, commodities which must find their buyers in the market, Rand, the self-proclaimed ardent pro-capitalist, was thoroughly sickened with such courting of 'public opinion' and de facto proposed the incongruous notion of a capitalism which flouts the market imperative. Hence the fantasy of a capitalist-artist, refusing the slightest concession to the mob and remaining at all times perfectly aloof from the market. Correspondingly, her capitalist heroes were not ones producing mass consumer goods, vulgar artifacts like nails, brooms, cars or—heaven forbid!—paperback bestsellers, but rather exclusive products that only the cream of the crop can afford. Roark, for example, was an architect of unique, irreproducible houses, masterpieces that only millionaires of excellent taste could acquire to supplement their unique individualities. Such an elite market, which accepts and understands the greatness of the one-time commodity, projects and realizes (in fiction, that is) the utopia of capitalism sanitized of all its dirty, ignominious, *market* traits: production lines, advertising, public-opinion surveys, cheap journalism and so forth. It is, above all, capitalism emancipated from the masses.[74]

Rand's crusade against the 'statism' of the New Deal, which she saw as an advance in socialism as against the supposedly pure, nineteenth-century model of capitalism, was marked by a similar paradox. It was in reality an all-capitalist affair, a struggle between the individual capitalist, for whom immediate personal interest is the only consideration, and the existence and reproduction of capitalism as a class system, which requires, over and above individual capitalists, a large measure of collective action, at least a partial suspending of immediate considerations, which can be achieved only by state intervention:

> By their individual action [capitalists] can endanger the basis for accumulation. . . . They are then forced to constitute themselves as a class—usually through the agency of the state—and to put limits upon their own competition. . . . The contradiction within the capitalist class between individual action and class requirements can never be resolved within the laws presupposed by the capitalist mode of production.[75]

Since Rand, however, was working with an idealistic conception of capitalism, she had to misrecognize these inner tensions and put the blame on the perceived rise of a pernicious socialist statism, postulating it as the anti-American reverse of real capitalist competition.

Rand is important also in another sense, in providing evidence of the actual, Nietzschean connection, at the heart of the American capitalist ethos. Far from representing some bizarre fanaticism, Rand's doctrines belong to the very heart of the American neoliberal discourse. Her philosophy of 'objectivism,' mediated by numerous objectivist official and semi-official clubs and institutions, exercises a considerable influence on many youths throughout the United States, who are initiated into Nietzschean capitalism and learn to look up to the ideal of the entrepreneur-hero (this, quite apart from the unrivaled success of her two main novels, *The Fountainhead* and *Atlas Shrugged*, 'the two absolute best-sellers of the century'[76]). Professed 'critics' of popular American Nietzscheanism, such as Allan Bloom or, more recently, Thomas Hibbs, who impugn the destructive influence of the German 'nihilist,' come themselves from the center right, and therefore understandably choose to keep silent about Rand, probably the single most important American Nietzschean in popular culture. In *The Closing of the American Mind* Bloom mentioned her in passing and belittlingly: 'There is always a girl who mentions Ayn Rand's *The Fountainhead*, a book, although hardly literature, which, with its sub-Nietzschean assertiveness, excites somewhat eccentric youngsters to a new way of life.'[77] Rand is therefore trivialized as girlish stuff, inspiring some marginal youngsters to a very loosely described 'new way of life,' of whose more precise substance—intransigent capitalism—we are told nothing. Hibbs, for his part, ignores Rand altogether.

Both Bloom and Hibbs, though the former much more unambiguously, misrepresent Nietzsche's influence as some foreign import, alien to true American values and, moreover, as an essentially *leftist*, nihilist relativism, which gnaws at the heart of America's healthy hierarchical instincts (in the process ignoring or misstating the fact that Nietzsche was in truth a determined fighter *against* what he referred to as 'passive nihilism,' which, he thought, finds its political expression in democracy and socialism).[78] Hibbs, to be sure, presents nihilism as dangerous to *both* left and right, threatening the very foundations of communal life, however differently the ideal of the community is understood across the political spectrum. Yet his analysis of Nietzscheanism in American popular culture is not predicated on a probing of the power structure of American capitalism, terms such as elitism, inequality, racism or exploitation rarely if ever surfacing in his discussion; rather, his starting point is 'the subtle link between democratic liberalism and nihilism'[79] and the unvarying undertone of his discussion is that of a lament, in the spirit of Tocqueville and Nietzsche, on the elimination of excellence in modern, mass society. The breeding ground for nihilism is thus 'political equality,'[80] 'the modern emphasis on historical progress,'[81] the Cartesian extirpation of 'the influence of tradition, convention and authority from one's reasoning,'[82] 'the advent of democratic nihilism,'[83] 'our insatiable pursuit of equality,'[84] and so on. Hibbs does not venture to offer any decisive way of transcending the predicament he describes, yet, given the way such problem is construed, any consideration of socioeconomic transformation is inevitably excluded. The remedies he discreetly points at are of an essentially cultural and moral kind, such as the recuperation of religious seriousness[85] and 'a sense of the presence of the past.'[86] Since, according to Hibbs, the social problem in American life involves *an excess* of equality, it is only logical to suggest, along with Tocqueville which seems to represent his political ideal, 'ways to temper our passion for equality of conditions.'[87] Bloom, in turn, depicted Nietzsche as a fatal German virus, which infiltrates

America through its vulnerable rear, incompetently guarded—if not willfully deserted—by leftist slouches, pacifists and other politically correct individuals. Having successfully contaminated the system, the virus steadily advances towards the center, threatening to transform America into a veritable nihilistic, mass society, in which no tradition, no canon, no sound values—that is, no *social distinctions*—are left intact. This is most eloquently expressed by the title of Bloom's article 'How Nietzsche Conquered America'—later expanded into his influential bestseller.[88] Rather more realistic would have been to document how *America conquered Nietzsche*, that is—how Nietzsche's teachings were deeply compatible with dominant trends in 'American' ideology from the start, and were therefore swiftly incorporated into its canon. Consider, in that regard, the lasting influence on Nietzsche of a quintessential American thinker like Emerson, who, in that sense, directly contributed to 'Americanize' Nietzsche; nor could the fact that Kaufmann's rehabilitation of Nietzsche, as early as 1947, took place in America of all places, be attributed to sheer coincidence.

Given such theoretical premises, it is quite appropriate that, as a positive counterexample to the purported nihilism sweeping over American popular culture and perverting the nation's ethical-standards, Thomas Hibbs should recommend Disney's *The Lion King* (1994).[89] Paradoxically, however, the film happens to be one of the most salient examples of popular Nietzscheanism in the last twenty years at least. It is the tale of a literally mighty 'blond beast', the lion king Mufasa that reigns supreme at the top of the natural hierarchy, but is threatened by the dark schemes of his (physically, as well spiritually) darker brother, Scar, consumed by envy of the monarch's grandeur. Scar becomes the paradigmatic preacher of *ressentiment*, plotting against the natural 'circle of life.' He incites the mass of the lowly hyenas into a socialist slave revolt against Mufasa's noble rule. The fact that the story takes place in the savannas of Africa occasions no change in proper racial ordering either; the vile and lazy hyenas, 'dangling at the bottom of the food chain,' speak and behave unmistakably like caricatures of poor African Americans and Latinos, while Simba, Mufasa's son and the rightful inheritor of nature and all its treasures, is the perfect image of the fair and delicate WASP. The movie's message is archconservative and racist, so retrograde ideologically as to espouse a return to a monarchic creed of the times preceding the revolution, not of 1917, but of 1789; certain scenes portray the murderous hyenas, laughing hysterically as blood drips from their jaws, in a way which easily calls to mind the vicious anti-Semitic caricatures of the Nazi era. To kill Mufasa, Scar and his henchmen excite a *herd* of mindless gnus into a frenzied stampede, which runs down the supreme individual: the power of numbers disastrously triumphs over individual eminence.

Once the revolutionary regicide of Mufasa is completed and the masters enslaved, a communist regime under Scar's totalitarian domination takes over. Simba, the rightful heir, perniciously escapes into the jungle where he leads a life of Hakuna Matata, 'a trouble free philosophy,' a nihilistic, pleasurable shirking of duty, proper to Nietzsche's 'last man.' Thereby is also exemplified Nietzsche's contention that: '*The decadence of the rulers and of the ruling classes* has caused the greatest mischief in history!'[90] In the absence of the king the land, once a prospering paradise, demises, symbolizing socialist infertility (as if the anti-communist fable were not transparent enough, the filmmakers took care to provide the categorical proof: as Scar incites the hyenas with flamboyant gestures, he appears ominously to rise to the heavens, until his figure combines with the moon's sickle and the red flames to briefly form the Soviet flag). It is only after the restoration of hierarchy, made possible by a counter-revolution led by the now grown-up Simba—a true *master revolt*—that nature resumes its destined course, along the inviolable pattern of eternal hierarchy. And it is with such 'morally serious' films that Hibbs proposes to *resist* the impact of Nietzschean nihilism, through the example of 'Simba's somber and edifying affirmation of his role in the cycle and hierarchy of nature.'

Bloom and Hibbs gallantly rise, in the best of the Leo Strauss tradition, to defend hierarchy against Nietzscheanism and the egalitarian disintegration it entails, as if the German philosopher was but a devout champion of the French Revolution. This purported anti-Nietzscheanism in fact surreptitiously contributes to perpetuate the Nietzschean hegemony. As Geoff Waite suggested, addressing the issue of Straussian anti-Nietzscheanism, such interpretation is propelled by a properly Straussian double play on the exoteric level of writing—that which appears on the surface and targets or distracts the unwary multitude—and esoteric writing, which conceals one's deeper meaning for strategic reasons and purposes, in the service of those happy few who are, or are meant be, in the know. Hence, by exoterically attacking Nietzschean nihilism and the corroding effects of excessive egalitarianism, such authors esoterically help to conceal and further enhance proper, rightist Nietzscheanism, operative at all levels of American life, political, social and economic.[91] In the case of Hibbs, this truth is actually fairly easy to perceive since, to do him justice, the real Nietzscheanism underpinning his anti-nihilist position is never kept too strenuously out of sight. As in the following statement:

> The difficulty, then, with inviting nihilism, the 'unwelcome guest,' into the heart of civilization is that it deprives us of any grounds for retaining the elevating and ennobling aspect of Nietzsche's thought. The heroic confrontation with nihilism may be inspiring for a time, but its long-term result is likely to

be the trivialization of all aspiration, the inability to distinguish between higher and lower.[92]

Thus, *with* Nietzsche, in the name of social distinction and of order of rank, we are invited to take a stand *against* Nietzsche. Such statement would seem thoroughly to confirm Waite's argument that

> . . . the Straussian and post-Straussian tradition really objects to Nietzsche not on grounds that are either philosophical or poetic but rather *pragmatic*. It seems Nietzsche blew—or almost blew—the cover of the means of communicating the 'Noble' doctrine: in other words, the subtlety with which 'order of rank' must be transmitted to have maximum transformative and positive effect on the elite, while having maximum hegemonic and negative effect on the supporting, laboring 'Base.'[93]

For a genuine (*and* non-nihilist) attempt to defy the Nietzschean hegemony one should turn to another highly successful animated film, *Ice Age* (2002), which reads as an ideological rejoinder to *The Lion King*. Here too we have a literal blond beast, the prehistoric tiger Diego, a ruthless predator who reluctantly joins Manny the mammoth and Sid the sloth, in a journey through the icy wilderness, which confronts us with a compelling image of our own age of ice-cold, survival-of-the-fittest global scene. Diego furtively contemplates betrayal of his companions, until his frosty cynicism begins to melt down in a scene which deconstructs one of the greatest anathemas of our, Nietzschean, times: the herd. Diego's life is saved by Manny, who puts his own life on the balance. Astonished, he asks for an explanation for such altruism and gets the terse answer: 'That's what you do in a herd. You look out for each other.' To which Sid the sloth—himself a triumphant vindication of one of our age's most reviled specimen: the (poor) freeloader—immediately adds: 'I don't know about you guys, but we are the weirdest herd I've ever seen.'[94] *Ice Age* attempts to transcend the Nietzschean branding of the herd as a locus of mediocrity, anonymity and cowardice. The herd in the film, by contrast, is composed of three distinct, but equally valued personalities, that complete and enhance each other, providing much-needed solidarity, aid and affection, to go through the harsh winter of social Darwinism. As Sid declares, after outsmarting a large predator: 'Survival of the fittest? I don't think so!'[95] As against *The Lion King*'s insistence on eternal, sacrosanct hierarchy, *Ice Age* challenges the alleged laws of natural order of rank. As if to spite Hibbs-cum-Nietzsche, it stubbornly refuses 'to distinguish between higher and lower.' Beyond the fact that the herd admits no such distinctions—its premise being equality *in* difference—the powerful master of the natural world, Man, the supreme hunter, is taught a lesson in compassion by the three brutes, who return to him his lost baby.

Nietzscheanism vs. anti-Nietzscheanism in popular culture; images of herds, blond beasts, and noble capitalists in texts consumed by the rabble. Yet it remains to be explained how it came to pass that the great patron of elitism got 'entangled' in the culture of his despised mob. As I wish to argue, the internal logic of Nietzscheanism, so to speak, actually necessitates for it to get involved in popular culture, notwithstanding all avowals of entrenched elitism, and disavowals of foul-smelling, mass books. To comprehend why this is the case we need, however, to engage in a slightly methodological discussion of popular culture, in order to try and define an area of potential fusion between 'the high' and 'the low.' This will be our mission in the next chapter.

3

Popular Nietzscheanism: Aesthetics for Everyone and No One

The debate on the significance of popular culture, regarding both its aesthetic as well as social merits, has been historically presided over by two contending groups, 'the populists' who celebrated popular culture and 'the pessimists' who decried it.[1] This rough dichotomy is quite instrumental at a preliminary stage of classification, in setting apart two main responses to popular culture. Yet, for the purposes of a more precise ideological analysis, it is a far too narrow one. Most restricting proves the impossibility to address properly and systematically, on such binary terms, the most vital question of all, *ideologically* speaking: the deeply ambiguous relation of capitalism to modern popular culture. For capitalism is, on the one hand, the historical breeding-ground of mass society, *hence a vehicle of political and cultural egalitarianism*; while, on the other hand, it is no less the generator of enormous social disparities, hence the great *eliminator of equality*. Thus, it becomes vital to identify, in any given response to popular culture, what precisely is the position taken. What, in other words, is being rejected, or embraced: the egalitarian tendency or the un-egalitarian one, the closing or the opening of gaps?

I. CAPITALISM AND POPULAR CULTURE

This ambiguity historically opened the way for a number of different, often quite confused and contradictory responses to capitalism and to popular culture that need to be broadly distinguished from each other, even if, in reality, they only rarely manifested themselves in theoretical, or political, 'purity.' In order to attempt and distill a clearer notion of the precise substance of each position I therefore propose to further divide the binary opposition between 'populism' and 'pessimism'—the latter term I will replace by 'elitism,' since this seems to me to be the proper antonym.[2] The following list classifies the social content of four main approaches in accordance with their ideological response to capitalism (C), juxtaposed with their response to popular culture (P):

1. **Outright populism**: affirming both capitalism and popular culture (C+ / P+): this response consists of an optimistic idealization of capitalism and popular culture (and mass society in general) as nothing short of an earthly paradise, in which all get what they wish for: the industrialists get rich by selling to the customers at accessible prices precisely the commodities they crave. Adherents of this approach typically endorse the market as the sole legitimate arbiter of culture, for it alone can 'give the public what it wants,' thus discarding any interference with the imperative of 'the ratings.' Theoretically, this is a position defended essentially within 'the entertainment industry' while generally lacking explicit support on the part of academic 'theory.' However, certain practitioners of Cultural Studies have been accused of exaggerating the 'popular audience's capacity to resist the workings of hegemony,' to the point 'that capitalism had ceased to be a problem.'[3]

2. **Critical populism**: rejecting capitalism while affirming popular culture (C− / P+): this response rests on the premise that popular culture is not simply a tool or a reflection of capitalist economy—being just a means and expression of exploitation—but possesses at least a measure of autonomy, even potential resistance, vis-à-vis the exploitative socioeconomic core. Thus, while opposing exploitation and inequality, popular culture, or elements of it, are still commended for their democratic significance and plebeianism, which are seen as undermining the hegemonic pretensions of the canon. The early, radical Richard Wagner, Walter Benjamin, Bertolt Brecht, Antonio Gramsci, Raymond Williams, Stuart Hall and Pierre Bourdieu would broadly belong here, as well as most work undertaken in the last 4 decades or so within the anti-disciplinary discipline of Cultural Studies, particularly its British variant, exemplified in the pioneering, and by now almost canonical work of R. Williams, E. P. Thompson and Stuart Hall.[4]

3. **Critical elitism**: rejecting both capitalism and popular culture (C+ / P−): to this category belong those critics who express their dissent towards both the exploitative economics of capitalism and the manipulative, degraded culture, concomitant to it. The assumption is

that the two cannot be separated and that mass cultural production under capitalism is inexorably but a reflection and an extension of the exploitative economy, thus becoming a reified, barbaric 'culture industry.' As a possible remedy notions of autonomous, high or 'serious' art are advanced, which eschew cultural commoditization. The names of Adorno and Horkheimer would come most naturally to the fore in connection with that critical line. In the American context, one could mention the literary critic Dwight MacDonald and the highly influential art critic Clement Greenberg.

4. **Outright elitism**: affirming capitalism while rejecting popular culture (C+ / P−): this response consists of an affirmation of the need for hierarchies, the inevitability of exploitation and the legitimacy and expediency of inequality at the socioeconomic levels, while lamenting the cultural deterioration in standards and the general levelling down implied by popular culture and democratic politics. The economic core is therefore accepted, directly or indirectly, whereas those cultural and political phenomena perceived as militating against the hierarchy are discarded. This is the properly Nietzschean response, denigrating *egalitarianism* as the root of *cultural degradation*, and here belong such conservatives as T. S. Eliott and Ortega y Gasset, or out-and-out fascist sympathizers as Wyndham Lewis, Ezra Pound or D. H. Lawrence. Other important critics of modern popular culture whom I would classify as, essentially, 'outright elitists' are Matthew Arnold and F. R. Leavis.

These four categories are not put forward as comfortable niches into which the attitudes of different theorists can be neatly classified. Only very few thinkers, if any, could actually be said to belong wholly and unambiguously to a single category. Thus, for instance, Bourdieu was here located in category 2, of critical populism, yet there can be no doubt that some aspects of his critique, say his analysis of television as 'manufacturing consent' (Noam Chomsky's term), are akin to that of category 3, of critical elitism, while Fredric Jameson would appear to waver and take a mediating position between categories 2 and 3. An eclectic and unsystematic thinker as Wagner could be claimed, in different phases of his career, for categories 2, 3 and 4. And examples for many other possible combinations could easily be thought of. Thus, these categories would be more usefully conceived of as main stations along a path, implying the existence of many other intermediary stations, situated in between these principal four, as well as the possibility of *movement* between them. To attain a clearer notion of the ideological relation between these four positions I add the following illustration, which is intended as mapping

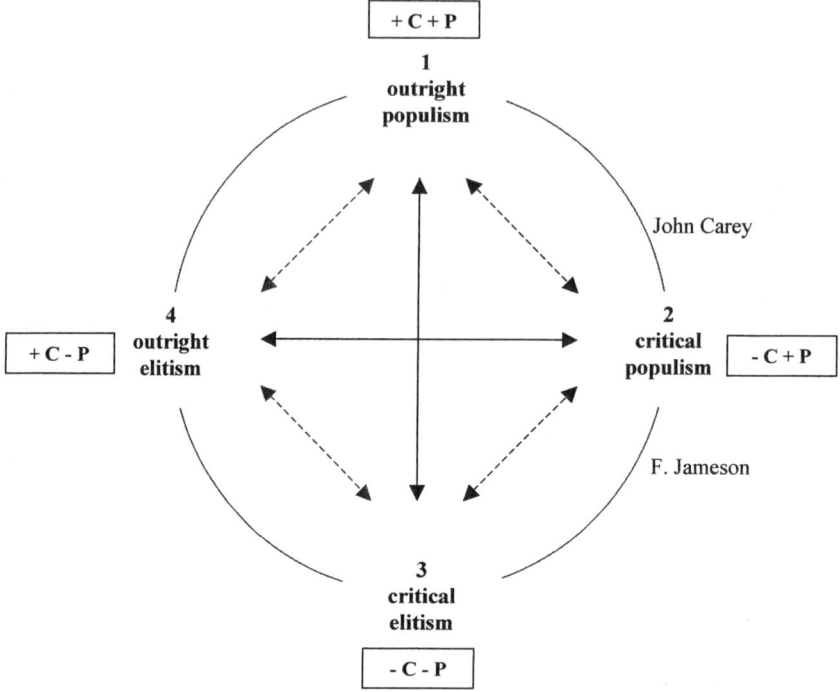

Figure 3.1.

down the 'spatial' relation between the different approaches, indicating their relative degree of affinity and hostility:

The circle along which the four stations are located is meant to indicate the dynamic nature of the different positions and the possibility of movement between them, as opposed to the relation obtaining between rigid doctrinaire stances (which they cannot in any case be, given that the set of categorizations corresponds not, of course, to the way different theorists define their own position, but is rather an 'external' theoretical construct, meant to characterize different stances from an outward perspective). The degree of affinity and hostility between the various positions can be gauged according to their relative proximity along the radius: hence, broken arrows represent the possibility of dialogue, say between positions 1 and 4, or between 3 and 2, while the two plain arrows represent the lines of sharpest division, between the antithetical positions:

(a) 1 (C+ / P+) and 3 (C− / P−)
(b) 2 (C− / P+) and 4 (C+ / P−).

These would be the theoretical combinations or alliances less likely to occur, although, as already said, exceptions are conceivable (see, again, the case of Wagner).

If the relation between these categories is seldom one of absolute and rigid opposition, this becomes even more the case once we consider two *structural* junctures of potential ideological intersection. What I have in mind is the possibility of ideological 'relapse' which seems to be lurking for both the categories described as 'critical,' namely 2 (critical populism) and 3 (critical elitism). The critical populist, for one, may objectively forfeit the critical edge of his position, and, *over*-celebrating popular culture, veer towards the 'station' of the outright populist. There appears to exist, in other words, a significant potential that theorists who subjectively and formally embrace popular culture while rejecting capitalism, will actually, whether cynically or unconsciously, tend to accommodate capitalism *tout court*, without acknowledging, or even realizing, as much. It is in that context that I have included John Carey's name on the circle. In his critique of elite culture (*The Intellectuals and the Masses*) Carey has provided us with a salient example of radical critical populism, which challenges the hegemonic ambitions of the elite and denounces its 'civilizing' claims. At the same time, however, he also appears to harbor at least a latent leniency towards capitalism as such. This is expressed, for example, in his somewhat belittling treatment of utopianism, left and right.[5] Thus, capitalist reality, in its capacity as that which is decidedly *not* utopian, is surreptitiously accepted as something of an (unacknowledged) default option. What the outright populist asserts explicitly, namely, the beneficial, consensual nature of capitalism, and its union with the masses, Carey—and other critical populists—seem to assume silently.

Similarly, yet in the opposite direction, there is a potential ideological nexus between categories 3 and 4, namely between an Adornian critique of popular culture and a Nietzschean one. For, while the elitist critic of popular culture as defined in category 3 may like to think of himself as a committed leftist, this may actually serve to alibi his actual conservatism. In that case, by *over*-criticizing popular culture, he may drift towards an outright affirmation of social hierarchy proper of station 4. An example for such ambiguity is provided by Dwight Macdonald, a classic critic of 'mass culture':

[Mass Culture] threatens High Culture by its sheer pervasiveness, its brutal, overwhelming *quantity*. The upper classes, who begin by using it to make money from the crude tastes of the masses and to dominate them politically, end by finding their own culture attacked and even threatened with destruction by the instrument they have thoughtlessly employed.[6]

Now, what did Macdonald actually reprehend here about 'Mass Culture'? Did he, in the spirit of *critical* elitism, regret the fact that the upper classes 'use it to make money,' and 'dominate the masses politically'? Or, perchance, in the sprit of *outright* elitism, did he lament the fact that such 'culture' eventually turns *against* the masters, threatens their cultural hegemony? Is popular culture, in other words, denigrated qua hegemonic or qua egalitarian? This oscillation, I contend, is not a mere conceptual confusion, but a profoundly strategic one, reflecting the structural nexus between categories 3 and 4 of elitism. It is not that Macdonald *cannot* decide between the two positions; rather, he *must not* decide between them. The whole point in navigating ideologically to and fro between stations 3 and 4 is precisely the fact that one is thereby allowed to maintain a position which is at one and the same time *both* radical *and* conservative. A refutation of capitalism remains at all time the formal presupposition of such a critique—hence vouching for the critic's radicalism; yet such assessment of capitalism appears to be predicated on actual conservatism:

> Like nineteenth-century capitalism, Mass Culture is a dynamic, revolutionary force, breaking down the old barriers of class, tradition, taste, and dissolving all cultural distinctions. It mixes and scrambles everything together, producing what might be called homogenized culture, after another American achievement, the homogenization process that distributes the globules of cream evenly throughout the milk instead of allowing them to float separately on top. It thus destroys all values, since value judgments imply discrimination. Mass Culture is very, very democratic: it absolutely refuses to discriminate against, or between, anything or anybody.[7]

It is noteworthy how Macdonald specifically rebuked popular culture's erosive, anti-hierarchical thrust. One does not miss, to be sure, the unmistakable irony in Macdonald's words: avoiding an outright conservative position, he decried mass culture because of its extreme, conciliatory commercialism, which renders it incapable of any true cultural or social critique. What he seems to have been saying is that mass culture cannot generate any radicalism because it is committed to perpetual neutrality; the commercial need to please everybody entails the injunction *not* to anger anyone. In this, he came very close indeed to the leftist critique of the so-called Frankfurt School with its stress on the lulling, placating effects of the 'culture industry' which stifle any rebellious drive. But is popular culture indeed as bereft of critical power as such detractors assume? And indeed, if this skeptic, utterly pessimistic view is correct, how can such docile culture come to constitute 'a dynamic, revolutionary force, breaking down the old barriers of class, tradition, taste'? As Dominic Strinati, defending the democratic thrust of popular culture, observed with keen irony regarding Macdonald's position:

The real problem sometimes appears to be that mass culture, unlike folk culture, refuses to stay in its place and stick with the masses, but has pretensions beyond its station or merits, and refuses to recognise traditional hierarchies of taste, and the cultural distinctions generated by those at the top.[8]

Use Value as a Locus of Dissent

Another critique of 'leftist pessimism' has queried the soundness of its allegedly Marxist analysis of capitalist cultural production. One of the vital grievances of the 'critical elitist' approach against 'the culture industry' is the latter's integration in the overall production of commodities, hence the necessary degradation of such culture. Yet, as Terry Lovell counterclaimed in an important work, this conclusion is hardly validated under the assumptions of the classical Marxist analysis of capitalism: 'Cultural production, from a left pessimist point of view, is the production of shoddy goods, once culture is transformed into commodities.'[9] To which she added: 'There is no suggestion to be found in Marx's writings that commodities are, as such, second-rate goods, nor that the wants which they satisfy are not "real" wants. For Marx there is no such category, essential to left pessimism, as "false needs."'[10] A genuinely Marxist approach to industrial culture must allow for the relative autonomy of the cultural product in its capacity of *use value* as opposed to its function in generating *surplus value*. There is, within a strict market economy system, a non-negligible degree of autonomy at the level of use value, at the level, that is, of the cultural product's aesthetic, informative, ideological, emotional, moral uses. A book by Noam Chomsky, for example, is produced in just the same way as a Friedrich von Hayek book; both are equally—from the point of view of the capitalist book manufacturer—commodities targeting potential buyers. Yet their respective use values, namely what the buyers purchase them for—which, in the case of Hayek and Chomsky, would be their informative and ideological uses— is hardly identical, nor equally subservient to the hegemonic ideology. Needless to say, the imperative to sell and extract surplus value is not without impact on the content of the product—it ought, for example, be 'accessible'—but this does not transform it ipso facto into a hegemonic means of indoctrination or subjection. Far from it, precisely because the commercial product is intended for mass consumption, it may have to make more concessions towards the political-emotional-aesthetical wishes of the mass clients, where high art, intended for the few, may with less fear of reprisal indulge in elitism, discrimination, endorsement of anti-democratic stances and so on.[11] Far from robotically subservient to the hegemonic ideology 'cultural commodities are likely to express a wide variety of ideas, emotions, values and sensibilities, only some of which will be drawn from

and articulated with the dominant ideology, and many of which will origi-
nate in class experience and class aspirations antithetical to capitalism.'[12]

Interesting results are obtained when the 'culture industry' and 'mass culture' theories are put to the test in relation to an enormously successful ar-
tifact for the children market, *The Smurfs*, 'consumed' both as comics and as
a cartoon-animation series. If the theories are correct, we should expect to
find either a reactionary indoctrination, preparing the children for life-time
submission, or idiotic, escapist enjoyment, disguising or ornamenting the
realities of an exploitative world. *The Smurfs*, however, and this applies particularly to the original comics version by the Belgian author Peyo, are actually nothing short of a militant Marxist allegory.[13] The village of the
smurfs, inhabited by members of equal economic status, although of distinct personalities and talents, is guided by a fatherly figure who appears to
stand for none other than Karl Marx himself: unlike the rest of the smurfs
who wear white trousers and white cap, 'Le Grand Schtroumpf' wears red
ones, in addition to his ample, Marx-like, white beard. But the resemblance
is by no means only physical: the smurf-village illustrates the possibility of
a communal life where money, private property and wage-labour are absent, and of principle. In one of the comic-book issues, *Le Schtroumpf Financier*, an overly clever smurf introduces money into the village's traditionally communal and egalitarian economy, disrupting the fabric of its
social life.[14] The inhabitants gradually learn the painful meaning of hitherto
unheard-of phenomena: inequality, exploitation, hunger, corruption, alienation, destitution, luxury and sycophancy. One of the episodes even comprises a neat exposition of the Marxist labour theory of value. Eventually,
the smurf population takes organized political action to restore things to
their previous order and abolish the new market economy. Le Grand
Schtroumpf explains: 'not everything that is good for humans, is also good
for us smurfs.' *The Smurfs* can thus hardly be seen as a neutral, uncritical,
value-free work; nor does it 'absolutely refuses to discriminate against, or
between, anything or anybody.' It rather involves a radical political stance,
discriminating wholeheartedly against inequality, exploitation, and the entire market system. It illustrates how a product designed for mass consumption can inculcate in millions of innocent children a theory completely inimical to capitalism, the very mode of production under whose
conditions it was manufactured. A fact which accounts for the shocked indignation of one unsympathetic customer:

> Saturday morning cartoons. The last refuge for our children. . . . But amongst
> the vibrant colors of a certain cartoon there is a tiger lying in wait. A red tiger,
> one who is both stealthy and corrupting. Yes, communism exists in your chil-
> dren's cartoon fantasies. . . . Indeed, Peyo was a clever man for submerging
> Marx's views in an innocent seeming cartoon. Why the NBC television network

allowed such a man to impress young minds with such garbage, we'll never know, but the truth has come out and hopefully, future generations will be able to avoid the hidden threat of Communism forever.[15]

No doubt, a myriad of counter-examples could be mustered to demonstrate how products of mass culture can be rather less critical of the prevailing hegemony. The point, however, is that the problematic of popular culture cannot be reduced to some sort of economic determinism. Or, put more correctly, it is *economic determinism itself* which creates the basis for the irreducible ambiguity in popular culture. For it is precisely here that the capitalist mode of production, if let alone to proceed entirely on its economic logic, may constitute a field of comparative democracy and egalitarianism (comparative, that is, to other domains of the 'superstructure'—the educational, legal, political and so on, which are relatively free of the imperative to sell and are under a much more direct control of the ruling-classes, thus more readily subservient to their aims). But this, of course, is an abstraction. Popular culture is not governed by the 'invisible hand of the market' but rather intervened in by many means, some blunt other more sophisticated. An infamous piece of historical evidence for this was the intervention of McCarthyism in the American entertainment industry, which was not simply an irrational witch-hunt, a fringe phenomenon countering the true essence of American liberalism. At heart, McCarthyism was a highly functional intrusion into the making of popular culture, and an implicit recognition by the establishment that capitalism cannot simply be expected to reproduce itself at the level of culture and ideology. Though not necessarily communists, many of the blacklisted filmmakers were nonetheless dangerous dissidents indeed, 'guilty' of producing popular culture at loggerheads with the ideals of the ruling elite (the fact the most persecuted sub-group was that of scriptwriters, namely of those most directly in charge of ideological content, is hence by no means fortuitous). Hollywood before and after McCarthyism could never be quite the same, as even after the persecution subsided the lesson remained deeply ingrained that making films is not a simple, direct dialogue with the movie-watcher's wallet, as Adam Smith envisioned.

The contradiction between capitalist production and consumption, or between surplus value and use value, suffices in itself to create a condition in which it is never possible to determine *a priori* whether a cultural commodity, say a Hollywood film, will harpoon the American myth—as in the wild parody of America/Freedonia in the Marx Brothers' *Duck Soup*—or will pay it homage as in Spielberg's *Saving Private Ryan*. Only a concrete encounter with a given popular text can shed light on its ideological content. Yet such interrogation of the popular text presupposes a more discriminate, open-minded perspective than the entrenched, pessimist-elitist refutation of 'the culture industry.' I wish now to explicitly state a case for the advantage of the critical populist perspective, in particular in comparison with the critical elitist one, in appreciating popular culture in general and the role of *Nietzschean* popular culture more specifically.

Bourdieu's Aesthetical Theory: 'Critical Populism'

Our main point of reference in mapping the greatly disputed terrain separating high from popular culture will be the approach of Pierre Bourdieu, as expressed most systematically in his groundbreaking work, *Distinction: a Social Critique of the Judgement of Taste* (1979). Bourdieu's essential contention concerned the need for historicizing and socializing the aesthetic experience. He challenged commonplace notions about the aesthetic intuition, the reputed ability to appreciate the beauty of an artistic object directly, as it were, without the need for any social mediation. This, for Bourdieu, is itself an ideological construction, aimed at giving the false appearance that social differences merely correspond to different aesthetic sensitivities, rather than *generate* them. According to Bourdieu, 'The "eye" is a product of history reproduced by education.'[16] From this vantage point we must regard aesthetics as a sphere of social conflict, in which art is always a means of attaining, or affirming, *distinction*: 'Taste classifies, and it classifies the classifier. Social subjects, classified by their classifications, distinguish themselves by the distinctions they make, between the beautiful and the ugly, the distinguished and the vulgar.'[17]

Bourdieu saw in the cultural history of the last two hundred years a steady process in the course of which 'high art' has been constantly drifting apart from 'low art,' asserting its superior value vis-à-vis the popular taste. This was conceived of as an essentially Kantian project, inasmuch as it rests upon Kant's seminal opposition in the *Critique of Judgement* between coarse, sensual, animalistic pleasure—which cannot be admitted into the realm of the aesthetic proper—and refined, sublimated, disinterested pleasure, which alone is truly human.[18] A corresponding hierarchy was hence erected, classifying highly those who are capable of appreciating art for its own sake, denying its immediate, 'bodily' attraction, while placing on the lower cultural level those barbarously 'entrapped' in precisely such 'vulgar' enjoyment. By means of refusing carnal pleasures, insisting on the autonomous value of a work of art beyond any functional attribute and elevating form over content, the *ethereal-sublime* bourgeoisie managed to enclose its own exclusive aesthetic territory and assert its cultural preeminence against the *earthly profane* masses. Bourdieu used a quotation from Ortega y Gasset to illustrate how modernist culture was indeed entrusted with this social role. Considering the broad Nietzschean footing of this thinker, it is well worth including in our discussion:

For a century and a half, the 'people', the mass, have claimed to be the whole of society. The music of Stravinsky or the plays of Pirandello have the socio-logical power of obliging them to see themselves as they are, as the 'common people', . . . the inert material of the historical process, a secondary factor in the spiritual cosmos. By contrast, the young art helps the 'best' to know and recognize one another in the greyness of the multitude and to learn their mis-sion, which is to be few in number and to have to fight against the multitude.[19]

Modern art is hence 'a systematic refusal of all that is "human", i.e., generic, common—as opposed to distinctive or distinguished—namely, the passions, emotions and feelings which "ordinary" people invest in their "ordinary" lives.'[20]

Moving, however, beyond a mere critique of high art and its underpin-ning of hierarchy, Bourdieu was able to offer significant ways to escape the dead end of the pessimistic view of popular culture, associated chiefly, at least in its leftist incarnation, with the Frankfurt School (a similar position, though not committed to radical social critique, was advocated by the more conservative theorists of 'mass culture,' such as F. R. Leavis or, as in the ex-ample above cited, Dwight Macdonald). Advocates of this theoretical line traditionally argued that there is no longer much to be hoped for—in terms of subversive potential—from the working class, which has been incorpo-rated into the capitalist system, not least by means of popular culture, or 'the culture industry.' Paradoxically, mass-culture-cum-the-culture-industry thus became an anathema of *both the conservative right and the 'utopian' left*, with but slight differences in theoretical formulations and ideological stresses. In spite of the significant advances made by Cultural Studies, the Frankfurt-School approach remains prevalent among leftists, in however updated variants.

Fredric Jameson proposed, very incisively, to historicize both mass culture and high, modernist art, as the contradictory yet complementary products of capitalism: the former directly, as it is produced in the framework of the mar-ket and in conformity with its means, methods, and goals, the latter indirectly, as a protest against this very framework, as a resolve '*not* to be a commodity.'[21] He described the modernist stance as 'critical' 'although generally not revolu-tionary.'[22] Yet—accepting the basic accuracy of this description—one might ask: *why* is modernism not revolutionary? If mass culture is indeed the legiti-mate offspring of capitalism and modernism its outcast bastard, one should expect of the former a mere apologia for capitalism—which is not the case—and from the latter a vigorous resistance and critique of the market, indeed a *generally revolutionary* one—which hardly obtains, either. The reason for that, I argue, is that modernism was to a significant extent a—critical/outright elitist—refutation of the market's partial *egalitarianism*. Rejected by many mod-ernists was not so much, or at all, the economic factor of exploitation but the cultural factor of a consumer society, democratic inasmuch as the masses, on account of numerical superiority, are able to dictate aesthetic—and ultimately political—standards and policies.[23] On the other hand, the very opposite is sometimes the case with mass culture: often enough, its texts evince a—critical populist—celebration of mass society, a conscious glorying in the power of numbers, and a condemnation of capitalism precisely as a system which is founded on *mass* exploitation. We are confronted with a dialectical situation in which those who reject the methods of the market are (often) conservative mandarins, apprehensive that its unchecked proceedings may undermine social privilege, while those who work within the market-framework are (sometimes) committed plebeians, using its methods in order to contest its economic basis. Hence is resolved the baffling paradox of conservative foes of the market, 'critical but generally not revolutionary,' on the one hand, and dissident supporters of 'mass culture,' on the other.

We may easily invoke many cases of explicit and militant radicalism in popular culture (to arbitrarily cite two examples from among a virtually endless supply, think of the politically defiant lyrics of such rock groups as Rage Against the Machine or Ton Steine Scherben). But even in texts infinitely more innocuous, the utopian in popular culture may be sensed. As in the numerous popular songs, say ABBA's 'Happy New Year,' in which the hope for a future of friendship and brotherhood is expressed. Before we rush to dismiss texts such as these as banally sentimental and artistically null, we might do well to consider that they are, if nothing else, a call for fraternity, understood, moreover, as something yet to be realized and standing in opposition to a degraded present; and fraternity, as Marx stated as early as 1848, was the target for bourgeois attacks bent on 'abolishing this word and the illusions hiding in its ambiguous bosom.'[24] By endorsing the project of fraternity, no matter how *art*lessly, in an age of rampant individualism, neo-social Darwinism and the global 'risk society,' such texts can be read as a message in a bottle, keeping alive the hope and stubbornly clinging on to the *ambiguous illusion* of a better society. The message, moreover, was apparently better understood and appreciated by the millions of duped 'consumers,' while theoreticians of culture, even avowedly radical ones, often insist on undermining such communication. In that, they may be collaborating, regardless of their subjective self-image, with the bourgeois attack on fraternity.

At this point we witness the formation of an unholy alliance between the greatest of opponents, the outright populist and the critical elitist. For all the enormous disparities that differentiate their basic aesthetic and political outlooks, they manage equally well to eradicate the utopian voice from the sphere of popular culture. Developing their respective arguments upon diametrically opposed premises, their conclusions boil down to a strikingly similar ideological substance. The outright populist who celebrates the market, rules out in advance any utopian impulses in popular culture, precisely since his premise is that of the market *as utopia*; given that capitalism is the best of all possible worlds any dissenting voices defying such a system from within the market are bound to be refuted automatically, in fact utterly ignored, as a logical impossibility: the people love the market just as the market loves the people, and no discord can ever come to upset this perpetual honeymoon. The critical elitist, in turn, by condemning the culture industry or mass culture *a priori* as instrumental barbarism, is equally predisposed to rule out utopian popular culture as a structural oxymoron, a judgment which no amount of evidence to the contrary can put into question. In both cases the upshot is therefore a thorough silencing of the utopian voice in the popular. The only difference is that the optimistic populist stands with his face turned towards the masses and smiles complacently as he surveys his paradise, perfectly unable to perceive the defying gestures made in his direction, while the critical elitist, presupposing 'the thinly veiled identity of all industrial culture products,'[25] turns his back to the masses and assumes the grave countenance of the utopian liberator, all the while frowning with disgust at the insolent cries and desperate pleas raising from behind him, which he cannot but discard as barbaric havoc. Under such light, it becomes possible to appreciate how Bourdieu's verdict on Adorno hits the nail on the head:

> An arrogant theoretician who refuses to sully his hands with empirical trivia and who remains too viscerally attached to the values and profits of Culture to be able to make it an object of science . . . a submissive Marxist who goes in for vulgar Marxism when refinement is needed and elegant Marxism when vulgarity is called for.[26]

Bourdieu's Anti-Kantian Aesthetic: The Taste of Necessity

Neither a gullible 'populist' nor a hegemonic one, Bourdieu, possibly the most prominent theoretician of French Cultural Studies, was able to offer a valuable corrective to the anti-mass tilt of much of leftist theory. He managed to form a persuasive defense of the inherent merit of the popular taste itself. This merit was understood as stemming from a proletarian resistance to the criteria imposed by the elite, and a resolute ratification of its own popular aesthetic (to be sure, this is a primarily intuitive and spontaneous ratification, rather than one fully conscious of its objective status and goals, thus being an 'in itself' rather than 'for itself' aesthetic[27]). Whereas the elite insists that the category of the beautiful must stand strictly apart from those of the useful, the ethical, the agreeable and so on, popular aesthetics 'stubbornly' assumes their interdependence; the 'popular' beautiful is forever embedded in the concrete, always morally and practically contextualized, and expected to fulfill a function, *to meet* rather than *transcend* interests. In that respect, popular judgment springs 'from an "aesthetic" (in fact it is an ethos) which is the exact opposite of the Kantian aesthetic . . . working-class people expect every image to explicitly perform a function, if only that of a sign, and their judgments make reference, often explicitly, to the norms of morality or agreeableness. Whether rejecting or praising, their appreciation always has an ethical basis.'[28] High art, in contradistinction, by negating any commitment to such supra-aesthetic demands and asserting its unqualified independence, often demonstrates its aloofness by refuting any ethical restriction and flirting with moral transgression. Ingeniously, Bourdieu praised the popular taste and, by extension and to an extent, popular culture, precisely on account of what is usually perceived, even among leftists, as its degraded aspect, namely its *functionality*. He thus pointed at an affinity between the form of capitalist production, functionality, and the content of popular aesthetics. Whereas Jameson, writing at the same year in which *Distinction* was published, agreed with Adorno and Horkheimer and saw in mass culture 'the triumph of instrumentalization over that "finality without an end" which is art itself, the steady conquest and colonization of the ultimate realm of non-practicality, of sheer play and anti-use, by the logic of the world of means and ends,'[29] Bourdieu pointed at the class logic underlying this very conception of art as 'finality without an end.' He attempted to socialize the idea that art is 'sheer play and anti-use' and deconstruct its universal pretensions, by positing a counter-ideal of popular aesthetics, which always invests art with the useful. In consequence, what from a standard leftist perspective was deprecated as the demeaning aspect of popular culture, its instrumentality, was perceived by Bourdieu as a redeeming aspect.[30]

The conflict between bourgeois and popular aesthetic can be illustrated by comparing two antithetical reactions to Dashiell Hammett's thrillers. On the part of 'mass culture' theory, we find Dwight Macdonald lamenting the 'sensational style' instigated by Hammett and expressing nostalgia for the lost days of the polite detective:

> The sensationalists use what for the classicists was the point—the uncovering of the criminal—as a mere excuse for the minute descriptions of scenes of bloodshed, brutality, lust, and alcoholism. The cool, astute, subtle Dupin-Holmes is replaced by the crude man of action whose prowess is measured not by intellectual mastery but by his capacity for liquor, women and mayhem (he can 'take it' as well as 'dish it out'—Hammett's *The Glass Key* is largely a chronicle of the epic beatings absorbed by the hero before he finally staggers to the solution).[31]

For Raymond Chandler, however, examining the very same cultural object, it is precisely Hammett's 'crudeness' which constitutes a welcome improvement in comparison with the tradition of the intellectual detective:

Hammett gave murder back to the kind of people that commit it for reasons, not just to provide a corpse; and with the means at hand, not with hand-wrought dueling pistols, curare and tropical fish. He took murder out of the Venetian vase and dropped it into the alley.[32]

Where Macdonald, applying the yardstick of bourgeois aesthetics *within* popular culture, saw only a senseless orgy of violence, Chandler, from a rather more plebeian perspective, perceived the enhanced critical value of precisely such 'vulgarity.' Needless to say, such contrasting outlooks—refined, bourgeois anti-functionality, and plebeian, hard-boiled realism—are not simply the outcomes of an ideological class struggle taking place in a material vacuum, each side choosing or developing its distinctive sensitivities in opposition to the choices of its Other, but are rather grounded in material reality, in the lived social experiences of each group. In that respect, a critique of elitism is not necessarily, as Jameson suggested, 'an anti-intellectual thrust,' a 'negative position' with 'little theoretical content.'[33] It can rather be consistent with Jameson's own, wholly justified demand, for an approach to 'the dilemma of the double standard of high and mass culture,' which is not simply restricted to 'the subjective problem of our own standards of judgment,' but rather grasps 'an objective contradiction which has its own social grounding.'[34] For surely, the whole point of Bourdieu's sociologizing of taste is to show precisely how both 'bourgeois elitism' and 'mass populism' are not simply subjective reactions or a matter of personal sensibility but are best understood as *social practices*, objectively necessary within a context of class conflict. If the bourgeoisie tends to favor art isolated from material exigency it is anything but a matter of subjective, arbitrary inclination; rather, such 'choice' fundamentally corresponds to a social experience relatively free from the pressures of material necessity and the associated impulse to cash in on such freedom as cultural capital. By the same token, working people tend to demand that art should engage in the practical and the material precisely because both are much more pressing in their daily lives. Therefore, what we have are two major aesthetic postures, bourgeois and working class, which are ultimately regulated by their relative 'distance from necessity.'

From such a perspective the leftist aesthetic theory of the Frankfurt School is found, astonishingly, to abstract from its analysis of cultural consumption the very *materiality of class-experience*. Instead of taking as its starting point the lived social experience of a given class and proceeding from there to understand what such class finds as beautiful and for what reasons, the Adornian critic comes equipped with an *a priori* conception of 'serious' or 'utopian' art and expects the working class to conform to such standard, rooted in a social experience completely alien to its own. Bourdieu, by contrast, emulating Hammett, took 'the beautiful' out of the Venetian vase and dropped it into the alley. This was not a gesture of frustration, an empty provocation, but part of an endeavor to bring the beautiful back into material context while at the same time depriving the aesthetician of his privilege to arbitrate in matters of taste in the name of a meta-historical and meta-social standard.

In referring to the eating habits of different social groups, Bourdieu distinguished between a working-class 'taste of necessity,' which 'favours the most "filling" and most economical foods,' and a bourgeois 'taste of liberty, or luxury,' which emphasizes the manner of serving, presenting and eating.[35] Such theoretical contrast between *aesthetics of necessity* and *aesthetics of liberty/luxury* applies not only in the domain of gastronomic preferences but also holds equally well across the broad horizon of consumption, including that of culture. The sociological significance of many cultural phenomena can be substantially clarified by situating them between these two poles, on condition that the scheme is not employed rigidly, expecting any given input to perfectly match one pole or the other. Rather, it should be recognized that all aesthetic positions inevitably fluctuate between necessity and liberty/luxury, incorporating, in some constellation or another, elements of both extremes. This must be so, not only since no cultural expression is ever likely to be purely bourgeois or purely working class, particularly within an hegemonic culture whose essence is compromise,[36] but also because both aesthetic positions contain each other from the very start, albeit in a repressed form: bourgeois aesthetic of liberty/luxury, to start with, may strive energetically to deny the material and to rise into the pure realm of incorporeal beauty, but precisely this uncompromising effort to banish the material betrays the fact that it remains at all times its hidden presupposition, that which must be denied at all costs. No liberty and no luxury are conceivable in the absence of the anathematized potential of necessity. Thus, bourgeois aesthetics can be described as the paradoxical *necessity to deny necessity*. On the other hand and by the same token, nor can working-class aesthetics of necessity constitute an autonomous, as it were unadulterated, paradigm. Needless to say, such aesthetics does not make a fetish of necessity, perversely relishing the inscrutable beauty of hard toil, poverty or hunger; rather, it is all about the effort to break away from these predicaments, and to attain, in fact, liberty and luxury. But this 'collective struggle to wrest a realm of Freedom from a realm of Necessity'[37] is done upon the premise of confronting material reality rather than suppressing it. It is the therefore the *necessity to recognize necessity*.

Perhaps the quintessential literary example of the taste/aesthetics of necessity is *Lazarillo de Tormes* (anonymous, 1554)—it is generally considered the first picaresque story, but may equally be regarded the great forefather of modern realism in literature. Radically materialistic, the story delivers a devastating critique of the cruelty, hypocrisy and idiocy of the Spanish ruling classes, their morals, economy and politics—surely the reason that it was published anonymously. Lazarillo, the lowly son of a prostitute mother and a convict father, is confronted desperately, continually and inexorably not with the task of giving his life meaning, making a mark on the world, nurturing his reputation through great deeds or impressive appearance, but rather with the search for a daily meal. The protagonist's sole ambition, by necessity, is a piece of bread. Living constantly at the brink of starvation Lazarillo does not harbor any illusions of heroism: bread becomes the root, the firm foundation of happiness and its securing takes precedence over any fancy. The bread-seeking scenes at the house of the tightfisted pastor are some of the most convincing, ruthless depictions of hunger in world literature. By comparison, the impoverished, good-hearted nobleman who treats Lazarillo kindly appears childish with his inflated self-esteem and the fact that, even in ruins, he still takes care to preserve a lofty demeanor. Ultimately, it falls to Lazarillo to supply his 'benefactor' with some nourishment. Doubtless, this is an early formulation of bourgeois challenge to the aristocratic class, as 'honor' and knightly ideals sink into obsolescence, a theme, of course, which will find its masterly development in Cervantes, greatly influenced by *Lazarillo*.[38] But, importantly, it is the bourgeoisie at a stage when it still endorses a radical, critical alternative to the nobility and therefore represents with great authenticity the figure of the wretched boy, at the very bottom of the social heap. Certainly, it is possible to situate the narrative broadly within the popular tradition of grotesque realism, with its 'vulgar' emphasis on the body, as expressively described by Bakhtin. Yet at this early historical stage an alliance is possible between nascent bourgeois ethics and the age-old popular lore, in joint opposition to absolutism. Lazarillo, free from any scruples of honor and reputation, ultimately marries the maid of an Archpriest and endures with perfect equanimity her adultery with her former master, provided that food is regularly served to his table: 'We got married and I've never been sorry because, besides her being a good and attentive girl, the priest is always very kind to me. Every year I get a whole load of corn; I get my meat at Christmas and Easter and now and again a couple of votive loaves or a pair of old stockings.'[39]

Yet is the 'popular' also 'popular'? Is the popular aesthetic as defined by Bourdieu, an aesthetic of necessity, also popular, in the sense of modern, popular culture? To be sure, once we turn to examine products of contemporary popular culture (and by this I mean specifically what is yielded by the capitalist mode of production, this most commercial and hence 'degraded' field of 'mass culture,' in contrast to the romantically envisioned and standardly better evaluated 'purer' folklore) one should beware not to apply Bourdieu's scheme too sanguinely. It would be an obvious mistake to assume without further ado that modern popular culture is indeed a terrain dominated by working-class aesthetic preferences to the exclusion of bourgeois involvement (or, by the same token, that high art is nothing but ostentatious formal experimentation). For all its elitist indignation, the culture industry thesis is not lacking in real insights into the nature of capitalistically produced culture, which it would be unwise to write off. Commercialization, standardization, instrumentalization, manipulation and so forth are all existing phenomena, as Bourdieu himself would have readily admitted and which, in fact, he helped to document and analyze.[40] The very dominance of middle-class artists at the level of production of popular culture, as well as a massive bourgeois presence at the level of its consumption, clearly indicates that it will not conform to any simple class-pattern, and that it must be acknowledged as a complex, heterogeneous, and contradictory cultural sphere. To assume an identity between the cultural 'popular' and the social 'popular' would therefore amount to an *outright populist* imposition of a vacuous harmony, an idyllic and apologetic uniformity, upon a vast array of cultural expressions which are in truth fraught with profound antagonism. To be avoided are both the complacent enthusiasm of 'outright populists' as well as the despairing condemnation of 'critical elitists,' the former entrusting popular culture with 'the popular' as such, the latter denying it any authenticity whatsoever. If popular culture is indeed a sphere of conflict and ideological contention, the proper task would be to gain consciousness of such discord, rather than negate it, from either a populist or elitist standpoint.

It is for the purposes of precisely such an endeavor, however, that Bourdieu, to my mind, proves considerably more helpful than Adorno. Whereas Adorno drains popular culture of all inherent value, contending that emancipatory art can only be 'serious' art—with the dire conclusion that the masses in our time are bereft of real culture and thus hardly in a position to contribute to radical politics[41]—Bourdieu enables us to approach popular/ mass/industrial culture more realistically, being attentive to the tensions it encompasses. With the aid of the basic categories, aesthetics of liberty/ luxury and aesthetics of necessity, it becomes easier to distinguish methodically between what is predominantly bourgeois in popular culture, including its manipulative and indoctrinating implements, and that which agrees more genuinely with popular needs and sensitivities; to differentiate, in Stuart Hall's terms, 'the culture of the oppressed' from 'the culture of the power bloc.'[42]

My proposition is to further implement Bourdieu's definition of bourgeois vs. popular aesthetic, by expanding its reach *into* popular culture itself. If it is not simply an arena of working-class taste, and bourgeois taste makes its presence, attempting to dominate and transform the proletarian class taste of necessity, it becomes pertinent to split popular culture itself into two main poles which may be tentatively referred to as *high popular culture* and *low popular culture* (thereby, needless to say, completely junking the usual normative baggage associated with such adjectives, if not, in fact, reversing its usual axiological significance). 'High popular culture' would consequently cover those aspects, themes and ideologemes in popular culture which are permeated by the taste of liberty/luxury and correspond to the bourgeois predilection to banish material necessity from the aesthetic experience and to relish a luxurious, privileged existence; 'low popular culture' will encompass the contrasting effort to socialize and materialize the beautiful so that it reflects and engages in the struggle of those oppressed by want and exploitation. In Gramscian terms, it becomes a matter of radically unraveling the apparent unity of hegemonic culture, sorting out those elements which are of a predominantly containing and bourgeois function from those which are fundamentally working-class and disruptive.

The next step will be to evaluate Nietzsche's position and the significance of popular Nietzscheanism with the help of this set of definitions, thus putting the abstract to the test of the concrete.

2. THE POLITICS OF PLEASURE: NIETZSCHE BETWEEN ELITISM AND POPULISM

When turning to examine Nietzsche's aesthetics from a Bourdiean point of view, what we encounter is an intriguing intermixture of the elitist and the popular. On the one hand, Nietzsche was certainly the archenemy of anything plebeian. We can believe Peter Sloterdijk when he asserts (with patent approval) that, as far as elitist disdain of the masses is concerned 'it will hardly be possible at any point in the future to provide a more eloquent delegate than Nietzsche.'[43] Similarly, if Ortega y Gasset has taken such a pronounced anti-popular stance in favor of Stravinsky and Pirandello, he has done so from an unmistakable Nietzschean standpoint. Nietzsche's version of aesthetic elitism was in fact so extreme that, far surpassing any mere expulsion of the masses from the domain of genuine culture, he explicitly expressed his conviction that the many should be enslaved for the purpose of facilitating the production of art by, and for, the few. In that respect, Nietzsche greatly simplifies the work of the critical sociologist; what Bourdieu usually needed to extract from between the lines of the works and theories of high art he discussed, namely—the social function of high art in subjugating the masses and ratifying hierarchy—Nietzsche stated in the most unambiguous terms imaginable: 'The misery of men living a life of toil has to be increased to make the production of the world of art possible for a small number of Olympian men.'[44] In *Beyond Good and Evil*, among other places, Nietzsche salutes the cultural finesse of the French and expresses his admiration for their historical commitment to unadulterated art, to pure form as against the plebeian taste: 'the capacity for artistic passions, for devotion to

"form", for which . . . the term *l'art pour l'art* has been devised—it has been
present in France for three hundred years and, thanks to their respect for the
"small number", has again and again made possible a kind of literary
chamber music not to be found anywhere else in Europe—.'[45] Thus, it may
seem obscene to claim Nietzsche for popular culture, to insist and embroil
him with his hated rabble. By contrast, it appears only appropriate to concede Nietzsche's position of *outright elitism.* On the other hand, however, it
should be remembered that Nietzsche ultimately *disavowed Kantian aesthetics,* departed from the high-art emphasis on art as an autonomous, disinterested, disembodied activity. In order to grasp what was at stake in such
refutation of ethereal beauty, a useful first step would be to recall Nietzsche's most systematic utterances on this theme from *The Genealogy of
Morality*:

> Kant said, 'Something is beautiful if it gives pleasure *without interest.'* Without
> interest! Compare this definition with another made by a genuine 'spectator'
> and artist—Stendhal, who once called the beautiful *une promesse de bonheur.*
> Here, at any rate, the thing that Kant alone accentuates in aesthetic matters: *le
> disinteressement,* is rejected and eliminated.[46]

Complementing this rejection of the presumed aloofness of the aesthetic experience, Nietzsche specifically censured bourgeois aesthetics on
account of its ascetic denial of the erotic component in the beautiful. Here,
Schopenhauer was taken as the cardinal representative of the attempt to
suppress carnal desire with the calming, quasi-sedative effect of artistic
spirituality:

> . . . as our aestheticians never tire of weighing in on Kant's side, saying that un-
> der the charm of beauty, *even* naked female statues can be looked at 'without
> interest,' I think we are entitled to laugh a little at their expense. . . . There are
> a few things which Schopenhauer speaks about with such certainty as the ef-
> fect of aesthetic contemplation: according to him, it counteracts *sexual* 'inter-
> estedness,' rather like lupulin and camphor, and he never tired of singing the
> praises of *this* escape from the 'will' as the great advantage and use of the aes-
> thetic condition.[47]

In place of both Kant's detachment and Schopenhauer's asceticism, Nietzsche adopted a grand, 'Stendhalian' aesthetics which shuns neither interest
nor the libido, instead extolling both as the very essence of what is beautiful:

> As I said, Stendhal, no less a sensualist than Schopenhauer but with a more
> happily adjusted personality, emphasized another effect of beauty: 'beauty
> *promises* happiness,' to him, the fact of the matter is precisely the *excitement of
> the will* ('of interest') through beauty.[48]

In passages such as this Nietzsche manifested a fundamental dissension vis-à-vis the predominant current of modern, elitist art and aesthetic theory. Whereas the elite attempted to demarcate the domain where art gains its independence from the senses and to disentangle the elevated from the vulgar, Nietzsche celebrated the sensual pleasures as aesthetic and the *interest* in enjoying art, *the heroic* as opposed to dry, functional scholarly activity. In that, he comes much closer to popular aesthetics, as understood by Bourdieu, with its refusal to refuse the body, its emphasis on art as an extension of life, as opposed to an ascetic interlude, and on the unity of the beautiful and the agreeable. We find ourselves, in other words, with the paradox that the *philosopher of the elite* was contemplating a cultural project in many ways incongruent with *the culture of the elite*. What is the source of this contradiction?

The False Consciousness of the Bourgeoisie

In full compliance with Nietzsche's just quoted assertion that the beautiful is rooted in the interest that it 'excites,' I suggest that an understanding of Nietzsche's standpoint must once again entail its historical contextualization. For Nietzsche, the principal political weakness of the post-aristocratic elites facing mass society was their incompetence *as* elites. What he doubted was the ability of the *ruling* classes to *rule*. Just as political liberalism, with its emphasis on democracy and the common good, was at odds with economic liberalism, so was bourgeois culture, weighted down by residues of its revolutionary and fraternal past, hardly up to the tasks of strong leadership, capable of stemming the tide of barbarism. As is so often the case with Nietzsche, what one finds is Marxism in reverse: 'The development of Modern Industry, therefore, cuts from under its feet the very foundation on which the bourgeoisie produces and appropriates products. What the bourgeoisie, therefore, produces, above all, is its own grave-diggers.'[49] Yet what Marx and Engels envisaged as a reassuring prospect, was for Nietzsche a vision of apocalypse. The modern, bourgeois elite, suffered from the false consciousness of a class still perceiving its task in some vaguely universal terms, as rendering service to the cause of humanity; a genuinely aristocratic consciousness, by contrast, consists in perceiving oneself as an end, not as a means. An elite worthy of the name recoils at the idea of rendering service and ruthlessly *exacts* service, priding itself on its *parasitic* existence:

> The crucial thing about a good and healthy aristocracy, however, is that it does *not* feel that it is a function (whether of monarchy or community) but rather its *essence* and highest justification—and that therefore it has no misgivings in condoning the sacrifice of a vast number of people who must *for its sake* be oppressed and diminished into incomplete people, slaves, tools. Its fundamental

belief must simply be that society can *not* exist for its own sake, but rather only as a foundation and scaffolding to enable a select kind of creature to ascend to its higher task . . . much like those sun-loving climbing plants on Java (called *sipo matador*) whose tendrils encircle an oak tree so long and so repeatedly that finally, high above it but still supported by it, they are able to unfold their coronas in the free air and make a show of their happiness.[50]

This poetic elevation of parasitism (1886) into the very essence of 'what is noble' reads—in the context of Bismarckian society and closely following the pioneering social legislation introduced by the Chancellor, such as health insurance (1883) and accident insurance (1884)—as Nietzsche's condemnation of an elite that betrays its mission and turns itself into a tool of the community. That the main purpose of Bismarck's welfare programme, as one historian affirmed, 'was to avoid revolution through timely social reform and to reconcile the working classes to the authority of the state,'[51] did not, as far as Nietzsche was concerned, change the fact that it was nevertheless an objective concession to the masses and hence a further step in the quicksand of egalitarianism. It might successfully stave off the immediate advance of socialism but not its eventual victory. In *The Twilight of the Idols* the issue was defined in the most straightforward manner possible. Addressing the social gains of the workers, the fact that they were 'allowed to form unions and to vote,' Nietzsche stated: 'If one wills an end, one must also will the means to it: if one wants slaves, one is a fool if one educates them to be masters.'[52] The relative mildness of Nietzsche's position in social matters, as expressed in the transitional *Human, All Too Human*, was here retracted in favor of a strategic reaffirmation of ruthless subjugation, proper of the earlier tract, *The Greek State*.

Obviously, such social and political inadequacy of the Reich's ruling classes went hand in hand with a fundamental *cultural* deficiency. In cultural terms, the problem Nietzsche identified was that cowardly, unmanly bourgeois philistinism cannot muster proper resistance to set off barbaric egalitarianism. To illustrate this point, let us consider one of Nietzsche's most concentrated attacks on the cultural elite of his times, found in his early work, the first of his four Untimely Meditations, *David Strauss: The Confessor and the Writer*. Traditionally perceived, this essay, written in 1873, is an uncompromising rebuff of the cultural triumphalism prevailing in the recently unified German Reich. Thus construed, it is readily incorporated into the mainstream of Nietzsche-interpretation, that as a rule makes much of the philosopher's anti-political commitment to rescue genuine culture from the asphyxiating clutch of the Reich's aggressive nationalism. Upon more critical probing, however, it becomes evident that if Nietzsche found the cultural atmosphere in the Reich objectionable, it was not for any excess in belligerence. Rather, it was the elite's spinelessness, its cowardice and lack of class-resolution, which troubled him. For Nietzsche, the Hegelian David Strauss and his book (*The Old and the New Faith: A Confession*) embodied everything which was foul about the cultural atmosphere in the new Reich, with its jubilation at the new-gained national and military status. True culture, Nietzsche averred, consists not in self-indulgent celebration of the past geniuses of German culture, such as Lessing, Hölderlin or Goethe, but precisely in the recognition that these towering figures were 'seekers', not 'finders'; with them, German culture was asking questions, instead of congratulating itself it has attained answers.[53] This seems indeed to be fully in line with a cosmopolitan, 'enlightened critique' of the ungainly combination between conceited nationalism and smug philistinism. Yet 'seeking', Nietzsche added, is not *invariably* a synonym of culture. There are times, he made clear, when it becomes crucial *to repress seeking*, not promote it:

> 'All seeking is at an end' is the motto of the philistines. There was a time when this motto was to some extent sensible: the time when, during the first decade of the present century, so much confused seeking, experimenting, wrecking, promising, surmising, hoping was going on in Germany that the spiritual middle class was right to fear for its own safety.[54]

That is, during the years of the Napoleonic Wars, when the ideals of the French Revolution 'intoxicatingly' stormed Europe, a resolute arrestment of 'seeking' was required, the abandoning of undisciplined experimentation for the sake of (class) survival. The problem, however, was that this sour remedy of conservative, static attitude was then taken on a regular basis, far beyond the state of emergency which legitimized it in the first place: 'With the craftiness pertaining to baser natures, however, [the philistine] took the opportunity thus afforded to cast suspicion on seeking as such and to promote a comfortable consciousness of having already found.'[55] The bourgeoisie had suppressed the fact that cultural passivity was a temporary tactics, useful only for attaining the victory in a specific battle, but in no way to be confused with a proper strategic response, suitable for all times and conditions. Hence, it began to drift into a sweet slumber of material comfort and spiritual numbness, believing itself to have reached a safe shore and failing to appreciate the dangers lying ahead. Such philistine complacency displeased Nietzsche not simply because it excluded the possibility of a livelier cultural climate. Rather, as was clear in Nietzsche's mind already at that early stage, it had the most lamentable social consequences. What once proved a winning anti-revolutionary tactics, was now turning, albeit inadvertently, into complicity with the next challenge to hierarchy. In the face of the second revolutionary upsurge, the ascendancy of social democracy, an elite concerned simply with preserving 'peace and quiet' will not do. Strauss is taken as a 'shining' example of the anti-heroism of the middle class, which, for all its eagerness to preserve its social advantages, cannot but be accommodating towards the egalitarian tendencies of the age. Philistinism is bound to prove an easy prey to socialism:

> [I]t is in the highest degree instructive to see why, in one solitary passage, Strauss for once presents himself as the daring defender of the genius and of the aristocratic natures of the spirit. Why does he do it? From fear, this time fear of the social democrats. He refers them to Bismarck, Moltke . . . 'In the domain of art and science too', Strauss goes on, 'there will never be a lack of kings who build and who give work to a host of carters.' Good—but suppose the carters themselves start to build? It does happen, metaphysical Master, you know that—then the kings will have to grin and bear it.[56]

According to Nietzsche, Strauss's negation of social democracy in the name of Bismarckian heroism remains an aberration in the overall pattern of his vision, which as a rule strives at the very opposite of heroism, at the minimizing of conflict and the guaranteeing of a brotherly, harmonious, danger-free society. Nietzsche admonished him that, with his inconsistent, arbitrary application of heroic ideals, 'the kings' will find themselves denuded of any effective countermeasure, once 'the carters start to build.' With the soft-hearted Strauss in command, the elite will be incapable of deterring the march of the new barbarians. In opposition to that, Nietzsche propounded a genuine German culture, not optimistic and cowardly, but pessimistic and courageous. It is therefore only consistent for Nietzsche to have been impatient with Strauss's benevolent interpretation of Darwin's theories, from which the veteran Hegelian sought to induce some fraternal ethics. Against Strauss's 'cowardly' denial of Darwin's 'real' insights, his devotion to old Enlightenment tenets such as universality, equality and brotherhood, Nietzsche took an unequivocal *social Darwinist* stance. 'Here was an opportunity,' Nietzsche reprimanded Strauss, 'to exhibit native courage: for here he ought to have turned his back on his "we" and boldly derived a moral code for life out of the *bellum omnium contra omnes* and the privileges of the strong.'[57]

Significantly, the notion of *courage* (or lack thereof) was absolutely central to Nietzsche's cultural critique, as time and time again he referred to the philistine culture as weak. Strauss, who was described as 'a degree less cowardly' than the average cultural philistine, is himself but a natural coward, as 'reveals itself especially in the inconsequentiality of those assertions which it takes courage to make; there is the sound of thunder, but there follows no clearing of the air.' Strauss, as the elite he stands for, 'cannot manage an aggressive act, only aggressive words . . . when his words have died away he is more cowardly than he who has never spoken. Even the phantom form of actions, ethics, reveals that he is a hero only of words . . .'[58]

Here, Nietzsche's idea of heroism, its nature and its social functions, as discussed in the preceding chapter, are again manifest. To check the progress of the socialists, one will need *consistent heroism*, a unified style, rather than the good-natured, cultural mishmash of the decadent elite. In this light, to come back to our main question, Nietzsche's aesthetics of involvement rather than seclusion reveals itself as an attempt to spur the elite to actively defend its status. Therefore, Nietzsche could not concur with the relegation of the aesthetic to an autonomous enclave, drawn apart from the world, but must ultimately demand for art to take a stand; art must be *militant*, not *ascetic*. This will become a common-feature in his later writings where the Reich is repeatedly accused of faint-heartedness, a renunciation of greatness, which is political at least as much as it is cultural. In *The Twilight of the Idols*, for instance, several thoroughly unflattering comparisons are drawn between the culture and politics of modern Germany and Nietzsche's own counter-ideal:

> The decay of our hostile and mistrust-arousing instincts and that is what constitutes our 'advance'—represents only one of the effects attending our general decay of *vitality*: . . . Here everyone helps everyone else, here everyone is to a certain degree an invalid and everyone a nurse. This is then called 'virtue'—: among men who knew a different kind of life, a fuller, more prodigal, more overflowing life, it would be called something else: 'cowardice,' perhaps, 'pitiableness,' 'old woman's morality.'[59]

Following such general refutation of modern cultural and moral feebleness, Nietzsche proceeded to a more concrete censuring of the prevailing politics corresponding to such cultural decline, a politics which is *not* aggressive and brutal but democratic and egalitarian:

> Our virtues are conditioned, are demanded by our weakness. . . . 'Equality' . . . belongs essentially to decline: the chasm between man and man, class and class . . . characterizes every *strong age*. . . . All our political theories *and* state constitutions, the 'German *Reich*' certainly not excluded, are consequences, necessary effects of decline. . . .[60]

From the heights of an endmost social Darwinist position, Nietzsche felt entitled to look down at none other than Herbert Spencer, the very man who coined 'the survival of the fittest' catch-phrase, and reduce him to a '*décadent*—he sees in the victory of altruism something desirable!'[61] Finally, we find Nietzsche extolling—in what can count as a neo-Burkean attack on radicalism—the *organic-conservative* solidarity between generations past and present against the *mechanic-revolutionary* solidarity between humans here-and-now. As the only remaining example of the former, healthier, organic society, Nietzsche singled out—in a preference which goes far to disprove those interpreters who are all too ready to count him among anarchists, as well as those who seek to turn him into a champion of individual freedom—the Czarist regime:

> I have already . . . characterized modern democracy, together with its imperfect manifestations such as the 'German *Reich*', as the *decaying form* of the state. For institutions to exist there must exist the kind of will, instinct, imperative which is anti-liberal to the point of malice: the will to tradition, to authority, to centuries-long responsibility, to *solidarity* between succeeding generations backwards and forwards *in infinitum*. If this will is present, there is established something such as the *Imperium Romanum*: or such as Russia, the *only* power to-day which has durability in it, which can wait, which can still promise something. . . .[62]

Similarly, much of Nietzsche's later critique of Bismarck closely corresponds to this pattern. What Nietzsche came to abhor was the Chancellor's *lack of true heroism*, the fact that in the end he renounced 'great politics' in favor of what were, in Nietzsche's estimation, humiliating compromises with the masses. As Zarathustra declares: 'And I turned my back upon the rulers when I saw what they now call ruling: bartering and haggling for power—with the rabble!'[63] For Nietzsche, imperial expansion was to be counted among the organic functions of life and, at least in principle, a valid expression of the will to power: 'At least a people might just as well designate as a right its need to conquer, its lust for power, whether by means of arms or by trade, commerce and colonization—the right to grow, perhaps. A society that definitely and *instinctively* gives up war and conquest is in decline: it is ripe for democracy and the rule of shopkeepers.'[64] Indeed, for a philosopher holding such views, a statesman had to fall out of grace who expressed his foreign-policy credo in the following, unassuming terms: 'Here lies Russia, and there lies France, and we are in the middle. That is my map of Africa.'[65]

The Taste of Necessity Refuted

Nietzsche's rejection of the elite's self-complacent cowardice, and his insistence on the bodily and the heroic seem to drive him close to a working-class posture, as understood by Bourdieu. But here one must also register the crucial difference, which alone suffices in reasserting Nietzsche's opposition to such aesthetics even while clearly sharing some of its premises: namely, the complete, principled *refutation* of the *taste of necessity*. Nietzsche celebrated the bodily and the sensual, but he did so nonetheless from the point of view of the luxurious, the non/anti materialistic, that emphasizes heroism. Thus, if Nietzsche's approval of Stendhal's binding together of art and happiness led one into thinking that Nietzsche endorsed a proletarian taste, the very ensuing passage in the *Genealogy* quickly redresses such a potential misreading:

> Every animal . . . instinctively strives for an optimum in favourable conditions in which fully to release his power and achieve his maximum of power-sensation; every animal abhors equally instinctively, with an acute sense of smell which is 'higher than all reason,' any kind of disturbance or hindrance which blocks or could block his path to the optimum (—it is *not* his path to 'happiness' I am talking about, but the path to power, action, the mightiest deeds, and in most cases, actually, his path to misery).[66]

The supreme goal of every living organism is a 'maximum of power-sensation' whose consummation necessitates, to be sure, an 'optimum in favorable conditions,' but only as a means to achieve power. In this way, power is ontologized, becoming not an instrument to obtain happiness but rather the end itself (as well as the beginning). Nietzsche formulated an aesthetic outlook in opposition to both the elitist and the popular, while incorporating important elements of both into some sort of a new synthesis. His endeavor could be described as an attempt to *translate elitist politics into popular language*. Herein lies the justification of analyzing Nietzsche within the popular and the relevance of such annexation. From a Nietzschean position, in contradistinction to a 'standard' elitist one, the popular is not simply dismissed as inconsequential or vulgar; rather, one reserves the possibility of partaking in the popular, instilling it with aristocratic ideals. It is in this light, I would suggest, that the subtitle of *Thus Spoke Zarathustra*, 'a book for everyone and no one,' can best be appreciated, for it neatly encapsulates the dialectical relation between Nietzscheanism and popular culture, the contradiction both stated and transcended in a single breath.

Nietzscheanism represents within the popular the aristocratic ethos of adventure as immaterial, the overflow of energy and might, the will to power, all of which become ends in themselves and not just means to satisfy want or attain safety. Popular Nietzscheanism is rooted, inasmuch as its celebration of bodily prowess, competition and struggle are concerned, in the aristocratic ethos of yore, its hedonism on a grand scale, which are upheld as an alternative to the stagnation of modernity, with its obsessive, decadent concern with the minimizing of danger. This role of Nietzscheanism as a proxy of elitism within the popular, and the very need for such cultural mediation, can be explained historically, and integrated into the sociopolitical development of modern aesthetics. The vital factor with which bourgeois art had to contend was the large-scale entrance of the masses onto the cultural arena, their increasing participation in art consumption following the industrialization of culture. From now on, it was chiefly for them, for the plebs constituting the bulk of the consumers, that cultural production was intended. The bourgeoisie understandably needed to find a means of distancing itself from the art of the masses, indeed from *the popular*, but at the same time of assuring that popular culture will not become, in the absence of bourgeois guidance, dangerously subversive and unruly. In other words, it had to maneuver effectively between the contradicting aims of excluding the masses *and* of incorporating them, between the affirmation of its eminence, on the one hand, and the fulfillment of its hegemonic, *inclusive* function, on the other. This awkward position of the ruling classes springs equally from the inherent contradiction in capitalism between the level of consumption, where a notable 'democratic' drive is predominant, corresponding to the need to expand the market and sell to as many consumers as possible, and the level of production, where the need is, on the contrary, to preserve the exclusivity in the owning of the means of production and limit democracy. Capitalism is hence obliged to maneuver between ultimate totalitarianism at the sphere of production and utmost democracy and equality at the level of consumption and exchange. Thus, capitalism gives rise to a culture which is at odds with itself, torn between its exclusive and inclusive imperatives.

To meet the first objective necessity, that of exclusion, the elite needed to distinguish between 'our art'—the neo-aristocratic one—and 'their trash,' the plebeian, vulgar pleasures.[67] The main strategy for attaining distinction was to enclose a territory of highly inaccessible art, by means of the separation of form from content, elevating the former into the sphere of pure pleasure, while relegating the latter to the level of vulgar art, fit only for mass consumption. But such a strategy is found fundamentally lacking because it can snobbishly keep the barbarians at bay but it cannot retract the flourishing of popular culture in its own ghetto, an *expanding* ghetto at that, with its ominous, antagonistic ethos. The bourgeoisie thus required a representation within popular culture, so that such tendencies may be curbed and modified. For that purpose, the Nietzschean notion of culture proves far more productive than the traditional 'Kantian' one, as it does not simply remain content with disdainful reclusion but, firmly criticizing such weakly asceticism, dares to infiltrate the enemy camp. Nietzschean heroism, although having in common many 'vulgar' attributes, is essentially, in its social function, an alternative aesthetics. Thus considered, we may begin to locate it within what we have above referred to as *high popular culture*. That popular Nietzscheanism is no oxymoron, constituting a perfectly feasible option, is shown emphatically by Ayn Rand, who sold millions of books while decrying the debased, mediocre, demagogic, populist nature of the very medium—popular culture—which made her success. She could gain a massive influence on American culture only by making her rampant elitism *popular*; that she did, by adopting the Nietzschean strategy, by abandoning the confinement of high art, and *forsaking elitism for the sake of elitism*. In that Nietzschean, anti-popular populism, however, she was certainly no exception. For capitalism cannot do either with or without the masses; the cultural 'solution' of Nietzschean aesthetics addresses and reflects precisely this structural ambivalence.

Nietzscheanism and Popular Ethics: *Gut und Böse, Gut und Schlecht*

Another aspect of Bourdieu's theory which has strong implications for Nietzsche's relation to the popular is the ascription of moral transgression, or at least moral indifference, to high culture while claiming an ethical dimension to popular sensitivity. If, according to Bourdieu, the popular aesthetic is by definition ethically involved, the Nietzschean aesthetic is a transgressive one, immoral or at least amoral. In this, Nietzsche's position is typically representative, indeed an apex of the aesthetics of high art:

> The Pure aesthetic is rooted in an ethic, or rather, an ethos of elective distance from the necessities of the natural and social world, which may take the form of moral agnosticism (visible when ethical transgression becomes an artistic *parti pris*) or of an aestheticism which presents the aesthetic disposition as a universally valid principle and takes the bourgeois denial of the social world to its limit.[68]

Yet, must one see in Nietzschean transgression a firm opposition to the popular 'ethic'? Would it not be better understood rather as a like-minded effort to transcend the narrow horizon of bourgeois respectability? Bourdieu's idea of 'the ethical' certainly does not imply that proletarian morals are identical with good bourgeois manners. To recall his words, 'working-class people always appeal to morality or agreeableness'; if we add to this his insistence on the corporeal, 'profane' pleasures which they take in art the result is a notion of a popular 'morality' which is above all concerned with the idea of spontaneity, of doing what is agreeable and 'comes natural,' which may actually fly in the face of what is considered fit and proper from a bourgeois point of view. Working-class people, what is more, may find particular pleasure in ethical transgression when this is aimed, consciously or spontaneously, against the attempts of the 'better classes' to impose upon them a 'civilizing' bourgeois etiquette. Huckleberry Finn, for one, would sooner to go to hell than be cultivated:

> The widow Douglas . . . allowed she would sivilize me. . . . Pretty soon I wanted to smoke, and asked the widow to let me. But she wouldn't. She said it was a mean practice and wasn't clean. . . . Her sister, Miss Watson . . . would say, 'Don't put your feet up there, Huckleberry . . . why don't you try to behave?' Then she told me all about the bad place, and I said I wished I was there. She got mad, then, but I didn't mean no harm. All I wanted was to go somewhere; all I wanted was a change, I warn't particular. She said it was wicked to say what

I said . . . *she* was going to live so as to go to the good place. Well, I couldn't see no advantage in going where she was going, so I made up my mind I wouldn't try for it.[69]

Popular ethics may find expression in an irreverent Bakhtinian carnival of 'grotesque realism,' whereby the lower part of the body rebels against the upper one, the concrete and earthly asserting itself against the abstract and spiritual. Ethics, in short, no less than aesthetics, must be socialized and historicized. At this point, Nietzsche and the popular seem to have much in common, for Nietzsche's view of the amoral is likewise a protest against the 'taming' moral control of the Judeo-Christian tradition and his vision of the new morality, one that will rise beyond the traditional dichotomy of good and evil, is also recurrently justified as being more natural, inhibitions free, sensual rather than frugal and so on.

But, resembling as they may be as far as their common appeal to nature is concerned, the Nietzschean supra-moral project and popular ethics reveal themselves as quite antithetic when more substantially compared. As was seen, Nietzsche's 'anti-elitist' aesthetics, for all its seemingly popular attributes, was at heart an endeavor to radicalize, aristocratize, heroize the bourgeois aesthetic stance so that it may successfully face the socialist peril; it was an attempt to redress the defensive line of the elite from above, even while recognizing the need to abandon some of its traditional traits. A homologous design underpins Nietzsche's revision of bourgeois morality. I have already discussed the general meaning of the Nietzschean break with the morals of the Enlightenment in the second chapter, and emphasized how the bourgeoisie could no longer abide by the universalistic, fraternal ethos with which it launched its revolution. Kantianism, namely, had to be rectified in regard to *both aesthetics and ethics*. What remains is to recall specifically how Nietzsche's transvaluation of all values was from its very inception intended as the same revitalization of hierarchy, *not* its undermining. To do so, we need to briefly return to Nietzsche's most schematic exposition of his transvaluating project.

In *The Genealogy* Nietzsche famously argued, by way of etymological analysis, that the conventional, modern use of the concepts 'good' and 'evil' is the outcome of a slave revolt which has reversed the natural, noble meanings of the terms and assigned them with ignoble significance. According to Nietzsche, the modern, slavish, Judeo-Christian opposition between good and evil—*gut und böse*—was preceded by the healthier opposition between good and bad—*gut und schlecht*. Whereas the later approach wishes to divide the world between the 'good' weaklings and the 'evil' strong individuals and classes, the more primordial one did not implement any such moral yardstick but was rather aesthetically motivated. For the noble Greeks and Romans, as well as for the pagan Germanic tribes, good meant simply *den*

Göttlichen (godlike), i.e. noble, aristocratic, elevated, while bad referred to the lower echelons of society, to the common people, which makes sense especially in Nietzsche's native language since *schlecht*, the German word for 'bad,' is indeed quite similar to *schlicht*, which means 'simple,' or 'plain': 'The pathos of nobility and distance, . . . the continuing and predominant feeling of complete and fundamental superiority of a higher ruling kind in relation to a lower kind, to those "below"—that is the origin of the an-tithesis "good" and "bad."'[70] And so, whereas the masters were simply expressing their aesthetic distaste at the vulgarity of the plebs, the slaves attempted to compel their masters into their moral straitjacket. In order to deliver the enslaved masters, Nietzsche wished to recuperate this higher form of ethics/aesthetics and to transcend the moral ploy of the slaves/ democrats/socialists: 'it has been sufficiently clear for some time what I *want*, what I actually want with that dangerous slogan which is written on the spine of my last book, *Beyond Good and Evil* [gut und böse]. . . at least this does *not* mean "Beyond Good and Bad [gut und schlecht]."'[71] Niet-zsche's critique of accepted morality should therefore not be mistaken for anti-elitist but rather recognized as a pledge to upgrade bourgeois morality, to rearm it against the rabble. Far from enhancing the working classes in their struggle against the bourgeoisie, Nietzsche's new morality was specifi-cally anti-popular, devised to combat modern 'plebeianism.'[72] Once again, the clear dividing line is Nietzsche's adherence to an aesthetic of liberty/ luxury while contemptibly dismissing that which is simply useful, comfort-able, and safe: 'Man does *not* strive after happiness; only the Englishman does that.'[73]

It is highly instructive, particularly in the context of discussing Nietzsche's anti-plebeian militancy, to contrast his extremely low opinion of English culture with his overall admiration of the French one. This preference may appear rather paradoxical in someone wholeheartedly opposed to French radicalism, while longing for a more rigid, conservative, 'organic' class soci-ety, which, especially to modern eyes, appears closer to the English model. Nietzsche, however, with some historical justification, traced back the source of modernism and its pernicious leveling-down process to English capitalism and the spectacular rise of the English bourgeoisie which have rung the knell of the aristocratic order and set off the tidal flow of vulgar-ity: 'let us not forget that the English, with their profound averageness, have once before brought about a collective depression of the European spirit: that which is called "modern ideas" or "the ideas of the eighteenth century" or even "French ideas"—that is to say, that which the *German* spirit has risen against in profound disgust—was of English origin, there can be no doubt about that.'[74] Nietzsche grieved over the ailing French culture of his times, the remainder of the magnificent aristocratic culture of the absolutist regime, this golden epoch preceding the fatal tide of English, bourgeois vulgarity. He went as far as decreeing that the coup of 1789 was actually an *English Revolution* fought by French soldiers:

> The French have been only the apes and actors of these ideas, also their finest soldiers, also unhappily their first and most thorough *victims*: for through the damnable Anglomania of 'modern ideas' the *âme française* has finally grown so thin and emaciated that today one recalls her sixteenth and seventeenth centuries, her profound passionate strength, her noble inventiveness, almost with disbelief. . . . European *noblesse*—of feeling, of taste, of custom, in short *noblesse* in every exalted sense of the word—is the work and invention of *France*, European vulgarity, the plebeianism of modern ideas, that of—*England*.[75]

Thus, and although the hostility towards France united most backward forces in Germany of the time, whether conservative, romantic or nationalistic, Nietzsche's veneration of French culture cannot be regarded as a true departing from this pattern, not *politically*, that is. Nietzsche created his idiosyncratic, ideal image of France by purging its history and culture specifically of its revolutionary tradition, ingeniously ascribed to England. For that reason, there can be no question of Nietzsche posing a fundamental opposition to the German rejection of French *radicalism*. Appropriately, what Nietzsche found most distasteful about English culture was its typically utilitarian creed, the belief in the greatest happiness for the greatest number. The Nietzschean dichotomy between happiness (goal of the Englishman) and power (goal of proper man) essentially corresponds to the contrast between the (mundane, English) taste of necessity and the (glamorous, French) taste of liberty/luxury.

But of course, Nietzsche did not simply confront power and happiness as opposites. He rather wished to conflate them into a higher conceptual unity; against the *schlecht*/common/English/modern/democratic/socialistic notion of happiness he advanced another, a reputedly nobler and more natural one, worthy of the *Übermensch*. Genuine happiness, he proposed, has nothing to do with the petty pursuit of a full belly, harmony, comfort, safety, affection. It rather must admit a 'maximum of power-sensation' as the superior form of happiness, the unsurpassable pleasure and the endmost expectation of life, even if it mostly leads to strife and misery. With this powerful temptation, this intoxicating assurance, Nietzscheanism could participate in popular culture and enjoy real bargaining power. For here the ascetic and defensive strategy of most high art expressions was replaced by a magnificent and daring challenge. Whereas the proponents of high art could only snobbishly, and rather fearfully, defend their shrinking status in the name of an alleged spiritual superiority, a claim towards which the masses could not but remain generally indifferent, Nietzscheanism enlisted into its ranks nothing less than *pleasure itself*—to be attained through competition, exploitation, overpowering. Nietzsche's particular notion of pleasure constitutes an explosive encounter between the 'high' and the 'popular,' introducing a comprehensive alternative to the popular taste of necessity. With this ethico-aesthetic discourse, Nietzscheanism attempts to convert the taste of necessity, to implode the moral consensus of the masses. Unlike standard elitist transgression, which remains a fringe-experience, a Nietzschean ethos of 'beyond good and evil' well within the popular domain can have a bearing on the mind-set of the 'great number.'

At that point, it is possible to return to the illustration mapping the relation between different approaches to capitalism and popular culture, in order to suggest the ideological location of most popular Nietzscheanism:

As shall be substantiated in detail, in the concrete discussion of Nietzschean heroes in chapters 5 and 6, the popular instances of Nietzscheanism consist of an attempt to reconcile a neo-aristocratic elitism with the reality of mass society, indeed to, *popularize elitism*. For the time being, we can give this apparent paradox a 'spatial' expression, by situating popular Nietzscheanism somewhere in between 'outright elitism' and 'outright populism.' In that respect, the popular Nietzscheans' work can be seen as a logical realization of Nietzsche's aesthetical and ethical critique of bourgeois Kantianism.

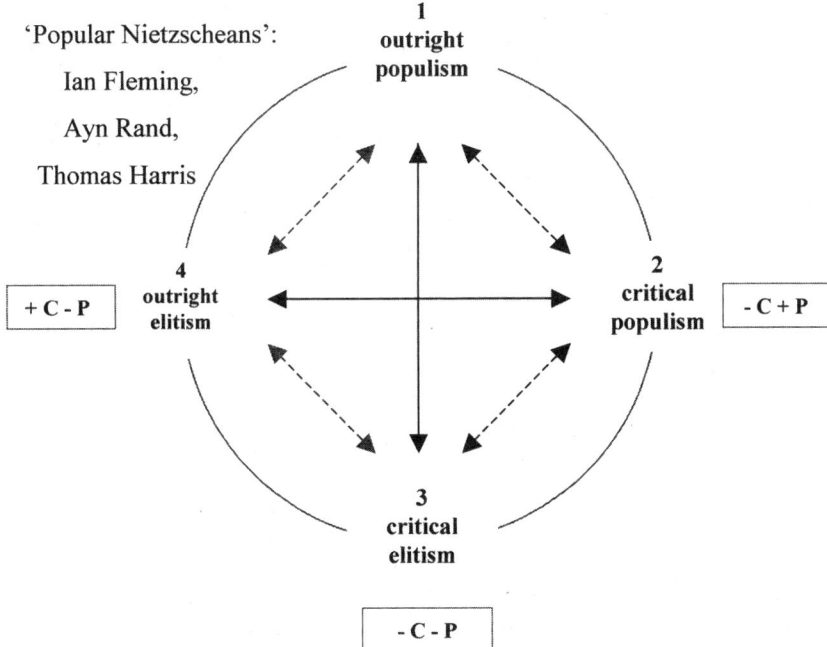

Figure 3.2.

An Aesthetic for Winners (and Losers)

Yet what is the precise ideological impact of Nietzschean 'pleasure'? And how does it actually work to obtain a maximal hegemonic effect? Malcolm Bull, in a valuable essay, has defined Nietzsche's promise of a maximum of power-sensation as the option of 'reading for victory'. Under this heading he characterized the first and most obvious of the two possible responses by readers to Nietzsche's gospel, the response of the would-be winner. The would-be winner becomes a shareholder in Nietzsche's project; he identifies with Nietzsche's elitism, placing himself squarely in the position of the *Übermensch*, in the belief that he is one of those exceptional few who are meant to relish the pleasures inaccessible to the mass. With equal perspicacity, Bull has characterized a second, opposite response to Nietzsche's proposition, of those who 'read him like losers', that is, identify themselves, contrary to Nietzsche's intentions, with the misfit, the silenced other in his scheme:

> Reading like losers will make us feel powerless and vulnerable. The net result, of course, is that reading Nietzsche will become far less pleasurable. . . . Rather than being an exhilarating vision of the limitless possibilities of human emancipation, Nietzsche's texts will continually remind us of our weakness and mediocrity, and our irremediable exclusion from the life of joy and careless laughter that is possible only for those who are healthier and more powerful.[76]

Bull provides us with a piercing insight into the very heart of the Nietzschean temptation and its mode of dominating and subjugating, illuminating its forceful psychological workings. Less convincingly, however, he goes on to extol this second reading as the only genuine alternative to Nietzsche. Reading like a loser, assuming without reservations the position of the subhuman, is to begin to subvert the Nietzschean narrative since 'Reading for victory is the way Nietzsche himself thought people ought to read'.[77] Nietzsche's, however, was by no means just an appeal to the future elite to 'read for victory'; it was at the same time a quite consistent enterprise to infuse into the masses, those 'ordinary men, . . . the great majority, who exist for service and general utility and who *may* exist only for that purpose',[78] a sense of their inferiority and thereby compel them to submission. That Nietzsche strove to breed the *Übermensch* is well known; that he was equally committed to the breeding of the *Untermensch* is hardly acknowledged, but, as I would argue, no less substantial to his project. Far from failing to foresee the potential danger from the direction of those who would read him 'like losers,' the *incitation* of precisely such a response was an indispensable complement to Nietzsche's pledge of happiness/power. Always implied, it surfaced at times in uninhibited blatancy: 'A doctrine is needed powerful enough to work as a breeding agent: strengthening the strong, paralyzing and destructive for the world-weary.'[79] In 1888, Nietzsche claimed that 'Nothing would be more useful or more to be encouraged than a thoroughgoing *practical nihilism.*' Which, as he continued to clarify, means nothing but an inculcation of the 'reading like a loser' response:

> Problem: with what means could one attain to a severe form of really contagious nihilism: such as teaches and practices voluntary death with scientific conscientiousness (—and *not* a feeble, vegetable existence in expectation of a false afterlife—)?
>
> One cannot sufficiently condemn Christianity for having devaluated the value of such a great purifying nihilistic movement, which was perhaps already being formed, through the idea of the immortal private person: . . . in short, through continual deterrence from the *deed of nihilism*, which is suicide—[80]

And on a similar vein, in *Twilight of the Idols*, the philosopher makes clear that not all forms of social parasitism are welcome:

> *A moral code for physicians.*—The invalid is a parasite on society. In a certain state it is indecent to go on living. To vegetate on in cowardly dependence on physicians and medicaments after the meaning of life, the *right* to life, has been lost ought to entail the profound contempt of society. Physicians, in their turn, ought to be the communicators of this contempt—not prescriptions, but every day a fresh dose of *disgust* with their patients. . . . To create a new responsibility, that of the physician, in all cases in which the highest interest of life, of *ascending* life, demands the most ruthless suppression and sequestration of degenerating life—for example in determining the right to reproduce, the right to be born, the right to live.[81]

Nietzsche openly and extravagantly meditates on how best to induce the 'reading like a loser' reaction, ascribing to it a clear social significance (once again, the decadent, cowardly, and defeatist bourgeois elite, far from serving the cause of ascending life and removing the 'parasitic' 'invalid,' has done the very opposite and, as if to spite Nietzsche, introduced the *Invalidenversicherung* in 1889). The misfits, those who are not worthy of life, ought to be given an education in dying. Nietzsche, though, was willing to implement more subtle, less 'ruthless' tools, to produce the required result:

> From love of *life* one ought to desire to die differently from this: freely, consciously, not accidentally, not suddenly overtaken. . . . We have no power to prevent ourselves being born: but we can rectify this error—for it is sometimes an error. When one *does away* with oneself one does the most estimable thing possible: one thereby almost deserves to live. . . . Society—what am I saying! *life* itself derives more advantage from that than from any sort of 'life' spent in renunciation, green-sickness and other virtues—one has freed others from having to endure one's sight, one has removed an objection from life.[82]

Nietzsche now turns away from the physicians to address the 'patients' and 'invalids' directly (and it is clear that for Nietzsche such categories do not cover merely the physically unfit but also those judged psychologically ill or even, perhaps especially those, who are simply *common*, 'mediocre' people, 'failures' in the business of life. As Zarathustra claims: 'The earth is full of the superfluous, life has been corrupted by the many-too-many. Let them be lured by "eternal life" out of this life!'[83]; or in the passage entitled *Of Voluntary Death*: 'For many a man, life is a failure: a poison-worm eats at his heart. So let him see to it that his death is all the more a success. . . . Many too many live and they hang on their branches too long. I wish a storm would come and shake all this rottenness and worm-eatenness from the tree!'[84]). Nietzsche encourages the patients to kindly remove themselves in the name of 'ascending life,' of which they can obviously take no further part. As he appeals to the good sense of the invalid he is willing to negotiate with him, to allure him into accepting death. The promised reward is a moment of glory and power, authenticated by the vitalist philosopher, a grand panoramic vista of the promised land of the *Übermensch*; Nietzsche declares that he who will be so brave and beneficial as to extinguish himself voluntarily will not go away empty-handed: loser though he is, he would still be privileged to say his last farewell knowing that he '*almost* deserves to live' (Oh, sweet 'almost'!). The master of all new physicians is, of course, none other than Nietzsche himself, the architect of the new moral code, who considers it his task to sift those fit for life and those who aren't. In order to carry out this act of selection, he has to *create the corresponding consciousness for each sort*; the fit will 'read for victory,' the misfit will 'read like losers.' Alongside Nietzsche's avowal to 'give the strong man a clear conscience' is hence discernible an attempt to give the *weak* man a *bad* conscience. To these examples could be added those remarkable passages in *The Anti-Christ,* where Nietzsche actually entreats the 'true' Christians to climb voluntarily on the cross, leaving any petty *ressentiment* behind them;[85] or the no-nonsense statement: 'The weak and ill-constituted shall perish: first principle of *our* philanthropy. And one shall help them to do so'[86]; or the following shock-treatment recommended by Zarathustra:

> But you world-weary people! You should be given a stroke of the cane! Your legs should be made sprightly again with cane-strokes!
>
> For: if you are not invalids and worn-out wretches of whom the earth is weary, you are sly sluggards or dainty, sneaking lust-cats. And if you will not again *run about* merrily, you shall—pass away!
>
> One should not want to be physician to the incurable: thus Zarathustra teaches: so you shall pass away!

> But to make an end requires more *courage* than to make a new verse: all
> physicians and poets know that.[87]

The *Übermensch* and *Untermensch*, finally, are the two inseparable poles of
a *single* project; presupposing each other, the existence of the one necessi-
tating the subordination/elimination of the other:

> Let us look a century ahead, let us suppose that my *attentat* on two millennia
> of anti-nature and the violation of man succeeds. That party of life which takes
> in hand the greatest of all tasks, the higher breeding of humanity, together with
> the remorseless extermination of all degenerate and parasitic elements, will
> again make possible on earth that *superfluity of life* out of which the dionysian
> condition must again proceed.[88]

That such a complementary side to Nietzsche's project exists should not,
considered politically, come as a terrible surprise. Every ideology which is
to serve as a means to cement a hierarchy cannot simply teach the masters
that they are superior; it must with at least equal urgency convince the subjects to accept their own subordination. If Nietzsche's promise of victory
and his condemnation of weakness are to be effective as ideological means
it is clear that they must reach a great number of people and not remain
some secret code. Social Darwinism must replace egalitarian creeds not
only in the minds of the chosen few; it must uproot the widespread belief
in human rights, fraternity, equality and so on, which is *the popular suste-
nance of democracy*. In this context, the role of popular culture again transpires: a far more substantial service to hierarchy would be rendered if the
masses would learn to see their *own* baseness as well as the eminence of
their 'betters'. This would truly mean a vital blow to democracy, for what
could be better, considered from a hegemonic point of view, than a *democratic, mass* support for *elitism*? Flaubert, in a 1852 letter, exactly pinpointed
the problem:

> Human consciousness did not protest in antiquity; victory was holy, it was
> awarded by the gods, it was just. The slave despised himself no less than his
> master despised him. . . . What, then, is equality if not the negation of all lib-
> erty, all superiority, of nature itself? Equality is slavery.[89]

The basic task emerges in great clarity: to re-teach the slave to despise
himself. Or, in other words, to make him read like a loser. Nietzsche—like
others of his class—thus needed to instruct the masses in their position in
the caste system, so that they may assume, if possible more or less voluntarily, their role of pariahs. He wanted to instill into them a sense of their

own 'weakness and mediocrity' very much like the Manu-ideologues—whom Nietzsche appropriately held in some esteem[90]—regarded it as necessary that the 'untouchables,' members of the Chandala subclass, shall be acutely aware of their 'filth,' that their unworthiness be indelibly branded onto their minds: 'But this organization too needed to be *dreadful*—this time in struggle not with the beast but with *its* antithesis, with the non-bred human being, the hotchpotch human being, the Chandala. And again it had no means of making him weak and harmless other than making him *sick*—it was the struggle with the "great majority."'[91] The depressing effect of such indoctrination upon its objects can thus hardly be seen, like Malcolm Bull suggests, as a sign that Nietzsche's plan somehow malfunctions. On the very contrary: taken by itself, it rather indicates that 'the disgust' was successfully communicated to the 'patient' by his 'physician'; that the patient, indeed, has been successfully *made* sick. In order for Bull's anti-Nietzschean transvaluation of values to galvanize, it is not enough for the readers simply to respond like losers. Bull absolutely insists that reading like a loser must 'not involve treating the text with scepticism or suspicion,' and that it cannot imply a 'questioning' of Nietzsche's 'extravagant claim.' Yet, although the loser's response may be—perhaps *must* be—a starting point, for it doubtlessly has the potential of triggering a process of critique and of awakening consciousness, I cannot see how it can possibly *replace* critique. Sooner or later the 'misfits' must begin to probe and deconstruct the Nietzschean ontologization of strong and weak, hero and coward, healthy and sick, applying, precisely, 'scepticism and suspicion,' if its effects are ever to be contravened.

Bull's considerable accomplishment, however, remains the dual definition of 'reading for victory' and 'reading like a loser,' as these can be used to great effect in the analysis of the ideological impact of Nietzscheanism. I wish, at this point, to reaffirm the fact that the Nietzschean strategy of inviting one to read *for victory* is not a simple elite discourse, cultivating a closed-quarters ethos of privilege; although definitely fulfilling such function, it is also tremendously effective when embraced by members of the mass. If the masses are allured into power-aesthetics, this inevitably results in the weakening of their political commitment to the cause which genuinely corresponds to their material reality. There is no contradiction, at least not as far as ideological usefulness is concerned, between Nietzsche's individualist message and its 'popularity,' that is, between the appeal to the uniqueness of the supreme individual and the fact that *every* individual may identify with the 'unique.' The same strategy, of course, is the bread and butter of advertising, whose appeal to the unique individual above the multitude is at the same time the appeal to *everyone*, by definition to the greatest possible number of consumers who can purchase a given product. '*You* are not ordinary,' '*you* deserve *the best*' for '*you* will not settle for something *lesser*' and so on. As an actual commercial brochure informs the targeted consumer:

Congratulations

Dear Mr [X],
You are the publisher's choice.
You have been selected from among a distinctive group of individuals to enjoy a generous discount on TIME, special issue, free gift and a free home delivery.
Why you? The reason is quite simple. Because TIME was created for the kind of person who likes to keep up with today's fast-moving world. The kind of person who likes to discuss key issues intelligently and impressively. The so-phisticated reader.
And, if I am correct, Mr [X], you are one of those people.

An appeal to 'read for victory' if ever there was one. The impact of this strategy, looking beyond the immediate commercial interest and addressing it from a social point of view, is to further atomize the individual, to create and nurture a conviction in one's superiority, to endorse a disdainful distance in regard to others, necessarily 'unsophisticated' and 'nondistinctive' individuals, thus diminishing the willingness to associate with them on equal terms or to draw from one's 'private' experience collective, social conclusions. When such an appeal is heeded by one who actually, in socioeconomic terms, belongs to the elite, then, apart from any ethical or psychological costs which may be speculated about, it will not prove counterproductive at the material level, so to speak. Rather, it will probably integrate quite well into the consciousness of an actual 'winner,' namely, one who enjoys a position of privilege in society. It may help him to reassert, in his day-to-day interactions with 'the mass,' his elevated position. The results are different, however, when such temptation of power 'seduces' individuals from the 'underprivileged' class. Here I am not talking necessarily about the personal fate of a given individual: in certain cases such a conviction in one's abilities may in fact, as advocates of capitalism do not tire of emphasizing, endow one with the proper, 'positive attitude' and help one to 'advance.' From a broad social perspective, however, taking in consideration the essential class structuring of society, this is precisely what guarantees the stability of the system; if most or many individuals of the working class come to consider themselves as winners in the capitalist sense, this will result in the principled acceptance of the hierarchy: that some working-class members may rise up the social ladder, provided this mobility remains fairly limited, does not constitute a threat to the stability of the system, for it clearly does not compromise the further existence *of a working class as such*, the social condition under which, as Nietzsche put it, the worker 'and his descendants will continue to work for our descendants.'[92] But if, by contrast, members of the working class reject this option of individual supremacy altogether and insist on the antiquated notion that human beings are to be socially equal, then they may organize to reject, or severely restrict, the 'freedoms' of the capitalist class as a whole and on a principled basis.

Possibly the finest illustration of this inner tension in the Nietzschean discourse and in the capitalistic liberal notion of individualism in general is the case of Jack London, the working-class writer who was an enthusiastic reader of Nietzsche and other social Darwinist thinkers, such as Huxley and Spencer. A restless youth, leading a life of adventure as a sailor, hunter and gold-seeker, among other short-lived quests and occupations, London responded with great zest to the Nietzschean image of the blond beast:

> Not only was I not looking for Socialism at the time of my conversion, but I was fighting it. . . . I was a rampant individualist. It was very natural. I was a winner. . . . I could see myself only raging through life without end like one of Nietzsche's *blond beasts*, lustfully roving and conquering by sheer superiority and strength.[93]

Although of proletarian origins, the young London saw himself as a future victor and felt destined to enjoy the pleasure reserved to the powerful. His position as an isolated individual, far from driving him into hopelessness, became a source of pride and expectation. He exalted in this solitude and was convinced that he may seize his happiness and success by his own means and talents, regardless of the social context and obstacles. Being 'young and callow,' he was fully incorporated into the hegemonic ideology and its discourse of heroic capitalism, in which Nietzscheanism was a key factor:

> . . . I was proud to be one of Nature's strong-armed noblemen. . . . The pride I took in a hard day's work well done would be inconceivable to you. It is almost inconceivable to me as I look back upon it. I was as faithful a wage slave as ever capitalist exploited. . . . [M]y joyous individualism was dominated by the orthodox bourgeois ethics. . . . I doubt not, if other events had not changed my career, that I should have evolved into a professional strike-breaker (one of President Eliot's American Heroes).[94]

However, as he moved from the 'open-frontier' of nomadic existence to the Eastern urban centers of the United States, and made his first serious encounter with the hard reality of properly modern and industrial America, the inadequacies of the Nietzschean tenet of individual sovereignty became clear to him and, moreover, in an unequivocal class-context:

I fought my way . . . to the congested labor centres of the East, where men were small potatoes and hunted the job for all they were worth. And on this new *blond-beast* adventure I found myself looking upon life from a new and totally different angle. . . . I found there all sorts of men, many of whom had once been as good as myself and just as *blond-beastly*, sailor-men, soldier-men, labor-men, all wrenched and distorted and twisted out of shape by toil and hardship and accident, and cast adrift by their masters like so many old horses.[95]

This was the crucial juncture, according to London's retrospective account, in which he began to shift from individualism and Nietzscheanism to collectivism and socialism. The depictions of his 'conversion' are truly remarkable in their profound reversal of the Nietzschean narrative. For one thing, it was likened to a move *from* paganism *to* Christianity: 'It is quite fair to say I became a Socialist in a fashion somewhat similar to the way in which the Teutonic pagans became Christians—it was hammered into me.'[96] Still more astonishing is the description of a move from the 'reading for victory' stance to that of 'reading like a loser.' The precondition for the transformation was London's terrifying realization that he may not end up a victor after all, that the promise of triumph was a great illusion. The spell of bourgeois orthodoxy was therewith broken, and London refused to be a proletarian any longer:

And as I listened my brain began to work. . . . I confess terror seized me. What when my strength failed? When I should be unable to work shoulder to shoulder with the strong men who were yet babes unborn? And there and then I swore a great oath. . . . *I shall do no more hard work, and may God strike me dead if I do another day's hard work with my body more than I absolutely have to do.* . . . But, just as I had been an individualist without knowing it, I was now a Socialist without knowing it, withal, an unscientific one. . . . Since that day I have opened many books, but no economic argument, no lucid demonstration of the logic and inevitability of Socialism affects me as profoundly and convincingly as I was affected on the day when I first saw the walls of the Social Pit rise around me and felt myself slipping down, down, into the shambles at the bottom.[97]

In *The Sea-Wolf*, London's most famous and complex fictional dealing with Nietzscheanism, there is a similar realization of the insufficiency of Nietzscheanism as a means by which a man of the working class may ascend. The Nietzschean captain of lowly origins, Wolf Larsen, also believed, like the young London, that only through amorality, sheer power and ruthless determination one may hold his sway in the 'yeast of life,' the social Darwinist metaphor that the sea-wolf uses to describe the struggle for survival. But, as his antagonist reminds him, these policies have not taken him at all far:

Why is it that you have not done great things in this world? With the power that is yours you might have risen to any height. Unpossessed of conscience or moral instinct, you might have mastered the world . . . And yet here you are, at the top of your life . . . living an obscure and sordid existence . . . Why, with all that wonderful strength, have you not done something?[98]

Gerd Hurm, in an otherwise excellent and cognizant overview of London's adaptation of Nietzsche, made the error of assuming that the reason that 'Nietzschean individualism falters' is its anachronism. He claimed that 'London's challenge to Emerson's Oversoul and to Nietzsche's Overman . . . occurs at the very historical moment when the conditions that had originally nurtured these individualist philosophies ceased to exist.'[99] A rather odd conclusion, given the fact that London was actually experiencing a social condition of a more *advanced* stage of individualist monadization than Nietzsche, let alone Emerson. Early on in his essay, Hurm lucidly explicated the hierarchical commitment of Nietzsche's thought, and, even more expressly, how it 'projects the *bellum omnium contra omnes* of industrial capitalism onto nature.'[100] That from there he went on to suggest that Nietzsche's view corresponded to some early epoch of a purportedly purer individualism is hence quite incoherent. Hurm thus repeats London's own 'mistake,' in failing to see that Nietzsche was not behind his times, but rather *untimely*, and that his vision was specifically suited to an age of advanced capitalism. The root of the difficulty was therefore not in a contingent, historical constellation, but rather in the intrinsic, political purpose: the young London was a genuine captive of Nietzscheanism, inasmuch as he believed in the compatibility of a Nietzschean outlook with plebeian ambitions. His subsequent disappointment was therefore the inevitable outcome of experiencing the objective gulf between the two perspectives, in coming to discern very vividly the rupture between the 'reading for victory' option and the material condition of the worker. Nevertheless, London's heroes, much like their author, 'overcame' Nietzscheanism politically, but not emotionally, and remained marked by this dilemma into the later works, such as *The Iron Heel* or *Martin Eden*. In the former novel, London insisted on a formally Nietzschean hero, the unconquerable Ernst Everhard, but one who for all purposes, apart from his unbending resolution, is a thorough anti-Nietzschean, with his struggle for socialism, the eradication of capitalism and the profound aversion he takes—'moral,' 'altruistic' and 'decadent' through and through—to exploitation and injustice. In *Martin Eden*, the mourning over the intoxicating Nietzschean gospel, the bitter lament that it cannot fulfill its promise, is at the very core of the novel, which is greatly pessimistic and melancholic. It reads as the author's semi-autobiographical confession of a soul torn between two poles, socialism and Nietzschean individualism, which were known to be irreconcilable but could not be satisfactorily mastered or mediated.[101]

This, then, is the enhanced weapon which Nietzscheanism applies upon entering the popular arena; on the one hand, there is the promise of triumph, which divides and rules the working class, by converting its members to the hegemonic ideology. Complementarily, Nietzscheanism engenders the opposite sentiment, one of self-contempt and reverence vis-à-vis the grandeur of the winners. If the masses read for victory they end up losing by forfeiting their genuine class interests; if they read like losers they lose again, this time by resigning to their fate as subordinates (unless they can, like Jack London, somehow transform their dismay into an alternative ethos). I wish now to turn to a more concrete dealing with the Nietzschean hero, in order to see how such forceful strategy was brought into practice and to evaluate its success.

II

THE NIETZSCHEAN HERO ON THE GROUND

4

Realism, Romanticism, Byronism: The Genealogy of the Nietzschean Hero

As a first step in sketching the development of heroic Nietzscheanism the theory of the great literary critic Northrop Frye proves very helpful. In his seminal resuscitation of Aristotle's typology of the hero from the *Poetics*, Frye has provided us with a useful register of literary heroism, in which the hero is classified according to his 'power of action.' Five basic categories of hero are designated, along with the literary modes or genres corresponding to them[1]:

1. Myth: the hero is superior in *kind* to other men, a divine being; this is a story about a god.
2. Romance: the hero is superior in *degree* to other men and to his environment—laws of nature slightly suspended; corresponding literary genres are legend, folk tale, *Märchen*.
3. High mimetic mode: the hero is superior to other men, a leader, but subordinate to nature; most epic and tragedy.
4. Low mimetic mode: common humanity, hero is one of us; comedy and realistic fiction.
5. Ironic mode: hero inferior to us in power or intelligence; most 'serious literature' of the twentieth century.

Frye's typology is both synchronic, inasmuch as all five major kinds of hero are said to be perennial archetypes dating back, at least, to Classical literature, and diachronic, inasmuch as 'European fiction, during the last fifteen centuries, has steadily moved its center of gravity down the list,'[2] namely towards the ever greater predominance of realistic, average or less-than-average heroes and the ever-shrinking role of majestic, outstanding heroes, whether godlike or socially eminent. The relevance of such an historical/generic account for our purposes should be obvious once it is re-called that the Nietzschean hero was characterized precisely as a vindication of the supreme hero of the past as against the realistic, mediocre protago-nist, which has dominated nineteenth-century realism. In these terms, the Nietzschean hero might be seen as an attempt to resist the unremitting de-crease of the hero's power of action and climb back up the ladder, from the domains of realism and irony to the levels of romance and myth, in an at-tempt to recuperate a hero who is also *heroic*. For, as Frye tells us, at the be-ginning of the low mimetic era 'the difficulty in retaining the word "hero," which has a more limited meaning among the preceding modes, occasion-ally strikes an author. Thackeray thus feels obliged to call *Vanity Fair* a novel without a hero.'[3] Along this scale, the Nietzschean hero would be located somewhere in between level 3 and 2, occasionally 'ascending' even onto the summits of level 1, where he makes a claim for a semi-divine status. Such is the case of E. R. Burroughs' hero, Tarzan, for example (whose Nietzschean affinities will be discussed in the next chapter), who, though a human be-ing, is gifted with such physical prowess that make him a godlike figure, as is recurrently underscored:

> His straight and perfect figure, muscled as the best of the ancient Roman glad-iators must have been muscled, and yet with the soft and sinuous curves of a Greek god, told at a glance the wondrous combination of enormous strength with suppleness and speed.[4]

The Nietzschean hero, though assuming many traits of previous heroes, constitutes not simply their reproduction but a new, historically specific, heroic type. In what follows, in this as well as the next chapters, I will at-tempt to explain what is specifically new about the Nietzschean hero, even though he may exhibit many remarkable parallels to, notably, the 'Byronic hero' of romanticism.

NARRATIVE AND THE CLASSLESS SOCIETY

A second aspect of Frye's approach which has important implications for our discussion is the emphasis on the social embeddedness of literature. Frye advanced a theoretical model within which literary modes, for all their alleged synchronic fixedness, are explained fundamentally as *socially condi-tioned* constructions. Literature and society being inextricably intertwined, a social and historical perspective is the precondition for a truly scientific un-derstanding of literature. Thus, at one point in *Anatomy of Criticism*, Frye claimed that 'no discussion of beauty can confine itself to the formal relations of the isolated work of art; it must consider, too, the participation of the work of art in the vision of the goal of social effort, the idea of complete and classless civilization.'[5] In *Anatomy of Criticism* Frye, in fact, came very close indeed to the insight, later to stand at the basis of Fredric Jameson's work, that the key for deciphering narrative is the social, more specifically Marxist kind of literary scrutiny. 'Criticism,' he wrote, 'seems to be badly in need of a coordinating principle, a central hypothesis which, like the theory of evolution in biology, will see the phenomena it deals with as parts of a whole. The first postulate of this inductive leap is the same of that of any science: the assumption of total coherence.'[6] He went on to attack 'the absurd quantum formula of criticism, the assertion that the critic should confine himself to "getting out" of a poem exactly what a poet may vaguely be assumed to have been *aware of* "putting in,"' thereby opening up the space for a theory of the unconscious, not only in the subjective process of literary production, but in the 'objective,' socially symbolic, weaving of texts.[7] To join these three elements together—first, the search for a *totalizing critical principle*, then the negation of *authorial primacy* and, finally, the call for considering 'the participation of the work of art in the vision of . . . *classless civilization'*—is very nearly to obtain the outline of a theory of 'narrative as a socially symbolic act' (which is, of course, the subtitle of Jameson's *The Political Unconscious*).[8]

To read Frye, with Jameson, as an insightful explorer of the inexorable social immanency of literature and to add to that his Aristotelian theory of literary heroism, is to find him especially rewarding in shedding light on the *social* significance of the Nietzschean *hero*. How, then could we account for him on Frye's terms? The Nietzschean hero, to start with, came to do struggle with realism. For Frye, modern realism was allied with the rise of the bourgeoisie. Following the pre-medieval age of myth, medieval romance and renaissance high mimetic began an epoch of distinctly bourgeois narrative: 'Then a new kind of middle-class culture introduces the low mimetic, which predominates in English literature from Defoe's time to the end of the nineteenth century. In French literature it begins and ends about fifty years earlier.'[9] Frye, however, does not elaborate on the specific historical connection between the low mimetic and the bourgeoisie; he does not, that is, undertake to explain why, of all classes, it had to be the bourgeoisie which advanced a hero of mediocrity, neither superior nor inferior to the reader, and representative of common humanity. Nor does he provide us with a consideration of such a mediocre hero's 'participation in the vision of a classless civilization.' We will have to account, however generally, for such historical development, to understand the social function of the realistic hero, before we can assess the significance of the *Übermensch* bidding to replace him.

NIETZSCHEANISM AND REALISM:
THE ADVENTURER VERSUS THE ANTI-HERO

The nineteenth century saw the culmination of an age of realism in Western literature, during which the hero in the classic sense, the overpowering figure, engaged in exciting and perilous exploits, has dwindled into something of an endangered species. Paul Zweig, in his defense of adventure stories, has regretted such demise:

> The oldest, most widespread stories in the world are adventure stories, about human heroes who venture into the myth-countries at the risk of their lives . . . The modern world's dismissal of adventure as an entertaining but minor experience is unprecedented.[10]

Zweig's critique of the 'modern world,' however, is not absolute; he distinguishes between modern high literature, deemed guilty of 'arrogance,' while commending mass literature for subversively preserving and nurturing the heroic narrative. Whereas the bourgeoisie has developed its quintessential literary medium, the novel, allegedly characterized by domesticity, politeness and social realism, the 'popular imagination' hungered after 'Gothic horror, exotic tales of struggle and warfare, stories of crime and the underworld. Not "realistic" chronicles of polite behaviour and budding individuality, but fantasies of risk and high adventure.'[11] Nineteenth-century realism, according to Zweig, is thus not only bourgeois but conservative and anti-popular. The endeavor to restore the lost status of adventure stories is accordingly presented as carrying radical social implications: 'The conservatism of so many great novelists is not accidental: Balzac, Jane Austen, Henry James.'[12] This sort of political taxonomy, however, is a double-edged weapon which can turn just as easily against Zweig's own argument. For, if the allegedly conservative essence of realism is disclosed by the political creed of key novelists, what can we learn about *adventure literature* from the political affiliation of those who—according to Zweig—are *its* greatest patrons? The likes of E. A. Poe, Joseph Conrad or, first and foremost, *Nietzsche*?

> With the doctrine of recurrence, as with the will to power, Nietzsche broadens his lifelong preoccupation with struggle into a theory of adventure which unifies his thought and justifies the apparent excesses of his language. It was Nietzsche's genius to have conceptualized what previously had been a countercultural ambiance, a half-articulate hybrid of popular fantasy and demonic romanticism.[13]

Zweig dedicates an entire chapter, 'Nietzsche: The Philosophy of Adventure,' to substantiate this reading of Nietzsche as the greatest champion of the adventure principle. Nietzsche is said to have 'created a stylistic medium, using the language of epic and high adventure, which the novel [the realistic novel of the nineteenth century] had relegated to the badlands of popular literature . . .'[14] Zweig's suggestion is, in that respect, highly interesting, although he clearly exaggerated the role of this dimension of Nietzsche's work, which on this account becomes, no less, that which 'unifies Nietzsche's thought.' While agreeing with Zweig that Nietzsche was indeed a formulator of a substantially new 'adventurous' language, which was also to some extent a regeneration of past traditions, I radically differ from him as concerns both the historical as well the political meaning of this new discourse. Historically, I do not think that Zweig's view can be accepted, as if Nietzsche was a medium through which the timeless theme of the heroic quest has found its way back into modern culture. On the contrary, Nietzsche was acutely a philosopher of his time, his thinking a product of the modern era, giving expression to its very particular conditions and concerns. Hence, the Nietzschean adventurer is not an existential one, a proxy of the eternally human. I should like to take issue with Zweig's historical interpretation of realism and its social and political significance, and, consequently, also with his rather sanguine view of Nietzsche's role.

In my view, the rise and fall of realism—the consolidation of the low mimetic mode during the eighteenth and nineteenth centuries and its subsequent succession by what Frye called irony (namely, of twentieth-century literature of the absurd, existentialism, surrealism, stream-of-consciousness narrative etc.)—are to be explained as a process organically linked to the changing historical needs of the bourgeoisie. The twentieth-century demise of realism cannot be accounted for on purely aesthetic grounds, as pertaining strictly to literary history and the immanent evolution of genres it embraces, nor as a purely epistemological issue, involving modernist and post-modernist questioning of our very ability to objectively grasp and faithfully portray what was in the past naively referred to as 'the reality.' We must rather insist on the social origins of realism with its characteristic 'hero' or rather, anti-hero. His was, of course, no abrupt entrance upon the scene, but rather the culmination of a long process of realistic advance, or, formulated negatively, a steady diminution in the hero's stature, until virtually all exceptional qualities are denied to him. To be sure, agreeing with both Frye and Zweig, the nineteenth-century mediocre hero of realism is, fundamentally, a *bourgeois hero* (not necessarily in terms of his or her own class background, but in the sense of the class whose standpoint the hero ultimately represents).

From the very beginning of its historical and cultural ascendancy, in the early sixteenth century, bourgeois literature advances this alternative of the un-heroic hero as a genuine spokesman of its distinct world-view and aesthetic perspective. The first major landmark of this modern artistic tendency is *Don Quixote*, a novel (conventionally regarded the first properly modern novel) which signifies the first large-scale challenge—however ideologically ambivalent—to aristocratic values.[15] Anecdotally, yet tellingly, we might cite Thomas Paine, this greatest of anti-aristocrats, who on the eve of the French Revolution referred to the ancien régime as the 'quixotic age of chivalric nonsense.' We have already noted, in a slightly different context, the seminal realistic significance of the first and greatest picaresque story *Lazarillo de Tormes* (a key influence on Cervantes) and its humoristic subversion of the knightly ideals of the nobility. An additional case in point would be Molière's famous *bourgeois*, claiming that he has always spoken prose without realizing it. The rise of the bourgeoisie and the rise of prose are seen to be historically inseparable, already at the seventeenth century, and recognized in the nineteenth by no other than Balzac, who has one of his heroes state that: 'I must see life . . . through bourgeois spectacles, and make my calculations with the most prosaic realism.'[16] But, given Frye's opinion quoted above of the significance of Daniel Defoe, we may do well to concentrate shortly rather on *Robinson Crusoe* (1719), a further milestone in the development of realism's artistic medium par excellence—the novel. By returning to this historical junction we can see how this concrete reduction in the hero's power of action was clearly the result of a social and ideological position.

Upon embarking on a bold career as a seaman the young Robinson confronts his father, the prosperous merchant, who attempts to persuade him to give up the dangerous idea. This fatherly advice succinctly embodies the ideology of the rising bourgeoisie, providing a striking manifesto of sober materialism, proud mediocrity and, most importantly for our purposes, conscious *anti-heroism*:

> My father, a wise and grave man, . . . made me observe . . . that temperance, moderation, quietness, health, society, all agreeable diversions, and all desirable pleasures, were the blessings attending the middle station of life; that this way men went silently and smoothly through the world, and comfortably out of it, not embarrassed with the labours of the hands or of the head, not sold to the life of slavery for daily bread, or harassed with perplexed circumstances, which rob the soul of peace and the body of rest; not enraged with the passion of envy, or secret burning lust of ambition for great things. . . .[17]

The rest of the novel can be read as a confirmation of the father's 'middle station' outlook. The enthusiastic young dreamer, who insists on disregarding middle-class wisdom, is severely punished for his reveries, cast away from civilization and human company. Alone on his island, he learns to appreciate the real merit of the bourgeois thrifty way of life, vindicated as the true, solid—we may add, realistic—ground upon which happiness can be constructed, in contrast to puerile, heroic fantasies, which are doomed to grief. Importantly, Crusoe's mastering of nature upon his island, which he turns into his prosperous 'kingdom,' is not a product of a special, 'heroic' personal ability, but precisely of a mediocre, common human talent made to bear fruit through labour:

> So I went to work; . . . and by making the most rational judgment of things, *every man* may be in time master of every mechanic art.[18]

> I was yet but a very sorry workman, though time and necessity made me a complete natural mechanic soon after, as I believe it would do *anyone else*.[19]

In direct contrast with aristocratic contempt at work and commerce, labour is enshrined at the very center of the bourgeois ethos. This middle-class creed, to be sure, is formulated not only as a rejection of aristocratic heroism but also as clear taking of distance from the 'lower part of mankind'; the bourgeois father is here clearly the mouthpiece of an ideology of safety and prosperity which excludes *both* aristocracy and populace, demarcating a distinctly bourgeois territory. And the question arises: cannot heroism be associated with the working class as well as with the aristocracy, and be seen as an anti-bourgeois challenge *from below*? Paul Zweig, not failing to appreciate the bourgeois nature of *Robinson Crusoe*, indeed went on to deprecate it on such grounds: '*Robinson Crusoe* undermines the ethos of adventure. It does not glory in the episodic life. Its hero is exasperatingly cautious, paralyzed with terror at the dangers he encounters, forever regretting the "mistakes" of his past life.'[20] For Zweig, the change from myth and romance into realism is clearly a descent:

> This is the peculiar originality of *Robinson Crusoe*. Its hero is not an Odysseus, 'skilled in all ways of contending'; he is not a Beowulf, dragon-slaughterer, or a Hercules, or a Gawain. Its hero is an old earthenware pot; its hero is Robinson Crusoe, whose character resembles a homely piece of hardware. But here is the rub. In the world of *Robinson Crusoe*, old earthenware pots survive, and adventurers do not. Old earthenware pots have an unimaginative way of conquering the wildness of the world where adventurers are apt to get lost while losing all their money.[21]

In this way the demise of aristocratic heroism, the change from the warring skills of Beowulf and Gawain into the potting skills of the bourgeois hero of realism, is presented as the depressing triumph of a narrow-minded, petty and materialistic world-view. To dispossess bourgeois realism, to oust the bourgeois tyrant with the help of Nietzsche's adventurous philosophy and the 'live dangerously!' imperative, is to regain the qualities of a heroic humanity. But it is precisely in this enticing, 'anti-bourgeois' claim, that Zweig's argument is misleading. He capitalizes on the modern, negative connotations of the adjective 'bourgeois,' inviting his reader to treat *Robinson*

Crusoe as if it were a contemporary novel. Defoe's novel, written at a period when the third estate was just beginning to mount its challenge to the aristocracy, is judged to be conservative by the standards of an age in which the bourgeoisie is the long-established ruling class. In its original context, however, the novel was part and parcel of a world-view informed by an essentially egalitarian and democratic impulse, if not necessarily and simply revolutionary one; the *mediocrity* of the bourgeois hero corresponded to his *universality*. The 'universal class'[22] developed a prototype of a universal hero, a common individual of average qualities, with which it could launch its assault on the privileges of the aristocracy. It is, after all, only with the advance of bourgeois realism that a hero of lowly origins could become a central object of artistic depiction in the first place. Thus we can draw a very concise lineage from Lazarillo de Tormes, to Don Quixote, to Robinson Crusoe, to Gil Blas (Lesage), to Tom Jones, to Roderick Random (Smollett), to Scott's 'mediocre heroes.' Seen in its original social context, the rejection of all things fantastic, fanciful, improbable and supernatural was anything but conservative and elitist. This was realism as preparing the ground for, and then as embedded in the Enlightenment, postulating reason, scientific research, embryonic atheism. In that regard, it was clearly a weapon of a progressive movement, and not one which was battling or excluding the plebs. Far from it, this very universalistic ethos enabled the bourgeoisie, however incompletely and contradictorily, to join the common people and conduct the great Revolution in its name.

Zweig's analysis therefore lacks a properly historical perspective, in the absence of which we are left with idealistic, supposedly eternal contradictions such as adventure/safety, heroism/mediocrity and so on, which we can then apply as ready-made yardsticks to the content of given texts. In order to appreciate how the truth of the matter must exclude idealist, synchronic categories, it is useful to consult again the advice given by Robinson's father, and look more closely at the exact class position it endorses. Granted, the father's admonition to his adventurous son indeed postulates bourgeois anti-heroism as against the heroism of both aristocracy and the commoners. Thus, it is tempting to ossify this into a rigid dichotomy between bourgeois anti-heroism and aristocratic-cum-popular heroism, as Zweig does. By so doing, however, we overlook the fact that the father's discourse, far from simply uniting lower and upper classes, actually articulates a sharp *distinction* between them. For, although both the upper and the lower classes can be said in some basic sense to be 'heroic,' the respective motives behind their adventurous drive are so radically different that they undermine any such match-making. Instead of binding the two outlooks together under the common title of 'Nietzschean heroism,' it would make more sense to speak of *two kinds of heroism*, an aristocratic and a plebeian one, which are separated, moreover, along markedly Bourdian lines: aristocratic heroism is one motivated and founded upon 'pride, luxury, ambition, vicious living, extravagances' and so on. It is *heroism of liberty/luxury*; 'popular' heroism, by contrast, accompanies 'hard labour, want of necessaries, and mean or insufficient diet,' the lot of those 'sold to the life of slavery for daily bread.' This, clearly, is *heroism of necessity*.

Befittingly, Zweig's celebration of adventure situates itself, in spite of its popular ambitions, within aristocratic heroism of liberty/luxury. According to Zweig, the craving for adventure is a timeless psychological reality, an inherent human need, which has found a due recognition and satisfaction in all ancient cultures. Unfortunately, in our 'own domestically inclined culture'[23] adventure has come under attack. In trying to render tangible the phenomenological experience of adventure and its exciting potential, Zweig appeals to everyday sensations: 'Haven't all of us, now and then, experienced moments of abrupt intensity, when our lives seemed paralyzed by risk: a ball clicking around a roulette wheel; a car sliding across an icy road . . . For a brief moment we are like warriors, charged with the energies of survival.'[24] The author proceeds to explain the special significance of such rare moments:

> Ordinarily we don't endow these excursions with overmuch importance . . . Yet it is possible of [sic] think of these moments in another way. The gleams of intensity which invest them have an otherworldly quality, as if a man's duel with risk were not a 'vacation' at all, but a plunge into essential experience. They offer us heroes obsessed by risk and confrontation, who spell out a choice we glimpse only fleetingly in ourselves: the choice to pursue adventures, to interpret life itself as a series of solitary combats, with death as the adversary.[25]

Adventure is thus definitely *not* something which is imposed on us by material necessity; on the very contrary, our material and humdrum existence is precisely the abolition of adventure. Rather, risk is a luxury, to be pursued and cultivated as a cultural ideal. The precious risk of adventure is individual, metaphysical and aesthetical, bearing no social or political implications apart from a cultural protest against bourgeois timidity. Zweig has distilled one element, that of adventure, out of the Nietzschean discourse; I would contend that such a move remains organically tied with the dynamics of market society, because risk itself, when it is idealized, is very much a capitalistic ideal: when Zweig wrote his book he could still refer to risk as a wish to shatter the crust of bourgeois ossification, and to reclaim for the individual a more fulfilling and vivacious experience. In bitter irony, however, the very notion of 'risk' has since then become central to theories which analyze the structural volatility of capitalism, its permanent state of flux, notably Ulrich Beck's 'the risk society.' According to such sociological theories, risk is not what bourgeois society withholds from the individual but precisely what it enforces upon him or her.

At the same time, it is not my intention to claim that adventure stories, by emphasizing what is heroic and extraordinary, are by definition reactionary and elitist. Instead of clinging to idealistic fixities, we need to interrogate the Nietzschean hero for the concrete social content he embodies. Rather than take a stand for or against 'adventure,' we need to ask what exactly did the Nietzschean adventurer rise up against. Was it—as Zweig assumed—bourgeois domesticity and snobbery in the name of heroic mass egalitarianism? Or, perhaps, did he challenge the leveling egalitarianism of mass society from a perspective of heroic neo-aristocratism?

ODYSSEUS, THE HERO,
REPLACED BY GRAECULUS, THE SLAVE

Nietzsche's attitude to realism leaves little doubts: already in *The Birth of Tragedy* he had articulated a fierce critique of realistic 'mediocrity' in the name of an aristocratic ideal of cultural excellence. A discussion of the alleged deterioration of Greek tragedy, perfected by Aeschylus, into the Euripides-Socrates unholy alliance of morality and dialectics, served Nietzsche to launch an assault upon realism as the characteristic art of the Enlightenment, including a specific censuring of its typical narrative model—the novel:

> Plato really did bequeath the model of a new art-form to all posterity, the model of the *novel*, which can be defined as an infinitely intensified Aesopian fable where poetry has the same rank in relation to dialectic philosophy as, for centuries, philosophy had in relation to theology, namely that of *ancilla* [handmaid]. This was the new position into which Plato forced poetry under pressure from the daemonic Socrates.[26]

Realism, compared with poetry and myth, is said to be no longer attuned to the hardcore, tragic, brutal realities of existence, which underlie the world of phenomena. Instead, it focuses shallowly and un-aesthetically on the surface of phenomena, insisting on reason and morality whereas existence is irrational and amoral. Of utmost significance for us is Nietzsche's view of the realistic, mediocre hero, as a marked aesthetic depreciation compared to the noble literary hero. Such decline, moreover, is not simply confined to the aesthetic domain but is as surely a sign of pernicious sociopolitical *massification*. The mediocre hero championed by Socrates and Euripides, 'the seducers of the people,'[27] is the delegate of the crowd as it becomes the democratic sovereign over art and society alike:

> Thanks to [Euripides] people from everyday life pushed their way out of the audience and on to the stage; the mirror which once revealed only great and bold features now became *painfully true to life*, reproducing conscientiously even the

lines which nature has drawn badly. In the hands of the new poets *Odysseus, the typical Hellene of older art*, now sank to the level of the *Graeculus figure* who, as a *good-natured and cunning domestic slave*, is the centre of the dramatic interest from now on.[28]

Yet more remarkably, Nietzsche recognizes the *bourgeois* nature of such 'Euripidean realism,' and *denounces* it on account of its *democratic* essence:

Bourgeois mediocrity, on which Euripides built all his political hopes, *now had its chance to speak*, whereas previously the character of language had been determined *by the demi-god in tragedy* . . . Thus Aristophanes' Euripides praises himself for the way he has represented *general, familiar, everyday life and activity, things which everyone is capable of judging*. If the *broad mass* now philosophizes, conducts trials, and *administers land and property* with unheard-of cleverness, then this was his achievement, the successful result of the wisdom he had injected into the people.[29]

Realism is deemed the artistic branch of democracy. And when the masses begin to 'administer land and property,' great culture inexorably degenerates:

[T]he fifth estate, that of the slaves, now comes to power; at least as far as principles and convictions are concerned. If one can still speak of 'Greek serenity,' then only as the cheerfulness of slaves . . . [T]his pink glow of cheerfulness continued to colour the prevailing view of the ancient Greek world . . . for centuries, as if there had never been a sixth century, with its birth of tragedy, its Mysteries, its Pythagoras and Heraclitus, as if indeed the works of art of the great period simply did not exist.[30]

Although Nietzsche writes about the Greek masses of ancient times the real object lesson clearly concerns the modern masses and their repelling, democratic orgies 'of senile and slavish enjoyment of life and cheerfulness.'[31] The story of the decline of tragedy is a thinly veiled homily on degraded, modern mass culture (indeed, this is very much the 'mass deception' story that Adorno and Horkheimer will tell some seven decades later from a position that we have termed 'critical elitism.' The crucial difference, however, is that for Nietzsche, the 'outright elitist,' it is *the masses* that get to deceive their superiors). Realism and Socratic optimism, then and now, lead to the 'belief that thought, as it follows the thread of causality, reaches down into the deepest abysses of being, and that it is capable, not simply of understanding existence, but even of *correcting* it.'[32] Replacing 'metaphysical solace' it prompts people to look 'for an earthly resolution of the tragic dissonance.'[33] This optimism, in turn, fatally leads to a humanistic, materialistic and earthly politics; i.e., socialism:

[T]he true magic of . . . this new form of art [opera, in its degraded, pre-Wagnerian and non-tragic form, I.L], lay in satisfying an entirely un-aesthetic

need, in the optimistic glorification of mankind as such, . . . an operatic principle which gradually transformed itself into the threatening and terrible *demand* which we, faced by the socialist movements of the present, can no longer
ignore.[34]

Genuinely 'aesthetic' art, instead, pessimistic through and through, induces
one to renounce such false hopes and accept the world of phenomena (including society and politics) which is produced, not by some historical or social contingency, but the eternal Dionysiac element of existence: music and
tragic myth, Nietzsche affirms, 'justify by their play the existence of even "the
worst of all worlds." Here the Dionysiac shows itself, in comparison with the
Apolline, to be the eternal and original power of art which summons the entire world of appearances into existence.'[35] Here we see how Nietzsche's dismissal of realism and his attendant praise of tragic heroism were meant as
anything but a siding with mass sensibility; if Nietzsche, indeed, took the
bourgeoisie and its realistic novel to task, it was precisely because this novel
made Graeculus the slave its protagonist, at the expense of Odysseus, the
heroic master. Bourgeois realism was therefore discarded qua egalitarian, the
adventurous philosophy upheld qua aristocratic. It should therefore not surprise us that Nietzsche's teachings have in that respect fared generally well
with the bourgeoisie. Much of twentieth-century fiction, both high and low,
has objectively corresponded to this Nietzschean, proto-existential agenda.
The characters were no longer examined, as during the heyday of realism, in
the historical and social specificity of their conditions but rather with a view
to the synchronic 'human condition,' posited as floating above historical time
and social and material circumstances. The modern writer largely took on
Nietzsche's proposal, as it were, and began to explore the myth, the primordial truth, rather than the mere contingencies of history and society. Essential
is that which remains constant while the dialectics of history can barely
scratch the surface of existence. Hence, to cite just a couple of salient examples, Conrad's plunge into human nature, the 'heart of darkness' represented
by Africa, the continent presumably secluded from civilization and history; or
Proust's paradigmatic search for lost, Bergsonian, genuine, inner and personal
time, as opposed to historical, collective time.

As far as twentieth-century mass culture is concerned, the Nietzschean
anti-realism could be observed in the rise of the neo-aristocratic hero, accompanied by the demise of the picaresque buffoon; in the shift from Dumas's Balzacian musketeers, with their democratic 'all for one and one for
all,' their frivolous appetites and human frailties, to the super-heroes towering above the mass. Realism is thus jettisoned once it is no longer useful.
Weakness was the ideal of the bourgeoisie when it was itself weak; it corresponds to its revolutionary phase, when it had the ability, certainly the desire, to speak for 'the people.' But, as the bourgeoisie obtained and cemented

a position of dominance and to the same extent that it gradually discarded so many obsolete political, ideological and cultural tenets of its juvenile age, so too was this realistic, weak, common, democratic hero losing much of its appeal. The time was once again ripe for a renaissance of a bourgeois hero on a grand, aristocratic scale.[36]

FROM BYRON TO NIETZSCHE

A cultural protest against the prosaic bourgeois ethos was not, to be sure, a new phenomenon of the late nineteenth century. The gist of romanticism, after all, was precisely such a revolt against the limiting of the imagination which many perceived was concomitant to the 'age of reason,' the barrenness and cruelty of utilitarianism, and the cold, calculating instrumentalism of *laissez-faire*. Much of romanticism, from Rousseau's vital contribution to radicalizing the French Enlightenment in the name of spontaneity and creativity, to the visionary and irreverent revolutionary enthusiasm of the English romantic poets Blake, Wordsworth, Shelley and Byron, to the critique of bourgeois cynicism in Hugo's *Les Misérables* and the denunciation of utilitarian, 'rational,' systematic exploitation in Dickens's *Hard Times*, to cite but a few notable examples, was decidedly an attempt, not to destroy the benefits of reason or deny the ethos of egalitarianism, but to infuse the Enlightenment with radical passion, melt the glacial walls of capitalist instrumentalism. Romanticism, immensely eclectic and contradictory, was irreducibly *both* radical and reactionary, not only in the diametrical differences of political outlook between, say, a Shelley and a Kleist, but also as expressed within the work of a single artist, where conservative and radical tendencies are often confused as was the case, for example, in Novalis, Byron, Hugo, Dickens and Wagner.

For Northrop Frye, the essence of romanticism was a rebellion against the dominant, realistic current of modern literature. It was an attempt to resuscitate myth and romance in an epoch of low mimetic. Countering the tendency of realistic irony to portray the modern individual as weak and antiheroic, the romantic hero was a glorification of the individual as unique and noble, repelling the social forces operating to subdue his will. As against the realistic acknowledgment of social constraints, projecting a hero who is typically a character coming to realize the folly of his subjective ambitions and hence adjusting to the social pattern (Robinson Crusoe, Scott's middle-of-the-road heroes, Balzac's naïve youths, learning the ways of society, etc.), the romantic hero clings ferociously to his individual essence which is sanctified as artless and pure in the face of arbitrary social injunctions and artificial conventions. Even the failure of the romantic hero can thus be hailed as the admirable defeat of a misunderstood, sensitive genius

(Goethe's Werther as a prototype, Alfred de Vigny's Chatterton, etc.). To the same degree that the romantic hero is alienated from society, he enjoys a 'pantheistic rapport with nature.'[37] Nature becomes the projected antithesis of a corrupt civilization, and the romantic hero is hence, fundamentally, a 'noble savage' even amidst civilization, maintaining his naturalness and wholeness while surrounded by modern, urban decadence. This heightened and militant sense of individualism doing battle with social mediocrity also lays the foundations for the Nietzschean, elitist discourse, in which the genius confronts the herd. As Frye observed, characterizing the classical romantic posture:

> [The romantic poet] thinks socially in terms of a biological difference between the genius and the ordinary man . . . He confronts nature directly, as an individual . . . the romantic poet is often socially aggressive: the possession of creative genius confers authority, and its social impact is revolutionary. Romantic critics often develop theories of poetry as the rhetoric of personal greatness. The central episodic theme is the analysis or presentation of the subjective mental state, a theme usually taken to be typical of the literary movements accompanying Rousseau and Byron.[38]

In view of this, the Nietzschean hero battling the masses emerges clearly as a sub-specimen of the romantic and the Byronic heroes. We can corroborate the relevance of Frye's characterization as concerns the Nietzschean hero by taking a look at Howard Roark, the hero of *The Fountainhead*, whose author, Ayn Rand, was an avowed Nietzschean as well as a proclaimed romantic.[39] Roark is indeed a human being whose integrity and self-sufficiency catapult beyond the realm of the mediocre, mass man, and onto a semi-god position. The opening scene of *The Fountainhead* depicts him a naked figure majestically surveying nature while standing at the edge of a cliff. In the next scene, Roark, a young architecture student, presents himself (fully clothed) at the office of his dean, only to be thrown out of the college for attempting to defy the stale conventions of the métier. The rest of the story takes place almost exclusively in the urban heart of America amongst the skyscrapers of Manhattan, but it was from the outset impressed upon us that Roark is a creature of nature; he remains, in the midst of degraded civilization, a formidable, healthy being, beyond society. Like the romantic poet, who 'is apt to think of literary tradition as a second-hand substitute for personal experience,'[40] Roark's architectural designs consist of a bold denial of artistic traditions, which he sees as obsolete vestiges. The truly creative genius must express himself by inventing art anew, and Roark's style is appropriately absolutely unique, impulsive, irreverent and inimitable. Roark is by necessity 'socially aggressive' for he must defy atrophied conventions to remain loyal to the inner vision that compels him forward. But his 'social impact' can only be described as 'revolutionary', if we accept that a revolution can be undertaken to cement capitalism and fight for the endangered prerogatives of American big business.

At this point we must confront the crucial question of the connection between Nietzscheanism and romanticism; more concretely, we must address the issue of the Byronic hero, the romantic predecessor of what we have termed the Nietzschean hero. What is the relation between the two? To what extent—the Byronic hero being indeed a forefather of the Nietzschean one—are we allowed to speak at all of a qualitatively new brand of heroism? Perhaps it would make more sense to conceive of their relation in terms of a literary continuum rather than a paradigm shift, of the sort implied above? The following, 'Zarathustrian' lines from Byron's *Childe Harold's Pilgrimage*—referring to Napoleon, a romantic paradigm in his own right—would seem strongly to support such continuity-claim:

> He who surpasses or subdues mankind,
> Must look down on the hate of those below.
> Though high *above* the sun of glory glow,
> And far *beneath* the earth and ocean spread,
> *Round* him are icy rocks, and loudly blow
> Contending tempests on his naked head,
> And thus reward the toils which to those summits led.[41]

In order to offer a more precise articulation of my position on that vital question, I suggest a brief consideration of Byron's Manfred, a character whom Nietzsche ranked more highly than Goethe's Faust, and of Lermontov's Pechorin, the most notable example of Byronism in Russian literature. In both cases outstanding parallels with the Nietzschean hero are readily identifiable. Manfred, to start with, is unequivocally 'Nietzschean' in his proud independence, ruthless self-knowledge, self-inflicted torment, and, above all, in his titanic, super-human stature, his contempt at the petty concerns of common mankind. So as to do justice to that which the *Übermensch* had in common with Manfred, if not directly owed to him, here follows a selection from Manfred's unmistakable proto-Nietzschean utterances. Consider, firstly, his dismissal of conventional Christian virtues such as endurance, which is accompanied by a division of mankind into two qualitatively different groups, the servile multitude and the majestic elite:

> Patience and patience! Hence—that word was made
> For brutes of burthen, not for birds of prey;
> Preach it to mortals of a dust like thine,—
> I am not of thine order.[42]

Manfred feels humanity as a hindrance on his 'long pursued and super-human art'[43]:

> For if the beings, of whom I was one,—
> Hating to be so, crossed me in my path,
> I felt myself degraded back to them,
> And was all clay again.[44]

Finally, we must register Manfred's explicit repudiation of 'the mass' and 'the herd':

> I could not tame my nature down; for he
> Must serve who fain would sway . . .
> And be a living lie—who would become
> A mighty thing amongst the mean, and such
> The mass are; I disdain'd to mingle with
> A herd, though to be leader—and of wolves.
> The lion is alone, and so am I.[45]

Equally anticipating the Nietzschean hero is Pechorin, the protagonist of *A Hero of Our Time*, by Russia's foremost disciple of Byron, Mikhail Lermontov. Pechorin exhibits numerous affinities with the Nietzschean heroes of the twentieth century, and indeed, he appears to have been one of the models for James Bond (as we shall shortly see). These parallels are evident, for instance, in his warlike love affairs, his solitary, anti-social existence, his courting of adventures and perils, and, above all, in his immensely competitive, domineering nature. Reflecting on his need to conquer and subjugate his lovers, Pechorin all but yields a philosophical/psychological formulation, in embryo, of the will to power as the motivating force in his soul:

> [A]mbition is nothing else than thirst for power, and my main pleasure—which is to subjugate to my will all that surrounds me, and to excite the emotions of love, devotion, and fear in relation to me—is it not the main sign and greatest triumph of power? To be to somebody the cause of sufferings and joys, without having any positive right to it—is it not the sweetest possible nourishment for our pride? And what is happiness? Sated pride. If I considered myself to be better and more powerful than anyone in the world, I would be happy.[46]

Compare this with Nietzsche's definition of the 'ego' as a thing which 'subdues and kills: it operates like an organic cell: it is a robber and violent . . . It wants to give birth to its god and see all mankind at his feet.'[47] Or compare Pechorin's praise of enmity . . .

I love my enemies, although not in a Christian sense: they amuse me, they quicken my pulses. To be always on the lookout, to intercept every glance, to catch the meaning of every word, to guess intentions, to thwart plots, to pretend to be fooled and suddenly, with one push, to upset the entire enormous and elaborate structure of cunning and scheming—that is what I call life.[48]

. . . with Nietzsche's:

What is noble?—That one constantly has to play a part. That one seeks situations in which one has constant need of poses . . . That one knows how to make enemies everywhere, if the worst comes to the worst even of oneself.[49]

Even such a partial selection from Byron and Lermontov amply suffices to attest the organic link between Nietzscheanism and the Byronic branch of romanticism (at the same time that it dispels the romantic myth of the artist as a unique, isolated genius transcending his time and his society[50]). Yet, having outlined the parallels, we must equally stress the important differences. Literary kinship, in the first place, ought not be confused with sociopolitical one. Seen from the point of view of the history of ideas, the Nietzschean hero is clearly the descendant of the Byronic one; examined, however, from the perspective of the historical development of the bourgeoisie, the discrepancies outweigh the similarities. The Byronic hero was a product of post-revolutionary pessimism. Both Byron and Lermontov were outspoken supporters of radical social change greatly dispirited by the ebb of the revolutionary wave, the post-Napoleonic Restoration in Byron's case, the Czarist triumph over the Decabrists in Lermontov's one. For Byron, the defeat of his greatly admired Napoleon was the hated triumph of philistinism over freedom, a profoundly depressing age of darkness after a brief glimpse of liberty. The dark, brooding, even suicidal mood typical of Byron's heroes was closely bound up with this feeling of having fatally passed up a historic opportunity.[51] The revolutionary individual, apparently betrayed by society and history, thus resorted to retreat from common humanity, asserting the superiority and nobility of his failure vis-à-vis the pettiness of the triumphant social order. In *Manfred*, for instance (published 1817), the poet provides us with a compelling vision of the Restoration as the work of Nemesis, the Greek goddess of revenge:

> FIRST DESTINY: Say, where hast thou been? . . .
> NEMESIS: I was detain'd repairing shatter'd thrones,
> Marrying fools, restoring dynasties, . . .
> Shaping our oracles to rule the world
> Afresh, for they were waxing out of date,
> And mortals dared to ponder for themselves,
> To weigh kings in the balance, and to speak
> Of freedom, the forbidden fruit.[52]

Hence, if Byron was protesting against mediocrity and the herd, he was doing so very much in lament of the Revolution's demise and still cherishing its crushed ideals, and not, as would be the case in Nietzsche, in attack precisely on a society which is said to fulfill the egalitarian, decadent ideals of the Revolution. For Byron, who from his hereditary seat in the House of Lords supported the cause of the Nottingham Luddites, if society was denounced as mediocre it was on account of banishing the Revolution's utopian spirit and sinking into narrow-minded, conservative routine. In his 1816 *Song for the Luddites* Byron thus compared the proletarian rebels with the French revolutionists and saluted the only legitimate monarch—popular, revolutionary sovereignty:

> As the Liberty lads o'er the sea
> Bought their freedom, and cheaply with blood,
> So we, boys, we
> Will *die* fighting, or *live* free,
> And down with all kings but King Ludd![53]

Neither did Byron glorify Napoleon in the manner of later romantics, Nietzsche included, simply as an individual genius, ignoring—or indeed condemning—his historical role as spreading the ideals of the Revolution. Nietzsche famously remarked that 'the Revolution made Napoleon possible: that is its justification. For the sake of a similar prize one would have to desire the anarchical collapse of our entire civilization'[54]; as far as Byron was concerned, the greatness of Napoleon was inextricably bound up with the revolutionary project as a whole, perceived as enhancing, not countering, civilization. In *Don Juan* he takes the Duke of Wellington to task for rendering a disservice to liberty:

> Never had mortal man had such opportunity
> Except Napoleon, or abused it more.[55]

For Byron, there can be no question of a statesman's 'greatness' abstracted from the historical role he plays, and so Wellington, who has snuffed out the revolution, is not a real hero, whatever his personal qualities, but merely 'The Best of Cut-Throats'. He has sided against 'humanity' and committed himself to a corrupt and self-serving elite:

> Oh Wellington! . . .
> You have obtained great pensions and much praise;
> Glory like yours should any dare gainsay,
> Humanity would rise and thunder 'Nay!' . . .
> Though Britain owes (and pays you too) so much,
> Yet Europe doubtless owes you greatly more.
> You have repaired Legitimacy's crutch,
> A prop not quite so certain as before.[56]

In contrast to Zarathustra's claim that 'it is the good war that hallows every cause,'[57] Byron accuses Wellington of conducting an unjustified war, precisely inasmuch as it served the masters and not the people, understood, moreover, as the great, international masses:

> War's a brain-spattering, windpipe-slitting art,
> Unless her cause by right be sanctified.
> If you have acted once a generous part,
> The world, not the world's masters, will decide;
> And I shall be delighted to learn who,
> Save you and yours, have gained by Waterloo?[58]

Byron's 'satanic hero' was a radical rebel, a modern version of Milton's mutinous Satan refusing to resign himself to God's despotism and it was precisely on that account that he was vilified by Coleridge and Southey once these turned conservative beneficiaries of the Restorative establishment. Significantly and befittingly, Nietzsche's general admiration of Byron did not extend to embrace the latter's social radicalism; *this* was an aspect of romanticism which he dismissed as tomfoolery. In a passage from 1887 titled 'Critique of modern man (his moralistic mendaciousness),' Nietzsche mentioned Byron, along with Victor Hugo and George Sand, both of whom he held in contempt, as striking a 'romantic pose,' which involved the 'siding with the oppressed and underprivileged.'[59] In fact, to strip Nietzsche's outlook of its Byronic, titanic and defying trappings, is to remain with a political position not unlike that of Byron's Tory foe, Robert Southey, with his condemnation of 'the leveling principle of democracy' and his concern in the face of 'a great and increasing population . . . a class of men aware of their numbers and of their strength' and moved by 'resentment and indignation.'[60] Admittedly, the solutions Southey outlined to these social evils were nowhere near as bold as what Nietzsche would devise; in that regard, it is tempting to define Nietzscheanism as a Byronism turned *against* 'Liberty,' a term understood by Byron's contemporaries as encompassing the Revolution's ideals.

Lermontov's Pechorin was likewise a rebel against the Russian aristocracy and the Czarist establishment, rather than a crusader against the masses. His central love affair, for instance, consists in cruelly taunting and subduing a haughty Moscow princess. But this is just a detail; more importantly, as the novel's title indicates, Pechorin was not posited as an ideal figure to be contrasted with a decadent society in the name of a future promise of glorious heroism: as explicitly stated in the authorial introduction, Pechorin, rather than an antidote, is himself the surest symptom of his age's malaise: '*A Hero of Our Time*, gentlemen, is indeed a portrait, but not of a single individual; it is a portrait composed of all the vices of our generation in the fullness of their development.'[61] For Nietzsche, the *Übermensch* was supposed to be the antithesis of his age, the *overcoming* of the vices of his generation, to be materialized in the future: '*I teach you the Superman.* Man is something that should be overcome . . . What is the ape to men? A laughing-stock or a painful embarrassment. Just so shall man be to the Superman: a laughing-stock or a painful embarrassment.'[62] For Lermontov, the 'overmanly' Pechorin *was* the present, the summation of its ills. What Nietzsche posited as an ideal of health and a protest against decadent society, Lermontov described as a *manifestation of society*.

Here, over and above the significant respective differences in personal outlook, 'temperament' and political orientation between Byronists and Nietzscheans, the different historical moments are of decisive importance.[63] The Byronic hero emerges at an earlier stage of capitalist development and individualistic monadization, when the memory of a previous, more properly communal existence is still very much vivid and powerful. Hence, individualism itself, the very fact of individual and society drifting mutually apart, is still felt as a historical process, rather than a given 'fact of life.' This enabled both Byron and Lermontov, even as they took the side of their individualistic heroes against society, to record the painful aspect of individualism, the *Ichschmerz* and *Weltschmerz* foundationally articulated in the Ur-Romantic *The Sorrows of Young Werther*. Their work objectively reflects the social trauma involved in laying the ground for individualism, and expresses a certain nostalgic yearning for the lost community, without reverting to its idealization. Theirs is therefore by no means an outright celebration of the supreme individual but also a confrontation with his very existence as a kind of sickness, a state of disease. Again, the famous verdict of the later Goethe on romantic art as sickness is pertinent, the more so when the mutual admiration of Goethe and Byron is recalled. The individual's 'authenticity,' later to become the pillar of the existential celebration of the individual as opposed to *das Man*, communal existence, was here still an object of highly critical treatment. The hero, who in Byron and Lermontov is still a means of at least indirectly criticizing individualism and capitalism, becomes in Nietzscheanism a glorification of individualism and, at least tacitly, of the capitalist present. In the latter instance, capitalism is ironically confirmed *in the very act* of the clamorous *rejection* of the present. This apparent paradox is clarified, once it is understood that the glorious, super-human future promised by Nietzsche was at bottom the very present of a rapidly evolving and inexorably consolidating market society. Seen from that vantage point the protest against the herd was the ideological counterpart of the objective *elimination* of the herd, of the community, in social reality as, in their daily lives, the newly constituted monadic individuals were increasingly immersed in the competitive war of all against all. With Nietzscheanism, however, they could comfortingly invert their real condition into an imaginary triumph, turning their defeat and submission to reality into its heroic overcoming. The incompatibility of actual pity and human solidarity with objective social conditions, the fact that the principle of universal competition turned these into obsolete and even obstructive emotions and values, was therefore presented as a triumph over human weakness, the ascension from the tepid mire of the human-all-too-human into the icy summits of individual autonomy.

In that sense, it is possible to read *A Hero of Our Time* as a critical confrontation with the ideal of the will to power as characteristic of an age of intensifying competitive individualism. For Byron, as well, romantic individualism was highly problematic. This is patent, for instance, in Manfred's conversation with the chamois hunter, the commoner who had prevented him from committing suicide at the beginning of the dramatic poem. Certainly, the hunter, a humble man of the people, can never aspire to the supreme heights of Manfred's lonely and tormented soul; yet he is by no means a despicable, let alone disposable, mass man. He can defend his ground against Manfred's loftiness, and his voice is not bereft of wisdom and an evident share of the author's sympathy when he responds to the accusation of lowliness:

> CHAMOIS HUNTER: Thanks to heaven!
> I would not be of thine for the free fame
> Of William Tell; but whatsoe'er thine ill,
> It must be borne and these wild starts are useless.
>
> MANFRED: Do I not bear it?—look on me—I live.
>
> CHAMOIS HUNTER: This is convulsion, and no healthful life.[64]

This, in hindsight, can be read as the verdict of Byron's man of the people upon the *Übermensch*'s claim of representing the cause of ascending life, health and vitality. No doubt, the author's concern ultimately lies with his convulsive, individualistic hero, but by no means unambiguously as the harbinger of a glorious future. A true dialogue is still possible between the individual and 'the people,' in contradistinction to Zarathustra's monologist preaching, his unqualified and uncontested hatred of 'the rabble.' A longing for a healthier human condition preceding the divorce between society and individual can be sensed throughout the entire poem. And it falls again to commoners, Manfred's valets Manuel and Herman, to pass a negative judgment over their master's excessive, sickly seclusion within himself. Manuel, who has served under Manfred's father, unfavorably contrasts his present master's character with the brighter and more sociable disposition of his forefathers:

> MANUEL:
> Count Sigismund was proud, —but gay and free,—
> A warrior and a reveller; he dwelt not
> With books and solitude, nor made night
> A gloomy vigil, but a festal time,
> Merrier than day; he did not walk the rocks

And forests like a wolf, nor turn aside
From men and their delights.

HERMAN:
Beshrew the hour,
But those were jocund times! I would that such
Would visit the old walls again.[65]

Manfred, no less than Pechorin, was therefore a hero of his time, and an ailing one at that: 'Byron gives us alienation and nostalgia for death. In Shelley consciousness is raised, transfigured; in Byron it is *diseased*, disheveled, finally obliterated . . . Byron has stated the price of absolute autonomy.'[66] For all their charismatic appeal, both Manfred and Pechorin were presented not as objects for unqualified admiration, but as ambivalent figures, products of the contradictions of their age. Considered thus, it is not surprising that Byron's final masterpiece, *Don Juan*, was a good deal more picaresque, realistic and satirical than 'heroic' or 'romantic,' nor that Lermontov's profound influence on Russian literature did not result in a romantic tradition of flamboyant heroes but rather in a realism immensely sympathetic to the anti-hero. This predominant tendency in Russian literature owed even more, to be sure, to the influence of Lermontov's two great contemporaries and literary trailblazers: to Pushkin's ironic treatment of the Byronic hero (notably in *Evgeny Onegin*) as well as to Gogol's mightily influential 'little-men,' from under one of whose overcoats the entire Russian literature was famously said to have come out. But it was also a result of Lermontov's narrative itself. Therefore, as is conventionally recognized in Russian literary criticism, Lermontov's legacy, far from entailing some model of heroic overman, left its imprint in the realistic, distraught, socially misfit, 'superfluous man' of Turgenev, Goncharov or Chekhov's works.[67] The anti-hero so characteristic of nineteenth-century Russian literature also corresponded to a pre-revolutionary situation in that country, as compared with western European countries where feudalism and absolutism were shattered, if not altogether overthrown, much earlier. This explains much about the social need for and the abiding popularity of a universal, democratic, anti-despotic hero, and the continuance of a powerful tradition of critical realism at the very center of Russian literary production well after, in West European literature, realism has been displaced to the margins of art, challenged by a host of modernisms.

It is only at a later and more advanced stage of capitalist development that individualism is accepted as a given, natural condition, at any rate as *a desirable one*, to be defended against the unlawful intervention of the democratic and socialist collective. Thus it fell to a patently anti-revolutionary twentieth-century writer like Ian Fleming to tease out the properly *Nietzschean* side of Pechorin, which informed the character of James Bond, one of the most significant of all Nietzschean heroes in twentieth-century popular culture. In *From Russia with Love* Bond's boss, M, informs him that a girl from the ranks of the Soviet intelligence has madly fallen in love with him:

> She said you particularly appealed to her because you reminded her of the hero of a book by some Russian fellow called Lermontov. Apparently it was her favourite book. This hero chap liked gambling and spent his whole time getting in and out of scraps.[68]

James Bond's unlikely Russian ancestry can be discerned throughout Fleming's thrillers, in the affinity of his outlook and disposition with those of Pechorin. Pechorin, most notably, is a youth suffering from the typical Byronic affliction—boredom. This he tries to alleviate, never with more than temporary success, by a life of permanent traveling, adventures and love-affairs.[69] The same applies to Fleming's secret agent: 'boredom,' as we are told, 'was the only vice Bond utterly condemned'[70]; similarly, in *The Man with the Golden Gun*: 'Bond . . . decided that he was either too old or too young for the worst torture of all, boredom.'[71] The only difference in that respect is that, for Lermontov, boredom was an attribute of the triteness of Czarist Russia while Fleming's anathema was socialism in its twofold manifestations: Soviet Russia, on the world scene, and, at home, welfarist England of the post-War. If we add to this Nietzsche's own highly favourable treatment of Czarist Russia as a bulwark of conservatism we can see how, in spite all important points of convergence and influence, the Nietzschean hero signified a fundamental *break* from the Byronic hero when it comes to the essential sociopolitical and ideological parameters.[72]

Vladimir Nabokov's evaluation of Pechorin is most instructive in this context. As ever a champion of literary formalism, Nabokov advises us not to 'take, as seriously as most Russian commentators, Lermontov's statement in his Introduction . . . that Pechorin's portrait is "composed of all the vices of our generation."'[73] We are asked, in the name of proper literary reading, to suspend the historical and social dimension of the text (even though, in that case, it is not some ill-advised literary critic but the narrator himself who explicitly states the social and historical embeddedness of his tale). Nabokov further asserts that 'the point to be marked in a study of *A Hero of Our Time* is that . . . the "time" is of less interest to the student of literature than the "hero."'[74] Once Pechorin is abstracted from his time we are left with an avowedly synchronic literary hero, supposedly in possession of timeless appeal. In truth, however, this timeless essence is firmly rooted in the ideological climate of the times in which Nabokov's critique was penned. Writing in 1958, one year after the publication of *From Russia with Love* (and, we presume, in complete ignorance of it) Nabokov suggests explaining this appeal to us; he produces a description of Pechorin which would apply equally well, if not better, to Fleming's secret agent:

> . . . a fictional person whose romantic dash to cynicism, tiger-like suppleness and eagle eye, hot blood and cool head, tenderness and taciturnity, elegance and brutality, delicacy of perception and harsh passion to dominate, ruthlessness and awareness of it, are of lasting appeal to readers of all countries and centuries . . .[75]

Interesting here is not so much the characterization of the hero per se, nor could it be said that Nabokov (or Fleming) have read anything into Pechorin which could not in fact be corroborated by the text; instructive is rather what they *did not* perceive or preferred to exclude—the tormented, anti-heroic, indeed sick side of Pechorin, the scars his soul carry as a token of the traumatic social atomization signified by modern individualism. For both Nabokov and Fleming, both members of their countries' upper classes and having a common enemy in the Soviet Union, it was convenient to posit Pechorin as a figure of dazzling, immaculate heroism, 'tiger-like suppleness and eagle eye.' By doing so they usefully confirm a qualitative difference between the Nietzschean hero and the Byronic one, the former being the latter's *further heroization*. What for Byron and Lermontov was a problematic, perturbed, highly ambivalent type of heroism verging in fact on the anti- or mock-heroic, became with Nietzsche, Rand and Fleming a paragon of health, the antithesis of modern decadence. This holds true even if we consider that Nietzsche's great individual was often described as deeply suffering, a battlefield of painful contradictions. For in Nietzsche such tensions were in no way scrutinized as *themselves* symptomatic of modernity's ills. Rather, they were elevated into an ideal, an overcoming of the trouble-free, benumbed, lifeless life of the nihilistic last man of the present. Whereas in modern, competitive and alienated life, the actual suffering of every individual, the self-doubts, the insecurity and the constant discord, all come built-in and free of extra-charge, with Nietzsche the individual could congratulate himself that he has *transcended* modern society and proven his special 'greatness' precisely in and through the anguish. Such sense of achievement, of course, is conditioned on the individual's acceptance of his or her torment as an existential condition and as a mark of spiritual vigor; for only lesser individuals, according to Nietzsche, wish to escape from this situation into the ignoble, cow-like happiness of the herd, to say nothing of those people of *ressentiment* who seek the causes of suffering in some social depravity, and attempt to reform society. Thus, the lofty suffering of the *Übermensch* became an apology for the humdrum suffering of the modern individual, eliminating the critical potential of Byronism.

Fleming was probably unaware of the fact that his 'Pechorian' Bond was but one possible reading of Lermontov's novel, in fact one standing in opposition to a century of literary criticism. Nabokov, being an insider to Russian literature, knew better. With him, it consequently became a conscious endeavor to revise the accepted reading, to *transvaluate*—indeed, in the properly *Nietzschean* sense of the term—our notion of Pechorin:

> It is unnecessary to discuss here Pechorin's character. The good reader will easily understand it by studying the book; but so much nonsense has been written about Pechorin, by those who adopt a sociological approach to literature, that a few warning words must be said.[76]

As can be seen, Nabokov's own approach to Pechorin was neither more 'literary' nor less 'sociological' than the critiques he dismissed as nonsensical. The difference is rather in the very different social and ideological content of his critique, which consisted, precisely, of an attempt to transform the Byronic hero into a Nietzschean one. What is Byronic, i.e. troubled and desperate about the hero, is suppressed in favor of a far more narrow sense of Nietzschean excellence. Nabokov is here supplying a textbook case for the illustration of Nicos Poulantzas' definition of ideology has having 'the precise function of hiding the real contradictions and of *reconstituting* on an imaginary level a relatively coherent discourse.'[77] The real historical contradictions embodied in Pechorin were smoothed by Nabokov into seamless heroism after he has transferred Lermontov's figure onto an ahistorical vacuum, endeavoring to make him a hero of *all times*.

THE NINETEENTH-CENTURY TRANSITION TO 'COMPETITIVE INDIVIDUALISM'

The emphasis in these pages on the difference between the Nietzschean hero of the twentieth century and the realistic or even Byronic hero of the nineteenth century should not be taken to imply that modern heroism *as such* was a belated product of the twentieth century and that Nietzschean agency, however mediated, was playing the decisive role in bringing it about. However much the Nietzschean hero radicalizes and transforms the nineteenth-century hero, the latter could himself be seen as breaking with former heroic models, and as laying the grounds for what Jerry Palmer, in an important study of popular culture, has termed 'competitive individualism':

> [T]he conception of heroism typical of the nineteenth century was very different from that of the earlier period, and . . . the distinction centered on the notion of whether success was deserved or not. The new system, with its overwhelming emphasis on success, has the notion of competition at its heart. This

indicates that it is the transition to the nineteenth century that is the critical period.[78]

Palmer argued that the hero of the twentieth-century thriller, whose main characteristic is his competitive individualism corresponding to the values of a fully fledged market-society, began to develop in the nineteenth century as an ideological product of the industrial revolution. Trying to trace the historical evolution of the thriller's individualistic hero, Palmer began by refuting the conventional idea that he constitutes merely a modern, technological restatement of the medieval knight. Using the figure of Amadis of Gaul—the hero of extremely popular chivalric tales of fourteenth-century Spain—as a main point of reference in assessing medieval notions of heroism, Palmer claims that such were centered on a radically different set of assumptions as compared with the modern model. Above all, what separates Amadis from the modern hero is the firm refutation of personal gain or interest. Amadis operates in the service of a normative code revolving around the crucial notion of honor, an unconditional commitment to an ideal which totally contradicts the modern sense of individualism. Even while protecting his lady, Amadis cannot expect to obtain her love. For that would involve the illegitimate desire—under feudal norm—for reward: 'To act in order to obtain reciprocated love would be to act in view of a reward . . . In the traditional romance, to act in order to obtain reciprocation is half-way to rape.'[79] According to Palmer, the romance notion of heroism thus excludes precisely what would come to constitute, under the capitalist normative discourse, the ultimate motivation behind all human activity: the self-interested strive for personal profit. With the increasing competitiveness and individualization accompanying the industrial revolution and the new predominance of liberal ideologies, the medieval, chivalric hero abiding by a non-materialistic code of honor is no longer suitable as a conduit of the hegemonic ideology. If the hero is to represent the ethos of individual merit corroborated through the act of social competition, he must himself be an icon of competitiveness and convey the delights of winning. Thus, Amadis of Gaul must give way before Prince Rodolphe, the hero of Eugene Sue's popular novel *Mysteries of Paris*, which Palmer considers a milestone in the development of the modern hero. From fourteenth-century Spain to nineteenth-century Paris, the emphasis shifts from disinterested chivalry to the imperative of winning: 'In the renaissance version, success in an endeavor had to be validated by purity of heart . . . In the modern version, purity of heart involves only acting in accordance with a set of external demands, and the critical emphasis is on winning.'[80] The intense personal and emotional stake which Rodolphe has in his fight against the diverse figures of the Parisian underworld such as the heinous Schoolmaster, is the gratification he derives from inflicting punishment upon them—the Schoolmaster, for example, in a famous scene, is blinded by the prince. And it is precisely this emotional involvement, the personal gratification Rodolphe derives from punishing his enemies, which breaks with the chivalry of 'renaissance standards' and looks forward to the thriller hero.

However, for all the significance of Sue's character as a precursor of the modern popular hero, he remains only that, a precursor. In order for Rodolphe's transitional type of heroism to become a truly modern, namely twentieth-century, one, a crucial shift in sociopolitical alliance must still materialize: 'Rodolphe de Gerolstein is not in fact quite a fully fledged thriller hero. One further transition remains to be analysed. Rodolphe and his imitators avenge the wrongs of the poor and the oppressed. In Sue . . . it is the system of class hierarchy that is held responsible.'[81] Sue's radical affiliation emulates the radicalism of the Byronic hero, who, all across Europe, harnessed his angry individualism not against the slaves but against the masters. But, whereas the nineteenth-century competitive hero is revolutionary, his twentieth-century counterpart becomes the guardian of the present social order. Drawing a vital distinction, Palmer argues that Rodolphe and his contemporary romantic heroes represent a utopian alternative to society:

> [A]s is common in Romantic literature, it is an appeal to an ideal universal, a universal which exists *outside* the actual social order . . . the ideal kingdom of Gerolstein—with which France can be compared unfavorably, as it could with an equally fictitious China or Persia in the eighteenth-century *philosophes*—of which Rodolphe is the equally ideal king; or the ideal Fourierist farm to which he sends Fleur de Marie . . . Correlatively, the forces that Rodolphe and his imitators fight are the forces of an unjust social order: wealth and privilege at the service of lust are only the most obvious.[82]

The twentieth-century hero, by contrast, far from championing some utopian alternative, is the entrenched proponent of the status quo: 'In the thriller the villain is judged in terms of an already existing order; it is the hero who represents society, whereas in the earlier novels it is the villain who represents the social order, which is thereby conceived as a form of corruption.'[83] This shift from a subversive individualism to an apologetic one is precisely what has been specified above as the move from radical Byronism to containing Nietzscheanism. And indeed, our major Nietzschean heroes in the stories of Rand, Fleming or Clavell—as shall be closely examined in the next chapter—are all ultraist champions of the social order, while the villains they contend with are usually presented as evil representatives of social upheaval, threatening the stability of the class system and clogging the smooth workings of capitalism. Moreover, the logic underlying modern competitive heroism is quite consistent with the beyond-good-and-evil position of the Nietzschean hero, who discards morality to consecrate power.

For, once winning becomes the hero's sine qua non, relegating all strictly 'ethical' considerations to a secondary plane, a hero becomes possible 'whose intentions are not even good in the conventional sense, who is established as the hero purely on the grounds of his competitiveness.'[84] This basically amoral approach, the fundamental substitution of a competitive code for an ethical one, is immanent to all Nietzschean heroes, in some cases becoming their most salient characteristic. And to this latter variant of the Nietzschean hero, the hero as a criminal genius transcending herd morality, we shall turn our attention in the last chapter.

In this light, we can appreciate how the role of Nietzscheanism was not to invent the competitive hero, who was the objective literary product of modernity rising on the scene well in precedence of any Nietzschean intervention, but in facilitating the turn to the far more militant and ideologically unabashed hero of the twentieth century. Thus, if the nineteenth century commenced the movement towards competitive individualism, the twentieth century brought it to completion; and it was here that the role of the Nietzschean hero proved vital, in accelerating the process as well as in providing its most emblematic and ideologically pregnant expression. It would be both possible and useful, in that sense, to conceive of the Nietzschean hero as an exacerbated example of the thriller hero, taking 'competitive individualism' to its outmost limits.[85] As Fredric Jameson once argued, 'radical breaks between periods do not generally involve complete changes of content but rather the restructuring of a certain number of elements already given: features that in an earlier period or system were subordinate now become dominant, and features that had been dominant again become secondary.'[86] Indeed, such emphasis on restructuring and reorganizing would be the best way to grasp the significance of Nietzschean heroism as compared with nineteenth-century heroic models, whether realist or Byronic.

FROM CAPTAIN NEMO TO DOCTOR NO

A fine illustration of the historical move from revolutionary Byronism to containing Nietzscheanism, from a utopian drive to a basically apologetic one, could be attained by comparing the literary figures of Captain Nemo in Jules Verne's *Twenty Thousand Leagues under the Sea* and the eponymous villain of Ian Fleming's *Dr No*. They have much in common yet the differences are just as revealing; both are larger-than-life individuals, possessing immense powers and abilities, creating their own invulnerable refuges from the world, Nemo on board his unique submarine, the *Nautilus*, Doctor No on a Caribbean island upon which he instituted a small empire. It seems not unlikely that Verne's hero has influenced the creation of Doctor No (who, in addition, appears to combine elements of Wells's Dr Moreau and Sax Rohmer's Fu Manchu), although the existence of such a direct link is not crucial to our argument. Among other marked similarities, both Nemo and No entertain their guests/captives in their staggeringly luxurious, submarine kingdoms: Dr Aronnax, Nemo's captive, is astonished by the splendor of the spectacle seen from Nemo's board as the sea is illuminated by powerful floodlights[87] while James Bond, No's guest, is likewise amazed by the landscape in No's living room, which comprises a huge, underwater aquarium, also artificially lighted.[88] Both Nemo and No are described as ageless: 'whether [Nemo] was thirty-five or fifty years of age, I could not say'[89]; 'It was impossible to tell Doctor No's age.'[90] Nemo, an unmistakable Byronic hero and something of an *Übermensch avant le mot*—the story was published in 1868, only four years before the publication of Nietzsche's first book, *The Birth of Tragedy*—is an extraordinary, tormented genius: 'Captain Nemo seemed to grow enormously, his features to assume superhuman [*surhumaines*] proportions. He was no longer my equal, but a man of the waters, the genie of the sea.'[91] Similarly, Doctor No is a person of unique genius: 'What an amazing man this must be who had thought of this fantastically beautiful conception.'[92] Both geniuses, furthermore, are misanthropic recluses who seek to isolate themselves from society and who zealously protect their privacy and anonymity:

'You like the sea, Captain?'
   'Yes; I love it! The sea is everything . . . In it is supreme tranquility. The sea does not belong to despots. Upon its surface men can still exercise unjust laws, fight, tear one another to pieces, and be carried away with terrestrial horrors. But at thirty feet below its level, their reign ceases, their influence is quenched, and their power disappears. Ah! Sir, live—live in the bosom of the waters! There only is independence! There I recognise no masters! There I am free!'[93]

Doctor No is possessed by a the same longing for privacy, yet even as he expresses such need his words convey that which ultimately separates him from Nemo:

'Mister Bond, power is sovereignty. Clausewitz's first principle was to have a secure base. From there one proceeds to freedom of action. Together, that is sovereignty. I have secured these things and much besides. No one else in the world possesses them to the same degree. They *cannot* have them. The world is too public. These things can only be secured in privacy. . . . And how do I possess that power, that sovereignty? Through privacy. Through the fact that nobody *knows*. Through the fact that I have to account to no one.'[94]

As can be appreciated, Nemo's aspiration is to escape the injustices of the social order, to evade the power of despots and the horrors of the earth, whereas Doctor No uses his refuge as a 'secure base' from which to launch his criminal attacks on the outward world. With Verne, the Byronic hero is an ambivalent one: Nemo (as is clarified in the sequel, *The Mysterious Island*) is an Indian prince who has fought to no avail against the English occupation of his country. He is imbued with hatred of despotism and employs his riches to clandestinely sponsor the fight of oppressed peoples throughout the world. In that sense, the Nautilus is clearly a 'secure base' too, a subversive headquarter plotting against the rulers of the earth; yet the cause is morally vindicated, at least partially so. Nemo's crew is an international community of freedom fighters sharing a deep bond of love and loyalty. Verne certainly criticizes the revengeful passion that guides Nemo, his 'terrible' desire for retribution. In that sense the Captain is a transitional figure, uniting the heroic and the demonic. His humanistic, egalitarian, compassionate sides are marred by his vengeful, destructive, ominous aspects. Yet he is ultimately a noble and admirable man, and his faults are the products of the injuries inflicted on him by the 'civilized' world: 'I had guessed that whatever the motives which had forced him to seek independence under the sea, it had left him still a man, that his heart still beat for the sufferings of humanity, and that his immense charity was for oppressed races as well as individuals.'[95] Doctor No, by contrast, is 'only cruelty and authority.'[96] He, too, commands a loyal stuff of workers, yet their relation is grounded merely on fear, blind obedience and common, vile, material interests. While the noble Nemo represents a utopian alternative to the inequities of the social order, a romantic rebel who preserves in the womblike depths of the ocean the ideals of social justice once they have been defeated on earth, Doctor No, so similar to him in all outward details, is a sheer evil transgressor against the established hierarchy. Palmer's insight is wholly confirmed: Nemo, the Byronic hero of the nineteenth century, crusades against corrupt society, whereas Bond, the Nietzschean hero of the twentieth century, defends society against Doctor No, a grotesque, evil caricature of Nemo. What is alluring and charismatic about Nemo, his one-man defiance of authority, is the very crime of Doctor No: 'I changed my name to Julius No—the Julius after my father and the No for my rejection of him and of all authority.'[97]

CONAN DOYLE'S DEFENSE OF COWARDICE

A remarkable response to the emerging trend of Nietzschean heroism can be found in Arthur Conan Doyle's tale of fantastic adventure, *The Lost World*, published in 1912. Conan Doyle ironically contests the arising, heroic ethos of the twentieth century in the name of a more properly nineteenth-century stance of moderation. Two ideologies are doing battle:

the old bourgeois ethos of realism and mediocrity defending itself against the new, vanquishing discourse of flamboyant heroism. At the beginning of the story the young and unexceptional reporter Edward Malone is passionately courting the girl he loves, Gladys Hungerton, but cannot advance beyond mere 'comradeship.' Frustrated by this state of things, he utters a Nietzschean avowal concerning the proper relationship between the sexes, which must consist of violent, belligerent passion rather than easy-going friendship. He speaks in the name of the primordial instinct, the call of the wild, which civilization cannot wholly domesticate:

> She sat with that proud, delicate profile of hers outlined against the red curtain. How beautiful she was! And yet how aloof! . . . My instincts are all against a woman being too frank and at her ease with me, it is no compliment to a man. Where the real sex feeling begins, timidity and distrust are its companions, heritage from old wicked days when love and violence went often hand in hand. . . . Even in my short life I had learned as much as that—or had inherited it in that race-memory which we call instinct.[98]

By implication, therefore, Malone falls short of true, assertive manliness, at least in the eyes of the girl he wishes to win over. And indeed, to his desperate inquiries, the reluctant girl answers that she cannot love him since his character fails to correspond to her 'ideal' of a man. Malone is eager to comply and transform himself:

> ' . . . Well, what is it that he [Gladys' ideal-man] does that I don't do? Just say the word—teetotal, vegetarian, aeronaut, Theosophist, Superman—I'll have a try at it, Gladys, if you would only give me an idea what would please you.'[99]

It is noteworthy that one of the 'ideals' spontaneously occurring to the enthusiastic youngster is that of a 'Superman.' This attests the very early grip Nietzschean imagery managed to take of European (not only German) imagination, an influence clearly permeating contemporary popular culture. The girl—to return to our story—explains that she would love a true hero, a man of great deeds and glories, 'who could do, who could act, who would look death in the face and have no fear of him.' Rejecting Malone's objection that heroic opportunities are scarce she continues to expound her vision:

> 'But chances are all around you. It is the mark of the kind of man I mean that he makes his own chances. You can't hold him back . . . There are heroisms all round us waiting to be done. It's for men to do them, and for women to reserve their love as a reward for such men.'[100]

Malone answers that he would readily become an hero to please her or to earn his living, but Gladys declines such pretext: 'you shouldn't do it merely to please me. You should do it because you can't help it, because it's natural to you—because the man in you is crying for heroic expression.' Thus, at the conclusion of the opening chapter—significantly entitled 'there are heroisms all round us'—the young protagonist sets forth to 'make his own chances' and find an opportunity to live up to his lover's ideal. Yet, he obviously does *not* do it 'since the man in him is crying for heroic expression.' Rather, it is an alien wish that compels him to seek the allegedly ubiquitous heroisms around him. And the narrator already inserts a skeptical reflection on the spuriousness of this ideology of heroism:

> Was it hardness, was it selfishness, that she should ask me to risk my life for her own glorification? Such thoughts may come to middle age, but never to ardent three-and-twenty in the fever of his first love.[101]

Expectedly, Malone manages to find the adventure that would make his glory, by joining a scientific expedition to South America where a lost Jurassic world is discovered. The many exploits of this quest need not concern us here, apart from one significant scene. The hero takes upon himself to discover a path that will lead his company out of a plateau upon which they are stuck. And this opportunity serves the narrator to further deconstruct the heroic discourse of his times:

> I thought of Gladys, with her 'there are heroisms all round us.' . . . I thought also of MacArdle. What a three-column article for the paper! What a foundation for a career! A correspondentship in the next great war might be within my reach. . . . I had not gone a hundred yards before I deeply repented my rashness. I may have said somewhere in this chronicle that I am too imaginative to be a really courageous man, but that I have an overpowering fear of seeming afraid. This was the power which now carried me onwards. I simply could not slink back with nothing done. . . . And yet I shuddered at the position in which I found myself, and would have given all I possessed at that moment to have been honourably free of the whole business.[102]

Our 'hero' thus candidly confesses that he is not a Superman, but a victim of the ideology of heroism. It is not the manly instinct 'crying for heroic expression' but the power of society, 'the *overpowering fear* of seeming afraid,' which 'carries him onwards.' Malone is essentially the same bourgeois, mediocre, middle-of-the-road hero of Scott from a century ago, but one thrust into an alien and oppressive atmosphere that forces him to deny his nature. It is the anti-heroic bourgeois hero *forsaken by his class*, now exuberantly espousing heroism. Graeculus, the domestic slave, has to feign the greatness of Odysseus: the weak hero, once a representative of his class, now becomes a hindrance to its expansionist ambitions and must conceal his weakness behind a facade of boldness. In the character of Edward Malone,

Conan Doyle thus embodied the transformation of the bourgeois ethos in the very process of its dramatic splitting.

As a consequence of this ideological transmutation, the fears of Conan Doyle's average hero are therefore no longer self-evident, expounded as a matter of course in the context of an overall realistic literary climate and ideology. They are rather specifically stated in opposition to the heroic, predominant vision (note that Byronism, even at its heyday of mass appeal, could never have become quite *the* dominant ideology, being always a sort of counter-fashion/culture. This is another indication that one is dealing here with a new kind of heroism, one which is essentially compatible with the needs of the establishment. Not heroism from below, of embittered and tormented outcasts and rebels, but heroism from above: well channeled, organized and highly functional). Because the ideology of heroism is already prevailing, the anti-hero of *The Lost World* must explicitly, ideologically, as it were, state his un-heroic nature.[103] That Conan Doyle was here taking an anti-Nietzschean stance, so to speak, does not mean, to be sure, that he was a firm critic of the bourgeoisie. It was rather from a classical bourgeois position that he opposed the new tendencies, but now articulating a self-conscious posture vis-à-vis the tidal flow of heroic militancy. Instructively, however, even this perfectly moderate adherence to the quintessential bourgeois values of the Enlightenment comes accompanied by a certain critique of cynical, imperialist capitalism.[104] The woman for whose love Malone is willing to become a hero awaits him, upon return, married to a well-to-do solicitor. A sinister mismatch reveals itself between the glamorous rhetoric and the dreary, cruel reality:

> And Gladys—oh, my Gladys! . . . Did I not, in my truest thoughts, always recurring and always dismissed, see past the beauty of the face, and, peering into the soul, discern the twin shadows of selfishness and fickleness glooming at the back of it? Did she love the heroic and spectacular for its own noble sake, or was it for the glory which might, without effort of sacrifice, be reflected upon herself? Or are these thoughts the vain wisdom which comes after the event?[105]

In some profound and tragic sense, however, these reflections turned out to be wisdom *before* the event. Only two years after the story's publication Europe was drawn into the First World War, in which millions of youths were killed, Conan Doyle's son included. I read the story as a fatal premonition of the coming horrors and a protest against the enticing, militaristic furor and cynical promise of glory which led so many to their 'heroic' deaths. The figure of the tantalizing woman (if we are allowed to suspend the problematic of misogyny) would accordingly be the adulterous, cynical Nation, in whose name they die, and which is at bottom rather 'selfish and fickle,' and quite practical-minded, as the survivors learn only too late. For was not 'the Great War' that 'next great war' which Malone fantasized about as the opportunity to launch a glorious career? That selfsame war which stood under the sign of Nietzschean heroism, and, as we can see, not *only* on the German side (that, next to The Bible, most German soldiers carried with them *Thus Spoke Zarathustra* to the trenches, is a well-known anecdote)?

The examples of Verne's and Conan Doyle's heroes indicate how heroic models basically of the nineteenth century—the Byronic hero in Verne's case, the realistic hero in Conan Doyle's—stand in relation to twentieth-century Nietzscheanism. Yet they are still examples for what the Nietzschean hero resists, and not of what he actually is. We have by now, so I hope, attained an understanding of the overall significance of Nietzscheanism and gained an insight into its political and aesthetic meaning. This, however, is merely the general background from which the Nietzschean hero has emerged; but to know a species habitat is not the same as knowing the species. It is now time to turn to a concrete and sustained discussion of the Nietzschean hero proper.

5

The Bourgeois Renaissance of Aristocratic Heroism

An interesting case of early popular treatment of the Nietzschean heroic model, alongside Conan Doyle's *The Lost World*, are Edgar Rice Burroughs's Tarzan tales, bringing forth one of the most famous and enduring heroes of twentieth-century popular culture. Here we have a character corresponding much more closely to the Nietzschean model yet still 'resisting' it in some important respects. The ideological ambiguity of the Tarzan stories stem from their roots in two distinct and incompatible ideologies of nature as an alternative to corrupt society, the Rousseauvian notion of 'the noble savage,' on the one hand, and the Nietzschean, social Darwinist ethos, on the other. I describe them as incompatible, since, although evincing some superficial similarities, the first advances a critique of society on account of its 'unnatural' exploitative structure whereas the second censures society precisely on account of its 'unnatural' attempt to *curb* exploitation. In the figure of Tarzan, however, particularly as developed in the original novels, both conflicting ideologemes are simultaneously active, generating a singular dynamics.

1. TARZAN: THE BLOND BEAST MEETS THE NOBLE SAVAGE

For Nietzsche, as for all social Darwinists (and Rousseauvians, certainly, but for different purposes), 'nature' counted not so much in itself as it was useful as a model for society. Since the process of 'natural selection,' went the familiar argument, takes place under natural, wild conditions, civilization has no business interrupting and meddling with the wildness of nature as it expresses itself within society, namely, in the transactions of the free market. The attempt of the masses to regulate competition can only result in the fatal defeat of the evolutionary logic, which enhances the fittest. The pernicious outcome of such regulation, already apparent everywhere in the modern world, is the proliferation of the misfits, those whom unobstructed nature would have effectively, and beneficently, weeded out. The *ideology of the jungle* thus made sense as part of a bid to *'jungalize' society*. The class system was therefore projected as operating under nature's eternal blessing:

> The *order of castes*, the supreme, the dominating law, is only the sanctioning of a *natural order*, a natural law of the first rank over which no arbitrary caprice, no 'modern idea' has any power. In every healthy society, there can be distinguished three types of man of divergent physiological tendency which mutually condition one another and each of which possesses its own hygiene, its own realm of work, its own sort of mastery and feeling of perfection. Nature, *not* Manu, separates from one another the predominantly spiritual type, the predominantly muscular and temperamental type, and the third type distinguished neither in the one nor the other, the mediocre type—the last as the great majority, the first as the élite. . . .[1]

In keeping with such premise, Nietzsche often positively contrasted the animal world, where evolution proceeds unchecked, with human, modern civilization, which is characterized by its effort to arrest evolution. Hence, the animals are depicted as healthy and vital in comparison with man: '*Animals as critics.*—I fear that the animals consider man as a being like themselves that has lost in a most dangerous way its sound animal common sense; they consider him the insane animal, the laughing animal, the weeping animal, the miserable animal.'[2] Elsewhere, man is judged to be 'more ill, uncertain, changeable and unstable than any other animal, without a doubt—he is *the* sick animal.'[3] 'Every animal,' Nietzsche tells us, 'instinctively strives for an optimum in favourable conditions in which fully to release his power and achieve his maximum of power-sensation; every animal abhors equally instinctively . . . any kind of disturbance or hindrance which blocks or could block his path to the optimum.'[4] Animals, one is tempted to add, in their capacity of 'critics,' abhor socialism; except, of course, for the one animal that truly counts, the sick animal, man. Man is burdened by reason, which fatally tends to split apart from his 'sound animal common sense' his 'instinct.' This divide between reason and instinct is man's special predicament, and Nietzsche can therefore condemn 'progress' as a process whereby reason further alienates man from his natural instincts. The upshot is cultural, moral, social and political decline. Consequently, it is logical to demand that 'we begin to "naturalize" humanity.'[5] In what is a very important passage in the context of establishing the Nietzschean spirit informing the popular myth of Tarzan, Nietzsche also makes a distinction between 'the tropics' as a geographical site of vitality, the alleged youth of mankind and the abode of instinct, and the colder, northern zones, where humanity diminishes and loses much of its creative exuberance, succumbing before petrified conventions:

> In comparison with the temperate cultural zone . . . the past gives, on the whole, the impression of a *tropical* climate. Violent contrasts; abrupt alternations of day and night; heat and magnificent colors; reverence for everything sudden, mysterious, frightful; rapid onset of oncoming storms; everywhere the wasteful overflowing of nature's horns of plenty; and on the other hand, in our culture, a light, though not brilliant sky . . . : thus the two zones contrast with one another. When we see how the most raging passions are overcome and broken with uncanny power by metaphysical ideas, we feel as if wild tigers in the tropics were being crushed before our eyes in the coils of monstrous snakes . . .[6]

Considered thus, Tarzan can be seen as an attempt to recover man's instincts by returning to the tropics, that place of 'mystery' where he had lost them. Man becomes, through Tarzan, a healthy animal once again, regains his youth and vitality. Tarzan turns back the clock and naturalizes man, cures him of the effects of civilization. Burroughs repeatedly emphasizes this motif of recovery, achieved by shrugging off the constraints of civilization:

> To Tarzan of the Apes . . . civilization was at best but an outward veneer which he gladly peeled off with his uncomfortable European clothes whenever any reasonable pretext presented itself. It was a woman's love which kept Tarzan even to the semblance of civilization—a condition for which familiarity had bred contempt. He hated the shams and the hypocrisies of it and with the clear vision of an unspoiled mind he had penetrated to the rotten core of the heart of the thing—the cowardly greed for peace and ease and the safe-guarding of property rights. That the fine things of life—art, music and literature—had thriven upon such enervating ideals he strenuously denied, insisting, rather, that they had endured in spite of civilization.[7]

Whereas Nietzsche's civilized beast has dangerously 'lost its sound animal common sense,' Burroughs's *uncivilized man* penetrates 'with the clear vision of an unspoiled mind' the sham of civilization. Tarzan embodies health precisely because he was formed by the struggle for survival and has, under the pressure of natural selection, proven himself the fittest. He has not, like modern man, renounced war and strife and degenerated into an enervated weakling. Rather, he cherishes and thrives in 'the battle for existence':

> 'Show me the fat, opulent coward,' he was wont to say, 'who ever originated a beautiful ideal. In the clash of arms, in the battle for survival, amid hunger and death and danger, in the face of God as manifested in the display of Nature's most terrific forces, is born all that is finest and best in the human heart and mind.'

And so Tarzan always came back to Nature in the spirit of a lover keeping a long deferred tryst after a period behind prison walls. . . . He ate burnt flesh when he would have preferred it raw and unspoiled, . . . he craved the hot blood of a fresh kill and his muscles yearned to pit themselves against the savage jungle in the battle for existence that had been his sole birthright for the first twenty years of his life.[8]

This is Tarzan's recipe for retracting the modern process of a steady de-naturalization and emasculation. In accordance with such natural education, unencumbered by 'modern ideas,' the ape-man innocently embraces the war-of-all-against-all as the sound principle of jungle life: 'Tarzan of the Apes was no sentimentalist. He knew nothing of the brotherhood of man. All things outside his own tribe were his deadly enemies. . . . And he realized all this without malice or hatred. To kill was the law of the wild world he knew.'[9] Unlike modern man, enfeebled by morality, competition—even when life itself is at stake—does not produce in Tarzan the bitterness of *ressentiment*. He squarely accepts the rules of the game and recognizes the justice of jungle life. He signs no social contracts, for, like any animal in its right senses, he strives for an optimum in power sensation. The pleasure of killing, for such indeed it is, must be purchased by facing the risk of getting killed. Thus, in the jungle, quarter is neither asked nor given:

> Few were his primitive pleasures, but the greatest of these was to hunt and kill, and so he accorded to others the right to cherish the same desires as he, even though he himself might be the object of their hunt.
>   His strange life had left him neither morose nor bloodthirsty. That he joyed in killing, and that he killed with a joyous laugh upon his handsome lips betokened no innate cruelty.[10]

Tarzan is a laughing, innocent killer: 'When Tarzan killed he more often smiled than scowled, and smiles are the foundation of beauty.'[11] He evokes, in that respect, Nietzsche's noblemen who 'return to the innocent conscience of the wild beast, as exultant monsters' with 'their shocking cheerfulness, the depth of delight in all destruction, in all the debauches of victory and cruelty.'[12] It is only once 're-touched, re-interpreted and re-viewed through the posionous eye of *ressentiment*' that such noble men and cheerful murderers become 'evil enemies' and 'barbarians.'[13] Above all, Tarzan, the orphan scion of English Lords who grew up among the beasts, is the epitome of the natural master. He is destined to become the sovereign of the jungle and assert his inborn supremacy over all lesser species, beasts and black natives alike, due to the whiteness of his skin (Tar-Zan, in the language of the great apes, means white-skin) and the pureness of his blood. The social Darwinist and racist fable is here complete. Tarzan's aristocratic essence is stressed repeatedly, as in the following instance:

Tarzan of the Apes was seeking a kill. . . . [A]t last his nostrils were rewarded with the scent of the fresh spoor of Bara, the deer. Tarzan's mouth watered and a low growl escaped his patrician lips. Sloughed from him was the last vestige of artificial caste—once again he was the primeval hunter—the first man—the highest caste type of the human race.[14]

Here, certainly, a certain tension reveals itself between Tarzan's 'artificial caste,' the aristocratic title awarded him by civilization, and the genuine, primordial distinction, which goes back to the very origins of civilization, to the primeval hunter. 'The first man' is the unmistakable antithesis of the modern, dwarfed man, Nietzsche's nihilistic last-man, which modernity prizes as the 'meaning of history'.[15] Nobility, Burroughs assures us, must purge itself of the decadence of luxuries and mere conventions and recover its firm roots in nature, brute force, indeed in the literal sense, and true heroism.

The affinity between Tarzan and Nietzsche's perspective ought not be dismissed as an instance of colorful simplification of the philosopher's ideas by a popular author. In the work of a major Nietzschean of 'high culture,' Ortega y Gasset, we find, at times, striking parallels with Burroughs' vision. In *The Revolt of the Masses*, for example, Ortega addresses the historical problem of aristocratic crisis amidst defiant mass society but de-historicizes this into 'the tragedy of every hereditary aristocracy,' which consists of an alleged disparity between the original, active nobility of the primordial ancestor and the passive one or the heir:

The aristocrat inherits . . . conditions of life which he has not created . . . At birth he finds himself installed, suddenly and without knowing how, in the midst of his riches and his prerogatives. . . . They are the giant armour of some other person, some other human being, his ancestor. . . . What life is the 'aristocrat' by inheritance going to lead, his own or that of his first noble ancestor? Neither one nor the other.[16]

True nobility is therefore the one of the mythical 'first noble ancestor,' the aristocratic self-made man, who has earned his privilege overcoming adversity: 'All life is the struggle, the effort to be itself. The difficulties which I meet with in order to realise my existence are precisely what awakens and mobilises my activities, my capacities. . . . So in the "aristocratic" heir his whole individuality grows vague, for lack of use and vital effort'.[17] Precisely such disparity was dramatized by Burroughs—some fifteen years before Ortega, certainly—in the mismatch between Tarzan, the real Lord Greystoke who warrants his nobility amidst the perils of the jungle, and his cousin William Cecil Clayton, the hereditary nobleman. The advantage of fiction over philosophy, however, is that the former can actually arrange for the two representatives of aristocracy, the vital and the inert one, to meet, so as to demonstrate all the more palpably the gulf stretching between them. Having reached Africa with a scientific expedition, Clayton, the representative of 'artificial caste,' of enfeebled, civilized aristocracy, is accompanied by a handful of upper-class individuals whom he must protect from the threat of both natural, jungle forces, and the mob of insurrectionary cockney sailors, who reflect the growing audacity of the 'revolting masses.' Tarzan, surveying the camps of impending class war from a hiding place, decides to join the fight on the side of the endangered aristocracy:

> He did not understand anything of the motives behind all that he had seen; but, somehow, intuitively he liked the young man [Clayton] and the two old men. . . . For the sailors, and especially Snipes, he had developed a great hatred. He knew by their threatening gestures and by the expression upon their evil faces that they were enemies of the others of the party, and so he decided to watch closely.[18]

Though brave enough in the face of both natural and social danger, Clayton is powerless actually to defend himself and needs the saving intervention of Tarzan, his primeval ancestor. As in the following scene, where a leopard assaults him:

> He was no coward; but if ever man felt the icy fingers of fear upon his heart, William Cecil Clayton, eldest son of Lord Greystoke of England, did that day in the fastness of the African jungle.
> The noise of some great body crashing through the underbrush so close beside him, and the sound of that bloodcurdling shriek from above, tested Clayton's courage to the limit; but he could not know that it was to that very voice he owed his life, nor that the creature who hurled it forth was his own cousin— the real Lord Greystoke.[19]

In his 1940 long introduction to count Eduardo Yebes' book *Veinte años de caza mayor,* an essay translated into English under the title 'Meditations on Hunting,' Ortega y Gasset defended the practice of hunting as a quasi-religious, mystical ritual, whose thrills enhance human authenticity. His descriptions, at times, might have been copied down from a Tarzan book: 'When one is hunting, the air has another, more exquisite feel as it glides over the skin or enters the lungs, the rocks acquire a more expressive physiognomy, and the vegetation becomes loaded with meaning.'[20] The social Darwinist ideology embedding such praise for the elations of hunting is also unmistakable:

> A fascinating mystery of nature is manifested in the universal fact of hunting: the inexorable hierarchy among living beings. Every animal is in a relationship of superiority or inferiority with regard to every other. Strict equality is exceedingly improbable and anomalous.

Life is a terrible conflict, a grandiose and atrocious confluence. Hunting sub-
merges man deliberately in that formidable mystery and therefore contains
something of religious rite and emotion in which homage is paid to what is divine, transcendent, in the laws of nature.[21]

Neither Ortega nor Burroughs were truly aristocrats (nor was Nietzsche, of
course). They came from middle-class backgrounds and appealed to the myth
of nobility as a form of countering, precisely qua bourgeois, the advancement
of mass democracy. The very emphasis on the first nobleman as the *self-made
man* attests to the bourgeois remolding of aristocratic ideology. As we shall
shortly see, in this ideological refutation of egalitarianism Ortega was the more
thorough and consistent Nietzschean than Burroughs. Yet it is nonetheless significant that, even in the absence of a properly aristocratic class in his own 'plebeian' society, the American Burroughs was thinking in very similar terms on
the significance of blood-lineage, noble ancestry and caste hierarchy as the European Ortega. Given that the predicament of mass society was the same, in its
essential features, across national boundaries, and emerging throughout the
West as part of the dynamics of capitalism and its inherent class struggles, the
aristocratic ideology became useful everywhere, even in America, where a sense
of national identity had emerged very much in the course of a decisive struggle with the aristocracies of the Old World. Since the basic conflict was one between bourgeoisie and working class, the actual presence of a national aristocracy was a matter of secondary importance. In that respect, both Spanish
philosopher and American paperback writer furnish excellent examples for the
'bourgeois renaissance of aristocratic heroism.'

This does not mean that actual European aristocracies remained passive vis-
à-vis this social and ideological struggle; nor that Nietzsche, Ortega or Burroughs simply contrived a myth of nobility foreign to the experience and self-
conception of the aristocracies themselves. On the contrary, for all their
unbounded fantasy and escapism, the Tarzan stories, for example, provide a
surprisingly good porthole through which to inspect the mind-set of actual
contemporary aristocracies. The Jungle-Lord's delight in primitive nature, as
well as the thrills of hunting, corresponded to true aristocratic habitus. As
Stephan Malinowski shows in an excellent historical study of the German nobility in the first half of the twentieth century and its relationship to Nazism,
the aristocrats prided themselves on a rapport with nature—virile, continual,
commanding, bellicose, organic and profound—which was antithetical to
bourgeois fascination with nature—passive, ephemeral, submissive, contem-
plative, shallow. Hunting, in particular, an aristocratic practice from times immemorial, was now acquiring a special significance as a form of protest and
ritual of distinction against the alleged blandness of mass, city life:

The Prussian officer Rudolf von Gersdorff, who described 'writing-desk' life as
unbearable, indicated his love of nature as the foundation of his 'adventurous

soldier's life.' An aristocratic university professor described hunting as a singular 'intoxication,' which made his blood 'simmer.'[22]

The contrast conventionally drawn by both aristocrats and middle-class ideologues who were keen to cultivate the myth of nobility, was between (1) the countryside, a place of stability and tranquility combined—however paradoxically—with adventure and excitement, and (2) the urban loci of hectic change and permanent uproar, combined—again, no matter how contradictorily—with deadening, monotonous routine. There developed a ritualistic denigration of Berlin, the corrupt, nomadic, international, multi-racial city, even by members of the nobility who spent most of their time there. Many complained of Berlin's 'asphalt people,' 'asphalt culture,' and 'asphalt world.'[23] None other than Wilhelm II recalls in his memoirs 'having always felt like a "captive" in Berlin, "the great city with its sea of stone, away from nature."'[24] Yet such disparagement of the big cities coupled with an idealization of the countryside was no German idiosyncrasy, finding many voices throughout the West. We shouldn't, therefore, be surprised to find our nobleman of popular fantasy, Tarzan, 'echoing' the Kaiser's alienation in the metropolis, which happens on this occasion to be Paris. Tarzan loves to frequent a certain disreputable street of dire living conditions, yet he is not motivated by sympathy with its inhabitants—indeed, they would viciously attack him—but rather by the fact that its exceptional quietness reminds him of the jungle:

> Tarzan had been wont to traverse the Rue Maule on his way home at night. Because it was very quiet and very dark it reminded him more of his beloved African jungle than did the noisy and garish streets surrounding it. If you are familiar with your Paris you will recall the narrow, forbidding precincts of the Rue Maule. If you are not, you need but ask the police about it to learn that in all Paris there is no street to which you should give a wider berth after dark.[25]

Tarzan's partiality for this inhospitable street, no doubt, is also a reflection of the fact that, being a primeval nobleman in possession of all his powers and not an enfeebled modern, he doesn't fear, in fact he relishes, the challenge of the lower classes:

> 'Well,' said D'Arnot, 'among other things, it has taught you what I have been unable to impress upon you—that the Rue Maule is a good place to avoid after dark.'
>
> 'On the contrary,' replied Tarzan, with a smile, 'it has convinced me that it is the one worth-while street in all Paris. Never again shall I miss an opportunity to traverse it, for it has given me the first real entertainment I have had since I left Africa.'[26]

Animal-Critique: A Double-Edged Weapon

So far, it was shown how Burroughs' popular myth corresponded to the Nietzschean blueprint of a return to nature and the survival-of-the-fittest tenet. Yet when Nietzsche, like all social Darwinists, spoke about the need to naturalize humanity this was meant metaphorically, having in mind not man's actual return to primitive conditions but the naturalization of society. To be sure, this also accommodated an imperialistic discourse, 'nature' coming to mean that which lays outside 'home' and the Western, civilized world. Hence Nietzsche's affirmation that, noble, civilized men and races

> . . . are not much better than uncaged beasts of prey in the world outside where the strange, the foreign, begin. . . . [I]n the wilderness they compensate for the tension which is caused by being closed in and fenced by the peace of the community for so long, they *return* to the innocent conscience of the wild beast, as exultant monsters, who perhaps go away having committed a hideous succession of murder, arson, rape and torture, in a mood of bravado and spiritual equilibrium as though they had simply played a student's prank . . . At the centre of all these noble races we cannot fail to see the blond beast of prey, the magnificent *blond beast* avidly prowling round for spoil and victory; this hidden centre needs release form time to time, the beast must out again, must return to the wild.[27]

But Nietzsche never did contemplate an actual 'homecoming' to nature. 'The wilderness' in the above passage obviously cannot mean the actual jungle or desert, for there the opportunities for unleashing one's beastly nobility in, for instance, acts of rape or torture, would be even more scarce than at home. It rather must mean the colonies, where 'the strange and foreign begin.' The 'jungle model' was only useful for social Darwinists inasmuch as it permitted them to impose upon society a mould they purportedly derived from observation of nature and the fathoming of its evolutionary rules. Burroughs, however, took this naturalizing discourse literally, and 'truly' transferred an English Lord to the jungle. But by taking social Darwinism at its word and bringing humanity—via Tarzan—'back' to the wild, something unexpected took place: the Rousseauvian discourse began to infiltrate and subvert Tarzan's Nietzschean core. From a social Darwinist perspective, the purpose of sending a modern representative to the jungle was to extol the cruelty, the immorality of nature: for Nietzsche, the whole point in the struggle to 'reach nature' was in 'daring to be immoral like nature.'[28] Or, in a slightly different formulation which drives home the very same point against social 'degeneracy':

> Nature is not immoral when it has no pity for the degenerate: on the contrary, the growth of physiological and moral ills among mankind is the consequence of a pathological and unnatural morality. The sensibility of the majority of

men is pathological and unnatural . . . The body perishes when an organ is altered. The right of altruism cannot be derived from physiology; nor can the
right to help and to an equality of lots: these are prizes for the degenerate and
underprivileged.

There is no solidarity in a society in which there are sterile, unproductive,
and destructive elements—which, incidentally, will have descendants even
more degenerate than they are themselves.[29]

Yet such logic imploded once the jungle uncannily revealed itself a far
more habitable place than 'moral,' 'benevolent' and 'decadent' civilization.
For all his Nietzscheanism, Tarzan did something that Nietzsche, Malthus,
Spencer, Gobineau, de Lapouge and co. would never have dreamt of doing:
condemn society on account of its cruelty. Social Darwinists were always
striving to show how benevolent, sentimental social policies cannot but en-
gender calamitous consequences since they upset the natural, ruthless,
scheme of things. With Tarzan, taken as a social Darwinist metaphor, something unexpected occurs. In retreating to the jungle and taking a look at
modern civilization from a distance he discovers that it is, in fact, the worst
jungle out there. As Tarzan explains to a white man who, after years of cap-
tivity in the jungle, wishes to return to civilization:

'You do not know what you are talking about,' replied the ape-man. 'You have
been gone very long. You will find no friends left back there from whence you
came. You will find deceit, and hypocrisy, and greed, and avarice, and cruelty.
You will find that no one will be interested in you and that you will be interested in no one there. I, Tarzan of the Apes, have left my jungle and gone to the
cities built by men, but always I have been disgusted and been glad to return
to my jungle—to the noble beasts that are honest in their loves and in their
hates—to the freedom and genuineness of nature . . .'[30]

The first novel in the series, *Tarzan of the Apes*, was published in 1912, four
years after Upton Sinclair published *The Jungle*, a classic condemnation of
American capitalism and the working conditions in Chicago factories. For
Nietzsche, man is a sick animal since civilization subdues and castrates him.
We have seen how the 'return' to animal state entails the unleashing of the
most barbarous drives of cruelty and murder, saluted by Nietzsche, for all
their horror, as unmistakable marks of noble races. But for Tarzan, the
source of sickness lies elsewhere. Cruelty—whether noble or vile—cannot
be ascribed back to the animals. For 'being a man, he sometimes killed for
pleasure, a thing which no other animal does; for it has remained for man
alone among all creatures to kill senselessly and wantonly for the mere pleasure of inflicting suffering and death.'[31] Sadism is not an animal quality
which civilized man has forfeited, but a distinctly human attribute, absent
among the animals. It is in this context that the specifically human vice of

greed and the *unnatural* institution of property is repeatedly denounced by Tarzan as a curse afflicting modern civilization:

> Tarzan . . . hated the shams and the hypocrisies of [civilization] and with the clear vision of an unspoiled mind he had penetrated to the rotten core of the heart of the thing—the cowardly greed for peace and ease and the safe-guarding of property rights.[32]

The sine qua non of capitalism—property rights, that which the bourgeois civilization in its entirety is instituted upon, is refuted by Tarzan. Civilization is denounced not only on Nietzschean terms, but on those of the noble savage as well. In fact, both ideologemes are uttered simultaneously, the Nietzschean in Tarzan attacking 'cowardly greed for peace and ease,' the noble savage in him then censuring 'the safe-guarding of property rights.' Unlike Nietzsche, who would have 'the order of castes' written into nature, Tarzan—in this regard a follower of Rousseau—denounces the very foundation of the capitalist class system as an aberration, violating the law of the jungle.

Nietzsche's concept of nature, it should be quite clear, was not only different but antithetical to that of Rousseau.[33] Rousseau referred to nature as a revolutionary metaphor, inasmuch as the 'corruption' of society was contrasted with the innocence of nature, where property does not exist. A 'return to nature,' under such terms, would basically mean the abolition of property. In his multiple dealings with Rousseau, Nietzsche repeatedly charged against this metaphor and its radical social implications. As he once put it, 'good Europeans' understand 'return to nature' 'more and more decisively in the opposite sense from Rousseau's . . . [M]ore and more decisively anti-idealistic, more concrete, more fearless, industrious, moderate, suspicious against sudden changes, *antirevolutionary.*'[34] Rousseau was the archetype of the apostle of revolt: 'The French Revolution as the continuation of Christianity. Rousseau as the seducer: he again unfetters woman . . . Then the slaves and Mrs. Beecher-Stowe. Then the poor and the workers. Then the vice-addicts and the sick.'[35] Quite explicitly and programmatically, Nietzsche reversed both Rousseau's evaluation of nature and of civilization *and* its charge of affect:

> *Against Rousseau.*— *Unfortunately,* man is no longer evil enough; Rousseau's opponents who say 'man is a beast of prey' are unfortunately wrong. Not the corruption of man but the extent to which he has become tender and moralized is his curse . . . Rousseau . . . moralizes and, as a man of rancor, seeks the cause of his wretchedness in the ruling classes.[36]

Thus, if civilization is indeed 'corrupted' it is in the opposite sense of what Rousseau had meant; for Nietzsche, the problem is precisely that the beast of prey in man has been tamed, that the ruling classes are fettered by slave morality. Occasionally, however, Nietzsche admits that ruling class degeneration is not quite so pervasive, that society has not become all that tame, compassionate and egalitarian. He states: 'More natural is our first society, that of the rich, the leisure class,'[37] and optimistically adds, in the same passage:

> *In summa*: there are signs that the European of the nineteenth century is less ashamed of his instincts; he has taken a goodly step toward admitting to himself his unconditional naturalness, i.e., his immorality, *without becoming embittered*. . . . This sounds to some ears as if corruption had progressed—and it is certain that man has not come close to that *'nature'* of which *Rousseau* speaks but has progressed another step in civilization, which Rousseau *abhorred*.[38]

The abrupt oscillations between a critique of civilized decadence and a defense of civilization are, objectively seen, the result of the very phenomenon Nietzsche faces and its contradictions: modern, capitalist, mass society. The verdict hinges on the perspective Nietzsche happens to adopt: to the extent that he sees the empty part of the glass, mass power with its egalitarian ideologies, modern civilization is condemned as weakly, unnatural and decadent; inasmuch, however, as the full part of the glass is perceived—the inequalities inherent to capitalism, the exploitation and disciplining of the masses—Nietzsche is happy to announce 'naturalness' and 'progress.' At times, Nietzsche is driven to conceptualize these contradictions, for example by splitting the notions of 'culture' and 'civilization,' ascribing the former with excellence and the latter with mediocrity: 'The high points of culture and civilization do not coincide. . . . The great moments of culture were always, morally speaking, times of corruption; and conversely, the periods when the taming of the human animal ("civilization") was desired and enforced were times of intolerance against the boldest and most spiritual natures.'[39]

The Rousseauvian side of Tarzan explains why he could have been quite rapidly metamorphosed, in his extremely popular cinematic adaptations, into a rather leftist critic of civilization, a good giant, living in a world without money and exploitation. Tarzan of the films becomes less the ferocious predator that Burroughs initially conceived of and more of a defender of the weak, possessing an immaculate sense of moral integrity.[40] Being himself an animal, Tarzan is perfectly placed to represent the voiceless victims of civilization and, by extension, also the weak members of society. The subversive potential of the animal as critic lies dormant in the novels as well, and is sometimes materialized, for example when Tarzan, who in the jungle was worthy of the love of Jane Porter, the aristocratic damsel he saves from distress, becomes in civilization, in the far more ominous jungle of money and titles, an inferior alien:

Would either be happy in such a horrible misalliance?

'You do not love me, then?' he asked, in a level tone.

'Do not ask me. You will be happier without me. . . . [C]ivilization would become irksome to you, and in a little while you would long for the freedom of your old life—a life to which I am as totally unfitted as you to mine.'

'I think I understand you,' he replied quietly. 'I shall not urge you, for I would rather see you happy than to be happy myself. I see now that you could not be happy with—an ape.'

There was just the faintest tinge of bitterness in his voice.[41]

Splendidly above *ressentiment* while facing the beasts, human beings do manage to stir bitterness in Tarzan's magnanimous soul. True, at this stage the lovers are ignorant of the fact that Tarzan is in reality an aristocrat inheriting a huge fortune, both facts obviously removing the problem of a 'horrible misalliance.' Burroughs, at any rate, inspirationally avoids the banality of a happy ending: once realizing that he is in truth a wealthy Lord, Tarzan does not rush to claim his lawful share of finance and romance, and renounces both. He refuses to be loved on account of his blood and his money. And so the novel ends with an at least implicit defying of aristocratic values, as Tarzan answers the query of Clayton, who mistakenly assumes the identity of Lord Greystoke:

Here was the man who had Tarzan's title, and Tarzan's estates, and was going to marry the woman whom Tarzan loved—the woman who loved Tarzan. A single word from Tarzan would make a great difference in this man's life.

. . . 'I say, old man,' cried Clayton, 'I haven't had a chance to thank you for all you've done for us. . . . If it's any of my business, how the devil did you ever get into that bally jungle?'

'I was born there,' said Tarzan, quietly. 'My mother was an Ape, and of course she couldn't tell me much about it. I never knew who my father was.'[42]

In opposition to social judgment, based on a place in the social hierarchy, Tarzan, precisely from an ape's vantage point, represents an egalitarian ideal of humanity. In him are ambivalently united the Nietzschean hero, a patrician of 'superhuman strength,'[43] with the subhuman, the gorilla's son. And whilst the former perspective underpins hierarchy, the latter provides a steady democratic undercurrent. As is evident in the following exchange:

'Nor is the matter of birth of great importance to me,' he went on. . . . 'Raised as I have been, I see no worth in man or beast that is not theirs by virtue of their own mental or physical prowess. And so I am as happy to think of Kala as my mother. . . . To you, my friend, she would have appeared a hideous and ugly creature, but to me she was beautiful—so gloriously does love transfigure its object. And so I am perfectly content to remain forever the son of Kala, the she-ape.'[44]

This is a love for the subhuman inconceivable from the vantage point of an entrenched, undiluted Nietzschean such as Ortega.

The Tarzan films starring Johnny Weissmuller, which played an immense part in spreading the character's popularity, are conventionally dismissed by critics as a reactionary means of inculcating the myths of imperialism among popular audiences.[45] Though by no means an unfounded slander— the 'natives' are usually (though not in all films) portrayed as vicious and cruel cannibals, in many senses worst than the beasts—such views are incomplete precisely since they perceive the blond beast in Tarzan but overlook the noble savage. Often enough the films' more substantial ideological point is less a justification of imperialism than a critique of Western civilization in the name of an unspoiled, primordial, Rousseauvian alternative.[46] Tarzan's little ideal paradise upon an almost unreachable plateau is ritually invaded by arrogant, greedy and brutal agents of imperialism, usually with the intent of plundering the land for ivory. Apart from this underlying—and admittedly ambivalent—resistance to the imperialist discourse, some of the films actually go as far as criticizing, albeit indirectly, capitalism as such, the rule of money and profit. In *Tarzan Escapes*, for instance, Jane tries to explain the abstract idea of money to the ape-man, by using the metaphor of a trap. 'Lacuna?' Tarzan asks. 'No, not a real trap, but just as strong, just as horrible,' she answers.[47] Tarzan's black-and-white jungle was thus projected to the contemporary audience, amidst the Depression, as a utopian refuge fending the encroaching corruption of the modern world, a symbolic escape from a dreadful entanglement whose meaning viewers knew all too well. Similarly, Tarzan becomes an ally of the working class, as exemplified by his relation to the cockney Rollins, a servant in the colonialist safari. Rollins is mocked and tyrannized by his master and laughed at overbearingly by the rest of his upper class, articulate companions. He appears to be but a vicious caricature of the commoner. But, as the plot progresses, the caricature gradually dissolves, until it can no longer sustain the affirmation of class hierarchy. Captain Fry, the conspicuous embodiment of imperialism, is revealed as a greedy, deceitful individual, whereas Rollins turns out to be honest and kindhearted. He befriends Tarzan, who is likewise patronized by the civilized company as a peculiar sort of savage, and Jane says to him:

Jane: I believe you think more of Tarzan than the others do.

Rollins: Miss Jane, he is the finest gentleman I ever knew, trousers or no trousers.

Jane: Thank you. Tarzan would be proud of that.

When Rollins realizes that his captain is trying to double-cross Tarzan, he bravely attempts to intervene, for which the agent of imperialism cynically shoots him in the back. The working class thus finds in Tarzan a friend, identifying with his savageness and inarticulateness, behind which are concealed his gentleness and nobility of soul. Whereas social Darwinists looked to Africa as the *heart of darkness*: that cruel, imponderable, ontological substratum of human existence, upon which the superficial attempts to civilize man are bound to shatter, in Tarzan's jungle it is predatory civilization which threatens to extinguish the light that still flickers in the wild. Animals, in short, prove themselves rather unpredictable critics.

2. THE NIETZSCHEAN HERO AS A NATURAL ARISTOCRAT

As observed in the chapter 2, one of the main tasks of Nietzschean heroism was to impart at least something of that flair and glamour formerly associated with the aristocracy upon the rather uninspiring bourgeoisie, to make the mundane vocations of moneymaking, trade and industry appear admirable, noble enterprises. In the post-aristocratic age of the masses, the bourgeoisie was driven to substantiate class privilege by developing a neo-aristocratic discourse that John Carey has termed 'natural aristocracy': 'In response to the revolt of the masses, intellectuals generated the idea of a natural aristocracy, consisting of intellectuals.'[48] Yet Carey somewhat misrepresented this discourse as a defense mechanism employed by the intellectual lobby, if so it can be called, vis-à-vis massification and the vulgarity of market society. In truth, however, the neo-aristocratic ethos was not primarily the product of some marginalized and desperate anti-market sector but rather represented a major apology *on behalf of the market*, frequently celebrating the personifications of capital, the self-made man and the free entrepreneur. The capitalist, and not only or primarily the intellectual, was thereby turned into a natural aristocrat, a man whose inherent distinction elevates above the herd. Often enough, in fact, such *capitalistic* nobility was celebrated in explicitly *anti*-intellectual terms, contrasting the capitalist's direct power of action with the impotent, resentful and devious eloquence of the (often socialist) intellectual (in perfect harmony with Nietzsche's hostility towards the dialectician, the frustrated individual spreading rancor). If, as Nietzsche contended, socialism is born because the masses get 'the idea that it is only accident and luck that have elevated one person above another,'[49] then such dangerous illusion must be dispelled by showing how hierarchy in fact correctly reflects *intrinsic distinction*.

James Bond: A Nietzschean for the Cold War

In Tarzan, the lord-ape, the solution to that specific problem was rather unique, and ideologically ambivalent, inasmuch as the social Darwinist hero was taken out of the capitalist framework and transferred into nature, where, as we have seen, he became a partial critic of capitalism, 'betraying' his original class mission and inverting the sociopolitical logic of the blond beast. Ayn Rand's solution, as recalled, was ideologically rather more to the point, by postulating the capitalist-artist. But we can identify other methods of getting around this problem. One of them was to depict the natural aristocrat as an individual possessing an acute artistic and sensory sensibility. If the pea under the twenty mattresses could identify the princess of the classic legend, a similar process can authenticate the natural aristocrat in the modern one. In such terms, we can understand the social logic in operation behind James Bond's exquisite culinary demands condensed in the famous 'shaken, not stirred' phrase. Or in the meticulous details of one of his breakfasts:

> The single egg, in the dark blue egg cup with a gold ring round the top, was boiled for three and a third minutes. . . . Then there were two thick slices of deep yellow Jersey butter and three squat glass jars containing Tiptree 'Little Scarlet' strawberry jam; Cooper's Vintage Oxford marmalade and Norwegian Heather Honey from Fortnum's. The coffee pot and the silver on the tray were Queen Anne, and the China was Minton, of the same dark blue and gold and white as the egg-cup.[50]

This is the natural aristocrat as *Feinschmecker*.[51] A breakfast such as this may well be a good example of what Anthony Burgess had in mind when he referred to Bond's 'quiet joy in life.' But it is no less an example of Bond's highly refined taste of liberty/luxury.[52] As Bourdieu taught us, the more distinctions we make the more distinguished we are. The slightest nuance matters to Bond since he is a natural aristocrat. His hedonism is no less consistent with Zarathustra's claim that 'The best belongs to me and mine; and if we are not given it, we take it: the best food, the purest sky, the most robust thoughts, the fairest women!'[53] Bond's hedonism, moreover, is thoroughly *disciplined*, thus not conflicting with Nietzsche's contention that the '"predominance of suffering over pleasure" or the opposite (hedonism): these two doctrines are already signposts to nihilism.'[54] Bond's heroic way of life consists precisely of a fine balance between pain and pleasure, and the fact that he embraces both as an inevitable duality. Bond does not indulge in gastronomic or sensual pleasures for their own sake and certainly does not shirk suffering. Rather, he seeks to combine pleasure and pain in order to enhance life, intensify the quality of his experiences. Pleasure for its own sake would be simple, undignified debauchery, a symptom of decay, which provokes Bond's repulsion. He is not the usual moneyed and dissipated hedonist, but a *puritanical one*, a hedonist with a purpose. Bond, in that respect, incarnates what Nietzsche extolled as a 'fusion of a Stoic and a frivolous appearance of happiness, characteristic of noble cultures.'[55] Nor is Bond a libertine, for 'the libertinage . . . should not be confused with the will to power (—which is the counterprinciple).'[56] The British writer Anthony Burgess, reflecting admiringly on Fleming's hero observed that in Bond, the 'gusto is controlled: the banquet of the senses is a reward for dangerous work performed on behalf of a free world.'[57] The eclipse of noble culture, according to Nietzsche, manifests itself in the aimless, un-heroic, cowardly hedonism of the rich who are characterized precisely by shunning anything resembling 'dangerous work': 'Our time, with its aspiration to remedy and prevent accidental distresses and to wage preventive war against disagreeable possibilities, is a time of the *poor*. Our "rich"—are poorest of all. The true purpose of all riches is forgotten.'[58] Accordingly, after sharing a luxurious, 'purposeless' meal with a millionaire Bond cannot but feel disgust:

> Bond thought, I asked for the easy life, the rich life. How do I like it? How do I like eating like a pig . . . ? Suddenly the idea of ever having another meal like this, or indeed any other meal with Mr Du Pont, revolted him. . . . It was the puritan in him that couldn't take it.[59]

Fleming's hero illustrates an important Nietzschean strategy for reconciling the bourgeois principle of competition with the aristocratic ethos of heroism. This ideological element is considerably more 'positive' in emphasis than the simple stress on distinction, since the natural aristocrat is not merely shown as negatively asserting his superiority to the market herd, but, on the contrary, the market principle is hailed as the very sound basis underpinning the new hierarchy. This was undertaken already by the early Nietzsche, notably in the fragment *Homer on Competition*, where Nietzsche proclaimed that the distinguishing feature of ancient Greek greatness was the conscious construction of society and state around 'the finest Hellenic principle, competition.'[60] The Greeks, Nietzsche insisted, cherished competition as a life-enhancing force in stark and refreshing contrast to our own 'emasculated concept of modern humanity.'[61] Nietzsche characteristically found fault with the modern world, on the verge of sliding into global imperialist conflicts, in its allegedly decadent *negation of competition*. The Greeks knew better, for they acknowledged that cruel and horrible side of human nature as 'the fertile soil from which alone all humanity, in feelings, deeds and works, can grow forth.'[62] Modern, meek humanity, was encouraged to embrace competition in all spheres of life, spiritual as well as material. Not confined to spiritual excellence, competition is rather a general economic propeller, 'the permanent basis of life in the Hellenic state.' Nietzsche enthusiastically quotes Hesiod to that effect: 'She [Eris, the goddess of Strife] drives even the unskilled man to work; and if someone who lacks property sees someone else who is rich, he likewise hurries off to sow and plant and set his house in order; neighbor competes with neighbor for prosperity. This Eris is good for men.'[63]

Getting very close indeed to Adam Smith, Nietzsche even warned against the fatal consequences of halting competition through over-accumulation of power. No single man or state should come to possess too strong an advantage over the competitors so as to clog the fruitful dynamics of combat. Nietzsche referred to this as the danger of *Alleinherrschaft*, which Carol Diethe has tellingly translated as *monopoly*: 'That is the kernel of the Hellenic idea of competition: it loathes a monopoly of predominance and fears the dangers of this, it desires, as *protective measure* against genius—a second genius.'[64] Yet this celebration of competition should not be taken at face value. In truth, far from being universal, competition was by definition restricted to the handful members of the elite, 'the geniuses,' whereas the rest, the vile herd, can be said to 'participate' in the competitive struggle only as lubricant applied to the wheels of industry. This truth, though muffled in *Homer on Competition*, was frankly admitted, in fact trumpeted, in another fragment of the same period, *The Greek State* (both texts belong to a series of five fragments written in the course of 1872 titled 'five forewords to five unwritten books'), where Nietzsche, as will be recalled, declared that: 'In order for there to be a broad, deep, fertile soil for the development of art, the overwhelming majority has to be slavishly subjected to life's necessity in the service of the minority, *beyond* the measure that is necessary for the individual.'[65] This, then, is the rather *non-competitive* basis, comprising the 'overwhelming majority,' upon which the 'universal principle' of competition is predicated.

Competition can serve to identify the abler and nobler individuals for, as we are told, 'the greater and more eminent a Greek man is, the brighter the flame of ambition to erupt from him, consuming everyone who runs with him on the same track.'[66] That Nietzsche employed a metaphor from the world of sports is by no means accidental. Rather, he regarded the Greek concern with athletic triumph as epitomizing the healthy agonistic drive of their culture. In fact, the ancient combination between individual athletic achievement and the glory of the state was highly praised as an example of harnessing the ambition of the individual for the sake of a meta-individual, collective, i.e. national, cause:

> . . . for the ancients, the aim of agonistic education was the well-being of the whole, of state society. For example, every Athenian was to develop himself, through competition, to the degree to which this self was of most use to Athens and would cause least damage. . . . [T]he youth thought of the good of his native city when he ran a race or sang; . . . it was to the city's gods that he dedicated the wreaths which the umpires placed on his head in honour.[67]

This passage would alone suffice to demonstrate how, for all its alleged opposition to modern times and notwithstanding the reiterated effort to posit the ancient world as a radical counterexample to modernity, Nietzsche's critique objectively formed an ideological accommodation of already existing trends. For precisely the combination between sport and national pride, which Nietzsche acclaimed as specifically ancient and non-modern phenomenon, became soon enough—we may assume wholly independently of Nietzsche's reflections—one of the trademarks of modern, nationalistic society and culture. Only twenty-four years after *Homer on Competition* was written, modernity objectively manifested its affinity with Nietzscheanism by launching the first Olympic Games in Athens (1896).[68] These were, of course, followed by the twentieth-century institution of competitive sports at the individual, city and national levels as a mass phenomenon of great importance.

Instructively, Nietzsche implicitly concedes that 'emasculate' modernity is not all that lacking in the blessings of the agonistic spirit. Far from it, we suddenly learn that individualism and competition are so pervasive in our society so as actually to *surpass* the Hellenic standard. From an ascetic antithesis of antiquity, modern society is transformed into a place ruptured by agonistic mania:

> [Greek ambition] was not a boundless and indeterminate ambition like most modern ambition . . . individuals in antiquity were freer, because their aims were nearer and easier to achieve. Modern man, on the other hand, is crossed everywhere by infinity, like swift-footed Achilles in the parable of Zeno of Elea: infinity impedes him, he cannot overtake the tortoise.[69]

The formal structure of the argument remains the same—positive antiquity posited as a remedy to negative modernity—yet the content is completely reversed. Now the ancient world is recommended on account of channeling and restraining competition, whereas modern man is diagnosed as fatally tormented by the 'infiniteness' of his competitive ambition. Nietzsche, now, has to intervene and slow down the frenetic pace of modern competition, by introducing some Hellenic sense of purpose and moderation.

James Bond could be seen as a modern embodiment of the agonistic spirit, of Nietzsche's assertion that 'the cruelty of victory is the pinnacle of life's jubilation.'[70] He is, to start with, an athlete of sorts, not so much as regards physical prowess, but in his fascination with games. Golf, a test of shooting skills or, most frequently, diverse card and gambling games: they all furnish him with an opportunity to indulge his competitive appetite. Meticulously described, and greatly entertaining to read, the sheer pleasure-value of Bond's myriad 'games' should not allow us to overlook their deadly seriousness. Winning, for Bond, is a necessity; his whole personality is constructed around his sense of invincibility. To lose spells complete and irrecoverable ruin. Since Bond must represent the winner in the competitive formula, the one thing he can never do, by definition, is lose. Yet, at times, Fleming allows us a glimpse into Bond's mind on the very verge of defeat, so as to confirm the utter bitterness of such pill. At such moments, the ideological tightness of the narrative is somewhat loosened as the loser-perspective takes centre stage, however temporarily. Thus, in *Casino Royale*, Bond loses—that is, momentarily *thinks* he has lost,—a game of baccarat:

> Bond sat silent and frozen with defeat. . . . What now? . . . Back to the telephone call to London, and then tomorrow the plane home, the taxi up to Regent's Park, the walk up the stairs and along the corridor, and M's cold face across the table, his forced sympathy, his 'better luck next time' and, of course, there couldn't be one, not another chance like this.[71]

Similarly, in *Moonraker*, we are afforded the following, surprising deconstruction of the sacrosanct principle of victory: 'Bond, in a mood of anticlimax, had gone off to bed. . . . Before he slept he reflected, as he had often reflected in other moments of triumph at the card table, that the gain to the winner is, in some odd way, always less than the loss to the loser.'[72] Or, in a slightly altered formulation: 'the pain of failure . . . is so much greater than the pleasure of success.'[73] This is a profoundly anti-Nietzschean conclusion inasmuch as it subverts Nietzsche's standard argument in favor of competition and exploitation. The whole point of the Nietzschean justification of the suffering of the slaves is a particular economy of suffering and elation: however terrible the sacrifice demanded of the slaves, it permits the elite to ascend to the magnificent peaks of culture:

> If culture were really left to the discretion of the people . . . the iconoclastic destruction of the claims of art would be *more* than the revolt of the oppressed masses against drone-like individuals: it would be the cry of pity tearing down the walls of culture; the urge for justice, for equal sharing of the pain, would swamp all other ideas.[74]

Such argumentation, however, heavily suffers once it is assumed, instead, that triumph is something of an 'anti-climax,' and that the satisfaction of the winner never equals the desolation of the loser. Under *such* an assumption, one may feel rather less inclined to guard the 'walls of culture' against 'the cry of pity.' Hence, precisely on account of its subversive potential, such an insight must remain but an ephemeral glimmer in Fleming's narrative.

Such depictions of the psychological effects of competition show how misguided is the conventional, sanguine reading of Nietzsche as a defender of individual integrity in face of mass inauthenticity. For the celebration of competition which Nietzsche promoted and James Bond practices actually ratifies society as the last arbiter as regards individual value. The individual can only assert his or her 'inherent value' in and through the social process of competition. As Bond painfully realizes upon losing, his essence is not some internal, authentic core, which he can protect from social scrutiny. On the contrary, what he *is*, a winner or a loser, is what he can gain through competition. What counts is only what one is willing to deposit beside the roulette wheel, literally to put into circulation, for only that can potentially accrue surplus value. It is by no means a coincidence that gambling scenes are so central in the Bond stories. Just like Tarzan appears as the literal application of Nietzsche's call for naturalizing humanity, so does Bond provide the literal enactment of Zarathustra's proclamation that 'The devotion of the greatest is to encounter risk and danger and play dice with death.'[75] It is precisely the relative unimportance of the skill-factor and the comparative significance of pure luck involved in gambling games that make them all the more suitable for conveying the Calvinist logic of the ideology of competition. Within this ideological framework, luck is never, in fact, *pure* luck. 'Fortune as luck' and 'fortune as money' are bound together in an unfathomable, yet divinely ordained way. As Calvin put it: 'For all are not created in equal condition; rather, eternal life is fore-ordained for some, eternal damnation for others.'[76] This means that the dice are *metaphysically loaded*; whether one is predestined for salvation or for damnation can only be found out by entering competition to see which way the dice fall. The will of God manifests itself through the apparent contingencies and fluctuations of market transactions. It is hence that the casino becomes of all places the perfect arena for enacting the drama of competition; and it is hence that Bond is absolutely devastated after losing a 'mere' game of cards. His desolation reflects the shocking realization that he is after all not one of the elect, but bound for damnation; or, in Nietzschean: not an *Übermensch* but merely all-too-human.

That is why those moments in which the possibility of defeat is contemplated, let alone materialized, can only be striking exceptions in Bond's gaming experiences. As a rule, these scenes rather convey the exhilaration of competition and the gratification of victory, illustrating the thrilling adventure offered by the 'risk society':

> Bond was pleased. It was good to know that the fight was well and truly joined . . . he looked at himself in the mirror with inquiry. . . . the grey-blue eyes looked back at him from the tanned face with the brilliant glint of suppressed excitement and accurate focus of the old days. He smiled ironically back at the introspective scrutiny that so many people make of themselves before a race, a contest of wits, a trial of some sort. He had no excuses. He was ready to go.[77]

For all the fatality of defeat, Bond never shrinks from conflict or suspends it until no peaceful alternative remains open. On the contrary, being 'a man of war . . . peace was killing him.'[78] War, by contrast, possesses great therapeutic value; in *You Only Live Twice*, for example, Bond suffers from depression, having lost his interest in his job and his life. A renowned psychologist working with the British intelligence recommends, in *the absence of war*, extreme danger, as the only way of recovery for Bond:

> He knew how a desperate situation would bring out those nerves again, how the will to live would spring up again in a real emergency. He remembered how countless neurotic patients had disappeared for ever from his consulting-rooms when the last war had broken out. . . . Give [Bond] something that really matters to his country. It would be easy enough if a war broke out. Nothing like death or glory to take a man out of himself.[79]

This brings to mind Zarathustra's famous declaration: 'You say it is the good cause that hallows even war? I tell you: it is the good war that hallows every cause'[80]; or, among many other possible examples: 'One has renounced *grand* life when one renounces war.'[81] True, in his relatively moderate 'middle period,' especially in *Human, All Too Human* and *The Gay Science*, Nietzsche, as a rule, disapproved of the pleasure of war, defining it, in *The Gay Science*, as 'a detour to suicide, but a detour with a good conscience.'[82] In his later writings, however, from *Thus Spoke Zarathustra* onwards, his judgments on war were almost invariably positive and he had shown himself particularly appreciative of war's therapeutic value: 'War has always been the grand sagacity of every spirit which has grown too inward and too profound; its curative power lies even in the wounds one receives.'[83]

James Bond must necessarily war, not primarily because there is a good moral reason to do so, but because of his inherent need 'to live dangerously.' He therefore defiantly looks for trouble and plunges himself head-on into the heat of battle. Fighting for the cause of justice though he is, Bond is nonetheless almost invariably the aggressor, the one to draw first blood. Hence the ritual movie scene where Bond gallantly enters the casino to search and provoke the villain, who is at that stage usually unsuspecting and ignorant of his rival's identity and intentions. Bond often derives special pleasure from stirring up the enmity of his powerful adversaries. For instance, when taunting an agent of the crime organization SPECTRE, in a scene set yet again around the gambling table:

> Bond thought, I will see if an association of words does something to him. He said, 'When I came to the table I saw a spectre.' . . .
> The smile came off Largo's face as if he had been slapped. It was at once switched on again, but now the whole face was tense, strained, and the eyes

had gone watchful and very hard. His tongue came out and touched his lips. 'Really? What do you mean?'

. . . The table had gone quiet. The players and spectators felt that a tension had come between these two men. Suddenly there was the smell of enmity where before there had been only jokes. A glove had been thrown down by the Englishman.

Bond laughed good-naturedly. ' . . . Come on, your spectre against my spectre!'[84]

As Nietzsche stated, the 'mature man has, above all, weapons: he attacks.'[85]

While war is the equivalent of health, peace goes along with illness. Being sick, Bond is prone to flirt with the idea of pacifism, as happens in *Thunderball.* After showing some signs of deteriorating health Bond is sent by M, his boss, to a nature clinic, where he is expected to regain his fitness by assuming a strenuous diet and a perfectly serene routine. Already as he undergoes a preliminary medical examination, the stark contrast between Bond's intrinsic vitality and the spiritless dogma of the clinic comes forward, expressing itself as the classic conflict between sickly peace and robust war:

When [the doctor] saw the many scars he said politely, 'Dear me, you do seem to have been in the wars, Mr Bond.'

Bond said indifferently, 'Near miss. During the war.'

'Really! War between peoples is a terrible thing. Now, just breathe in deeply please.'[86]

The light diet begins to have a devastating, erosive effect. And what is at stake is more than a choice of menu. It is rather the alternative between ascending and declining life:

He took the horrible mug . . . sat down and sipped the thin soup while he watched some of his fellow inmates meandering aimlessly, weakly, through the room. Now he felt a grain of sympathy for the wretches. Now he was a member of their club. Now he had been initiated. . . .[87]

Even worse follows: now so overpowered by weakness, Bond starts to lose grip of even the *ideal*, the correct concept of healthiness, and drifts into the illusion that peace and quiet are really good for him:

It was all a world whose ghastly daintiness and propriety would normally have sickened him. Now, empty, weak, drained of all the things that belonged to his tough, fast, basically dirty life, through banting, he had somehow regained some of the innocence and purity of childhood. . . . It was really quite disturbing. Was his personality changing? Was he losing his edge, his point, his

identity? . . . Who was he in process of becoming? A soft, dreaming, kindly idealist who would naturally leave the Service and become instead a prison visi-
tor, interest himself in youth clubs, march with the H-bomb marchers, eat nut
cutlets, try and change the world for the better?[88]

Here, the fundamentally Nietzschean edge of Fleming's perspective surfaces forcefully. It is not that peace is unattainable since the Soviets are un-
compassionate brutes with whom only the bullet can negotiate, as the novels ritually assert. The truth is simpler than that: peace *is* attainable, but is
unwanted. Though offering some of the 'innocence and purity of childhood'
peace ultimately equals decadence. An existence free of 'any aches and
pains'[89] is perfectly possible, but on a meager diet which Bond cannot stomach. Peace is to Bond—and by extension to his employers, England and the
West—not the synonym of life but its antithesis. Thus, Bond rejects the ideal
of the anti-H-bomb marchers, not simply because it is unfeasible and naïve
but because, at bottom, he *craves* war. It is the one item on his menu that he
would not give up. As stated unswervingly in *From Russia with Love*: 'He was
a man of war and when, for a long period, there was no war, his spirit went
into a decline.'[90] In *Thunderball* Bond is only mildly unwell; he can therefore
muster up enough forces to contemplate the idea of leftist pacifism from the
safe distance of his basically healthy, conservative standpoint. But when severely ill, he sometimes collapses altogether, with calamitous consequences.
Fleming's last Bond novel, *The Man with the Golden Gun*, commences with
the narration of such a remarkable case. Bond returns to London after having been pronounced dead in his last assignment, and demands to tell his
story to M. The resurrected Bond, as it turns out, is not quite himself: he has
been captured by the Soviets, who have indoctrinated him, transforming
him into the would-be assassin of M, their great adversary. Bond had come
to believe in the Russian propaganda, and sees the West as a warmongering
power, merely resisted by the KGB. He then attempts to assassinate his boss
and, of course, fails. M, nonetheless, emphatically refuses to press charges:
'007 was a sick man. Not responsible for his actions. If one can brainwash a
man, presumably one can un-brainwash him.'[91] Once again, sickness is the
root of ideological lapse, and Bond will recover. All of this is in deep accordance with Nietzsche's diagnosis of socialism as the wretched, low-calorie
alternative to life, with which the slavish and weakly seek to pollute the consciousness of their masters.

This is the opening Nietzscheanism has exploited in order to pervade
popular culture. Whereas high culture, resenting the encroaching barbarians, has become ascetic and withdrawn, thus forfeiting any active power to
incorporate the masses, Nietzscheanism triumphantly appropriates pleasure. Far from denying life it professes to be a genuine *Lebensphilosophie*, unhindered by sickly mass morality which is discarded as a parasite on life: the

masses and the Soviets cynically manipulate the ploy of pacifism facing the aristocracy and the West respectively, so they may benumb their instincts and enslave them. Nietzscheanism tantalizes the masses with an intoxicating elixir, a sip of which is promised to those individuals who will join the cause of ascending life. To them will be reserved the delights of capitalism and power, while their opponents, if fortunate, could only aspire to the listless environment of a natural clinic, where the quest for power, the greatest enchantment of existence, is artificially amputated from life. Having taught that risk is what makes life worthwhile, Nietzscheanism prompts one to choose between the exciting insecurity of capitalism and the dull safety of socialism. In that way it becomes a powerful weapon against the masses and their corporeality, replacing the potential collective, anti-bourgeois hedonism, with a properly 'individualistic' one, fully compatible with the bourgeois order.

Anthony Burgess realized the political significance of the Bond stories as a vivacious protest against the puritanical welfare state emerging from the debris of the War. Fleming's oeuvre was said to have 'a kind of Renaissance gusto in it. It was a gusto which contradicted the socialist austerity of the fifties and yet did not endorse the permissiveness of the sixties.'[92] Indeed, an apposite enough summation of Bond's brand of popular Nietzscheanism, which attains a perfect balance between the hedonism of Dionysos and the restraint of Apollo: 'if Bond reports for duty with a hangover, there is always the retired admiral M to recall him to the ancient virtues of discipline and sobriety.'[93] Burgess commended the refreshing vitality of the novels, the way they honor the 'quiet joy in life': 'the joys are all the more intense for being fleeting: death may come at any moment for 007. If one of the tasks of the artist is to enhance life, then no one can deny Fleming the title of artist.'[94] And is not 'enhancing life' another way of saying: permitting life *to ascend*? The irony of *Lebensphilosophie* is here evident, precisely in what Burgess perceived as a harmless, 'quiet joy in life': it can only celebrate life under the shadow of death, war and destruction. Hence, we should not be shocked to hear Nietzsche, the philosopher-of-life *par excellence*, occasionally speaking warmly in praise of a return to something deeper and better than life—death:

> A fundamentally false *evaluation* of the *sensing* world against the *dead* one. Because *we* are this world! *Belong* to it! And nevertheless, along with sensation sets in *superficiality*, deceit: what do pain and pleasure have to do with the *real* procedure!—It is a side-thing [Nebenher] which does not reach the depths! But *we* call that *internal* and the dead world we regard as *external*— fundamentally false! The 'dead' world! Eternally moving and without error, force against force! And in the sensing world everything false and conceited! It is a *feast*, to pass over from this world to the 'dead world.' . . . The sense

[Sinn] of truth is to grasp sensation as an error of being, as an adventure. It lasts briefly enough for it! Let us see through this comedy and, as such, *enjoy* it! Let us *not* conceive of the return into non-sensation as a decline! We become fully *true*, we complete ourselves. Death has to be *newly interpreted*! We reconcile ourselves with the true, that is with the dead world.[95]

Yet why and for what purpose must death be 'newly interpreted'? Assuming, with Nietzsche, that death is indeed such a 'completion' and realization of the living, then such completion, surely, will come to us all regardless of whether we interpret death anew or not. Consequently, the true significance of Nietzsche's claim must have something to do with the way *we live* rather than the way *we die*. Quite as Burgess diagnosed in relation to Fleming, death existentially *intensifies* life. Life is an 'adventure,' a sour-sweet flirt, the dialectical consummation of which is death. This, moreover, in both Fleming and Nietzsche, is not a mere existential rumination. Rather, it is a recommendation to live reconciled to the idea of a death which might step in and complete us at any moment. This vantage point is given powerful expression in a scene from *Live and Let Die*, where Bond's plane runs 'into one of those violent tropical storms that suddenly turn aircraft from comfortable drawing-rooms into bucketing death-traps':

> Bond gripped the arms of his chair so that his left hand hurt and cursed slowly to himself. . . . There's nothing to do about it. You start to die the moment you are born. The whole of life is cutting through the pack with death. So take it easy. Light a cigarette and be grateful you are still alive as you suck the smoke deep into your lunges.[96]

Such acceptance of danger and lurking finality, once becoming a part of our life philosophy, turns into a means of 'reconciling' us not only with 'the true, dead world,' but also with the world *around us*, with the *world of sensation*, with a global system that taunts death continually, that perpetually generates strife and danger and war. The plane in which Bond is being shaken thus becomes, in the context of the Cold War, a fitting metaphor for a historical—as opposed to simply existential—situation in which the world, and human life with it, may come to a sudden end upon the press of a button. Consequently, and this Burgess overlooked, nothing could better spice up life in Bond's Nietzschean, competitive, capitalist universe, than the *death of others*. 'Great and fine things can never be common property: *pulchrum est paucorum hominum*.'[97] Like all pleasures worthy of their name, life itself, the ultimate delight, only makes sense when it is exclusive, a luxury. If everybody lives, if life is a mass commodity, then its value necessarily sinks. And thus, the Nietzschean life philosophy of James Bond becomes truly a case of *live and let die*.

Bond's 'Nietzscheanism,' as can be seen, manifests itself quite palpably and consistently in multiple ways throughout Fleming's stories, as regards the vitalist affirmation of war as essential to heroic life, the equation of pacifism with sickness, Bond's unquenchable competitive drive down to his exquisite gastronomic sensibilities; in the next chapter I will say something about Bond's sadistic amorous relationships and their affinity with Nietzsche's view of women's place. And yet, Bond's fundamental Nietzscheanism is nowhere openly manifested. Fleming does not flaunt a 'beyond good and evil' position, openly embracing the tenets of amorality: officially, Bond and England still stand for what is 'good' in the world, just as evil and amorality are still formally ascribed to the opposite side. 007's Nietzscheanism is ideologically encrypted, to the point where he is routinely presented as a true champion of herd morality, decency and self-abnegating patriotism against the beyond-good-and-evil rapacity of over-man-like arch-villains. Could it be that in Bond's case, as well as Tarzan's, popularization entails a remarkable subversion of the class-logic of the *Übermensch*? This is a possibility that we must now consider.

The Common Man Fighting the *Übermensch*?

The many bigger-than-life villains in the Bond stories are unmistakable caricatures of the *Übermensch*, obsessed with the conquest of absolute power and exhibiting utter disregard for the conventional inhibitions of herd-morality. This is the case of Mr Big, Goldfinger, Doctor No, Hugo Drax, and Ernest Stavro Blofeld, to name but the most formidable ones. Hugo Drax, 'a sort of superman,'[98] is further described in the following terms:

> Why should . . . this remarkable man cheat at cards? . . . Did he think that he was so much a law unto himself, so far above the common herd and their puny canons of behaviour that he could spit in the face of public opinion? . . . Spit in their faces. That just about described his manner at Blades. The combination of superiority and scorn. As if he was dealing with human muck so far beneath contempt that there was no need to put up even a pretence of decent behaviour in its company.[99]

Indeed, this seems to be a clear enough statement in refutation of Nietzschean, elitist hubris, accompanied by a defense of democratic 'public opinion' and the values and merit of the 'human muck,' of common humanity. Yet, on closer inspection, many ironies reveal themselves at the heart of such 'anti-Nietzscheanism.' For one thing, what is the nature of the 'human muck' Bond is willing to protect? These are, in truth, the very cream of the British upper classes, who enjoy exclusive membership at Blades, 'the most famous private card club in the world.'[100] Blades is not exactly the corner pub where 'the common herd,' as usually conceived, would gather to have its evening beer. Far from representing some democratic alternative to Nietzschean elitism, it is itself a temple of exclusivity, superiority and distinction. Being 'the standard of luxury of the Victorian age' Blades is hardly a place where true 'human muck' is admitted, with the significant exception of the servants, who form a vital part of the club's charm. Indeed, the finest among working girls are quite welcome there, as 'servants' of sorts:

> Club servants are the making or breaking of any club and the servants of Blade have no equal. The half-dozen waitresses in the dining-room are of such a high standard of beauty that some of the younger members have been known to smuggle them undetected into débutante balls, and if, at night, one or other of the girls is persuaded to stray into one of the twelve members' bedrooms at the back of the club, that is regarded as the members' private concern.[101]

In view of this, one can begin to appreciate how it is not Drax's scorn and contempt at his fellow human beings as such which unsettles Bond— himself the member of a patrician caste in a quite strict social hierarchy. The true outrage about Drax's 'superior manners' is rather the way he dares to mishandle the refined people of Blades as contemptuous 'human muck,' giving them a taste of the same treatment they accord everybody else. Which brings us directly to the second significant variation on the Nietzschean theme, concerning Drax's social origins. Drax is a self-made millionaire, a plebeian success story of a man rising from the ranks to the heights of British society. Whereas Bond sees in him a 'bullying, boorish, loud-mouthed vulgarian,'[102] the vile masses are delighted:

> And all the time he went on getting richer and the people simply loved it. It was the Arabian Nights. It lit up their lives. If a wounded soldier from Liverpool could get there in five years, why shouldn't they or their sons? It sounded almost as easy as winning a gigantic football pool.[103]

Hugo Drax is therefore a 'superman' of the people, a working-class hero, challenging the established order. In view of the pernicious example he sets, it is all the more vital to check his meteoric rise to glory, lest many more vulgar supermen present themselves at the gates of Blades. It is, hence, *in the service of hierarchy*, and *with Nietzsche*, not against him, that a maverick *Übermensch* like Drax must be exposed and ousted as a false, illegitimate, mad overman, a traitor to England, in fact a Nazi impostor plotting to eradicate London. If Drax is the Nietzschean as a plebeian Nazi, the Chinese Dr No— who reads as Fleming's version of Sax Rohmer's Fu Manchu, now with an appropriately *German* father—is likewise a perverse and destructive overman, rising to defy authority. He craves absolute power and rejects Bond's charges of lunacy with Nietzschean aloofness:

> 'Mania, my dear Mister Bond, is as priceless as genius. Dissipation of energy, fragmentation of vision, loss of momentum, the lack of follow-through—these are the vices of the herd. . . . I do not possess these vices. I am, as you correctly say, a maniac . . . with a mania for power. . . . That . . . is the meaning of my life.'[104]

As against such deranged will to power, Bond utters a refutation of key Nietzschean tenets. To start with, he argues against No's ambition to have overcome common humanity by reminding him that, whatever his achievements and eccentricities, he remains inexorably a mere human: 'you are still a man who sleeps and eats and defecates like the rest of us.'[105] Still more remarkably, Bond goes as far as embracing a philosophical negation of the concept of power altogether, advancing his argument, moreover, in the name of the community: 'Other people beside you have murdered in secret and got away with it. A greater power than they possess is exerted upon them by the community. . . . I tell you, your search for power is an illusion because power itself is an illusion.'[106] Yet No clings to his Nietzschean perspective: 'So is beauty, Mister Bond. So is art, so is money, so is death. And so, probably, is life. These concepts are relative. Your play upon words does not shake me. I know philosophy, I know ethics, and I know logic—better than you do, I daresay.'[107] The Doctor embodies the entire gamut of ugly traits which can be gathered under the title of 'evil Nietzscheanism': he is an immoral atheist, who can summarily dismiss the threat of a punishment in the next world: 'Mister Bond, I do not admit the existence of hell'[108]; a cynical sadist, he endorses the Nazi experimentation with human beings claiming that they were 'of great benefit to science'; he collaborates, inevitably, with the Russians (just like Drax enjoyed Soviet support in his plot to destroy London); most significant, perhaps, is his nihilistic refutation of all hierarchy: 'I changed my name to Julius No—the Julius after my father and the No for my rejection of him and of all authority.'[109] This rebellion against the father figure is a recurrent feature of Fleming's evil overmen, so that a relatively minor one, Scaramanga, is likewise diagnosed as 'a paranoiac in subconscious revolt against the father figure (i.e. the figure of authority).'[110] Mr Big is a racial rebel into the bargain, a black giant, standing for 'negro emancipation.' And he is, no doubt, a thorough Nietzschean:

> 'It is unfortunate for you . . . that you have encountered the first of the great negro criminals. I use a vulgar word, Mister Bond, because it is the one you, as a form of policeman, would yourself use. But I prefer to regard myself as one

who has the ability and the mental and nervous equipment to make his own laws and act according to them rather than accept the laws that suit the lowest denominator of the people. . . . I am by nature and predilection a wolf and I live by wolf's laws, naturally the sheep describe such a person as a "criminal." . . . The fact that . . . I survive and indeed enjoy limitless success against countless millions of sheep, is attributable . . . to an infinite capacity for taking pains. Not dull, plodding pains, but artistic, subtle pains.'[111]

Another menacing overman from below is Ernst Stavro Blofeld, to whom we shall return shortly. At present we only need to register how the commoner Blofeld is obsessed with ascending to the ranks of the aristocracy and attempts to procure himself a title of nobility, as described in *In Her Majesty's Secret Service*. Here, again, we find the motif of the evil *Übermensch* transgressing on social boundaries.

Strangely, yet most instructively, for all his alleged 'manias' the typical Nietzschean villain is in many respects but a negative duplicate of Bond himself. His vices are but Bond's virtues, the same drives and obsessions now condemned. Take the necessity of winning. The following could perfectly have been said of Bond's gambling fascination: 'What's he trying to prove with it? That he can beat everyone at everything? He seems to put so much passion into his cards—as if it wasn't a game at all, but some sort of trial of strength.'[112] Yet the reference is not to Bond but to Hugo Drax. Similarly, 'boredom . . . was the only vice Bond utterly condemned.' Yet Mr Big, who is supposed to be Bond's antithesis, suffers from the very same affliction: 'Mister Bond,' he tells him, 'I suffer from boredom.'[113] Moreover, Nietzscheanism, however evil, exercises an enormous appeal for Bond. For all the enmity, he cannot but admire the greatness of his adversaries, for instance Mr Big's: '[Bond] shivered at the beauty of it all, at this fabulous petrified ballet. . . . His eyes came back to the square of green baize and the great zombie face and into the wide yellow eyes with awe, almost with reverence.'[114] In such passages, the paradoxical ideological substance of the Bond stories manifests itself with an objective clarity. Bond's own obsessions are conveniently displaced onto his enemies: 007 remains the good Nietzschean, whereas Drax, Mr Big, Doctor No and co. are the evil Nietzscheans.

Working Undercover

But why such a divide in the first place? Why should Bond be the anti-Nietzschean Nietzschean rather than dispense with such intricate maneuvers and proudly brandish his Nietzscheanism? Bond's ambivalent perspective reflects the historical context in which the novels were written; following the triumph over world fascism, the Western world was ideologically driven to assume a double identity, whereby its structural Nietzscheanism—revolving around competition, elitism and contempt for mass democracy—had to go undercover, and a formal refutation of at least the most notorious Nietzschean creeds was espoused. The secret of Bond's double standard is such a division between the good, and unspoken, Nietzscheanism of the West, and the evil, explicit one, of old Germany, still sprouting mischief, and the Communists. This displacement of evil Nietzscheanism towards the Cold War adversary was of major ideological significance in the attempt to deal with the disturbing social Darwinist heritage of the liberal West. So now Soviet agents such as Kronsteen were presented as machine-like, beyond-good-and-evil social Darwinists 'not interested in human beings—not even in his own children. Nor did the categories of "good" and "bad" have a place in his vocabulary. . . . To him all people were chess pieces. . . . Their basic instincts were immutable. Self-preservation, sex and the instinct of the herd—in that order.'[115] His partner, Rosa Klebb, is no less of an evil Nietzschean: 'In her, the herd instinct would also be dead. Her urge for power demanded that she should be a wolf and not a sheep.'[116] The English and Americans, by contrast, embody the congenial alternative to such inhumanity. Bond becomes an icon of the crusade against totalitarianism, and Anthony Burgess could therefore have commended him for fighting 'on behalf of a free world.' As a rule, however, Bond was fighting to keep the world free, not for, but *from* democracy. If Bond manifested nothing but disdain at social democracy at home, democracy *as such* was discarded when turning to the so-called Third World. As in the case of Turkey, called on during one of the campaigns for a free world. Fleming refrained from letting Bond himself condemn the idea of Turkish democracy; instead, he permitted local friends of Bond, insiders to native 'mentality,' to convey the message, while Bond quietly acquiesces. It was left to Darko Kerim, a Turkish friend of England and a 'remarkable fellow' (M's judgment), to teach the reader something about Turkish democracy:

> Kerim harangued the waiter. He sat back smiling at Bond. 'That is the only way to treat these damned people. They love to be cursed and kicked. It is all they understand. It is in the blood. All this pretence of democracy is killing them. They want some sultans and wars and rape and fun. Poor brutes, in their striped suits and bowler hats. They are miserable. You've only got to look at them.'[117]

To remove democracy from Turkey would on this logic by no means disagree with the noble concept of a 'free world'; on the contrary, such a measure would greatly enhance the freedom of the Turks themselves. It would be a mistake to dismiss such political content as part of half-humorous jingoism by a diehard British conservative. Rather more ominously, it reflects the very consensual approach of the Western political elites towards the very idea of Second and Third World democracy, the way the free world shakes itself free of democracy, when party politics forms an obstacle to its economic prerogatives. Apart from the famous fact that the Bond novels were favorites of none other than President Kennedy himself—which one may discount as mere anecdote—the very pattern of American foreign policy in most of the Third World closely followed, as it were, Darko Kerim's perspective. Indeed, one need not travel further than Turkey; as one historian of modern Turkey informs us, the 1980 elimination of Turkish democracy and its replacement for three years by a military regime was endorsed by the U.S. foreign ministry and welcomed by the International Monetary Fund, as indispensable measures if Turgut Özal's neo-liberal economy, widely resisted by the population, was to benefit Turkey: 'Özal knew that little would be accomplished under normal party politics. . . . One of the aims of the military intervention was precisely that: to provide the period of tranquility . . . marked by an absence of politics and dissent in all forms.'[118] 'Parallel with an economic policy virtually dictated from Washington, the 12 September regime also adopted a foreign and military policy designed to serve Western interests in the region.'[119]

It is instructive to note how, only a few years before Fleming began depicting the *Übermensch* as an outcast attacking the West, a racial and social rebel, Norman Mailer firmly anchored Nietzscheanism at the very heart of America's Military-Industrial Complex, condensed in the figure of General Cummings from the great Second World War novel *The Naked and the Dead* (1948). The entire novel could be read as a prolonged, tormented, almost hopeless grappling with the sense that a Nietzschean power morality is inexorably overtaking the world, a force in the face of which resistance is almost unthinkable. As the General tells Lieutenant Hearn, his subordinate of radical leanings: 'Man's deepest urge is omnipotence . . . the only morality of the future is a power morality, and a man who cannot find his adjustment to it is doomed.'[120] General Cummings, a keen student of philosophy[121] and a reader of Nietzsche[122] posits, in the words of one commentator, 'the will to power as the monism through whose thrustings all human activities can eventually be explained. . . . This is straight Nietzsche.'[123] This is not the place to engage in a discussion of Mailer's important work and the full implications of its complex dealings with Nietzscheanism; here I wish only to establish how, as far as Mailer was concerned, far from signifying any defeat of fascism, the Second World War rather meant a handing over of the torch, the onset of an era of fascism on a truly global scale, taken over by the United States. General Cummings's formulation of this idea is worth quoting at some length:

> 'Historically the purpose of this war is to translate America's potential into kinetic energy. The concept of fascism, far sounder than communism if you consider it, for it's grounded firmly in men's actual natures, merely started in the wrong country [Germany], in a country which did not have enough intrinsic

potential power to develop completely. . . . But the dream, the concept, was sound enough. . . . America is going to absorb that dream, it's in the business of doing it now. . . . Your men of power in America, I can tell you, are becoming conscious of their real aims for the first time in our history. Watch. After the war our foreign policy is going to be far more naked, far less hypocritical than it has ever been. We're no longer going to cover our eyes with our left hand while our right is extending an imperialist paw.'[124]

This is the manic *Übermensch* working for the West, not against it; with Mailer, it is as if Dr No or Mr Big are running the show, rather than spoiling the party.

The most symptomatic case of schizophrenia between good and evil Nietzscheanism in Fleming is the showdown between James Bond and his greatest adversary, Ernst Stavro Blofeld, in the last Bond story actually completed by Fleming, *You Only Live Twice*. Here the ideological paradox surfaces most blatantly, and with its consideration I will conclude the discussion of Bond.

Of all Bond's foes, Blofeld is the only one who explicitly mentions Nietzsche as a source of inspiration. Like Doctor No, Bond accuses him of being mad, to which he aloofly replies: 'So was Frederick the Great, so was Nietzsche, so was Van Gogh. We are in good, in illustrious company, Mister Bond.'[125] 007, by contrast, is belittled by Blofeld as a member of the common throng: 'On the other hand, what are you? You are a common thug, a blunt instrument wielded by dolts in high places.'[126] To extract from its context the direct confrontation between Bond and Blofeld, which constitutes the last part of the story, is to remain with what appears a militant anti-Nietzschean message. Blofeld gives the ultimate performance in the role of the evil Nietzschean: a caricature of the Nazi—described as a Hitlerite figure, and regularly listening to Wagner melodies—he embarks on a profoundly Nietzschean scheme. He heads for Japan, a land where suicide is a time-honored tradition, and founds a garden of death, where desperate Japanese youths who regard themselves failures can commit suicide choosing from amongst a variety of deadly traps and poisonous plants. There is no material gain in store for Blofeld; the naked, philosophical issue is here at stake. 'It is the concept that matters,' Blofeld insists: 'If my bridge, my waterfall, yields a crop of only perhaps ten people a year, it is simply a matter of statistics. The basic idea will be kept alive.'[127] Like Nietzsche—when encouraging the weak and sickly to remove themselves from life (as discussed in chapter 3)—Blofeld regards his garden a vital service for the preservation of culture:

'And so, Mister Bond, I came to devise this useful and essentially humane project—the offer of free death to those who seek release from the burden of being alive . . .'

'I saw one man being disgustingly murdered yesterday.'
'Tidying up, Mister Bond. Tidying up. The man came here wishing to die. What you saw done was only helping a weak man to his seat on the boat across the Styx.'[128]

Bond, reflecting bitterly and ironically on Blofeld's project, does not fail to realize its anti-democratic significance: 'perhaps, one day, they would get a Minister of Self Destruction appointed in the Diet! Then the great days of the Black Dragon *Kōan* would come again to save the Country of the Rising Sun from the creeping paralysis of *demokorasu*!'[129] Yet what are the values which Bond himself appeals to in his defense of democracy against the assaults of the devilish overman? These are conveyed via Bond's conversations with his two buddies in Tokyo, an Australian and a Japanese, who, like Darko Kerim, can say openly, mischievously and with impunity what Bond secretly thinks. For Fleming, as for James Clavell, who will be addressed in the next section, the Japanese 'way of life'—allegedly ruthless, non-sentimental and greatly deferential—serves as a positive example to counter the democratic laxity of the decaying West. The recurrent motif of Bond's 'lessons' in Japan is that stalwart and vital elitism must substitute the permissive mushiness of Welfare England. To start with, the unsentimental Australian, Dikko Henderson, explains to Bond the advantages of the Japanese, hierarchical way of doing things, in which absolute commitment to one's superiors, up to the final source of authority, the Emperor, is the decisive regulating principle. This allegedly 'Japanese style' immediately calls to mind, however, the fascist notion of the leader as ultimate point of reference. Significantly, Henderson goes on to equate the central authority principle with the mode of decision-making prevalent in big capitalist corporations:

'Got it? It's not really as mysterious as it sounds. Much the same routine as operates in big corporations, like ICI or Shell, or in the services, except with them the ladder stops at the Board of Directives or the Chiefs of Staff.'[130]

When Bond objects that: 'It doesn't sound very *demokorasu*,' Henderson, as if he were the Turkish Darko Kerim in disguise, promptly replies:

For God's sake, get it into your head that the Japanese are a separate human species. . . . Just because people play baseball and wear bowler hats doesn't mean they're quote civilized people unquote. . . . I fornicate upon thy *demokorasu*. . . . I stand for government by an *élite* . . . And voting graded by each individual's rating in that *élite*. And one tenth of a vote for my government if you don't agree with me!'[131]

Henderson's boisterous defense of elitism is mitigated by having him utter these scandalous truths under the effects of sake. The Japanese agent

Tiger Tanaka, by comparison, is decidedly sober when expounding his own, remarkably similar, social theories. Tanaka, educated in Oxford, learnedly compares Japanese vigor with the sickness of American mass society, which 'has become . . . more and more unattractive except to the lower grades of the human species to whom bad but plentiful food . . . and the "quick buck," often dishonestly earned, or earned in exchange for minimal labour or skills, are the *summum bonum*.'[132] Bond, a consummate culinary connoisseur who certainly does not belong to that inferior rabble for whom 'bad but plentiful food' is such a blessing, nevertheless finds fault with Tanaka's argument, on the grounds that Japan has also taken the path of Western decadence. But he is immediately corrected: 'Baseball, amusement arcades, hot dogs . . . are the tepid tea of the way of life we know under *demokorasu*. They are a frenzied denial of the spirit of the *samurai* . . . but fortunately they are also expendable and temporary. They have as much importance in the history of Japan as the life of a dragonfly.'[133] Yet when Tanaka begins to batter American plebeianism, Bond must seriously disagree. He champions the honor of his Trans-Atlantic cousins, yet introduces a telling distinction between genuine, aristocratic Americans, and the riffraff of the working-class immigrants:

> 'I've got a lot of American friends who don't equate with what you're saying. Presumably you're talking of the lower level GIs—second-generation Americans who are basically Irish or Germans or Czechs or Poles who probably ought to be working in the fields or coalmines of their countries of origins instead of swaggering around a conquered country under the blessed coverlet of the Stars and Stripes with too much money to spend.'[134]

Thus, despite the immensity of the cultural gulf which reputedly separates them, both Japanese and Englishman are united in their frustration about the comfortable life run by the workers worldwide, the disproportional relation between their meager skills and insignificant labour and the 'easy buck' they get in return. This odd, cross-cultural affinity may explain why Tiger Tanaka immediately withdraws his exaggerated accusations against the countrymen of President JFK: 'Forgive me, Bondo-san. Of course you are right. . . . There are many cultured Americans who have taken up residence in this country and who are most valued citizens.'[135] At another occasion, however, Tanaka, authentically Japanese though he is, delivers a remarkably *Tory* speech concerning the decay of the British class system in the postwar time and the pernicious advances of the indulgent British proletariat:

> I, and many of us in positions of authority in Japan, have formed an unsatisfactory opinion about the British people since the war. You have not only lost a great Empire, you have seemed almost anxious to throw it away with both

hands. . . . Further, your governments . . . have handed over effective control of the country to the trade unions, who appear to be dedicated to the principle of doing less and less work for more money. This feather-bedding, this shirking of an honest day's work, is sapping at ever increasing speed the moral fibre of the British, a quality the world once so admired.[136]

While protesting against being judged according to Japanese 'jungle standards' Bond is intimately 'smarting under Tiger's onslaught, and the half-truths which he knew lay behind his words.' Tanaka has nothing but contempt for the British 'so-called aristocracy,' the demise of the British elite, and he thus makes Bond a tempting, and highly instructive, offer. He suggests that, by defeating Blofeld, Bond will vouch for the abiding worth of the British elite:

> And, for your information, those are very similar to the words I addressed to my Prime Minister. And do you know what he said? He said, all right, Mr Tanaka. Put this Commander Bond to the test. If he succeeds, I will agree that there is still an *élite* in Britain.[137]

Thus, Bond's democratic, *anti-Nietzschean* and *anti-elitist* mission is formulated in terms which are decidedly *anti*-democratic, *Nietzschean* and *elitist*; the fight against Blofeld's 'evil Nietzscheanism' is undertaken under the latent premises of 'good Nietzscheanism.'[138] Fleming's ideological schizophrenia, reflecting the duplicity in Western, Cold War ideology, reveals the narratives as spy stories in more sense than one: James Bond is a secret agent in the service of Nietzscheanism. Fleming concocted a version of Nietzscheanism specifically suited for pleasurable mass consumption, diluting the bitterness of the original drug. This yields the benefit of espousing Nietzschean amorality without facing the trouble of admitting as much, and keeping up a benevolent facade. And indeed, from an ideological point of view, what could possibly be more useful than subscribing to vice under the banner of virtue? And is this not what ultimately hides behind Bond's famous '*license* to *kill*'? That Bond and the West continue to preserve the outward appearance of justice and freedom while being in fact ruthless and cynical, can be quite useful in reconciling an appearance of democracy with the essence of exploitation. Fleming—one is tempted to say: *along* with modern liberal democracies—has thereby put *Nietzsche* to a *Machiavellian* use. This strategy was obligatory in the post–Second World War era, when mere power could not suffice as a moral argument as it did during the bolder age of fascism, when outspoken subscription to the might-is-right principle and the culling of the weak were widely licit in the fascist countries as well as in large sections of the social Darwinist, liberal West.

Yet Bond, though a neo-aristocratic knight-errant in the service of the ideology of competition, is not a capitalist himself. He could only indirectly be seen as bestowing nobility upon the naked act, not of war, conflict, risk-taking and competition, but of net profit accumulation. At times, as in the critique of Drax, the plebeian millionaire, Fleming is even assuming something of an aristocratic critique of the bourgeois nouveau riche, an elitist disdain of the marketplace. In the novels of James Clavell, by comparison, it is precisely such a plebeian act that is glamorized.

King Rat: The Invisible Paw of the Market

James Clavell's abiding concern with the coupling of aristocracy to capitalism is manifest in the titles of many of his novels, notably *Noble House* and *King Rat*. This preoccupation predominates already in his first novel, *King Rat*, a perennial best-seller that has never been out of print since its publication in 1962. The novel recounts the story of a very peculiar natural aristocrat and monarch, an American corporal in Changi—the 'notoriously barbaric'[139] Japanese POW camp in Singapore where Clavell himself has spent three years during the Second World War (the prisoners were American, British and Australians). The American, whom we only know by unofficial title, 'the King,' has risen into a position of almost unlimited power and authority in the camp by making the most of his immense commercial sagacity and entrepreneurial ruthlessness. He amasses enormous capital—in terms of the camp's acute scarcity, that is—by way of much-needed food supplies and other vital goods, notably cigarettes, and commands a half-grateful, half-resentful workforce. His story becomes a moral and political fable: '*For the men, Changi was more than a prison. Changi was genesis, the place of beginning again*.'[140] The naked struggle for survival in conditions of dire need which constitutes daily routine in the camp provides the perfect laboratory conditions for a great social experiment. In Changi, all prior social and cultural conditions, privileges as well as handicaps, are reset to zero. Men can only resort to their intrinsic, quasi-animal qualities to save them. Hence, the fit, truly qualified for life, can be effectively distinguished from the misfit, less generously equipped by nature. Likewise, the respective value of competing economic systems can be judged. In that sense the narrative clearly belongs in the sub-category of a return-to-the-state-of-nature stories, of which William Golding's *Lord of the Flies* remains the quintessential representative. What is more, given its autobiographical component *King Rat* in fact enjoys a distinct advantage over comparable, but purely fictional, stories. The compelling force of *King Rat*'s bleak 'realism' in the depiction of the struggle for survival in Changi no doubt owes a great deal to the biographical fact of the author's actual imprisonment in the camp. Yet there are, in truth, serious doubts regarding the basic veracity of Clavell's depiction of conditions in Changi which, some argue, have been exaggerated beyond all proportion.[141]

The King, within the story's ideological composition, is the conspicuous representative of American democratic capitalism, understood as founded upon individual merit confirmed in and through free competition:

> The King . . . always . . . saluted officers, English and Aussie officers. But he knew they were aware of the vastness of his contempt for 'Sir' and saluting. It wasn't the American way. A man's a man, regardless of background or family or rank.[142]

> 'Nobody gives me nothing. What I have is mine and I made it. How I made it is my own business.'[143]

Opposing American meritocracy are, firstly, the British highborn officers, standing for antiquated and unjust hereditary aristocratic privilege. They would rather congeal the free-flowing play of competition in the name of traditional hierarchy and birthright. Their guiding ethos is that of *inequality*, both *formal* and *substantive*. The other, and even fiercer opponent of competition, is the plebeian Lieutenant Grey—also an Englishman—the preacher of socialist *ressentiment*, who, being himself naturally unqualified for competition, struggles to impose a strict egalitarian code to halt the King's rise: 'Unlike most of the officers, Grey had refused to convert his bed to a bunk, for he hated the idea of sleeping above or below someone else. Even though the added doubling up meant more space.'[144] Grey hence represents *equality*, both *formal* and *substantive*. These are the ideological forces—from above and from below—which the representative of the market must overcome, himself standing for *formal equality* and *substantive inequality*. In the course of the story the torch of nobility is passed over from the hereditary aristocrats, who have exhausted their historical role, to the self-made man, the heroic capitalist entrepreneur. The bourgeois revolution itself (certainly in its *American* version, as opposed to the French one) is thereby vindicated, substituting the values of meritocracy for the obsolete ideals of divine right or caste privilege. Yet Clavell's new conception of nobility, running through all his stories, does not so much undermine the principle of blood lineage as it replaces a decaying lineage for a vital, ascending one. Thus, for instance, the commerce empire which Dick Struan, the supreme merchant, has founded in *Tai-Pan* (the second novel in Clavell's so-called 'Asian saga'[145]) continues to be managed by his descendants in *Noble House* (the fifth novel), just as the Japanese samurai Lord Toranaga, from *Shōgun*, will remain in business more than two and a half centuries after his death through his direct descendant Lord Toranaga Yoshi, in *Gai-Jin*. The purpose, hence, is not to banish the concept of nobility altogether but rather to reintroduce the aristocratic principle, albeit in an updated, 'legitimate' guise, into the formally egalitarian mass society. There must absolutely be a king in Clavell's meritocracies (or a Tai-Pan, or

a Shōgun, all essentially aristocratic titles which designate ultimate authority), precisely because, while formal equality is endorsed, substantive equality is emphatically denied. That 'a man's a man, regardless of background
or family or rank,' by no means implies human equality. On the very contrary, now that true merit and talent separate one man from another, the
difference between the natural aristocrat and the common mass man becomes all the more evident and irrefutable. With the elimination of artificial, social inequality, and its many forms of protective, unnatural privileges, natural inequality makes the King stand out among men as a veritable
masterpiece of nature, unique and incomparable: 'Only by mutual effort
did you survive. To withhold from the unit was fatal, for if you were expelled from a unit, the word got around. And it was impossible to survive
alone. But the King didn't have a unit. He was sufficient unto himself.'[146]
Whereas everybody else in the camp owned the scarce resources in common, 'only the King owned alone.'[147] This distinction from the mass is
something which Clavell will equally insist upon in his other novels. This,
for instance, is the way the hero of *Shōgun* relates to his shipmates—his
equals in terms of social background but not as far as inherent stature and
quality are concerned: 'Blackthorne left. He had wearied of their fears and
hates and obscenities.'[148]

It is nonetheless significant that, in Clavell's first novel, where his neo-
aristocratic ethos is for the first time articulated, the King's nobility had to
be ratified, so to speak, by a legitimate authority, namely an aristocrat of the
old, hereditary kind. As if unwilling to overstate the King's challenge to traditional nobility, Clavell left it to Peter Marlowe, a young English officer of
high birth, to confirm the King's eminence. Marlowe thus mediates and facilitates the transition from the old sense of nobility to the new one. Initially, he finds the King's obsession with profit wholly deplorable, for such
vocation contradicts everything that he has learned to see as exalted and admirable. Like a true Nietzschean nobleman, Marlowe relishes the dangerous
life and would go a long way to enjoy a good 'danger-excitement.'[149] Yet, for
him, it is the sheer thrill of adventure that counts, rather than any material
calculation. We are repeatedly informed that members of the Marlowe family are complete illiterates when it comes to 'business': '"Well, I couldn't go
into business. Marlowes aren't tradesmen," Peter Marlowe said . . . "It's just
not done, old boy."'[150] And elsewhere: 'Peter Marlowe frowned, trying to
understand. "When anyone starts talking about business, I'm afraid I'm
right out of my depth," he said. "I feel such an idiot."'[151] Yet between the
first instance and the second, separated in the text by some fifty pages, a
marked progress has taken place. From the initial snobbish, complacent
refutation of business, Marlowe retreats into a defensive, self-criticizing posture. Keeping oneself clean of the mess of moneymaking is initially a virtue,
something that a proper nobleman takes pride in, only to become, as the

second quotation shows, a defect, a mark of incompetence, indeed 'idiocy.' Such difficulty in seeing the noble side to moneymaking, coupled with an attempt to overcome such aversion, we find in Nietzsche, too:

> *Trade and nobility.*—Buying and selling have become common, like the art of reading and writing. . . . One can imagine social conditions in which there is no buying and selling and in which this art gradually ceases to be necessary. Perhaps some individuals who are less subject to the laws of the general condition will then permit themselves to buy and sell as a *luxury of sentiment*. At that point trade would acquire nobility, and the nobility might then enjoy trading as much as they have hitherto enjoyed war and politics, while the esteem for politics might undergo a total change.[152]

True, Nietzsche here merely speculates about a strictly hypothetical possibility that trade, sometime in the future, may attain nobility, while Marlowe recognizes such development as a living reality in Changi. Yet the King's activity—as that of the rest of Clavell's majestic tradesmen—corresponds profoundly to Nietzsche's prescription of 'noble trade.' *Their* buying and selling is certainly anything *but* common, for they are exceptional talents, and can only prevail in business due to their unique vitality and astuteness. Profit extraction, for the King, is not a prosaic, mundane act of necessity but the utmost gratification, a veritable 'luxury of sentiment.' And he certainly enjoys trade as a traditional nobleman takes joy in 'war and politics,' namely as an act whereby one's will to power is invested and capitalized on. For this is exactly what the Nietzscheanizing of the bourgeois ethos entails: the elimination of its characteristic democratic vulgarity. And it is this heroic nature of the King that Marlowe comes to recognize and, in his capacity of the hereditary aristocrat, sanction as the mark of true nobility. The genuine nobleman is he who has paved his own way, ascending from humble origins. Far from colliding with moneymaking, genuine nobility manifests itself precisely in the act of capitalist triumph. Consequently, at the end of the story, Marlowe is fully converted to the meritocratic ideology of the market, celebrated as a precious American value, which combines an acceptance of formal equality with the refutation of actual, substantive one. This change is encapsulated in Marlowe's final conversation with the lowly and resentful lieutenant Grey:

> '. . . But you're right in one thing. [The King] did change me. He showed me that a man's a man, irrespective of background. Against everything I've been taught. So I was wrong to sneer at you for something you had no hand in [namely Grey's lower-class origins], and I'm sorry for that. But I don't apologize for despising you for the man you are.'[153]

Class snobbery is renounced only to be replaced forthwith with warranted contempt, which shuns a man on account of what he allegedly 'is,' his inherent value. From now on it will be 'merit'—i.e., one's performance in business—which will determine a given individual's value and insert him in the new hierarchy.

In some respects, Clavell's heroes show themselves to be not merely natural but *supernatural* aristocrats as well. No matter how adverse the social or natural circumstances, triumph is mystically written into their destiny. Come what may, they are virtually predetermined to prevail. Blackthorne, struggling on his own with a fierce storm (all his shipmates are by this stage wholly defeated and dejected, resigned to their fate) successfully defies the forces of nature (no doubt since he is one himself): '"Piss on you, storm!" Blackthorne raged. "Get your dung-eating hands off my ship!"'[154] And the King, even in a camp where death is omnipotent, can confidently assert his creed according to which, 'Most times, only suckers get killed.'[155] Those belonging to the majority of the dying are indeed pushovers. Not even in the living hell of Changi can they possibly be considered victims of exterior circumstances, beyond their control, such as starvation or infections. Rather, it is their own *inherent* weakness that has sealed their doom. A conversation between the King and the camp's doctor about a just departed patient powerfully drives this point home:

> 'What'd he die of?'
>   'Lack of spirit.' The doctor stifled a yawn. . . .
>   'You mean will to live?'
>   . . . The doctor glowered up at the King. 'That's one thing you won't die of, isn't it?'
>   'Hell no. Sir.'
>   'What makes you so *invincible*?' Dr. Kennedy asked, hating this huge body which exuded health and strength. . . .
>   The King despised weakness. That doctor, he thought, . . . won't last long. Like Masters, poor guy! Yet maybe Masters wasn't a poor guy—he was Masters and he was weak and therefore no goddamned good. The world was jungle, and the strong survived and the weak should die. It was you or the other guy. That's right. There is no other way.[156]

This is, of course, classical Malthus, applauding the natural elimination of the weak; but it is also a profoundly Nietzschean insight. For it was Nietzsche, anticipating Clavell, who has advanced a psychological and interior explanation of illness:

> A young man grows prematurely pale and faded. His friends say: this and that illness is to blame. I say: *that* he became ill, *that* he failed to resist the illness, was already the consequence of an impoverished life, an hereditary exhaustion.

. . . Every error, of whatever kind, is a consequence of degeneration of instinct, disgregation of will.[157]

Hence, the King survives on account of his intrinsic health, his indomitable will to life, which are only subsequently translated into exterior, physical as well as economical, well-being (similarly, a very sick Marlowe will later on battle 'with death. But he had the will to live. And he lived'[158]). As Malcolm Bull diagnosed in relation to the reader response to Nietzsche (see Chapter 3), either one reads *King Rat* like a winner, identifying with the invincible natural aristocrat and savoring that promise of victory, or one reads the novel like a loser, adopting the perspective of one of those great many who did not survive Changi. Either way, a powerful ideological service is rendered to the competitive discourse of capitalism. Certainly, capitalism is squarely admitted to be a dog-eat-dog universe, in contradistinction to the sanguine talk about a system serving 'the good of the greatest number,' yet it is precisely *as a jungle* that capitalism is vindicated, proclaimed both just and inevitable. For, even if one reads *King Rat* like a loser, there can be no other option, on the novel's terms, but to resign before one's own incompetence and surrender meekly as the invisible hand of the market does the culling. To deem the intrinsic quality of the individual the decisive factor in determining his success or failure regardless of external, objective conditions, is by definition to undermine the validity of any social critique.

Having said that, merely to expose the ruthlessness of life in Changi and the cynicism of the King may have driven some of the readers, especially those reading like losers, to question the moral soundness of the narrative and shift their sympathies towards the socialist Grey, who fights, however weakly and inadequately, to make the camp a more equitable place. If the King is to appear worthy of nobility he cannot remain a mere instrument of exploitation and self-serving economics. The ideological challenge is therefore to show not merely that Changi is a jungle, but also that it cannot possibly be anything else, and that those trying to improve conditions in the camp are bound to prove only destructive. Capitalism and its representative, the King, are therefore depicted as at once ruthless *and* benevolent. A series of paradoxical messages are conveyed whereby capitalism emerges as filthy but majestic, egotistic but altruistic, destructive but productive, cynical but generous, amoral but moral, exploitative but life-giving, godforsaken but divinely administered.

Let us briefly examine only the most significant of these paradoxes, the themes of atheism and of economic utility. As far as atheism is concerned, Clavell's story confronts the reader with an essentially post-theistic world, following, in Nietzschean terms, the death of God. The morality of good and evil is obsolete in both its old, aristocratic variant and new, socialist one, the former in its reliance on divine right, the latter on account of its belief in an egalitarian metaphysics which is wholly incompatible in the context of the jungle-like, god-forsaken camp. In full accord with the Nietzschean discourse, Grey's socialism is irrevocably rooted in Christian, life-denying values, for both socialism and Christianity share the unnatural predilection for favoring and protecting the weak, those whose very existence forms an objection to life. This would become a recurring motif in Clavell's novels as the rise of the vitalistic hero, the envoy of Nietzsche's 'ascending life,' will repeatedly be obstructed by the 'fanaticism' of Christian preachers (for example, the sinister Jesuit priest Alvito, Blackthorne's foe in *Shōgun*). The rules of Changi are those of natural selection, fundamentally inscrutable by conventional moral conceptions, the cruel but just rules of the market which recognize neither birthright nor a moral principle but merit, and merit alone (defined in the capitalist sense of the ability to make profit). Yet, considered from the point of view of ideological utility, such a renunciation of a benevolent deity in favor of a 'natural law' is fundamentally flawed, potentially even self-defeating, inasmuch as it ironically *calls for* moralistic intervention. Precisely *because* nature is decreed inhuman, cruel and predatory the objective need arises all the more urgently for a moral and social regulation of natural selection. Such regulation may be artificial but it offers the invaluable advantage of humanizing nature, so to speak, and making life far more bearable. For why should we live miserably in a jungle, when it can be turned into a pleasant park? Because, the Nietzschean answer will be, life looses its essence, forfeits the will to power, when democracy and socialism are allowed to benumb the exhilarating savagery of existence. Yet such argumentation can only appeal to those reading the Nietzschean narrative like winners, and imagining themselves in the *Übermensch's* position; it is less likely to attract all those whom capitalist competition is bound to devour. Hence, an essentially benevolent god must be sneaked back in, albeit in innovative guises. The consummate ideology of the market must therefore present the system, however paradoxically, as simultaneously (1) ruthless—so as to justify the rat-race reality under capitalism (2) benevolent—so as to counteract the dejecting impression created by the first assertion, and (3) inevitable—so as to peremptorily deny any attempt to better the present order.

Clavell's solution to that second requirement, the recuperation of a benevolent deity amidst the social Darwinism of unfettered competition, constitutes an interesting variation on the solution arrived at by classical liberal thought, with its notion of the invisible hand benevolently steering the wheel of market exchanges, putting order into apparent chaos. Peter Marlowe, the young officer, seriously injures his arm and is facing the terrible choice between amputation and death. Now that natural selection appears to condemn him, the merciless logic of Changi drives the desperate Marlowe into an incoherent, *atheistic* fit of rage against the cruelty of *God*. He thus engages in a telling dispute with Father Donovan, an exceptionally worthy priest:

> Father Donovan smiled. 'You should have more faith—'
>
> [Marlowe:] 'I'm tired of faith.' The words were sudden-raw and very angry . . . Then he whirled back on Donovan. '. . . Faith's a lot of nothing! What does it get you? Nothing! Faith's for children—and so is God. What the hell can He do about anything? Really do? Eh? *Eh?*' . . .
>
> 'He can heal,' Father Donovan said, knowing about the gangrene. . . .
>
> Peter Marlowe slammed his cards down on the table. 'Shit!' he shouted, berserk. ' . . . God! You know, *I* think God's a maniac, a sadistic, evil maniac, a bloodsucker. . . . God's nothing but evil—if He really is God. . . . Don't give me faith! It's nothing!'[159]

Yet for all his raging atheism Marlowe, now nature's prey, is obviously in desperate need of God, yearning for that benign intervention which will save his rotting arm. It is just that he is stuck between the Nietzschean affirmation of God's death, which he has accepted as part of the ideology of the market, and the burning necessity to revive God. And at that point Clavell provides the surprising resolution of the dilemma. Since God must absolutely come back to life he indeed reappears, but in a strange and mysterious new incarnation—the King:

> 'And yet you have faith in the King,' Father Donovan said quietly.
>
> 'I suppose you're going to say he's an instrument of God?'
>
> 'Perhaps he is. I don't know.'
>
> . . . Peter Marlowe laughed hysterically. . . . 'Listen, Priest. You're a joke . . . You're all an unholy joke, you and God. . . .' And then he scooped some of the cards off the table and threw them into Father Donovan's face and stormed out into the darkness.[160]

But, preposterous as the idea at first sounds, Father Donovan turns out to be right and the King does prove himself an instrument of God. He uses his commercial connections and attains antitoxin, whereby the gangrene is reversed and Marlowe's arm recovered. A reassuring divine harmony is reinstated, deus ex machina indeed, even in hellish Changi. Everything that happens in the camp, notwithstanding appearances to the contrary, is in prefect accordance with the divine scheme:

> Father Donovan . . . smiled at Peter. 'I'm glad your arm is healed, Peter.'
>
> Peter Marlowe smiled back. 'There's not much that goes on that you don't know about, is there?'
>
> 'There's not much that goes on that He doesn't know about.' Donovan was very sure and completely peaceful. 'We're in good hands.'[161]

The King, whose activities completely fly in the face of conventional morality, proves nonetheless—better said, *because* of such activities—to be that benign regulator which is supposed, in and through market forces, to guarantee a propitious outcome. He is the personification of Hegel's 'World Spirit,' of Adam Smith's 'invisible hand,' of Mandeville's self-seeking Bee that produces public honey, or, to go even further back in time, of the Protestant predestination. The fundamental uncontrollability of the capitalist mode of production is metamorphosed into a priceless virtue via a modern 'fable of the bees': the more egotistic the means, the more beneficial and harmonious is the result; the more absent is God, the more wild and forsaken the scene appears, so can we mysteriously sense His eminent presence. The King is God's proxy and a rat at the same time. This unlikely serendipity is symbolically expressed when the inmates catch a rat and turn to torture it, only for the King to interfere:

'That's a lousy idea,' said the King. 'It's okay to kill the bastard. No need to torture it, even if it is a rat. It never did you any harm.'
  'Maybe. But rats're vermin. They got no right to be alive.'
  'Sure they have,' said the King. 'If it wasn't for them, well, they're scavengers, like microbes. Weren't for rats, why the whole world'd be a stink-pile.'[162]

Under the King's inspired guidance the inmates keep the rat alive and, suitably naming it Adam, use the animal to found a 'rat farm' in which they produce and market rat-meat (naturally without letting the starving clients in on the true nature of the meat), to the great economic advantage of the unit. The usefulness of the capitalistic rat is thereby both metaphorically as well as literally corroborated. And as the story concludes, we are left with this final parable about the fate of the rats in the farm:

They were still there. Beneath the hut. And many had died . . . But the strongest were still alive . . .
  And Adam ruled, for he was the King. Until the day his will to be King deserted him. Then he died, food for a stronger. And the strongest was always the King, not by strength alone, but King by cunning and luck and strength together. Among the rats.[163]

In the face of such grim social Darwinist mayhem it is good for the reader to keep in mind that rats are actually useful, and that, through their kings, 'we're all in good hands,' as Father Donovan is peacefully confident of. The invisible paw of the market sees to that.

Another way of attracting the reader's sympathies towards the ambiguous American monarch is by eventually transforming the omnipotent capitalist into a tragic victim, just as Nietzsche's strong man is tragically subjugated by slave morality, infected by guilt and self-doubt. In such narratives, cruelty is condoned and pity condemned, *until* the perceived object of injustice becomes the master. When this happens, traditional morality recovers its validity, however obliquely. No matter how devastating the consequences of natural selection, they are stoically accepted, if not directly applauded; unnatural selection, by contrast, carried out by the illegitimate agents of society and morality, is melodramatically deplored. With Clavell this melodramatic turn takes place when, at the end of the war, the camp is liberated. Natural conditions, under which the King thrived, are suspended in favor of a return to civilization, where anti-natural morality reigns. The King is severely punished both by the agents of morality liberating the camp and by his own former workers who now obscenely bite the hand that fed them:

> Peter Marlowe . . . glanced towards the King's corner. 'Where's our fearless leader?'
> 'He's dead!' Max rocked with obscene laughter.
> 'What?' Peter Marlowe said, frightened in spite of himself.
> 'He's still alive,' Tex said. 'But he's dead all the same.'
> Peter Marlowe looked searchingly at Tex. Then he saw the expressions on all their faces. Suddenly he felt very sad.
> 'Don't you think that's a little abrupt?'
> 'Abrupt nothin'.' Max spat. 'He's dead. We worked our asses off for that son of a bitch, and now he's dead.'
> Peter Marlowe pounced on Max, loathing him. 'But when things were bad, he gave you food and money and—'
> 'We worked for it!' Max screamed, the tendons in his neck stretching.[164]

The great King thus fades tragically back into anonymity. Swallowed by the indifferent crowd of democratic mediocrity he loses his identity: 'Jesus God, he wept inside, give me back my face. Please give me back my face.'[165] In all this, it is important to stress, there is nothing which reflects a popular 'vulgarization' of Nietzsche or of liberal doctrines. Nor does it stem from some inadequacy or rudeness, literary or ideological, in Clavell himself, who was a very gifted storyteller. What is here reflected are rather the deep-seated paradoxes of the liberal discourse itself. The ubiquitous self-contradictions and manipulative ploys in Clavell's 'popular' narrative are therefore basically the same that can be found in the canonical works of Nietzsche or in those of the Nobel Prize–winning liberal theorist, Friedrich August von Hayek, to name but a couple of 'eminencies.'

We must now address the third and last element of the ideology of the market listed above—the ruling out of an alternative to capitalism. One of the principal means of fulfilling this requirement is the discrediting narrative of *ressentiment*.

3. TALES OF *RESSENTIMENT*

A useful way to identify the Nietzschean hero is to notice in his vicinity the presence of his archetypal foil—the *ressentiment* man. As Fredric Jameson determined, one of the major ideological containment strategies employed by the bourgeoisie in the latter half of the nineteenth century facing the advances of socialism was the narrative of *ressentiment.*[166] Known also by such aliases as 'the black tarantula' or 'the ascetic priest,' the man of *ressentiment* is held responsible for proletarian agitation. A failed, inferior individual, typically a dissatisfied intellectual, he finds his vocation in whipping up the emotions of the workers and inciting them to rebel. This was, to be sure, not an invention of Nietzsche, but if Joseph Conrad was described by Jameson as the 'epic poet' of *ressentiment,*[167] then Nietzsche was established as its 'primary theorist, if not, indeed, the metaphysician.'[168] The man of *ressentiment* becomes the preferred scapegoat for explaining social unrest and working-class consciousness. In their basic appreciation of the modern social condition, Nietzsche's views and Conrad's are practically interchangeable. Both were deeply nostalgic about the docile and manageable working classes of the past, and both were conscious of the fall signified by modernity. The working classes have taken a massive bite from the apple of knowledge, a sin for which the masters are expelled from Eden. As Conrad wrote in a personal correspondence in 1885, the same year that Nietzsche published *Beyond Good and Evil*:

> the International Socialist Association are triumphant, and every disreputable ragamuffin in Europe feels that the day of universal brotherhood, despoliation and disorder is coming apace, and nurses day-dreams of well-plenished pockets amongst the ruin of all that is respectable, venerable and holy. . . . Where's the man to stop the rush of social-democratic ideas? . . . England was the only barrier to the pressure of infernal doctrines born in continental back-slums. Now, there is nothing![169]

This historical conviction has subsequently found expression throughout Conrad's fiction. In order to exemplify the modus operandi of the ideologeme of *ressentiment* few texts are more pertinent than Joseph Conrad's *The Nigger of the 'Narcissus.'* In this early novel, Conrad provides a dramatic account of paradise lost and the fall of the modern worker. He glorifies the pious seaman of the past, untouched by socialism, while sternly portraying his deplorable modern successor. Singleton, a veteran sailor, 'a lonely relic of a devoured and forgotten generation' stands for the former, ideal vassal, as compared with the present generation. What had characterized the former generation, above all, was its imperviousness to the poison of *ressentiment*:

> He stood, still strong, as ever unthinking . . . the men who could understand his silence were gone. . . . They had been strong, as those are strong as know

neither doubts nor hopes. They had been impatient and enduring, turbulent and devoted, unruly and faithful. . . . [T]hey had been men who . . . knew not fear, and had no desire of spite in their hearts . . . voiceless men—but men enough to scorn in their hearts the sentimental voices that bewailed the hardness of their fate. . . . They were the everlasting children of the mysterious sea. Their successors are the grown-up children of a discontented earth: they are less naughty but less innocent; less profane, but perhaps also less believing; if they learned how to speak they have also learned how to whine.[170]

These are Conrad's (and, no doubt, Nietzsche's) ideal slaves, innocent, unthinking, undoubting, voiceless, enduring, faithful, and, importantly, with no desire of spite in their hearts, indeed, all qualities that no slave worthy of his name should come without. The anti-*ressentiment* narrative, importantly, presents the corruption of the modern workers not in terms of objective historical dynamics but as some subjective fancy getting hold of the workers' minds. At bottom, it is a matter of wrong ideas, the contamination of consciousness. As Singleton affirms: 'Ship! . . . Ships are all right. It is the men in them!'[171] It is not, therefore, an objective deficiency of the ship—of society—which is the decisive factor, but the defects of men, and, importantly, not of the men running these ships but of those serving aboard them. The ship of society will continue to sail safely as long as its crew assumes the right attitude—unthinking, undoubting, enduring, etc. And since the rot is ideological one has to look for the culprits at the level of ideology: the worker's mind has turned insidious, since a preacher of *ressentiment* has been messing with it, spreading doctrines of 'universal brotherhood, despoliation and disorder.' Nietzsche has furnished the ultimate philosophical analysis of such agitators, but usually at an abstract, theoretical level. It is in fiction that The Black Tarantulas become living, concrete persons, with names and faces. Conrad engaged with this theme in most of his works, generating a gallery of *ressentiment* men. If Nietzsche's abstract treatment of the apostles of revolt was severe enough, Conrad's 'concrete' dealings are even harsher. The fact that the man of *ressentiment* becomes a flesh-and-blood person does not imply a more nuanced, or lenient, depiction. If anything, the element of caricature becomes even more marked. Donkin—the man of *ressentiment* aboard the *Narcissus*—is not so much an individual human being as he is the personification of the cockney:

They all knew him. Is there a spot on earth where such a man is unknown, an ominous survival testifying to the eternal fitness of lies and impudence? . . . The independent offspring of the ignoble freedom of the slums full of disdain and hate for the austere servitude of the sea.[172]

Being the embodiment of the vile cockney, Donkin contradicts Conrad's earlier avowal that 'the infernal doctrines' of democracy and socialism are 'born in continental back-slums': such doctrines, as Donkin testifies to, emanate just as surely from the very heart of the noble British Empire, from the slums of its very capital. Donkin enkindles and relishes the slave revolt on the ship: 'The *Narcissus* was still a peaceful ship, but mutual confidence was shaken. Donkin did not conceal his delight. We were dismayed.'[173] The discontent of the crew is a symptom of a strange psychological affliction, hardly rooted in material conditions. The sailors mutiny, but they have scarcely an idea of what it actually is that bothers them. It is a vague, unarticulated, illusive ambition. As Captain Allistoun, usually referred to simply and eloquently as 'the master', somberly reflects, they lack the concrete drive of past rebellions, which were momentarily fierce but then easily subdued: 'Years ago; I was a young master then—one China voyage I had a mutiny; real mutiny, Baker. Different men, tho.' I knew what they wanted; they wanted to broach cargo and get at the liquor. Very simple. We knocked them about for two days, and when they had enough—gentle as lambs. Good crew.'[174] Things are more complicated with the current, fallen generation of seamen that aims for more than extra booze. With them, it is at bottom a question of over-refinement.[175] They have become spoiled through modernity and thus prone to resist the inevitable hardness of sea-life, of life as such, of existence:

> Falsehood triumphed. It triumphed through doubt, through stupidity, through pity, through sentimentalism. . . . [W]e were becoming highly humanised, tender, complex, excessively decadent: . . . as though we had been over-civilized, and rotten, and without any notion of the meaning of life.[176]

The seamen are diagnosed as diseased with morality, which incites them to an optimistic rejection of the tragic truth of life, just as Nietzsche maintained from the *Birth of Tragedy* to the *Will to Power*. The modern sense of compassion, for both Conrad and Nietzsche, is not beneficial, civilized improvement of the human character, but its corruption, a symptom of enervation, exhaustion and decadence. As Nietzsche affirmed: 'precisely pity I recognized as more dangerous than any vice. . . . One has to respect fatality— that fatality that says to the weak: perish!'[177] The crew of the *Narcissus*, however, rejects precisely such fatality, in its obsessive concern with the life of its sickly 'nigger', James Wait. One of the sailors, particularly thorough in tending to the sick, becomes 'as gentle as a woman, as tenderly gay as an old philanthropist, as sentimentally careful of his nigger as a model slave-owner.'[178] Modernity implies an unmanly deterioration of man, one more lamentable consequence of which is indeed the hyper-sensitivity to the suffering of slaves in general and black ones in particular. Singleton—the veteran seaman who is a relic of the lost golden age—makes this point abundantly clear as he magnanimously reproaches the rebellious, younger sailors:

> 'I have seen rows aboard ship before some of you were born,' he said slowly, 'for something or nothing; but never for such a thing. . . . And a black fellow,

too,' went on the old seaman, 'I have seen them die like flies.' He stopped, thoughtful, as if trying to recollect gruesome things, details of horrors, hecatombs of niggers; and they looked at him absorbed. . . . What would he say? He said:—'you can't help him; die he must.'[179]

Slavery, however horrific, pertains to the truth of life, while to refute it, to become infatuated with one more nigger, is a futile, overly civilized, defiance of existence.[180] Singleton's voice is that of man's ability to acknowledge his inexorable fate with resigned dignity rather than stoop to optimistic protestations. Where Donkin sows revolt, Singleton emanates existential resignation:

> [Singleton] radiated unspeakable wisdom, hard unconcern, the chilling air of resignation. Round him all the listeners felt themselves suddenly enlightened by their disappointment, and, mute, they lolled about with the careless ease of men who can discern perfectly the *irredeemable aspect of their existence*.[181]

The final pages of the novel bring the ideological dichotomy between Singleton and Donkin into completion. As the crew goes onshore to receive its payment, a telling reversal of roles occur. Singleton, who in sea was magnanimous and imposing, appears self-conscious and tamed on land:

> [H]is hands, that never hesitated in the great light of the open sea, could hardly find the small pile of gold in the profound darkness of the shore. 'Can't write?' said the clerk, shocked. 'Make a mark, then.' Singleton painfully sketched in a heavy cross, blotted the page. 'What a disgusting old brute,' muttered the clerk. Somebody opened the door for him, and the patriarchal seaman passed through unsteadily, without as much as a glance at any of us.[182]

Donkin, who as a sailor was a useless malingerer, correspondingly emerges onshore as easygoing and confident: 'Donkin . . . went straight to the desk, talked with animation to the clerk, who thought him an intelligent man. They discussed the account, dropping hs against one another as for a wager—very friendly . . . He had better clothes, had an easy air, appeared more at home than any of us.'[183] The cockney is thus truly a 'child of a discontented earth,' Singleton genuinely a 'child of the sea' (the novel was originally to be titled *Children of the Sea*). The ideal seaman/worker/slave in Conrad's social fantasy is one who is as indefatigable at work as he is awkward, meek and embarrassed when collecting his modest reward. But sadly, the Singletons of the world are replaced by the Donkins, lazy at work just as they are contentious and businesslike when claiming their paycheck. Into the bargain, Conrad adds a critique of general education, a fateful development that spoils the innocence of the laborers, robs them of their noble illiteracy. Conrad, the supreme master of words, the consummate linguist, fantasizes about the worker as a mute beast of burden, deprived of even such basic linguistic skills that may serve him when negotiating with his employers. The only poetry the slaves may practice is one of silent, arduous toil. The penultimate paragraph of the novel spells out the advantages of (working-class) silence as compared with loquacity:

> I never saw them again. . . . Singleton has no doubt taken with him the long record of his faithful work into the peaceful depths of an hospitable sea. And Donkin, who never did a decent day's work in his life, no doubt earns his living by discoursing with filthy eloquence upon the right of labour to live. So be it! Let the earth and the sea each have its own.[184]

The worker's literacy, inasmuch as he becomes militantly conscious of his aims, can never be more than 'filthy eloquence,' as opposed, overtly, to Singleton's majestic silence and, at a deeper level, to Conrad's own legitimate, clean eloquence.

For all the parallels between Conrad's narrative of *ressentiment* and Nietzsche's theories, what is essentially missing in the stories of the former is Nietzsche's positive counter-specimen, the *Übermensch*. In twentieth-century popular culture we will find them frequently coupled together, the Nietzschean narrative becoming one of the *Übermensch* battling with the man of *ressentiment*. The persistence of the motif of revolutionary *ressentiment* in popular narratives, from Ayn Rand to Disney's *The Lion King* (as discussed in chapter 2) appears to contradict Jameson's belief that this ideologeme has exhausted its historical life span.[185] In Ayn Rand's *The Fountainhead*, for example, the heroic architect Howard Roark is confronted with his antithesis, the socialist art critic Ellsworth Monkton Toohey who, recognizing Roark's greatness, musters up all his devious craft to destroy the budding *Übermensch*. They represent the two poles of the novel's ideological divide: majestic, individualistic capitalism vs. revengeful, wretched collectivism. Whereas Roark is the unmistakable Nietzschean hero, regally towering above the puny masses, Toohey is the epitome of *Ressentiment*, the innate, 'organic' foe of heroism.[186] Toohey's whole personality is constructed around a profound inferiority complex, both physical and spiritual. As a child, belonging to that group of children of 'substandard bodies,'[187] the defining moment in his development is the realization that he cannot stand up to the bullies in his class given his physical frailty. Indeed, inferior physique and imperfect manliness is one of the distinguishing features of *ressentiment* men. Donkin thus feels 'all over his sterile chin for the few rare hairs,'[188] Verloc in Conrad's *The Secret Agent* cannot hope to inspire erotic love in a woman and Lieutenant Grey in *King Rat* learns after the camp's liberation that his wife had cast him off and remarried during the war. In the absence of the real thing, true power, Toohey must exploit its surrogate: morality. Hence, his strategy is to stoke up the slave revolt, to feign altruism and care for others, in order to impede the rise of virile individuals. The trope of *ressentiment* serves Rand, as it did Nietzsche and Conrad before her, to discredit egalitarianism and leftist political activism as finally motivated, whether consciously or not, by the desire to impose universal mediocrity. At bottom, socialism is not out to achieve material, economic amelioration, but to advance a cultural refutation of greatness. For that purpose it harnesses the amorphous masses, gives shape and direction to their collective discontent. It is hence that Toohey forges a pernicious democratic alliance with 'the tremendous power of numbers, the power of the masses.'[189] His professed love for humankind is but a cynical veil behind which he conducts his venomous campaign to punish and subdue the unique individual and to destroy the prospects of Culture. Only superficially does Toohey oppose the likes of 'Rockefeller and Morgan'; for his real targets are rather 'Beethoven and Shakespeare.'[190]

Ironically, Rand speculated on socialist intellectuals doing clandestinely what she was doing quite brazenly all along: namely defending Rockefeller and Morgan, and American 'big business' as such, in the name of Culture. Perhaps nowhere as in Rand's Manichean tales can one get a finer illustration of what Jameson cannily called 'the autoreferential structure' of the *ressentiment* ideologeme: 'the theory of *ressentiment*, wherever it appears, will always itself be the expression and the production of *ressentiment*.'[191] This is a point of great importance, as the Nietzschean narrative is founded decisively upon the claim that envy and the desire to mete out punishment are attributes of the weak, whereas the strong are beyond such meanness. Even when they happen to inflict suffering they do it, as it were, innocently, free of wickedness and cruelty, just as a bird of prey delights on the flesh of a tasty lamb. Hence Zarathustra's denunciation of the very concept of punishment and the advocation of the need to rise above it:

> Revenge sits within your soul . . . with revenge your poison makes the soul giddy! . . . I speak to you in parables, you who make the soul giddy, you preachers of *equality*! You are tarantulas and deal in hidden revengefulness! . . . For *that man may be freed from the bonds of revenge*: that is the bridge to my highest hope and a rainbow after protracted storms.[192]

Many commentators have taken this and similar lyrical and appeasing avowals at face value, commending Nietzsche's high-mindedness. Merold Westphal, for instance, described Nietzsche's anti-*ressentiment* as a principled refutation of the desire to punish.[193] Yet Nietzsche's actual position, and the narrative of *ressentiment* in general, are in fact strewn with hatred and revengefulness. Thus we can hear Zarathustra threatening the rabble with horrible retribution: 'like a wind I will one day blow among them and with my spirit take away the breath from their spirit: thus my future will have it.'[194] It is tempting, in the face of such thundering threats, to invoke another

Zarathustrian counsel, form the very next passage: 'Thus, however, I advise you, my friends: Mistrust all in whom the urge to punish is strong!'[195] It makes little sense to abstract Zarathustra's utterances from their social context into an idealized 'magnanimity' for, certainly, nothing was further away from Nietzsche's intentions than the masters offering *their* other cheek. Clearly, it is not punishment and revenge as such which need be removed from the hearts of man but only the revolutionary sort of punishment, by those who 'raise an outcry against everything that has power!'[196]

The very same paradox of resentful anti-resentment and vindictive indictment of vendetta lies at the heart of Rand's tale. On the one hand, she makes much of the august poise of Roark, as compared with the scheming pettiness of Toohey. This fundamental difference between the two antagonists finds expression in the scene where they finally meet face-to-face. The man of *ressentiment*, burning with hate of the *Übermensch*, is curious to know what the archenemy thinks of him. Roark's casual, telegraphic response to his inquiry is all telling: 'I don't think of you.'[197] Whereas Toohey is a non-entity, little more than a shadow of his rival, the autonomous hero hardly even registers the existence of the embittered weakling.[198] This is a point which Rand is at pains to get across, and so we hear time and again of Roark's splendid equanimity in the face of rancorous schemes and defamations. But the aloofness of the hero is more than compensated for by the involvement of the fuming narrator. Productively, they divide labor between them, so that, whereas the hero admirably preserves his composure in face of the smearing campaign, the narrator meticulously describes its each and every detail. The inevitable result is a narrative soaked in resentment. The narrator, for example, insists that Roark ignored the vile attacks directed at him by the populist press, but then, rather than following the hero's noble example, proceeds to include the complete text of the wicked article, so as to ignite all the more the reader's ardent desire for retribution.

The sterility and impotence of *ressentiment* men obviously does not remain confined to the domain of erotic performance; rather, their sexual unproductiveness—women and erotic desire, for example, play no role whatsoever in Toohey's life[199]—is ominously suggestive of their social and political barrenness. In order preemptively to discard the alternative they represent they are described as inherently uncreative and incapable of performing any useful work; their only vocation is that of destruction. Toohey's natural profession must hence be that of the critic, the 'second hander' bar none, the medium of public opinion.[200] The man of action is confronted by a foil capable only of undoing. Donkin, as we saw, is equally a shirker, a freeloader, and, in his own way, a critic, filthily eloquent. Most objectionable is the fact that 'he could wallow, and lie, and eat—and curse the food he ate.'[201] Whereas the heroes are life-giving, labour-giving, their critics are ungrateful parasites, taking and complaining, eating and whining. Lieutenant Grey in

King Rat—who, for that matter, emerges as a somewhat more rounded figure, slightly more recognizably human when compared with the utterly flat
Donkin and Toohey—is not even credited with good subjective intentions.
It is vital that any genuine compassion in him, as in all *ressentiment* men, be
denied, that any true concern for social equity, however naïve and impracti-
cable, be exposed as disguised self-interest. His utopia is robbed even of
color, deprived of its allure and vividness even as a mere dream. It is not for
nothing that he is named, precisely, Grey.

The *ressentiment* man of the Nietzschean twentieth-century narratives
might be seen as the reclusive, embittered Byronic hero stripped of his heroism. His social defiance is at all times sheer frustration while heroism is
wholly on the side of the *Übermensch*, defending the established order. In
that respect there is an important difference between Fleming's villains and
the ones populating the stories of Conrad, Rand and Clavell. In Fleming, for
all his wickedness the villain still possesses greatness, arouses Bond's awe.
Doctor No, Mr Big or Blofeld may incarnate evil, but they are anything but
despicable and pathetic. Physically as well as mentally they are towering figures, well above the human average. Yet this does not imply an ideological
disagreement, a difference in social outlook between Fleming and the rest
of the authors discussed. All are basically united in lamenting a working
class that does not work and in grudging the 'easy buck' earned by the
pseudo-laborer. Rather, the disparity in the description of the villains is the
result of the different narrative mode operative in each case. Fleming's villains, namely, are decidedly *not* men of *ressentiment*; they are Nietzschean
villains whose greatness is precisely the result of their amoral, superhuman
status. Their challenge to the capitalist system is not predicated upon impotence and sterility but rather on the excess of the power they possess.
Bond's enemies are anything but inconspicuous non-entities, of the same
ilk as Donkin, Toohey or Grey. By the same token, the effeminacy and help-
lessness of the latter are exactly the reflection of their *anti*-Nietzscheanism,
the fact that they cling ferociously to the categories of good and evil. Theirs
is the ruse of morality substituting genuine potency, the inability to directly
strike back turned into a slow poisoning of the presuppositions of life. Yet
these ideologemes are two ways of skinning the same cat. The mad *Übermensch* of the Bond stories and the bitter weakling of *ressentiment* tales are
different ways of disarming a single enemy, whether utterly weak or horri-
fyingly strong: the insubordinate who comes *from below*.

Another important variety of the Nietzschean hero remains to be discussed, the hero as evil genius; the complexity and ramifications of this
theme, however, demand a separate chapter.

6

'The Joy of the Knife':
Nietzschean Glorification of Crime

Exploring the social origins of the crime story, Ernest Mandel has claimed that, roughly from mid-nineteenth century onwards, the outlaw, long enjoying the moral support of the middle class, began to forfeit his elevated cultural status. The rapid rise of urban crime was met with a corresponding upsurge in bourgeois sense of decency. It produced a fresh sympathy for law-enforcers—once considered, by the working and middle classes alike, as brutal lackeys of the aristocracy—and a steep decline in fellow feeling for 'criminals'—who up to this time were 'rebels with a cause.' The transgression that the bourgeois were romantically cheering on when directed against the feudal masters became quite inadmissible once their own social assets were nibbled at, as they assumed mastery. Consequently, 'there has been a dialectical somersault. Yesterday's bandit hero has become today's villain, and yesterday's villainous representative of authority today's hero.'[1] While agreeing with Mandel's basic historical account, I argue that alongside its undeniable endorsement of the punishment of criminals, bourgeois culture, in both canonical and 'minor' texts, has been regularly expressing a distinct *exaltation* of crime. I am not thinking here about the irrefutable persistence of the 'social bandit' narrative, albeit, arguably, on the peripheries of the cultural scene; what I have in mind is the consolidation of this specific branch of artistic *endorsement of amorality*, this admiration, not of the 'goodness' of the bandit, but rather of his outright 'evil' side.[2]

In what follows, I wish to account for the strange phenomenon that it was precisely within the headquarters of bourgeois culture, its entrenched and elitist ideological hub, that crime was frequently elevated and revered. This 'glorification of crime' was precociously expressed in the pariah writings of the aristocratic Sade, received an updated formulation by the plebeian

213

Stirner and then attained canonization in the works of the neo-aristocratic Nietzsche. The latter, in my view, recuperated *for bourgeois purposes* the forbidden delights of sadism, which were formerly the exclusive delicacy of the 'decadent' nobility. The nineteenth-century groundwork of aesthetic indulgence in evil, integral to the radiant murk of the *fleurs-du-mal* poetic mood, was to be thoroughly exploited throughout the following century, serving as a continual source of inspiration. A hegemonic middle class defending its privileges against the 'criminal classes' did not adopt *an indiscriminate* denigration of crime; the bourgeois tactic in defense of private property was highly intricate, bearing the dialectical upshot that the (literary) criminal was often transformed into a *guardian angel of private property*. To clarify how the criminal could have come to fulfill such an improbable function, I will begin by an outline of the ideas of Max Stirner and Friedrich Nietzsche, who between them have amalgamated a solid compound of crime, individualism and capitalism. The broad implications and significance of this Stirnero-Nietzschean theoretical complex will be further explored in the subsequent analysis of a number of 'secondary texts' informed by a similar spirit of crime-glorification.

FROM STIRNER TO NIETZSCHE

From *Human, All Too Human* (1878) to his letter to Jacob Burckhardt dating from January 5, 1889, two days after his mental collapse, Nietzsche consistently defended the notion that aberrant behavior contains emancipating potential. He appreciated the criminal as a rebel against modern society and his deviant action as a burst of healthy instinct amidst the vapidity of Western morality. In such a stifling atmosphere, a flare of this kind was doomed to quick extinction, but it was nevertheless seized upon as a worthy guiding principle, indicating valuable cultural alternatives: 'The criminal type is the type of the strong human being under unfavourable conditions, a strong human being made sick.'[3] Nietzsche wished to mend the myopia of accepted opinion that has labeled the delinquent a corrupt, ill-formed individual. According to him, the criminal, far from being substantially depraved, is actually a representative of an admirable human brand. This was allegedly acknowledged by Dostoevsky, who 'found the Siberian convicts in whose midst he lived . . . to be carved out of about the best, hardest and most valuable timber growing anywhere on Russian soil.'[4] The similarity Nietzsche recognized between his ideas and those of the Russian novelist was in all probability more than just a sign of spiritual kinship between a couple of 'free spirits.' Both Dostoevsky and Nietzsche drew nourishment from the common root of Max Stirner's thought. The maverick young Hegelian exercised a strong influence upon Nietzsche personally[5] and the Russian intelligentsia generally. His philosophy, condensed in his central book *The Ego and Its Own*, while paving the main road later to be taken by Nietzsche, at the same time furnishes a more bluntly composed variant of the same motifs, in which the inextricable linkage between crime-glorification and a particular notion of individualism can be more readily discerned.

Operating within the atheistic and, professedly, materialistic domain of left-Hegelianism, Stirner discarded any truth or ethics that rely for their jus-tification on some external, objective source—be it God, the state, society, morality or humanity. In their place, he enthroned subjectivity, the indi-vidual's inner world, as the only legitimate reference of truths, values and morals: '*I* decide whether it is the *right thing* in *me*; there is no right *outside* me. If it is right for me, it is right.'[6] Perpetuating bombastic and hollow fixed-ideas of 'the holy'—such as justice, duty, morality, rights and laws—the whole purpose of the social organism is to enfeeble the 'unique one,' as Stirner dubbed his sovereign individual. Consequently, Stirner rejected the very notion of crime as a product of a normative system, which is bogus by definition, a ghostly, but enslaving, presence. Stirner—and Nietzsche fol-lowing in his wake—saw the criminal as resisting the moral system itself, rather than any particular defect it may have, not some *ethical-abuse*, but the *abuse of ethics*.

In Stirner's thinking, the social realities of the early- and mid-nineteenth century increasingly industrialized and market-oriented era were faithfully translated into the epistemology of 'the egoist.' The very constitutive affir-mation, underpinning the whole of Stirner's critique, his celebrated '*Ich*,' ought to be seen as a historically bounded concept. The 'discovery' of the ego as the true ontological element hitherto unrecognized, the barricading of the ego against the world, society and other individuals, was not what it pro-fessed to be: a valiant insurrection against all forms of actuality. It was rather a registration in thought, a gaining of cognitive awareness, of what was for some time already a social reality: the isolation of individuals vis-à-vis the market. In Fredric Jameson's words 'the fully constituted or centered bour-geois subject or monadic ego' was the outcome of 'the dissolution of the older organic or hierarchical social groups, the universal commodification of the labor-power of individuals and their confrontation as equivalent units within the framework of the market.'[7] Once Stirner had taken 'the fully cen-tered subject' as his working assumption, he could move on to deal with what belonged to it, with the ego's *Eigentum*: property. Significantly, what Stirner referred to as property did not include exclusively material assets, as he clearly considered the individual's will, knowledge, talents, emotions etc., as forming a vital part of his possessions. This he did less in demonstration of the spiritual nature of property, as in the confirmation of the *material, ob-jectified dimension of spirituality*. He infused those qualities which are usually considered spiritual, intimate and immeasurable, with material substance; in other words, he reified them. He argued that an individual grown fully conscious of his uniqueness perceives the world as his property and all that is in it as commodities, as things to be used and manipulated to promote his 'ownness.' Quite explicitly, he established commerce and transaction of commodities as the sole legitimate rule of egoistical interaction. Stirner, who was also a translator of Adam Smith, painted a picture of society as a huge market where love, charity, compassion or any other human feeling are bargained for and exchange ownership just like ordinary goods:

> But love is not a commandment, but, like each of my feelings, *my property. Acquire*, that is, purchase, my property, and then I will make it over to you. . . . [A]nd I fix the purchase price of my love quite at my pleasure.[8]

Following the same principle, if the sick and old wish to obtain the reward of continued existence, they must successfully market themselves, barter a decent commodity:

> [W]e may perhaps actually go so far as to pay even the cripples and the sick and old an appropriate price for not parting from us by hunger and want; for, if we . . . want them not to withdraw this life from us, we can mean to bring this to pass only by purchase.[9]

In this manner, his philosophy was both a reflection and an advocacy of the reified reality of commodity production and social atomization. The 'materialistic' terminology which Stirner promoted to replace the 'idealistic' world conceptions of the sacred, thus established the premises of market-society as the sole authentic foundation for human relations.[10] Stirner concomitantly discarded the idea of an egalitarian society, claiming socio-economic equality to be another sacred ghost among other spooky despots, all demanding the subjugation of the egoist. He anticipated Nietzsche in formulating an ardent emotional revolt on behalf of the individual against equality, which was denounced as enforcing mediocrity, competition being the only adequate remedy:

> Now am I, who am competent for much, perchance to have no advantage over the less competent? . . . Against competition there rises up the principle of ragamuffin society—*partition*. To be looked upon as a mere *part*, part of society, the individual cannot bear—because he is *more*. . . .[11]

In affirming that 'the individual cannot bear to be looked upon as a mere part,' Stirner tacitly repressed his own postulate that it is only the *concrete* individual, as opposed to its abstract counterpart, who may rightfully decide what he may, or may not, bear. Here lies the most significant single inconsistency of Stirner's thesis, which happens to affect its very sustaining pillar: unconditional individual autonomy. He could only displace 'the holy' by invoking a new spectral entity, no less dictatorial than its antecessors, the Moloch of egoism, inescapably a metaphysical substance, to which any 'conscious individual' is then compelled to pay homage.[12]

Nietzsche's position was in essential agreement with Stirner's 'egoistic' view and with its sociopolitical inferences. Nietzsche, too, held fast onto the individual as the immutable ontological unit, the final deterrent at the face of any attempts to transform reality: 'The individual is, in his future and in his past, a piece of fate, one law more, one necessity more for everything that is and everything that will be. To say to him "change yourself" means to demand that everything should change, even in the past.'[13] Individualism, of course, is often referred to as confirmation of Nietzsche's essential pledge to personal freedom and unhindered development. Yet Nietzsche is not a very dependable champion of individual autonomy. Suffice to recall Zarathustra's appeal to warriors:

> To rebel—that shows nobility in a slave. Let your nobility show itself in obeying! To a good warrior, 'thou shalt' sounds more agreeable than 'I will.' And everything that is dear to you, you should first have commanded to you.[14]

Such an explicit plea for submission would have been out of place in the context of Stirner's principled rejection of authority. Nietzsche apparently realized the potential hazards of individualism, even egoism, if they are to be allowed unreserved command of social proceedings, especially as they may come to thrive among the lower classes. Since his position was decidedly more aristocratic than Stirner's, he needed to revise his theoretical model lest it shall present some unforeseen challenge to hierarchy. Hence, he characteristically took a binary stance, embracing individualism as a resolute check contra egalitarian creeds, but peremptorily denying its claims when implying some form of social defiance, say, disobedience in the military. Echoing Stirner, he classified two forms of individualism: the first was the immature and socialistic one, exorcising the spooks of state and church only to usher in the Holy of the social contract. The second, fully ripe expression of individualism remained to be attained: it will be individualism as unfettered from the burdensome demands of equality and solidarity. According to Nietzsche, individualism is only a means, not an end in itself, merely the 'modest form of the will to power.' Nietzsche's ideal of individualism paradoxically veered towards a decisively collectivist destination, though not, of course, in an egalitarian direction but rather in a hierarchical one:

> Individualism is followed by the formation of groups and organs; related tendencies join together and become active as a power; between these centers of

power friction, war, mutual recognition of one another's forces, reciprocation, approaches, regulation of an exchange of services. Finally: order of rank [*Rangordnung*].[15]

Individualism, that is, naturally unfolds into a hierarchy, not of isolated individuals, but rather of *groups of individuals*, 'groups and organs' of similar strength, which assert themselves against other groups, other 'centers of power.' Certain individuals are consequently to render en masse services to other groupings of superior individuals, resulting in a *Rangordnung*, a network of social factions, into which individuals are compiled. This was, in other words, Nietzsche's exposition of how *classes* are formed and how they faithfully represent the proportional diffusion of the will to power throughout society.

THE INDIVIDUAL AS CRIMINAL

Set against this background of 'unique individualism' as corresponding to an endorsement of competition and the unmitigated rule of the market, the specificity and functionality of the Stirnero-Nietzschean approbation of crime begins to transpire. Stirner expanded the customary notion of crime, in fact impregnated it with a novel significance, so that the criminal was no longer an individual who breaks the law but rather the individual pure and simple, the embodied *essence of individualism/egoism*. Stirnerian crime should therefore be grasped not so much as an *action*, but as a *state of being*. To cite three brief examples:

> Alongside right goes wrong, alongside legality *crime*. What are *you*?—*You* are a —*criminal!*[16]

> The unbridled ego . . . is the never-ceasing criminal in the state. The man whom his boldness, his will, his inconsiderateness and fearlessness lead is surrounded with spies by the state, by the people. I say, by the people![17]

> You do not know that an ego who is his own cannot desist from being a criminal, that crime is his life.[18]

This vision of the criminal as the egoist who spiritedly resists social claims and shakes off every collective bonding, the criminal as the individual's proxy, was largely assimilated into Nietzsche's system: 'The "ego" subdues and kills: it operates like an organic cell: it is a robber and violent. It wants to regenerate itself—pregnancy. It wants to give birth to its god and see all mankind at his feet.'[19] Both philosophers directed much of their criticism at the specific moral code of the Judeo-Christian tradition, which they commonly regarded as the nadir of Western culture's decline.[20] It was within modern, brotherly society (if we are to believe this version of history), that the individual had to become a criminal, a victim of either 'the Holy,' according to Stirner, or of the repressed will to power, as asserted by Nietzsche:

> What [the criminal] lacks is the wilderness, a certain freer and more perilous nature and form of existence in which all that is attack and defence in the instinct of the strong human being *comes into its own*. His virtues have been excommunicated by society. . . . It is society, our tame, mediocre, gelded society, in which a human being raised in nature, who comes from the mountains or from adventures of the sea, necessarily degenerates into a criminal.[21]

This is Nietzsche's casting of Stirner's theme of the subjugated individual in the more romantic and nostalgic mould of his moral genealogy. Nietzsche portrayed the delinquent as a remnant of past and glorious times, such as the Roman age or the Renaissance, when acts of violence represented not 'evil' but the natural drive for expansion and self-assertion.[22] But distortedly perceived through a *moral lens*, the once normative was branded anomalous. Within Nietzsche's undertaking to complete the 'transvaluation of values,' the criminal was rewritten as a clandestine representative of the will to power and a useful agent of revolt. The special task entrusted to him was to serve as a role model of genuine individualism.

Importantly, however, neither Stirner nor Nietzsche acclaimed *just any crime*. As we saw, under 'crime' Stirner understood a subversive state of being (and of mind) more than an actual illicit deed; something similar occurred with Nietzsche. He clearly avoided indiscriminate embracing of transgression. Instead, he singled out some criminal aspects and downplayed others:

> Nothing is more common than that . . . [the criminal] should slander and dishonor his deed under the influence of fear and failure—quite apart from those cases in which, psychologically speaking, the criminal surrenders to an uncomprehended drive and by some subsidiary action ascribes a false motive to his deed, (perhaps by a robbery, when what he wanted was blood).[23]

And, in a very famous and important passage:

> Behold, the pale criminal has bowed his neck: from his eyes speaks the great contempt. 'My Ego is something that should be overcome: my Ego is to me the great contempt of man': that is what this eye says . . . Thus says the scarlet judge: 'Why did this criminal murder? He wanted to steal.' But I tell you: his soul wanted blood not booty: he thirsted for the joy of the knife! But his simple mind did not understand this madness and it persuaded him otherwise. 'What is the good of blood?' it said. 'Will you not at least commit a theft too?

Take a revenge?' And he hearkened to his simple mind: its words lay like lead upon him—then he robbed as he murdered.[24]

Nietzsche anatomized crime, disassociated its elements, wishing to extricate the precious core, the truly meaningful aspect of crime, from the savorless peel enclosing it. Significantly, his analysis accorded substantial significance solely to the pure urge to slay, to the killing instinct, whereas the material factor was discarded as 'false motive.' The criminal desires blood exclusively, adding a robbery to murder only to excuse this obsession. To understand crime, Nietzsche argued, undivided attention ought to be directed at the psyche, which alone contains its solipsistic enigma. Matter, by comparison, was deemed immaterial. Crime, certainly, is said to be *bodily* instigated: 'Behold this poor body! This poor soul interpreted to itself what this body suffered and desired—it interpreted it as lust for murder and greed for the joy of the knife.'[25] And is not Zarathustra the prophet of the body, the great avenger of the long despised *Leib*? '"I am body and soul"— so speak the child. And why should one not speak like children? But the awakened, the enlightened man says: I am body entirely, and nothing beside; and soul is only a word for something in the body.'[26] This rings wholly materialistic, but Zarathustra, in fact, is an extreme idealist. What he calls 'the body' is actually a receptacle of abstract passions, a mortal robe that the will to power has to get into, like a ghost that must possess a living body in order to roam about. What the 'body desires,' according to Zarathustra, is scarcely corporeal; it may want to expand, to conquer, to bathe in the elixir of power, but it will never want to steal, so that it can appease its stomach or cover itself in warm clothes. It may *seem* to do just that, but this would be only a false rendition by the Christian mind, that cannot come to terms with the body's 'joy of the knife.' The body, from Nietzsche's perspective, seems less thirsty than *blood*-thirsty.

THE DISEMBODIED CRIMINAL

In this fashion, the scope of our object of inquiry, of Stirnero-Nietzschean crime, is tacitly, but dramatically, reduced. By definition, it must now exclude the huge majority of crimes in the course of which no blood at all is spilled, the knife, if at all employed, only facilitating the appropriation of money and goods. Nietzsche—without expressly disavowing such felons who do not exhibit any 'joy of the knife' as the pickpocket, the counterfeiter, the blackmailer, the smuggler, the peculator, or the unarmed thief—de facto restricted his interest to those cases displaying most vividly the requisite predilection for blood-thirst over avarice. In the dreary meadows of crime he treaded lightly, bending to pick only those roses fragrant enough to adorn the vest of the philosophical rebel in search of transgressive finesse. Closest to this model of crime as instinctually instigated are so-called 'crimes of passion,' which appear genuinely devoid of any material substance and, by contrast, are lavishly fertile with psychological, instinctual and symbolical potentialities. Sanction was granted principally to what might be called *Dionysian crime*, a pure, non-material urge. It is understandable why Nietzsche's pale criminal must ultimately have been the trespasser of the supreme taboo—the murderer. This was also confirmed by the philosopher's keen interest in the real homicide cases of Prado and Chambige, two murderers of women, the first a 'cynical adventurer' the second a 'decadent intellectual.'[27]

In this context, the category of 'material motivation' should encompass not merely hunger or poverty but everything that is *externally and socially triggered*, that is imposed upon the criminal, directly or indirectly, by social conditions. By contrast, the will to power, the underlying substance of Dionysian crime, is by definition immanent; it must be its own cause, a rudimentary, blind, spontaneous force, which propels any living organism necessarily *from within*. This basic attribute of the will to power bears ideological implications of utmost significance: any other interpretation, which deprives the will to power of its ontological status, perforce also denies the ontological necessity of struggle, competition and exploitation, which are no longer to be conceived as natural and inevitable but rather as perfectly historical and social. To be properly driven by the will to power means to transcend society's influence, just as to yield to society means to fail in the expression of a pure will to power. Hence, the category of material motivation must now expand to include such externally, socially bounded *psychological motives* as the ambition to climb up the hierarchical ladder; most notably, material motivation must include *ressentiment*, the surest symptom of an adulterated will to power.

Nietzsche's view of the superior criminal might be said to coincide with the predominant meritocratic ethos of the bourgeoisie, in the sense that entry into the upper echelons of crime was technically open to plebeians of merit. As Nietzsche put it, 'one should not hold against the criminal his bad manners or the low level of his intelligence.'[28] Crucially, however, the determination of what 'merit' actually means remains a strictly genteel affair. The 'vulgar' criminal ought to raise himself, as it were, to meet the demands of the elite. If he is to be granted admittance by his eminent colleagues, he must prove his immunity to 'external' influence, superseding all material motivation for crime by a properly psychological and instinctual drive. For that reason, a genuinely plebeian Dionysian criminal is ultimately an inherent impossibility, a fact that should be kept in mind as we shall shortly deal with Nietzschean criminals of literature and film. This aspect was likewise directly homologous to Stirner's position as regards the sanctity of property. Stirner indeed zealously negated right and sanctity as such, hence considering one's 'legitimate' property to be just what he is capable of appropriating, by *might* rather than *right*: 'Take hold, and take what you require! With this the war of all against all is declared. I alone decide what I will have.'[29] And yet, Stirner proposed to distinguish between the fake, 'ordinary criminal' and the genuine, 'egoistic' one. The difference between the two consisted in the commendable *abstinence* of the egoistic criminal who, in contrast to his ordinary, undeserving counterpart, shows himself quite *apathetic* in the face of worldly temptations:

> What is the ordinary criminal but one who has committed the fatal mistake of endeavoring after what is the people's instead of seeking for what is his? He has sought despicable *alien* goods. . . . Talk with the so-called criminal as with an egoist, and he will be ashamed, not that he transgressed against your laws and goods, but that he considered your laws worth evading, your goods worth desiring.[30]

So far, I have tried to establish the non-material dimension of the Stirnero-Nietzschean concept of crime. Yet this should not be taken to mean that their outlook corresponded to a curious need to flee to some escapist realm of idealized, imaginary, lofty crime. In truth, far from neutralizing the social dimension, the insistence upon crime being of extra-social and material origin is itself a *social statement* of great importance. Although the act of crime, the violent deed as such, emerges independently of social conditions, registering the incessant subterranean vibrations of the timeless will to power and expressing the perennial joy of the knife, it is up to society to assign meaning to this act in agreement with its historically developed ethics. Society may enter the picture only at the hermeneutic level, but this does not withhold its creative—or, in modern times, *destructive*—power, to encroach upon crime, to carve its eventual contours by the very act of interpretation. Hence, without producing delinquency, social forces certainly do fashion a certain *type of criminal*:

> Let us generalize the case of the criminal: let us think of natures which, for whatever reason, lack public approval. . . . The colour of the subterranean is on the thoughts and actions of such natures; everything in them becomes paler than in those upon whose existence the light of day reposes.[31]

From a Nietzschean point of view, there is therefore a sense in which one *can* speak of historically dependent crime, of a special sort and manifestation of transgression which is particularly modern. This is *underground crime*, the one practiced in secret because it lacks the normative approval to lift its head in broad daylight. What Nietzsche strove for was to change precisely this skewed normative system so that crime will no longer be consid-

ered depraved, so that what we condemn as 'crime' will come to be understood as a manifestation of meritorious strength and legitimate joy. There is
no good reason to believe that Nietzsche genuinely yearned for a burst of
instinctual violence, an actual unsupervised surge of individual will to
power; the criminal was for him at essence a metaphor, a propitious harbinger, but dispensable once the good tidings have been conveyed. What
counted, notwithstanding Nietzsche's occasional admiration of real criminals, was the *message embodied* in the criminal, not the *body of the messenger*.
The presence of the actual, physical perpetrator might even upset the neat-
ness of this idealized construction, of crime as a discarnate, metaphysical
protest. That Nietzsche's concern for this 'hero' was limited to his higher
role becomes clear once we consider his quite ruthless verdict as regards the
felon's earthly fate:

> One should not deprive the criminal of the possibility of making his peace
> with society; provided he does not belong to the race of criminals. In that case
> one should make war on him even before he has committed any hostile act
> (first operation as soon as one has him in one's power: his castration).[32]

Since Nietzsche construed genuine crime as thoroughly different from
the dwarfed delinquency of his times, *the times needed to change* in order for
'big crime' to be reinstated. Once society, culture, morality and politics
transform themselves, the criminal, at present dealing with obscure, covert
enterprises, will rise again to the level of Renaissance crime, the warlike, illustrious feat of the past. Herein lies the core of the matter as an ideological means and the whole point of adopting the criminal as an unruly hero;
Nietzsche's underlying goal was, through a heretical rendering of crime, to
give birth to a new social ethos, in radical opposition to the relentless
drift—or so he believed—towards the nihilistic, leveling creeds of modernity. Once such a hero is instituted, a new order will have to arise in order
to accommodate him, an order evolving around aggression, competition
and exploitation, postulating the unobstructed dominance of 'the strong'
over 'the weak':

> *To restore a good conscience to the evil man*—has this been my unconscious en-
> deavor? I mean, to the evil man in so far as he is the *strong* man? (Dostoevsky's
> judgment on the criminals in prison should be cited here).[33]

Like nineteenth-century humanist reformers Nietzsche condemned society and sympathized with the criminal. Yet he did so from a diametrically
opposed vantage point. In his view, the proliferation of crime does not reflect some injustice in distribution of wealth, fierce competition, generalized materialism and greed, degraded living standards, etc. The Dionysian
criminal reversed such objections to the capitalist system. The modern

criminal is rather a product of nihilism, democracy and proto-socialism, since even the restricted welfare measures under Bismarck were seen by Nietzsche as a concession to the masses, leading to the triumph of the herd. The universal uniformity imposed by mass society prevented the strong individual from satiating his lust for blood. Whereas the humanists typically sympathized with the plight of the criminal as underdog, Nietzsche prized the protest of the potential, shackled overman:

> *Crime* belongs to the concept 'revolt against the social order' . . . there is nothing contemptible in revolt as such—and to be a rebel in view of contemporary society does not in itself lower the value of a man. There are even cases in which one might have to honor a rebel, because he finds something in our society against which war ought to be waged—he awakens us from our slumber.[34]

Crime is hence a cultural revolt against spiritual stultification, not material injustice: 'The rascal has this advantage over many other men, that he is not mediocre.'[35] Unlike the typical conservative clamoring for law and order, Nietzsche did not negatively and defensively deny the need for social reforms; far more ingeniously and 'positively' he went on the offensive and used the metaphor of the Dionysian criminal to promote a neo-aristocratic social critique and advocate social reforms which will enhance human *inequality*. If crime is material and social, then an improvement in social conditions may abolish or restrict the need for crime, hence reducing crime itself. But if the need that crime satisfies is construed as the lust for blood, then no such change in social conditions, as Nietzsche repeatedly emphasized, may abolish crime, *least of all* a construction of a fraternal society outlawing and inhibiting man's natural aggressions; on the contrary, such a society is only bound to *foster* crime. Nietzsche takes distance from the socialist-humanist approach to crime: he attacks the man who 'will not be responsible for anything, to blame for anything, and out of an inner self-contempt wants to be able to *shift-off* his responsibility for himself somewhere else. This latter, when he writes books, tends today to espouse the cause of the criminal; his most pleading disguise is that of socialist sympathy.'[36] It is clear that Nietzsche's own partiality for the criminal has nothing to do with such '*religion de la souffrance humaine*.' The socialist's sympathy is *moral*, Nietzsche's is *aesthetic*. He seems to have Victor Hugo foremost in mind as a writer of that kind, with his ordinary criminal, Jean Valjean, stealing a loaf of bread to relieve his hunger. Yet the same would apply for Dickens, who had Magwitch exclaim: 'they measured my head, some on 'em—they had better a measured my stomach.'[37] This, for Nietzsche, would have been beside the point. Though not an outright advocate of phrenology—the criminologist pseudo-science of skull measuring—Nietzsche took what criminologists refer to as the 'positivist approach to crime,' namely a theory which conceives of crime as separate from politics and society, rooted in some purely individual attribute, whether genetic or psychological.[38] In his vision of the criminal as a suppressed genius, in his notion of crime as an inner drive, Nietzsche was ultimately a Lombrosian of sorts, a phrenologist of the psyche, as it were.

Stirner and Nietzsche may be considered the *bêtes noires* of the bourgeoisie inasmuch as they ostentatiously dismissed the dread of 'psychopathic crimes' like murder (if we choose to disregard Nietzsche's utterances in support of the most typically conservative penal severity). Psychopathic offences, however, and homicide of any sort, is an aberrance in the overall balance of crime statistics, each murder case eclipsed—quantitatively speaking—by several thousand thefts. The substantial, enduring, 'existential' apprehension on part of the bourgeoisie is to crimes against property, but such, as we have seen, did barely exist from Stirner and Nietzsche's point of view. Above all else, what the bourgeoisie apprehended was one crime in particular, *the socialistic scheme*, which aims not at concrete property, which can be insured, but at the pillars of private property as a social institution. Socialism was plotting to pull off the most extravagant heist in history, putting to shame every past effort from the ordinary criminal—not to mention the Dionysian one. Yet even the ordinary, petty criminal, can be seen as posing an existential threat to bourgeois society. As Vautrin, Balzac's Machiavellian hero, instructs his would-be-protégé about the class basis for the distinction between 'big' and 'petty' crime and the need for the ruthless prosecution of the *latter*:

> The enemies of social order . . . yelp at justice and, in the name of the people, get angry because a burglar or a chicken-stealer in an inhabited area is sent to the gallows, whereas a man who ruins whole families by fraudulent bankruptcy gets off with a few months imprisonment at the worst. But these hypocrites know full well that by sentencing the burglar the judges are upholding the barriers between rich and poor. If these were overthrown social order would come to an end. Whereas the bankrupt . . . is merely an instrument by which fortune changes hands.
> Thus, my son, society is forced, for its own sake, to make distinctions . . .[39]

In that regard, the Stirnero-Nietzschean selective glorification of crime contained a massively lucrative recompense for any potential annoyance it might occasion, as it engendered a vision that ultimately justifies bourgeois domination and endorses its perpetuation. By transforming the criminal into an existential rebel, he ceased to trespass the barriers separating the rich from the poor and became a fighter, not against society as such, but against *mass* society. Hence, however unlikely it may have appeared at first glance, the criminal was truly transformed from a perpetrator upon the rights of private property to their very devoted sentinel, like a police agent working undercover.

VAUTRIN AS A BYRONIC CRIMINAL

Yet was not Vautrin himself not just a 'disciple of Machiavelli'[40] but a proto-Nietzschean character as well? It was Gramsci who once suggested that in Balzac's work, along with that of Alexandre Dumas, one can discover 'the popular origin of the "superman."'[41] And few characters in the *Comédie humaine* appear closer to the overman than Vautrin, the genius of the Parisian underworld. And if not of the overman downright, he is surely an anticipation of the Dionysian criminal, resisting humanity's mediocrity. A first examination will readily reveal many similarities between Balzac's hero and Nietzsche's ideal, from the physical grandeur—Vautrin's 'Cyclopean power'[42]—to the more substantial, moral aspects, such as the comparisons with Napoleon,[43] Vautrin's avowed atheism,[44] his critique of 'men in the herd,'[45] and, finally, the avowal that 'I myself love power for power's sake!'[46] The kinship is certainly there. 'Culturally,' as Gramsci put it, 'the real nexus seems incontrovertible'; a lineage stretches to Nietzsche's criminal which is not to be overlooked. Equally incontestable, however, should be the changes that have taken place along the way, Nietzsche's far-reaching transubstantiation of the original model, if so it could be termed, to the point where only surface resemblances remain, covering a strikingly different content. In Balzac, to start with, the last thing we have is a Nietzschean clash between a moralistically petrified society and the supreme individual becoming a criminal to break the stalemate. For the French novelist, the path to crime follows the very opposite direction. The usual pattern he depicts is that of innocent, provincial youths such as Eugene Rastignac and Lucien Chardon de Rubempré, who are *initiated* into *social depravity*. Vautrin's role is typically that of the sage mentor who lifts the veils from these youths' eyes, teaching them the ways of society. Whereas Zarathustra professes to lead us *away from and beyond* contemporary society into the realization of a higher aim, Vautrin is our guide *into* society. Nowhere is this more apparent than near the end of *Lost Illusions*, in the prolonged conversation between Vautrin, disguised as a Spanish priest, and the desperate Lucien, on the verge of suicide:

> 'You horrify me, father!' said Lucien. 'This sounds to me like a code for highwaymen.'
> 'You're right,' said the Canon, 'but it's not of my invention . . . When you sit down to a game of *bouillotte*, do you argue about the rules? They exist, you accept them. . . . What would you say to a player who was generous enough to inform the others that he held four aces? . . . "Monsieur, you should never play *bouillotte*." Is it you who make the rules in the ambition-game? . . . '[47]

Vautrin instructs his naïve apprentice how to play according to the devious rules society dictates. For both Balzac and Nietzsche contemporary society compels the individual to become a criminal; yet in Nietzsche, crime means daring to defy society's benevolence; in Balzac, it is daring to equal its corruption: '"Why did I tell you to measure-up to society? Because in these days, young man, society has gradually arrogated to itself so many rights over the individual that the individual finds himself obliged to fight back against society."'[48] In this 'égaler à la Société' is epitomized the true gulf that separates Balzacian amorality from its Nietzschean 'offspring.' Balzac, if anything, had documented the way society *has given birth* to Nietzscheanism, and as a legitimate child rather than an unwanted bastard. The market society ushered in under bourgeois rule enforced the beyond-good-and-evil position which Nietzsche will herald as a radical overcoming of the present. The abolition of Judeo-Christian morality, the transvaluation of values which Nietzsche would passionately advocate more than a generation after Balzac is, in the post-revolutionary France of the *Comédie*, a living —and squalid—reality, not a noble vision of regeneration. 'Present-day society,' Vautrin observes, 'no longer worships the true God, but the Golden Calf!'[49] Elsewhere, the narrator reflects on the generalized amorality of market-society: 'The Charter has proclaimed the reign of money, success justifies all in an atheistical age.'[50] This historical vantage point allows us to perceive, once again, the fundamentally apologetic function of Nietzsche's teachings, which have urged modern man to support an allegedly world-shattering project which was in truth, for some time already, a *fait accompli*.

Indeed, for all his cynicism, Vautrin, like his creator, is not truly complicit with the wild *bouillotte* of nascent capitalism. This, though already sensed in *Le Père Goriot* and *Lost Illusions*, becomes perfectly clear in *Splendeurs et misères des courtisanes*, a novel in which Vautrin is the central hero. Closely behind the ruthless cynicism of his position hides a rebel, fighting and punishing the strong. He tells Esther, the harlot he uses to milk the capitalist Baron de Nucingen dry: 'Be sly, extravagant, pitiless with the millionaire I'm sending to you. Listen! . . . this man is a thief on the World Market, he's been without pity for a great many people, he's grown fat on the fortunes of widows and orphans, you will be their Revenge!'[51] Vautrin, 'this man of the people in revolt against authority,'[52] stands in relation to the Dionysian criminal in basically the same way that the Byronic hero relates to the Nietzschean hero, as discussed in Chapter 4. Vautrin's Byronism, for that matter, was explicitly established: 'The ignoble convict who yet embodied a poem shadowed forth by so many poets, by Moore, by Lord Byron, by Mathurin, by Canalis.'[53] And he takes pride, likewise, in being Rousseau's pupil, daring 'to raise his voice against the colossal fraud of the Social Contract.'[54] Furthermore, Balzac's authorial compassion is reserved throughout his novels for the victims of capitalism, not only for Esther or Lucien, but also for the still more helpless, aging and ill-adjusted figures such as Old Goriot or cousin Pons, precisely such 'weak and ill-constituted' individuals to whom Nietzsche will 'fatally' say: 'perish!'[55] Compare such posture with Balzac's: '*Death to the weak!* That is the watchword of what we might call the equestrian order established in every nation of the earth, for there is a wealthy class in every country, and that death sentence is deeply engraved on the heart of every nobleman or millionaire.'[56]

The most distinguishing trait of the Dionysian criminal, as we must finally observe, the non-materiality of his rebellion, is conspicuously absent in Vautrin. He is described, for example, as the 'representative of the interests of the empty belly, the bloody, swift protest of hunger!'[57] For Balzac, namely, it is not the thirst for blood which produces crime, as Nietzsche will argue; it is plain hunger, rather, that produces bloodshed. The entire social conflict Vautrin embodies is articulated in terms of 'theft and property.'[58] The act of thieving, for Balzac, is basically an admirable one, a form 'of vital protest . . . of the *state of nature* against society.'[59] The thief is the utopian as a man of deeds, the social reformer turned activist:

> It is not in sophistical books that the thief calls property, heredity, the social safeguards, into question: he suppresses them sharply. For him, to steal is to enter into his own. . . . Modern reformers write wooly, long-drawn, nebulous treatises, or philanthropic novels; but the thief acts! He is clear as a fact, he is logical as a blow with the fist. And what style![60]

As if to counter in advance any notion of criminals stealing only to excuse their 'joy of the knife,' we are told that criminals are 'made cruel by the need to suppress witnesses, for they commit murder only to destroy proofs.'[61] Balzac also celebrates the remarkable inventiveness of underworld vernacular, preemptively gainsaying Nietzsche's insistence that only the masters assign value and are linguistically fertile: 'At least a hundred words of slang belong to the language of Panurge, who, in the work of Rabelais, symbolizes the people, for his name is made up of two Greek words meaning: He who does all.'[62] And so, in a slight modification of Gramsci's helpful suggestion, we may say that, to the extent that the origins of the overman may indeed be tracked backwards to Balzac, it is because the *Comédie* at the same time powerfully suggests—in its description of a society *de facto* busily immersed in a transvaluation of all values—the *capitalist origins* of *Nietzscheanism*.

PRISON AS HAVEN

In her 1996 book, Martha Grace Duncan proposes an explanation to what she describes as 'A Strange Liking: Our Admiration for Criminals.'[63] If *we*— all of us—admire criminals, this has little to do with social reasons but because the criminal serves us to confront our existential orphanhood: 'we . . . use criminals and prisons to exalt our lives, to comfort ourselves in the face of our finitude, to defend against despair.'[64] This is something that criminals are able to do essentially on account of their beyond-good-and-evil status: 'Because they ignore the limits and moral compunctions that bind ordinary people, they are easily assimilated into the category of greatness.'[65] *We* might tell ourselves, by way of 'rationalization,' that the criminal, in life or fiction, appeals to us because he champions a worthy or noble cause, such as 'justice' or 'freedom.' Yet in truth, these are only superficial reasons, covering up a much more basic, psychological yearning. This yearning can only be addressed by applying a properly psychoanalytic and existentialist critical apparatus rather than a sociological one. Though never quite as blunt as Nietzsche was in his repudiation of the tepidity of mass society, for Duncan, as well, the fascination with crime reflects 'a desire to escape from the mundane world-as-it-is into a nobler and more meaningful time and place.'[66]

Without by any means dismissing the potential of psychoanalysis to shed light on criminals and what they signify, I maintain that it can never completely replace an analysis of objective social conditions. For whatever 'greatness' one ascribes to criminals cannot be separated from the way *one*, rather than *we*, perceives the social role of the criminal. One's social condition is bound to condition one's admiration (or dislike) of a given criminal, again, whether real of fictional. For example, it is unlikely that, from a bourgeois perspective, a given criminal will be appreciated in the same way as from a working-class standpoint. He may appall the former while inspiring the latter and vice versa. Whether the criminal emerges as a hero or as a villain is thus inextricable from the perspective from which he is being evaluated, one which is seldom, if ever, a merely human perspective, in the abstract, and usually class- and gender-bound. Take, for instance, the way Charles Bukowski, in his semi-biographical novel *Ham on Rye*, describes the way people in a blue-collar Los Angeles neighborhood at the time of the Great Depression, related to criminals such as Dillinger:

> 5th grade became 6th grade and I began to think about running away from home but I decided that if most of our fathers couldn't get jobs how the hell could a guy under five feet tall get one? John Dillinger was everybody's hero, adults and kids alike. He took the money from the banks.[67]

Yet obviously, not 'everybody' in America at the time, no imagined collective 'we,' was as disposed as Henri Chinaski's (Bukowski's alter-ego) neighbors to cheer on Dillinger's 'greatness' (compare this heroization with the FBI bulletins demonizing Dillinger in the name of decency[68]). By the same token, the Dionysian criminal, targeting mass society and democracy, is liable to have a greater appeal among those feeling ill at ease in democracy, oppressed by the purported power of the masses, while those identifying with the masses may find him either a curiosity or a threat. Certainly, I do not believe that 'our' response to criminals will always, or even normally, lend itself to a neat classification along class lines. Yet I *do* hold that any focus on the unconscious is bound to lead to gross abstractions, which fails to consider the *political* unconscious. In Duncan's book there is one particularly symptomatic example of such abstractions. She reports on a interview conducted with one James Garvey Jr., a warden in a New York penitentiary, in which she requested him to elaborate on his statement in the *New York Times* that people 'have to come back to jail to regain their self-respect.' Obviously, Duncan contacted Garvey hoping to garner some support for her thesis that prison can become a place of spiritual healing. The warden, however, apparently expecting the run-of-the-mill social worker rather than an existentialist cultural theorist, answered in a way which put decisive stress not on some metaphysical quest on part of the prisoners, but rather on quite concrete social and material conditions:

> In prison, he observed, the correctional personnel *must* listen to the prisoner. They must make sure the prisoners get their special diet. . . . The prisoners have a right to a job. . . . If a woman has a cold, she has the right to go to a doctor. . . . Thus, when they leave prison, the women are clean, they have money, they weigh more. Once they hit the streets, they begin selling themselves and they are treated with disrespect by everyone. . . . The warden then remarked: '*The confusion is that jail to them is freedom and society is the jail. They can't operate in society because society has turned its back on them.*'[69]

Now surely, what greater indictment could there be of a society in which, for some people, regular meals, a safe job, dependable medical services, clean clothing as well as a minimal sense of communal belonging and individual value, are to be found in jail, whereas outside the prison walls are only deprivation and alienation? For Duncan, however, the lesson to be learnt from this interview is quite different: 'The point here, of course, is not the objective veracity of Warden Garvey's description, but rather the way he *imagines* the offender and the prison experience.'[70] She concludes this part of her discussion by asserting that 'my analysis . . . demonstrates that there are individuals . . . whose newly acquired serenity and happiness is conditional on their remaining in prison.'[71] Far from being an occasion for pondering the need for some social reforms which will make society, for poor people, at least half as habitable as jail, her interview leads Duncan to practically recommend life-imprisonment for certain, abstract, 'individuals.' This is a fine example of the pitfalls awaiting those who are willing to abstract crime from its objective social context, at the same time that it illustrates the essential compatibility, if not outright utility, of such purified crime-conception with the requirements of the powers that be.

THRILL VERSUS SELF-PRESERVATION

Now that we have familiarized ourselves with the Dionysian criminal and possess a better understanding of his quest, let us accompany him through some of his most remarkable escapades in the last century, in the realms of both literature and film. As a preamble, I suggest to examine one famous incident in which Nietzsche's philosophy and real life interpenetrated, the theory, as it were, brought into practice. I am referring to this notorious homicide case in which two well-to-do youths, Richard Loeb (age 18) and Nathan Leopold (19) (L/L), were sentenced for life for the murder of their younger peer, Robert Franks (14) in 1924 Chicago. Leopold was a keen reader of Nietzsche, 'encouraged' by him to violate the injunctions of herd morality. Throughout the years, this case has inspired several plays and films, notable among them Hitchcock's *Rope* (1948). Here, however, I wish to consider not any literary narrative—at least not in the strict sense of the term—but the trial's very protocol.

From our vantage point, the most outstanding aspect in the L/L trial is the surprising common front assumed by defender and prosecutor alike as regards the premises of the Nietzschean discourse. Like enthusiast readers of Nietzsche—which Clarence Darrow, the celebrated American lawyer acting as the boys' defender, actually was—they jointly presumed that crime committed for material benefit is completely inexcusable, whereas Dionysian crime, a product of sheer passion or mania, might be somewhat tolerated. Accordingly, Darrow's successful defensive strategy in impeding capital punishment consisted substantially in attempting to show that money was not the motive for the murder; correspondingly, Robert Crowe, the state's attorney, insisted that money most certainly *was* the motive. Darrow, first:

> The state itself in opening this case said that it was largely for experience and for a thrill, which it was. In the end the state switched it on to the foolish reason of getting cash. Every fact in this case shows that cash had almost nothing to do with it, except as a factor in the perfect crime; and to commit the perfect crime there must be a kidnapping, and a kidnapping where they could get money, and that was all there was of it.[72]

And the prosecutor:

> Money is the motive in this case . . . All through this case is money, money, money—blood . . . 'In March, 1924, the patient conceived the idea of securing' —What? Thrill? The excitement? No. 'Conceived the idea of securing the money by having it thrown off of a moving train.' . . . I used to think that the most impelling motive in life was passion, but in this case passion and a desire for revenge is swept aside for money. Money is the controlling motive in this case.

Darrow emulated Nietzsche in striving to prove—what in this particular case was probably true—that the robbery was merely a relation of 'a false motivation to the act' whereas the real allurement was the intoxicating scent of blood. Nietzsche, moreover, once claimed that 'A criminal's lawyers are seldom artists enough to turn the beautiful terribleness of the deed to the advantage of him who did it.'[73] Darrow's line of defense, however, seems to reflect precisely such an artistic stratagem:

> Babe [Leopold] . . . is a boy of remarkable mind—away beyond his years . . . He became enamoured of the philosophy of Nietzsche. Your Honor, I have read almost everything that Nietzsche ever wrote. He was a man of a wonderful intellect; the most original philosopher of the last century. . . . In a way he has reached more people, and still he has been a philosopher of what we might call the intellectual cult. . . . At seventeen, at sixteen, at eighteen, while healthy boys were playing baseball or working on the farm, or doing odd jobs, he was reading Nietzsche, a boy who never should have seen it, at that early age.

Leopold's philosophizing, for all its disastrous consequences, was used to prove his actual saliency. He sinned out of eminence, not pettiness, collapsing under a mighty weight of intellectual rumination which he was too immature to sustain. His effort therefore remains somehow noble, worthy of admiration; he has read philosophy while other, lesser youths, 'healthy' but mediocre, were 'doing odd jobs.' The class basis of the conflict between vile material crime and Dionysian crime was strongly stated by Darrow in more than a single occasion. Continuing his discourse, he pushed the odd class-logic of the trial to its limits, construing L/L as nothing less than victims of society for *no other reason* than their eminent social status:

> If we fail in this defense it will not be for lack of money. It will be on account of money. . . . There are times when poverty is fortunate. . . . We are here with the lives of two boys imperiled, with the public aroused. For what? Because, unfortunately, the parents have money. Nothing else.

The prosecutor, in turn, struggled to dismiss the notion that the deed might have been Dionysian one, agreeing with Darrow that this would, in fact, constitute an excuse for it:

> Was this killing done, as we have been led to believe, by the defense, merely for the thrill, Your Honor, or the excitement? . . . The original crime was the kidnapping for money. The killing was an afterthought, to prevent their identification and their subsequent apprehension and punishment. He said he did not anticipate the killing with any pleasure. It was merely necessary in order to get the money. . . . That is the motive for the murder: self-preservation; the same as a thief at night in your house, when suddenly surprised, shoots to kill.

Remarkably, not in some gathering of sadist libertines, but in an American court of law and by a conservative state's attorney, L/L were actually rebuked for 'not anticipating the killing with any pleasure' while for his part, the defender insisted that they most certainly *did*! Much like Zarathustra who argued, wanting to *exculpate* the 'pale criminal,' that his theft was merely a pretext for killing, so did the state's attorney, in trying to *inculpate* L/L, claim that their killing was merely an 'afterthought,' an attempt to disguise the theft. My point in all this is not to somehow reassess the actual murder and the motive behind it; the protocol is rather a valuable piece of evidence as a historical testimony, hinting at the deep correspondence of the Nietzschean view with mainstream bourgeois values. Zarathustra's speech seemed to have echoed in the courtroom as some divine affirmation, obeyed by the tuneful duet of prosecutor and defender. To 'kill for thrill, for excitement,' may not be commendable, but to kill in 'self-preservation' like 'a thief at night' is utterly indefensible. It might be argued, of course, that both Darrow and Crowe were not earnestly holding to any philosophical, moral or social theory, that it was for them simply a matter of proving or disproving the possibility of insanity as a mitigating circumstance. Then again, it is precisely this moral convention inscribed in criminal law, this acceptance of insanity and uncontrollable passion as mitigating circumstances, which emerges in a new, questionable light. From this angle, it appears that 'insanity' is considerably less threatening as far as the dominant classes are concerned than 'sanity'; inasmuch as the 'sane' criminal is able to see through the arbitrariness of the hegemonic social arrangement and act upon it, sanity involves a threat to private property; we come again to Balzac's point that the thief 'calls property, heredity, the social safeguards, into question: he suppresses them sharply'; by comparison, it is precisely of such a dangerous unveiling that insanity and abstract passion, for all their excesses, are quite incapable.

M: DISTINCTION IN OBSESSION

The next example of Dionysian crime which I would like to address is *M* (1931), one of the earliest and most influential instances of the serial-killer film.[74] Fritz Lang's hypothesis, stated for instance in his essay 'Why I am Interested in Murder,' was that murder pertains to human nature, a repressed desire built into the psyche: 'Gradually, and at times reluctantly, I have come to the conclusion that every human mind harbours a latent compulsion to murder.'[75] Universal though the virus might be, its carriers in Lang's films happen predominantly to be tormented and isolated bourgeois individuals. The social status of Hans Beckert, *M*'s obscure protagonist (played by Peter Lorre), is not specified, but his manners and lifestyle, elegant dressing and musical gusto—he famously whistles a distorted version of a theme from *Peer-Gynt*—are those of a typical bohemian. Having escaped from a mental asylum and apparently not holding any job, he can nonetheless afford spending his days roving the streets of Berlin in search of young girls whom he seduces, violates and slays. His 'carefree' existence is contrasted by the gloomy conditions in a working-class district, the dwelling of little Elsie Beckmann, the only victim with whom we are actually acquainted in the film.

The plot unfolds a singular showdown between the compulsive delinquent and his materially motivated counterparts, the members of the Berlin's underworld, from the big Mafiosi right down to the destitute beggars. As one organism, they, the 'ordinary criminals,' embark on a meticulously planned operation to capture 'the unique one,' the child murderer. Although their coalition is partly motivated by strictly professional considerations, as they are bothered by increasing police intervention in their affairs resulting from the incessant efforts to find the elusive murderer, they likewise rely on some basic moral consensus. As a female innkeeper declares, sharply drawing the line between legitimate crime, which is perpetrated to earn a living, and inadmissible, 'gratuitous' violence and cruelty: 'All my customers are furious about that bloke; especially the girls. They may be streetwalkers, *Geschäft ist Geschäft*, but every one of them shares a mother's feelings. And plenty of crooks go all soppy when they see kids playing.'[76] However, once the united herd has successfully hunted down the wolf, and Beckert faces a popular trial by his unauthorized captors, the narrative takes a remarkable twist. The abhorrent murderer and pervert turns into a miserable victim, abused by the fanatic, bloodthirsty mob. This final scene of the improvised underworld court in which Beckert, constantly interrupted by the roars and jeers of the crowd, delivers a memorable speech and unburdens himself of his obsession with murder, is not only the dramatic climax of the film but its ideological one as well. The spectator, who up to this point saw in Beckert only a rabid dog on the loose, is compelled to consider his view on things, in effect, to sympathize with him: 'Nevertheless, though civilization may have tamed us and curbed our destructive desires in the interests of society at large, there is enough in most of us of the wild, uninhibited creature to identify ourselves momentarily with the outlaw who defies society and exults in cruelty.'[77] Thus, Beckert is extraordinarily converted into Nietzsche's pale criminal, the authentic, atavistic individual. Inexorably, this newborn identification with the murderer comes accompanied by a nauseating terror of the infuriated mob, which, up to this point in the plot was not a 'mob' at all but a rather likeable party of responsible, conscientious citizens, albeit of dubious careers. In his ecstatic confessional outburst Beckert is not merely absolving himself, pleading 'guilty, but insane'; he is also affirming his *merit* vis-à-vis his captors:

What do you know? What right have *you* to speak? Who are you, anyway? Criminals. Maybe you're even proud of . . . safe-breaking, burglary, card-cheating. You needn't be any of those things, if you learnt a proper trade, if you worked, if you weren't such lazy swine. But I can't help myself! . . . I'm forced to do it. *Will nicht, MUSS! Will nicht, MUSS!* [Don't want to, must!]

Avowing a middle-class work ethic, the bohemian harangues the unemployed poor of the crisis years for idly shirking a decent job. Without tackling the evasive issue of whether or not we are all psychopaths at heart, it is safe enough to assert that *M* cannot be viewed as simply the plunging into the mysteries of human nature that it alleged to be. The film should be appreciated just as much as a social drama, whose final scene enacts, two years before the triumph of Nazism, the most dreaded scenario of the increasingly impoverished middle class: proletarianization. In front of such tragic descent, the last resort of the bourgeois remains the rusty old armature which, years before, the aristocrat had abortively employed to try and repel the bourgeois himself. Namely, the bourgeois appeals to his 'distinction,' sheds a driblet of his blue blood, to emphasize, in lack of any material evidence for his vanished prerogative, his refined *inner caliber*. A no less tense rendition of the same social nightmare was provided by another important film from the period, *Der Blaue Engel* (1930, directed by Joseph von Sternberg). In one of the film's final scenes the once respectable Professor Immanuel Rath is reduced to a pathetic buffoon in front of his native town's throng which congregate in the local theater to relish his degrading fall, bombarding him with rotten eggs. Here as well, the fall of the bourgeois has to do with forbidden instincts and desires. The Professor's fall is instigated by his unbecoming sexual obsession with a working-class femme fatale, the tantalizing cabaret performer played by Marlene Dietrich. It appears as if, in the absence of a concrete materialist perspective, proletarianization is displaced onto the psyche and explained as a catastrophic succumbing before one's urges. Both films evince the same deeply rooted fear—much exacerbated by the specific historical constellation of acute crisis—of losing all class privileges and being exposed to the gaze of the mass, this monster with a thousand eyes, all staring at the naked, mortified bourgeois.

INDIVIDUALISM AND THE SERIAL KILLER

In the last twenty odd years, Hollywood has shown a ubiquitous fascination with serial killers that has spawned countless films, both 'thrillers' and 'horror movies,' to the point where it is possible to speak of serial killer fiction as a subgenre, perhaps *the* subgenre, of the thriller. The serial killer narrative is inherently compatible with the Nietzschean agenda and particularly well suited for the elaboration of the theme of Dionysian crime fundamentally because, in both instances, society is displaced as an object of inquiry and of critique in favor of a focus on an allegedly unique individual. The serial killer is apt to be a Dionysian criminal since they both appear essentially 'motiveless,' and are conditioned psychologically, metaphysically and philosophically but seldom socially. Whereas the thief or robber, motivated by hunger or greed, can be just about anybody in the herd, the serial killer, by definition, transcends the herd condition. He is more likely than any other criminal to embody the Nietzschean idea of the individual as the ultimate social outsider.

This coupling of individualism and serial murder is readily manifest in the police practice, developed to try to pinpoint serial killers, known as 'profiling': the attempt to sketch a profile of the elusive murderer, the idiosyncrasies of his crimes, his personal 'signature' etc., which will finally enable the police to isolate him in the crowd. Whatever its real merit in actual criminal investigation, which some have seriously doubted,[78] profiling has become a constant in serial killer fiction, where the mystifying 'text' written by the monstrous killer is slowly deciphered by a visionary 'critic,' the detective drawing the profile. This very practice, of course, is predicated on the assumption that the murderer *is* in fact unique, operating in accordance to a distinct personality structure, an idiosyncratic perversion, which normal people, including ordinary criminals, lack. Obviously, there would be no point whatsoever in profiling a burglar, even assuming the police could afford to spare the time and resources needed for such purpose, since greed is a universal motive in our society which would lead to all of us as potential suspects, or, at most, to the numerous members of a social 'underclass' who are in greater material need than others, but never to a given individual. To catch a burglar, therefore, requires taking fingerprints or drawing an identikit, not browsing through psychiatric records. As Philip L. Simpson observes, in his thorough overview and fine analysis of the serial killer subgenre, it is not the *motive*—external, material, social—of the murderer which counts in the serial killer thriller but his—internal, spiritual, personal—*psyche*: 'In contrast to the traditional mystery, the victims . . . have little to no prior connection to their murderer. No motive, as the classic mystery defines it, exists here for the police to uncover in plodding, linear fashion.'[79]

The serial killer story is thus inherently a story of *an individual*, whether disturbed or inspired—or both. In fact, it habitually confronts an individualist on the side of law enforcement with his criminal counterpart. Hence the recurrent theme of an exceptional and visionary detective battling with an equally remarkable foe, in some respects worthy of admiration: 'serial killers are imitating the qualities of individual initiative and resourcefulness —qualities highly valued in American society—so they are never quite as

Other as might be supposed at first glance.'[80] This focus on individuality is harmonious with the Nietzschean emphasis on crime as an internally motivated act, a personal predicament or subversive virtue, as was already seen in the case of *M*. I wish now to examine some of the most notable examples of the serial killer in popular culture through the prism of the Dionysian criminal.

HANNIBAL LECTER: THE NIETZSCHEAN AS SADIST

The most complex and intriguing instance of Dionysian crime in popular culture is surely Dr Hannibal Lecter, the literary figure created by Thomas Harris and attaining immense celebrity through Jonathan Demme's film *The Silence of the Lambs*, a multiple Oscar winner in 1991. His essentially Nietzschean defiance against the leveling down of mass society has not gone unnoticed by scholars. For example, explicitly connecting Lecter with a Nietzschean aesthetics of evil, Thomas Hibbs has claimed that Lecter's 'willing of destruction, of annihilation, as an end in itself is a response to the attempt to eliminate inequality, distinction, and freedom from human life.'[81] And Philip Simpson, without ever explicitly mentioning Nietzsche, at times nevertheless discusses Lecter in terms unmistakably Nietzschean, as when stating that 'The will to power which Lecter embodies defines itself in relation to mastery of the herd.'[82] Beginning *The Silence of the Lambs* as a caged abomination, Lecter ends it as a finely dressed aristocrat on the beach of some Caribbean island, his superior intellect having subdued the docile forces of the law. Lecter is a kind of Anti-Christ, a reverse father figure, a shepherd who slaughters his silent lambs instead of safely guiding them through the valley of darkness. His escape from prison, following a finely orchestrated carnage, is crowned with a symbolic defying gesture at Christianity: one of the slaughtered policemen is crucified on the cell's lattice. His murderous drives consent to the blueprint of Dionysian crime, having no material grounding whatsoever. Lecter is a psychiatrist by occupation, and a typical aristocrat by culture, relishing classical music and exquisitely washing down a cannibalistic meal not with beer but with Chianti. The unfortunate victim's error is also revealing—he visited Lecter for the purposes of making a population census, fatally attempting to drag the *unique* shepherd down into the anonymity of herd society.[83]

At the same time, Lecter, the torturer and killer, is at least as much a Sadian figure as he is a Nietzschean one. Yet this should not, in reality, be seen as an eclectic agglomeration of distinct themes or discourses. At a deeper level, as I wish to argue, Lecter rather 'exposes' the sadism that underlies the Nietzschean perspective as such. By 'sadism' I here mean not simply wanton delight in inflicting pain—sadism, as it were, *in itself*; rather, I have in mind cruelty with a philosophical basis, sadism *for itself*, which goes back to the theories of the Marquis de Sade. In what follows, my discussion of sadism will rely mainly on Gilles Deleuze's insightful account of Sade and Sacher-Masoch in his 1967 long essay, *Coldness and Cruelty*. Let us now examine the sadism of Lecter in conjunction with his Nietzscheanism, and see what new light such practice can throw on his psychosocial mechanism.

To start with, Lecter typifies—whether Harris intended it or not—what Sade distinguished as the 'intelligent libertine' as opposed to the vulgar one. As Deleuze tells us, Sade drew an important distinction 'between two kinds of wickedness, the one dull-witted and commonplace, the other purified, self-conscious and because it is sensualized, "intelligent."'[84] What marks the intelligent libertine apart from his inferior counterpart is that his evil activities are undertaken with 'apathy,' complete self-control and majestic aloofness, whereas the vulgar libertine is dominated throughout by 'enthusiasm': 'This apathy does of course produce intense pleasure, but ultimately it is not the pleasure of an ego participating in secondary nature . . . , but on the contrary the pleasure of negating nature within the ego and outside the ego. . . . It is in short the pleasure of demonstrative reason.'[85] This distinction between 'apathy' and 'enthusiasm' strikes me as grasping precisely that which differentiates the 'intelligent' serial killer, Lecter, from such 'vulgar,' 'vile' and 'obnoxious' perverts such as Buffalo Bill (in *The Silence of the Lambs*) and Mason Verger (in *Hannibal*). Whereas the vile criminal is controlled by his pleasures, Lecter's ultimate pleasure *is* control. He is never dominated by passion, and exhibits at all times utter composure, detachment and, indeed, 'demonstrative reason.' Nowhere is this better manifested than in the scene from *Hannibal* (in both book and film version) where, at the dinner table, he surgically removes the scalp of one of his guests, and, while the victim is still alive and oblivious to the procedure—thanks to the effect of partial anesthesia—goes on to cut off slices of his brain. While doing this, Lecter is not drooling in perverse and ignoble pleasure, but rather, impeccably dressed, remains perfectly composed, softly and learnedly expounding to Clarice Starling, the FBI agent, on what he is doing. Lecter's penchant for classical music stands in a similar relation to Buffalo Bill's preference for rock-and-roll. To each his own: high culture to the intelligent libertine, mass culture to the vile one. Beside the fact that Lecter's refined taste raises him above the culture industry whereas Buffalo Bill is a typical product of mass culture, classicism in music also indicates Lecter's self-control, the apathy and coldness of his sadism, whereas the erratic and disorderly rhythms of rock-and-roll designate the unworthy enthusiasm of the transvestite Buffalo Bill. A further pattern in Lecter's classicism is equally telling: he favors the intricate eighteenth-century Baroque constructions of Forqueray, Bach or Scarlatti, characterized by order, restraint and devout grandeur, rather than the sensual and emotional outbursts of nineteenth-century romanticism, say of Beethoven, Berlioz or Wagner. Helping Clarice Starling to capture Buffalo Bill he hints at the latter's dominant passion: covetousness. Lecter, by contrast, is beyond base material appetites, immune both to bodily urges and to greed. In *Hannibal* he hangs Inspector Rinaldo Pazzi, an Italian policeman, above the Piazza di Firenze, for attempting to sell him into the hands of his enemies. Greed is punished as an example, but no more so than mediocrity: the materialistic cop is the descendant of the Pazzi family which has attempted a plot against the Medicis in fifteenth-century Florence. Once again, the chasm is emphasized which separates the vulgar and inferior mass man and the neo-renaissance man of genius, Lecter emerging as a modern Lorenzo de Medici.

The purpose of Lecter's evil, hence, is not the indulgence in forbidden delights for their own sake but rather the negation of conventional morality and, in fact, of conventional humanity. The goal of his criminal undertaking is to elevate him beyond the sphere of the human-all-too-human into a higher form of existence. Importantly, the striving for ultimate mastery, for omnipotence, must also encompass *self*-mastery. This means that Lecter is not afraid of enduring excruciating pain and in fact pursues such tests of character in order to prove his over-humanity. Thus, as if in defiance of the most horrible of retributions, he lets himself be captured by his archenemy and former victim, Mason Verger, in *Hannibal*. This provides us with another unmistakable sign of intelligent sadism: as Deleuze pointed out, in contrast to the masochist, who seeks pain as a form of humiliation, expiation, and renouncement of the authority identified with the father-figure, the sadist is willing to go though torture to prove his mastery. Understood thus, far from signifying a concession of power, the act of surrendering oneself to torture is power's unsurpassable token. [86] Deleuze resists the popular misconception according to which the sadist enjoys inflicting pain while the masochist enjoys being hurt. This, he maintains, misses and distorts the real antinomy, which consists, rather, in the fact that the sadist enjoys *mastery* while the masochist enjoys *submission*. Consequently, to the extent that the act of enduring pain is construed as affirming mastery, the enlightened sadist will welcome it:

> [T]he 'masochism' of the sadistic hero makes its appearance at the outcome of his sadistic experiences; it is their climax, the crowning sanction of their glorious infamy. The libertine is not afraid of being treated in the way he treats others. The pain he suffers is an ultimate pleasure, not because it satisfies a need to expiate or a feeling of guilt, but because it confirms him in his inalienable power and gives him a supreme certitude.[87]

The parallels with Nietzscheanism should by now be obvious; the goal of the sadist, 'inalienable power,' reveals itself as strikingly similar to the goal of the Nietzschean. Sexuality and pleasure are here only means to an end.

This puts in a new light the pervasive Nietzschean insistence on the indispensability of pain, on the need, on part of an individual aspiring to transcend the general human condition, both to inflict as well as to endure suffering. Overt sadistic themes in Nietzsche are abundant, and what immediately springs to mind in that respect is of course the famous advice from *Thus Spoke Zarathustra*: 'Are you visiting women? Do not forget your whip!'[88] Yet there is more to this than just misogyny à la Schopenhauer. Rather, control of the woman is a sign of the natural master, a confirmation of his authority. Sexuality, here, is merely secondary. As Zarathustra elsewhere implies, *the libido* is an inferior form of an eternal essence:

> Never yet did I find the woman by whom I wanted children, unless it be this woman, whom I love, O Eternity!
>
> *For I love you, O Eternity!* [89]

By succumbing to erotic love, Nietzsche warns, the man of genius loses his vitality, surrenders to the parasite which is woman.[90] This corresponds profoundly to the sadistic universe in which the father-figure, the hero of the sadistic fantasy, rapes and kills the mother and places himself above the law (in stark contrast to the masochistic fantasy where the father figure is eliminated and a matriarchal—according to Deleuze proto-Communist!—order is instituted).[91] Hannibal Lecter provides an interesting variant on this theme, which confirms it even while appearing to take another path. Lecter, that is, unlike the 'classical' sadist, never kills or abuses women, choosing his victims only from among his own gender. Yet there is more to this than a mark of aristocratic courtesy, a gentlemanly treatment of ladies[92]; what Lecter actually proves thereby is that he has overcome sexual desire to remain focused on his ultimate goal, which is god-like empowerment. Instructing the detective Will Graham in the film *Manhunter* about the joy of killing, he discloses the rationale of his murders: 'And why shouldn't [killing] feel good? It must feel good to God. He does it all the time. . . . It feels good, Will, because God has power. And if one does what God does enough times, one will become as God is. God's the champ. He always stays ahead.'[93] Compare this to Nietzsche's assertion: 'I write for a species of man that does not yet exist: for the "masters of the earth." . . . In Plato's *Theages* it is written: "each one of us would like to be master over all men, if possible, and best of all God." This attitude must exist again.'[94] By victimizing only men Lecter testifies that the issue for him is indeed pure power, the completely sublimated libido, whereas the abuse of women might still indicate enslavement to pleasure. Nietzsche at one occasion described the connection between repressed sexual desire and increased power-sensation quite graphically and in pseudo-scientific terms: 'The reabsorption of semen through the blood is the strongest nourishment and generates perhaps most of all the stimulus of power. . . . The feeling of power has until now risen highest in abstinent priests and hermits.'⁹⁵ By contrast to such abstinence, what guarantees the ultimate disgrace of Lecter's lesser counterparts, the diverse commonplace libertines who also aspire to become human-gods, is largely their inability to transcend or successfully sublimate the crippling/humanizing libido. Francis Dolarhyde (*Red Dragon*), Jame Gumb (*The Silence of the Lambs*) and Mason Verger (*Hannibal*), are all sexual perverts (the first two victimize women, the third is a child molester and exhibitionist masturbator) and remain therefore dialectically enslaved by their victims, subconsciously guided as they are by the wish, however perversely expressed, to be loved and/or to experience sexual pleasure. This is most notably the case of Dolarhyde, who is surely the most 'sympathetic,' at least in Harris' terms, of all these lesser killers, and the one who comes closest to overcoming humanity. As he enlightens one of his victims before slaying him: 'Man to man. You use that expression to imply frankness, Mr. Lounds, I appreciate that. But you see, I am not a man. I began as one but, by the Grace of God and my own Will, I have become Other and More than a man.'⁹⁶ Dolarhyde, however, is finally humanized and consequently defeated by his romantic attraction to Reba, the kind woman whose blindness eases his paralyzing timidity. In Harris' universe, as well as in Nietzsche's, where the libido is assimilated into power, the ultimate sexual perversion is *sexual desire itself*. All non-sublimated expressions of sexuality are basically adulterated forms of power, hence being evidence of weakness. Lecter, with no sexual perversions but no sexual desire either, who cannibalistically consumes flesh but stands beyond carnal lust, prevails because he has truly given up the pleasure principle to embrace power. His final romance with Clarice Starling in *Hannibal* does not really alter this underlying truth, because it is depicted essentially as a platonic love, a spiritual liaison between two 'free spirits,' implying no 'dirty' lustful debasement.

Hannibal Lecter's sadistic willingness to go through torture as a proof of mastery, is likewise echoed, as it were, in the equation Nietzsche draws between pain, greatness and self-overcoming, as expressed succinctly in famous avowals such as 'What does not kill me makes me stronger,'⁹⁷ or, equally instructively: '*how* deeply human beings can suffer almost determines their order of rank.'⁹⁸ This was stated most blatantly in those passages in which Nietzsche espouses the practice of vivisection—recall Hannibal Lecter's lobotomizing at the dinner table—as a means of determining one's merit and rank: 'The *courage* of head and heart is what *distinguishes* us, European people. . . . Vivisection is a *test* [Probe]: he who does not endure it, does not belong to us. . . .'⁹⁹ Conversely, the inferiority of modern man finds appropriate expression precisely in his cowardly shirking of pain, his exaggerated sensibility:

> Now, when suffering is always the first of the arguments marshalled *against* life, as its most questionable feature, it is salutary to remember the times when peo-

ple made the opposite statement, because they could not do without *making* people suffer and saw first-rate magic in it, a veritable seductive lure *to* life.[100]

The infliction of pain and suffering is hence a precondition of life and of culture. Sadism, in that sense, renders a vital service to the advancement of civilization. As Nietzsche bluntly established early on: 'The misery of men living a life of toil has to be increased to make the production of the world of art possible for a small number of Olympian men'[101]; and, in *The Gay Science*: 'Who will attain anything great if he does not find in himself the strength and the will to *inflict* great suffering? . . . not to perish of internal distress and uncertainty when one inflicts great suffering and hears the cry of this suffering—that is great, that belongs to greatness.'[102]

Given that the Nietzschean ethos is imbued with sadistic elements, it should not surprise us that most of the Nietzschean heroes we have discussed exhibit certain sadistic propensities—quite apart from the Dionysian criminal, in whom sadism becomes the focal attribute. Tarzan, for example, takes pride in his ability to face torture and imminent death magnanimously:

> A little stream of blood trickled down the giant's smooth skin from the wound in his side; but no murmur of pain passed his lips. The smile of contempt upon his face seemed to infuriate the Russian. With a volley of oaths he leaped at the helpless captive, beating him upon the face with his clenched fists and kicking him mercilessly about the legs. Then he raised the heavy spear to drive it through the mighty heart, and still Tarzan of the Apes smiled contemptuously upon him.[103]

Though no active sadist himself—being a disciple of Rousseau and a creature of nature Tarzan does not inflict gratuitous pain—the jungle lord never loses his perfect self-mastery and shows the indifference to pain required of the sadist. In the more closely Nietzschean work of Ayn Rand, by comparison, sadism is at times quite overt. Love between the sexes, notably, is understood as an act of war, a clash of opposing forces, where the man vanquishes the woman, asserts his mastery over her through the violent possession of her body. Rape, for that matter, is as much the desire of the woman as it is of the man. As Roark's lover admits to herself while being manhandled, the rapture she desires, and which of course her heroic lover unerringly provides, has nothing to do with love or tenderness but with submission to a 'master' and a 'soldier,' possessing her 'shamefully' and 'contemptuously.'[104] In the Nietzschean-sadist universe rape, more or less explicit, is indeed the expression of genuine love, the only one worthy of the name.[105] Remarkable as this is, coming from a female author, this is no idiosyncrasy of Rand but rather a generalized feature of the Nietzschean discourse. Women, in their heart of hearts, and *pace* feminism, desire to be raped and be treated like whores.[106] As Contessa Teresa di Vicenzo, James

Bond's future wife, instructs him: 'Take off these clothes. Make love to me. . . . Do anything you like. . . . Be rough with me. Treat me like the lowest whore in creation.'[107] Marc-Ange Draco, the amiable Corsican Mafioso who would become Bond's father-in-law, tells him about the way he had met his English wife:

> ' . . . She had come to Corsica to look for bandits'—he smiled—'rather like some English women adventure into the desert to look for sheiks. She explained to me later that she must have been possessed by a subconscious desire to be raped. Well'—this time he didn't smile—'she found me in the mountains and she was raped—by me . . .'[108]

The underlying theory is expounded by Darko Kerim, Bond's Turkish id: 'All women want to be swept off their feet. In their dreams they long to be slung over a man's shoulder and taken into a cave and raped.'[109] A theoretical maxim which Kerim keenly practices: 'I got to her place and took away all her clothes and kept her chained naked under the table. When I ate, I used to throw scraps to her under the table, like a dog.'[110] There is greater wisdom and naturalness in the Turkish and Corsican brutal way of going about sex as compared with Western hypocritical timidity. Nietzsche's assertion from *Beyond Good and Evil* appears to loom large in all such essentially orientalist narratives:

> To blunder over the fundamental problem of 'man and woman,' to deny here the most abysmal antagonism and the necessity of an eternally hostile tension, perhaps to dream here of equal rights, equal education, equal claims and duties: this is a *typical* sign of shallow-mindedness, and a thinker who has proved himself to be shallow on this dangerous point—shallow of instinct!—may be regarded as suspect in general. . . . On the other hand, a man who has depth, in his spirit as well as in his desires . . . can think of woman only in an *oriental* way—he must conceive of woman as a possession, as property with lock and key, as something predestined for service and attaining her fulfillment in service—in this matter he must take his stand on the tremendous intelligence of Asia.[111]

Nietzsche's notion of Asian intelligence can clearly accommodate Darko Kerim's *minor*-Asian one. This combination of sadism and Nietzscheanism is by no means merely some 'philosophy of the boudoir'; it rather aspires to the condition of general social validity. As will be recalled, it was Darko Kerim who also suggested that not only women crave to be raped but the Turkish populace at large: 'That is the only way to treat these damned people. They love to be cursed and kicked. . . . All this pretence of democracy is killing them. They want some sultans and wars and rape and fun.'[112]

It is interesting in that respect that Primo Levi, the renowned novelist who survived Auschwitz, and who did not doubt the role of Nietzsche's philosophy in generally preparing the ground for the attack on conventional morality which was Nazism, nevertheless claimed that delight in causing pain was alien to Nietzsche:

> Nietzsche's message is profoundly repugnant to me; . . . yet it seems that a desire for the sufferings of others cannot be found it. Indifference, yes, almost on every page, but never *Schadenfreude*, the joy in your neighbour's misfortune and even less the joy of deliberately inflicting suffering. The pain of the *hoi polloi*, of the *Ungestalten*, the shapeless, the not-born-noble, is a price that must be paid for the advent of the reign of the elect; it is a minor evil, but still an evil; it is not in itself desirable. Hitlerian doctrine and practice were much different.[113]

Levi's argument is significant for our purposes since, precisely by implying that Nietzsche did *not* relish cruelty as such, the *social functionality* of his brand of sadism is highlighted. It suggests that its ultimate rationale was not a mere psychological condition or aesthetical predilection, but rather a hardened recognition of the social necessity of inflicting suffering. If the essentially gentle-hearted Nietzsche had to embrace sadism, in a sense against his own psychological and emotional inclinations, this attests all the more the structural, objective necessity to inflict pain which Nietzsche acknowledged and which, however reluctantly, he was bound to affirm and uphold. It also stands to reason that, actually to enact such sadism as a social practice as opposed to merely commend it as a necessary evil, would require the agency of natures far less squeamish than Nietzsche's.

Hannibal Lecter and James Bond are seen to be strangely akin; the former brings together the cannibal and the connoisseur while the latter is a latent sadist. It should be noted, in that respect, that Lecter's culinary refinement as well as his interest in art are not to be traced back to Sade, whose heroes were 'not art lovers, still less collectors.'[114] These aspects of Lecter seem to reflect a decidedly more Nietzschean trope, of a later historical stage, where it becomes increasingly pertinent to uphold good taste, indeed in all senses of the term, against the crudity of the enfranchised masses. Lecter's delight in good food, coupled with his sexual restraint, also appear to confirm Leo Strauss' Nietzschean claim that the 'wise man' is 'chiefly interested in the pleasures of eating . . . : for the enjoyment of food, as distinguished from sexual enjoyments, one does not need other human beings.'[115] Gastronomic pleasure is thus compatible with the *sine qua non* of wisdom, as Strauss understands it, namely 'the greatest self-sufficiency which is humanly possible.'[116]

The aura of Lecter's super-humanity hinges decisively on his god-like ability to decipher everybody else while remaining an enigma; like his deceased predecessor, the wicked human-god works in mysterious ways, too, his evil defying any rational or moral explanation. His spiritual distinction is matched and reflected by his physical, Houdini-like evasiveness, enabling him to escape and assert his autonomy even when kept under the strictest guard. Lecter, above all, as his name indicates can *read*, but is not read.[117] Thus, to interpret Lecter as obsessed with mastery is to puncture his super-human ambition, by showing his servility to the will to power. His aloof-ness and self-sufficiency, moreover, is fundamentally a sham, for, as Simp-son rightfully comments: 'Lecter would not exist without a herd to terrorize. . . . His lordship . . . implies psychological separation from the herd in or-der to manipulate its timid social structure all the more easily.'[118] This par-adoxical dependency of the Nietzschean shepherd on the herd which he despises calls to mind John Carey's insight into the shaky foundation of the Nietzschean majestic posture as such: 'We should see Nietzsche . . . as one of the earliest products of mass culture. That is to say, mass culture gen-erated Nietzsche in opposition to itself, as its antagonist.'[119] For all the al-leged autonomy of the Nietzschean would-be god, it is predicated through-out on the existence of the hated rabble, which lends it its very raison d'être.

The picture of Lecter, of course, cannot be complete without taking into account his dialectical foil/partner, Clarice Starling, the young FBI detective who embodies the traditional idea of the shepherd, truly devoted to the cause of imperiled lambs—both real and human ones; if Lecter represents evil than Starling represents the conventional notion of goodness. Signifi-cantly, good and evil are not made to pursue each other but rather enter into an odd liaison. If, in *The Silence of the Lambs*, Lecter and Starling were merely partners, collaborating to capture Buffalo Bill, in *Hannibal*, the se-quel, they become romantically engaged. Here, however, it is important to distinguish between the original story and the film version, whose endings, above all, are drastically different. In the film, Lecter reveals himself essen-tially a creature of Starling's universe; for all his cruelty, he operates very much *within* the boundaries of traditional good and evil, even if stretching them somewhat to accommodate his intransigent social critique. We learn, firstly, that there is a moral, as opposed to a merely aesthetical logic behind Lecter's crimes. The ruthless and creative punishments he administers are directed strictly against those members of mass society who may be termed *impure*: the vices he chastises are vulgarity, avarice and corruption. And he makes no distinctions between the simple, foul-smelling lowlife, the multi-millionaire (Mason Verger) or the corrupt policeman and would-be politi-cian (Paul Krendler). They are all equally sunk in the mire of inauthentic-ity, lust and greed. By contrast, those exceptional few who manage to preserve a purity of heart amidst mass society are perfectly protected from Lecter's wrath. Thus, a gentle male nurse who cares for every living thing and Clarice Starling, the compassionate shepherd, are as safe as they can be in Lecter's presence. Far from harming them in any way, he will even heal their wounds and nurse them, as well as join them in their fight against the agents of mass corruption. When Clarice, near the ending of the film, gets shot—significantly whilst attempting to rescue Lecter from his captor—the

Dr. applies his medical skills in a conventional fashion, to heal rather than kill. He lovingly operates on her, removes the bullet and stitches the wound. Lecter's adherence to his idiosyncratic moral code reaches a dramatic climax when, chained to Clarice, he prefers to cut off his own hand rather than harm her. Ultimate evil on the film's terms is not the opposite but the unlikely extension of faultless good. And it is only superficially that Lecter is a figure beyond good and evil. The Nietzschean reveals himself unexpectedly aligned with the herd, the principled neo-aristocratic gentleman as an antithesis to the hedonist and lecherous evil of capitalism. Lecter gives a particular twist to the theme of immaterial crime which, in Nietzsche's original conception, was all about undermining social criticism. Lecter's odd purity, by contradistinction, the fact that he is a thorough outsider to the pleasure principle of mass society, is precisely what allows him to punish social depravity.[120] To be sure, this surprising moral taming of the Nietzschean free spirit appears rather strained. It must, above all, suppress the fact that in order to maintain his aristocratic life-style, indulge his refined gastronomic demands and enhance his collection of rare artistic gems, Lecter must have recourse to the very same vile substance, the vulgar life-blood of market-society: money. This dependence on matter, though politely concealed from the viewer—we never learn how exactly Lecter came by his riches; he just seems to be intrinsically and naturally comfortable—severely compromises his proud aloofness. Yet such incongruity merely reflects the inherent contradiction in fusing the aristocrat and the moralist.

The novel, in that respect, is more coherent. The Nietzschean criminal is not forced to concede nearly as much to herd-morality. There, too, Lecter links with Clarice Starling in a common fight against the capitalist pervert, Mason Verger. Yet in this version it is Starling who is finally converted into Lecter's creed, becoming a dazzling new recruit, and Nietzschean amorality is vindicated rather than transubstantiated. The finale sees Lecter and Starling as an amorous couple, presiding over their luxurious mansion in South America. Clarice is weaned of her scruples and accepts Lecter's cannibalistic aestheticism: 'Clarice, dinner appeals to taste and smell, the oldest senses and the closest to the center of the mind. Taste and smell are housed in parts of the mind that precede pity, and pity has no place at my table.'[121] Shortly following this avowal, comes the scene described above where Lecter and Starling jointly savor the brain of a vulgar guest. And here also book and film significantly differ, for in the film, where good and evil are still formally held apart, Clarice does not eat but is merely compelled to look with obvious dismay at what Lecter is perpetrating.

The social implications of Sade's unlawfulness have often been described as radical and anarchist. Be that as it may, *Nietzschean sadism* revolves markedly around a sense of *Rangordnung*, a strict and irrefutable hierarchy. For all the ambiguous flirt with herd morality, *Hannibal* presupposes an undisputed chain of command. Thus, in Lecter and Starling's mansion the pertinence and mobility of mass society are perfectly contained: 'Morale is high among the servants in this house, but there is an iron discipline among them.'[122] The Nietzschean dream of producing a happy slave caste is seen to underpin the quest of the Dionysian criminal, even as he pretends to challenge the ignobility of capitalism by way of 'critical elitism,' as we have defined it above (chapter 3). Hannibal Lecter, in the final balance, is an 'outright elitist,' whose rejection of capitalism is the rejection of egalitarianism. Such 'anti-capitalism' sustains the conservative fantasy of reverting back to a condition where the boundaries between taste and vulgarity, eminency and lowliness, mastery and slavery are not up for grabs as they appear to be at present. As Hollywood inculcates the values of aristocratic elitism, popular culture, however paradoxically, is denounced *by means* of popular culture. This is true even if the film version of *Hannibal*, targeting larger and less 'distinguished' audiences as compared with the far more limited reading public, is driven to compromise with the popular sensitivity by mellowing down the unabashed elitism of Harris' original story.[123]

PULP FICTION:
EZEKIEL IN THE SERVICE OF THE *ÜBERMENSCH*

The theme of the over-human shepherd and his commanding relation with the herd, this reversal of the Christian conventional imagery which is at the heart of Nietzsche's discourse, was further developed by a salient Nietzschean in popular culture, Quentin Tarantino, in his immensely successful and influential film *Pulp Fiction* (1994). Here too, the atypical shepherd is a murderer: the hit man Jules (played by Samuel L. Jackson). Jules, who has often executed people in the service of his Mafioso boss, has a singular habit of reciting a biblical verse before liquidating his victims. One of the movie's opening scenes documents this eerie ritual:

> Jules: There's a passage I got memorized, seems appropriate for this situation: Ezekiel 25:17. 'The path of the righteous man is beset on all sides by the inequities of the selfish and the tyranny of evil men. Blessed is he who, in the name of charity and good will, shepherds the weak through the valley of darkness, for he is truly his brother's keeper and the finder of lost children. And I will strike down upon thee with great vengeance and furious anger those who attempt to poison and destroy my brothers. And you will know my name is the Lord when I lay my vengeance upon you.'
>
> The two men *empty* their guns at the same time on the sitting Brett. When they are finished, the bullet-ridden carcass just sits there for a moment, then *topples* over.[124]

On first sight, Jules and his associate Vincent Vega (John Travolta) hardly fit in the same category of the artists-assassins who kill for spiritual gratification, as Hannibal Lecter. In many ways, they are closer to the model of the picaresque anti-hero than to that of the Sadian tormenter: in contrast to the patrician psychiatrist, they are professional killers, having a solid material motive to hire themselves out as hit men. Nonetheless, in their own plebeian manner, they are no less keen on the aesthetic thrill in slaying. Jules' pre-execution-speech is a fine illustration of such a taste for the dramatic, which was no less evident as, shortly before killing Brett, they began to relish the delicacy of power-abuse:

Brett: . . . When we entered into this thing, we only had the best intentions — As Brett talks, Jules takes out his gun and *shoots* Roger three times in the chest, *blowing* him out of his chair. Vince smiles to himself. Jules has got style. Brett has just shit his pants. He's not crying or whimpering, but he's so full of fear, it's as if his body is imploding.

Jules (to Brett): Oh, I'm sorry. Did that break your concentration? I didn't mean to do that. Please, continue. I believe you were saying something about 'best intentions.'

This is a fresh restatement of Nietzsche's 'lust for blood' theme, something of a 'joy of the shotgun.' By the end of the film, however, Jules, inspired by a miraculous escape from a near-death situation is having second thoughts and begins to question his amoral existence. He embraces a new-found religious persuasion, which in turn necessitates his retirement from the killing-business. This transvaluation of his personal values is symbolically presented in the final scene of the movie; Jules has the power to kill a confused and pathetic couple of robbers, who attempted to steal from him, but he chooses differently:

Jules: There's a passage I got memorized. Ezekiel 25:17. [The verse is fully repeated: I.L]. I been sayin' that shit for years. And if you ever heard it, it meant your ass. I never really questioned what it meant. . . . But I saw some shit this mornin' made me think twice. Now I'm thinkin', it could mean you're the evil man. And I'm the righteous man. And Mr. .45 here, he's the shepherd protecting my righteous ass in the valley of darkness. Or is could be you're the righteous man and I'm the shepherd and it's the world that's evil and selfish. I'd like that. But that shit ain't the truth. The truth is you're the weak. And I'm the tyranny of evil men. But I'm tryin'. I'm tryin' real hard to be a shepherd.

Jules lowers his gun, laying it on the table.
This remarkable change-of-heart might be interpreted as a sharp turning away from the Nietzschean ethos, a thorough moral domestication of the Anti-Christ. Thomas Hibbs, for example, has commended the Christian

message underlying *Pulp Fiction*'s ending: 'The character of Jules suggests the possibility of reviving the premodern, especially scriptural, conception of man as a wanderer on the earth. . . . In Jules, we see the shift from God as vengeful to God as providential guide in a world where all are in need of mercy.'[125] This is basically true; yet, as I wish to argue, in Tarantino's theology the difference between a vengeful God and a merciful one is not particularly profound. The film's ending remains in truth *well along* the horizon of Dionysian crime. The structure of the Nietzschean discourse prevails intact inasmuch as Jules continues to take as his unquestionable premise hierarchical power-relations, refuting a specific use of power but not denying, in fact reasserting, its ontological supremacy. Still more importantly, he acquiesces in the crucial dichotomization of the strong vs. the weak, the first destined to rule, the latter to succumb, not because of some contingent, social configuration, but because of an immanent, natural division: the couple of petty robbers had the upper hand initially, had a gun pointed at Jules, but they *being* the weak and he *being* the strong, the natural order of things simply had to reestablish itself. It is a pithy illustration of the reification of power, of the insistence on its objective, intrinsic, independent nature; the gun does not bestow power—in the hands of a weak, 'unnatural' user it proves quite worthless; the gun rather finds its way back to its authentic master, is drawn magnetically into the hands of the strong, in much the same way that the Ring of Power seeks to reunite with Sauron, its master, in Tolkien's saga. This also calls to mind the theory expounded by the Nietzschean General Cummings in *The Naked and the Dead* in justification of uninhibited use of force:

> 'You've seen too many movies. If you're holding a gun and you shoot a defenseless man, then you're a poor creature, a *dastardly person*. That's a perfectly ridiculous idea, you realize. The fact that you're holding the gun and the other man is not is no accident. It's a product of everything you've achieved, it assumes that if you're . . . aware enough, you have the gun when you need it.'[126]

On such terms, power-abuse is a meaningless notion; power—which in our examples is objectified in a gun, but might equally find symbolic dwelling in money, possessions and authority—is never arbitrary or coincidental, but rather betokens value. Jules' final monologue is reminiscent of a scene from *Schindler's List* in which Oskar Schindler was guessing into the psychological mechanism of the Nazi butcher Amon Goeth. Schindler attempted to persuade Goeth that the best way of manifesting his awesome powers would be not by slaying his helpless prisoners but rather by majestically granting them clemency. This sort of mercy that is an emblem of power, the very *consecration* of hierarchy, was certainly authorized by Nietzsche, this harshest among the (philosophical) foes of pity, as one possible manifestation of true nobility:

> [A] man who has his anger and his sword and to whom the weak, suffering, oppressed, and the animals too are glad to submit and belong by nature, in short a man who is by nature a *master*—when such a man has pity, well! *that* pity has value![127]

Jules, therefore, has renounced his gun only all the more to confirm his *mastery*. Tarantino's filmmaking is often commented on as a marked example of postmodernist art, and *Pulp Fiction* in particular is certainly an intriguing play with perspectives, chronologies and contingencies. But this final scene—precisely where something of a fraternal message is supposed to have emerged after a series of intensely violent encounters—betrays an adamant hierarchical persuasion underlying much of the perspectivalist revelry. This conviction is encapsulated in the momentous sentence, 'the truth is you're the weak. And I'm the tyranny of evil men.'

If not a denunciation of power, is not *Pulp Fiction* at least an instance of *plebeian* Dionysian crime? It may seem strained to see in such rough lowlifes as Jules and Vincent undercover protectors of bourgeois property arrangements. Yet appearance can be misleading. For one thing, the implicit 'naturalization' of power and of hierarchies can hardly be understood unless within a class context, and, hence, as inescapably favoring the 'powerful' class. The coarse delinquents are, in that sense, decoys: they may be invested with this sort of immanent might *in the movie*, but they symbolize and justify power globally, that is, outside the cinema theater, where real power concentrates not in the slums but in the highest social echelons. More basically still, a truly plebeian Dionysian criminal, as discussed above, is a contradiction in terms: the plebeian, materially driven criminal is admitted in the company of his aristocratic superiors precisely to the extent that he renounces his annoying insistence on material benefit and supplants it with spirituality, with proper amorality. In that respect, what finally counts in the artistic presentation of the criminal is not the outside trappings—the way a criminal dresses, talks and behaves—but the internal content of his criminal activity, which is either moral/spiritual or material. In *Pulp Fiction*, the motivation behind Jules' criminal vocation is finally revealed to be moral, not material; his abandonment of crime is the outcome of an ethical maturation, a conversion of conscience, a religious illumination: when his interpretation of the Ezekiel verse changes, so does his vocation. His criminality was at bottom a *result of amorality*, was truly Dionysian, and now that he has turned 'moral,' crime is automatically transcended. Thus, for all its admirable mastery of street-vernacular, the wealth of verbal 'obscenities' and other plebeian gestures, the film remains a specimen of bourgeois representation of crime. It is a sort of a moral fable, a cinematic *Bildungsroman*, whose protagonists oscillate between two ethical alternatives, not material ones.

In the absence of a solid material and social basis to underpin their decisions, and in a postmodernist world in which the benevolent providence to which Jules would like to return appears no more than a fleeting chimera, the conversion from amorality to morality cannot but take the form of a whim. One may, indeed, take the route of virtue and choose for once to assume the role of the *good* shepherd, but then again one may choose *not* to. In fact, given the confirmation of power as the final horizon of human relations and the view of natural hierarchy irrevocably separating men, the natural and more coherent choice would be amorality rather than morality. The whimsical character of Jules' decision is thrown into a vivid relief when it is compared with the attitude of another Tarantinian murderer, Mickey Knox from *Natural Born Killers*. In Tarantino's original script (the final script for Oliver Stone's movie was heavily revised, becoming a nebulous satire on the mass media and violence in American life[128]), Dionysian glorification of crime is quite overriding, constituting something like the thematic core of the whole text.[129] I wish merely to sample one extraordinary enunciation of Nietzschean creed by Knox, the serial killer who defends his vocation against an obnoxious interviewer, who appears to be the representative of herd morality.

Wayne [the interviewer]: You just said an instant of purity was preferable to a lifetime lie. I don't understand. What's so pure about forty-eight dead bodies?

Mickey [the serial killer]: You'll never understand. Me and you, Wayne, we're not even the same species. I used to be you, then I evolved. From where you're standing, you're a man. From where I'm standing, you're a ape. I'm here, I'm right here, and you, you're somewhere else, man. You say why? I say why not?[130]

It is illuminating to invoke the 'original formulation' of this assertion, which seems with all probability to have echoed in Tarantino's mind as he wrote Knox's lines:

What is the ape to men? A laughing-stock or a painful embarrassment. Just so shall man be to the Superman: a laughing-stock or a painful embarrassment. You have made your way from worm to man, and much in you is still worm. Once you were apes, and even now man is more of an ape than any ape.[131]

Zarathustra's famous avowal situates Mickey Knox's in its broader philosophical context, against which it transpires as a true claim for the badge of the *Übermensch*. The tepid morality of mass society is challenged by the

Dionysian criminal, who affirms his distinction in and through transgression. In view of such a statement, Jules' repentance at the end of *Pulp Fiction* appears rather superficial, an arbitrary solution to the moral dilemma in question, since Knox's authentic amorality gives the impression of being far more sincere than Jules' virtuous commitment.

A SIGNIFICANT EXCEPTION: *AMERICAN PSYCHO*

The rules of a genre can sometimes be best observed by considering the exceptions to it. In our case, the boundaries of the serial killer narrative are sharply demarcated by a rare counter-generic instance, *American Psycho*, originally a novel by Bret Easton Ellis (1991) and later filmed by director Mary Harron (2000).

If most Hollywood serial killers are presented as either demonic aberrations or as individuals of higher stature (or, indeed, as some compromise between demon and genius), they are very seldom depicted with a basically realistic intent, in an attempt to reconstruct the psychological and social context in which a real killer acts. One consequence of this is that we hardly ever encounter killers who are neither demons nor geniuses, but pathetic individuals. As a rule, the killer emerges as beyond or below society, but not as an immanent piece of its construction, however ill-adjusted, frightening or undesirable. If he is a disturbed person, such films seldom attempt to look into that which actually disturbs him, much less imply that there may be some deficiency inherent in the social system which engenders such killers.[132] Far from it, in the traditional thriller, to dispatch the killer is usually the task of the protector of society, who purges a threatening element in defense of decent, law-abiding citizens. In such narratives society often proves an obstacle in catching the criminal by amassing legalistic and moral hindrances in the path of those entrusted with ensuring public safety, thus creating the recurrent theme of the heroic policeman or the fed-up civilian as vigilantes, brushing aside those leftists who would shelter killers. Don Siegel's *Dirty Harry* series featuring Clint Eastwood (first movie 1971) or the *Death Wish* movies with Charles Bronson as star (first movie 1974) would be the classic cinematic examples, all following in the wake of Mickey Spillane's hero Mike Hammer, the protagonist of classic hard-boilers from the early 1950s carrying all-revealing titles such as *I, the Jury*, *My Gun is Quick*, or *Vengeance is Mine!* The vigilante takes the law into his hands because the law is too lenient and humane, too much on the criminal's side. Sanguine liberals (in the American sense of the term), in their naïve belief in human perfectibility and the possibility to reform the criminal, are blind precisely to the demonic nature of the perpetrator, who must be ruthlessly extinguished, cudgeled rather than coddled. The social critique of the vigilante narrative targets permissiveness, excessive democratic sensibility and unwarranted squeamishness. Such tales obviously cannot depict the killer as a real and concrete human being since the entire ideologeme depends on thickening his monstrous aura. As a result, the killer typically becomes immensely clever, evasive and enduring. This lays the ground for the typical grand finale, the shoot-out between the heroic policeman, with or without a badge, and the monstrous killer; as Simpson notes: 'The super-criminal versus the super-detective is not a new dramatic convention, of course, but in the serial killer subgenre, the adversarial conflict between geniuses serves to illustrate both the magnitude of the menace and the need for saviors.'[133] Ritually, to kill the killer can never be accomplished with a single shot, for he has the super-human ability to recover, often enough virtually to resurrect, no matter how badly maimed or mutilated: 'it is the killer's ability to rise from the dead in film after film which . . . demonises him.'[134] The only reliable way of dispatching him is to chop off his head, and even this guarantees success only in 'realistic' thrillers and not in more fantastic horror movies.

The opposite, but in truth complementary model of the serial killer, that of the Dionysian criminal, which depicts the killer as an evil genius like Lecter or as a rebel like Mickey Knox, clearly does not entail any removal of the criminal super-human aura. Here as well, to eliminate the charisma is to render the entire ideologeme powerless. The whole point of using the murderer to chastise the mediocrity of mass society depends on the grandeur of the killer-genius. The Dionysian criminal accordingly possesses immense resources which make him almost impossible to capture. And when he is captured, he can dupe the police applying tremendous ingenuity and adroitness. Hannibal Lecter, for example, may be put in an iron cage, completely chained, his face under an iron mask, surrounded by an entire platoon of policemen. Yet such meticulous safety measures only serve to redouble the glory of the inevitable escape and establish all the more forcefully the prodigious might of Lecter's evil genius. Here, again, for all the differences between the demon and the genius, the latter is not presented as a symptom of society but as its refutation or its overcoming. Paradoxically enough, in both these guises the criminal finally exposes and serves to attack a single target: the pernicious egalitarianism of American mass society. In the first instance, society is shown to be too egalitarian and uniform to effectively fight the terrorizing demon, whereas in the second instance it is too egalitarian and uniform to accommodate the defying genius. Between them, these twin narratives appear to encompass almost all serial killer films (even fantasy versions of the serial killer, typically the series *A Nightmare on Elm Street*, with the figure of the indestructible monster Freddy Krueger, seem to belong here).

As might be expected, some critiques of this silent consensus have emerged during the 1990s, arguably the most notable among them Bret Easton Ellis's novel *American Psycho* (1991, the same year that Demme's *The*

Silence of the Lambs won the Oscar). Here, in marked contradistinction to the habitual patterns, the criminal's psychosis is linked blatantly with America and, moreover, *not* with its alleged egalitarian and humanitarian obsessions. Crime is here not *anti*-social, whether demonically or splendidly, but social through and through. The distinction of the killer as the ultimate outsider is done away with as he is located at the very heart of the American dream: Patrick Bateman is the prototype yuppie, a Wall Street broker, who leads a dreadfully empty life amidst status and abundance: 'I'm left with one comforting thought: I am rich—millions are not.'[135] Bateman is estrangement incarnated, completely incapable as he is of any human relationship, particularly love, which he can only profane by torturing and killing women. Nevertheless, it seems possible, at first sight at least, to read *American Psycho* as a Nietzschean critique of the elimination of individuality under conditions of modern nihilism, a sort of leftist-Nietzschean analysis of the 'one-dimensional man.' The theme of the protagonist's actual anonymity, the hollowness lurking behind his elegant façade, pervades the story. At one point, for example, he confesses his complete ordinariness to a girlfriend who mistakenly thinks that he is special:

> 'How many people in this world are like me?' I ask again ' . . . you know how they say no two snowflakes are ever alike? . . . Well, I don't think that's true. I think a lot of snowflakes are alike . . . and I think a lot of people are alike too.'[136]

This apparent affinity with a Nietzschean critique of the Frankfurt School mould seems still further confirmed when we consider that Bateman's cultural habitat is degraded pop culture, and the way the narration of his killings is regularly interlaced with his expert lectures on such musical icons of the 1980s as Phil Collins, Madonna or Huey Lewis. Clearly, for Ellis, the sham uniqueness of these entertainers is meant to reflect the fake individuality of Bateman. Along with mass society comes mass man, a standardized, soulless product of an endless assembly line. In all this, no doubt, Adorno, Marcuse and, at a second remove, Nietzsche, appear vindicated.[137] Yet, in my mind, such a rendering of *American Psycho* as simply a Nietzschean denouncement of mass nihilism, however 'leftist' and for all its partial applicability, would be greatly inadequate. The nihilism Ellis describes, crucially, is a reflection of the acute alienation of the American elite, of those in possession of power.[138] This is, if anything, a *Nietzschean nihilism*, the predicament of an elite which has followed Nietzsche's counsel and catapulted itself beyond good and evil only to gape into a void: 'He who sees the abyss, but with an eagle's eyes—he who *grasps* the abyss with an eagle's claws: *he* possess courage.'[139] The key distinction here would be that which Nietzsche drew between *passive* nihilism, which corresponds to the stupid, contented, cow-like happiness of the democratic Last Man, which the philosopher wholeheartedly condemned and sought to overcome, and the far better appraised *active* nihilism, which consists of a creative demolition of past values, particularly the slavish creeds of fraternity and compassion, without which the transformation into the overman would never come to fruition.[140]

I am not, it is important to clarify, suggesting that Ellis set out to criticize Nietzsche; my point rather concerns the objective import of his story, regardless of what may have been the author's subjective intentions. It is not so much the masses who are deceived in *American Psycho* as are the yuppies. A greater measure of humanity, decency and authenticity is found among secretaries, prostitutes, beggars and taxi drivers as compared with the desensitized elite. As Bateman reflects: 'My conscience, my pity, my hopes disappeared a long time ago (probably at Harvard) if they ever did exist.'[141] Life is more genuine and meaningful 'below' as it is in the privileged spheres of society. This is forcefully exemplified near the end of the novel, during a class clash between the prosperous killer and a taxi driver who robs him:

> 'You're a dead man.' I smile grimly at him.
> 'And you're a yuppie scumbag,' he says.
> 'You're a dead man, Abdullah,' I repeat, no joke. 'Count on it.'
> 'Yeah? And you're a yuppie scumbag. Which is worse?'[142]

In stark disagreement with the Dionysian criminal's claim to authenticity, Bateman is a social product from tip to toe. The novel takes as a motto Dostoevsky's words from *Notes from Underground* from which it is worth quoting: 'Both the author of these *Notes* and the *Notes* themselves are, of course, fictional. Nevertheless, such persons as the composer of these *Notes* not only exist in our society, but indeed must exist, considering the circumstances under which our society has been generally formed.' Easton Ellis invokes Dostoevsky to programmatically state the *Americanism* of his *psycho*. Whereas, in Nietzsche, the violence of the criminal is positively contrasted with the timidity of society and evil is endorsed as a kind of a last-resort stimulant, Bateman's brutality reflects the deadly apathy of an inhuman elite. The film version ends with the following confession:

> My pain is constant and sharp and I do not hope for a better world for anyone. In fact, I want my pain to be inflicted on others. I want no one to escape. But even after admitting this there is no catharsis. My punishment continues to elude me, and I gain no deeper knowledge of myself. No new knowledge can be extracted from my telling. This confession has meant—nothing.[143]

This reads as a statement on America's condition as a perverse super-power beyond punishment, all the more so as it closely follows a TV broadcast of a

speech by Reagan, lying about the Iran-Contra affair. Given that American nihilism is diagnosed as rooted in the obsession with power and decidedly not
in any excess of brotherly slave morality, the alternative indicated by the narrative, however weakly and intermittently given the story's all-enveloping
bleakness, is the very opposite of the remedy prescribed by Nietzsche. If the
nihilist aporia can still be escaped, the way out must go through a recuperation of the most elementary human sensibilities and not through the denial
and overcoming of humanity which has proven utterly dystopian: 'Justice is
dead. Fear, recrimination, innocence, sympathy, guilt, waste, failure, grief,
were things, emotions, that no one really felt anymore. Reflection is useless,
the world is senseless. Evil is its only permanence. God is not alive. Love
cannot be trusted. Surface, surface, surface was all that anyone found meaning in. . . . This was civilization as I saw it, colossal and jagged.'[144] *American
Psycho*'s most significant challenge to the Nietzschean project is probably in
the exchanges between Bateman and his apparently simple-minded assistant
Jean, who represents the closest thing in the novel to an alternative outlook.
In a very significant conversation her belief in goodness at first seems naïve
and hopeless besides the sober indifference of Bateman:

> Confused she says, 'I don't know. I guess . . . but one still has to maintain . . .
> a ratio of more good things than . . . bad in this world,' she says, adding, 'I
> mean, right?'[145]

The jaded Bateman initially treats Jean as his intellectual and emotional
inferior, someone who has not yet peered into the abyss, and can therefore
still maintain puerile notions of human empathy. As against such ingenu-
ousness, he plays the role of a tutor, enlightening her about the true, evil,
nature of the world:

> 'Sometimes, Jean,' I explain, 'the lines separating appearance—what you see—
> and reality—what you don't—become, well, blurred.'
>   'That's not true,' she insists. 'That's simply not true.'
>   'Really?' I ask, smiling.[146]

Reality, at that point, is on the killer's side, who slightly patronizes his immature interlocutor. Yet only to find himself unexpectedly shaken out of
balance:

> 'I didn't use to think so,' she says. 'Maybe ten years ago I didn't. But I do now.'
>   'What do you mean?' I ask, interested. 'You *used* to?'

In a momentous turnaround, it is Jean who now appears truly mature.
Nihilism is not something she has yet to experience but a condition she has

already grown out of. And this unsuspected perspective, a glimpse of a better existence, has a profound, if short-lived, effect on Bateman. The possibility opens that his bleak reality, so bitterly felt, is in fact illusive, that her human empathy is far more real than his reified indifference. This generates an inner struggle in which the male sadist stands on the verge of being dispossessed of his vital asset, control, by female affection:

> . . . a flood of reality. I get an odd feeling that this is a crucial moment in my life and I'm startled by the suddenness of what I guess passes for an epiphany. There is nothing of value I can offer her. For the first time I see Jean as uninhibited; she seems stronger, less controllable, wanting to take me into a new and unfamiliar land. . . . I sense she wants to rearrange my life in a significant way—her eyes tell me this and though I see truth in them, I also know that one day, sometime very soon, she too will be locked in the rhythm of my insanity. . . . yet she weakens me, it's almost as if *she's* making the decision about who I am, and in my own stubborn, willful way, I can admit to feeling a pang, something tightening inside, and before I can stop it I find myself almost dazzled and moved that I might have the capacity to accept, though not return, her love.[147]

The ambiguous alternative of female love, however, is bound to remain an episode: 'though the coldness I have always felt leaves me, the numbness doesn't and probably never will. This relationship will probably lead to nothing.' Unlike Nietzsche, however, who understands the male overcoming of female, 'parasitic' affection as the mark of genius and a sign of health, Bateman's inevitable rebuff of Jean's love bespeaks *his sickness*. Such rebuff is inevitable, of course, since the 'totally new and unfamiliar land' she briefly unveils is the complete opposite of the actual world of American capitalism which breeds the psycho, who is the inexorable result of 'the circumstances under which our society has been generally formed,' to refer again to Dostoevsky. In the figure of Bateman, the Dionysian criminal forfeits his iconoclastic claims to assume his place, in much greater accord with social reality, at the heart of bourgeois life. That which in the Nietzschean narrative is ambitiously advertised as the solution to the disease of modernity—namely the transcending of pity, justice, love—is identified in *American Psycho* as the very illness: 'my depersonalization was so intense, had gone so deep, that the normal ability to feel compassion had been eradicated, the victim of a slow, purposeful erasure.'[148] This pregnant sentence wonderfully encapsulates the novel's critique of ruling Nietzscheanism. The overman project has been completed; is it still possible to retrieve what it 'purposefully erased,' to get back, in other words, to the human, all-too-human condition?

'LIVING MEANS KILLING'

I have so far maintained that bourgeois laudation of crime should not be understood literally, as an approbation of actual transgression, but rather metaphorically, as a social fantasy, supplying the unique individual with the (imaginary) passport out of the herd's territory. It is therefore useful to consider a literary case—although not from popular culture—that goes further to support such a reading by portraying a protagonist who, unlike Beckert, Lecter or Knox, is truly a criminal *in mind alone*. Here, the trope of the authentic criminal is at its purest; and it may also serve to demonstrate how, for all the obvious differences in approaching the subject matter, the basic social concerns informing the notion of genuine crime remain very much the same whether treated in 'high' or in 'low' culture. Peter Handke's novel *The Hour of True Feeling* (1974) opens with the following question: 'Who has ever dreamt of becoming a murderer and continuing his normal life only in appearance?'[149] The novel reads like a literary exercise in Heideggerian philosophy, exploring most of its essential themes: the awakening to the real significance of one's mortality, the refutation of technology and mass culture, the rejection of political activity as a superficial meddling with 'ontic concerns,' and, of central importance, the conflict between authentic and inauthentic existence. Gregor Keuschnig, the story's somber (anti-)hero, is a reasonably affluent employee of the Austrian embassy in Paris who lives with his wife and little daughter in a huge, disaffecting apartment. He leads an uneventful life until a strange dream of murder totally alters its course; the imaginary killing of an old woman plays a decisive role in launching the hero out of the senseless comforts of his shallow existence and into the unsettling, but ultimately rewarding, experience of the title's 'true feeling.' Keuschnig is unable to resume his *das Man* involvement and is compelled to pursue to its last consequences the agitating authenticity of 'being-in-the-world.' Just like a true hunted felon, he has to lead a double life, strenuously to maintain a veneer of normality, under which the turmoil of his alienated, fearful, but concurrently ecstatic emotions is secluded. Keuschnig truly appears to be Stirner's 'never ceasing criminal in the state . . . surrounded with spies by the state, by the people.' He becomes an alien in the once-familiar streets of Paris, where the pointlessness of the ordinary way of life, hurled at him by every passerby, becomes a source of nausea: 'He went over the Avenue de Versailles and saw on one wooden-fence a poster, inviting to a meeting: "Isabel Allende speaks to us. . . ." "To us!," he thought. He turned away and spat.'[150]

Eventually, as in the more conventional crime story, the outlaw is captured and Keuschnig's crime, however internal, is publicly and shamefully exposed. Appropriately, taking in account the nature of the offense, the traditional role of the triumphant detective is performed by a writer with sharp psychological insight, who lays bare with Holmesian aplomb the culprit's inner corruption. After a painful family scandal, Keuschnig loses, first his wife, then his child. 'Losing,' however, must be cautiously applied in this case, as Keuschnig seems to have been determined from the start to disentangle himself from his familial obligations, right along with all other *das Man* relations, once they have been identified as non-existential shackles. Hence, the final pages depict an emancipated Keuschnig, who has recuperated something of the freedom of the child and stands excited on the verge of a fresh beginning; dressed in a newly acquired set of clothes he namelessly crosses the Place de l'Opéra, just 'a man' with a bright-blue suit, his 'loosely tied cravat swinging back and forth as he rapidly strides.'[151] These are the novel's final words, which seem, all told, to conclude a rather auspicious adventure.

Keuschnig's conflict with the collective does not evince the same acute class antagonism of *M*, for instance. The novel confronts the bourgeois individual not with a fanatic plebeian mob, but with society as a whole, with the Other as such, agreeing with Heidegger's broad outline, which was not class specified either. Yet a negation of equality vitally informs Keuschnig's authentic position; not formulated in socioeconomic terms, it nonetheless gives vent to the protagonist's psychological repugnance at the very *idea of being equal*, of seeing his own reflection in others and having to admit his ordinariness:

> How shameless they let themselves be looked at—as if everything has already been said about them anyhow and they had nothing more to fear. 'They were set up for life,' thought Keuschnig. Facing them, who were nonetheless so alike him, he couldn't imagine wanting to be anything else but dead.[152]

Sartre's affirmation, 'hell is other people,' appropriately from his existentialist phase, powerfully reverberates throughout the novel. The need to ascend above the mass, to reject one's 'mediocrity' and regain a sense of 'proper,' that is—unique and incomparable identity, is quite explicitly the need to compete, the need to have enemies. But, as enemies are not easy to find, *they must be created*: 'It occurred to him that he had never had a true enemy, someone that he would like to destroy without pity. "I will make myself as many enemies as possible!" he thought, strangely joyful.'[153] Indeed, the decisive import of the novel lies in this affirmation that the need to compete—condensed and heightened in the need to kill—is truly the genuine core of Keuschnig's nature, that authenticity is somehow deeply destructive:

> In the internal mirror of the taxi, he suddenly spotted his face. At first he would not recognize it, as it was so distorted . . . He immediately recalled with what alien pleasure he had once, in a dream, peed on a woman. At that occasion, as he woke up, he was troubled. 'It wasn't me,' he had immediately thought. To this newly

discovered face, however, such pleasure corresponded; it was not strange to him—this *was* him. And it became clear: with the exposed face, nothing, nothing could be strange to him. The excuse of estrangement was not valid any longer; but any regrets could also be spared . . . Keuschnig believed himself capable of anything, even of *Lustmord* [sexual murder]. Finally, he admitted to himself that the murder of the old woman in the dream had been a *Lustmord*.[154]

The respectable bourgeois conceals a killer, and the killer, moreover, is more genuine, more valuable than the respectable bourgeois.[155] In one of his earliest works, Slavoj Žižek has detected this same sensation of having made contact with the bedrock of one's soul only to discover the subdued 'joy of the knife,' in Fritz Lang's *The Woman in the Window* (1944). The film likewise dealt with a bourgeois who dreams he is a murderer, only that the imaginary nature of the murder did not become known before the very last scene, where the 'murderer,' on the verge of being apprehended and after swallowing lethal drugs, suddenly awakens. Žižek commented:

> The message of the film is not consoling, not: 'it was only a dream, in reality I am a normal man like others and not a murderer!' . . . [W]e do not have a quiet, kind, decent, bourgeois professor dreaming for a moment that he is a murderer; what we have is, on the contrary, a murderer dreaming, in his every-day life, that he is just a decent bourgeois professor.[156]

Our analysis of Dionysian crime would suggest that the bourgeois psyche, revolving around the principle of capitalist individualism and competition, is predicated on the notion that, in Ernst Jünger's words, 'living means killing.' [157] And if to live is to kill, *not* to kill is *not* to live, at least not truly and authentically. On these terms, the meaning of life is concentrated in the act of perpetual competition which, in turn, consummates itself in the final act of aggression, the killing act. Life in mass society is a living death, a state of spiritual coma. To break out of such vegetative existence one needs to compete, to create enemies, to assert the superiority of one's value, to wrest the sense of one's existence.

As the experiences of Lang's and Handke's murderers reveal, the dream of murder is by no means just a liberating, escapist gratification of long-restrained instinctual appetites; it is simultaneously a deeply threatening, unsettling dream. This unlikely junction of epiphany and nightmare corresponds to the schizophrenic division of the individual's psyche as he attempts to successfully perform his complicated role of a *social competitor*. Such haunted daydreams divulge the intrinsic tensions of a paradoxical situation in which the individual is constantly maneuvering between his interests as a 'unique ego'—which he perforce is, not because of reading Stirner but due to material and social necessity—and the no less abiding need to disguise this greed, selfishness and animosity. They radically unveil the 'egoist's' anxiety lest such 'authentic' content shall disastrously flood above the surface. What the individual fears, in other words, is to utter the confidential code of capitalism, precisely because he has come to consider it his *own terrible secret*, the incriminating reality of his desire. Upon finding the killer that has been, so to speak, implanted in his soul, the bourgeois cries with a mixture of horror and delight, echoing Gregor Keuschnig, 'this *is* me!' In Marx's terms, this is the predicament of the *bourgeois* in civil society, as he must, while ruthlessly competing, keep up the pretense of the kind, egalitarian, altruistic *citoyen*. Thus considered, such narratives that scrutinize the fear of exposing one's murderous, ugly side, may be powerful critiques of the basic contradictions of 'socialized individualism,' but not, of course, if these are construed as strictly psychological, natural and timeless phenomena.

American Psycho, once again, provides us with a valuable alternative to the standard explanation of a clash between taming society and the instinctual individual. When Patrick Bateman, finally collapsing under the burden of his furtive crimes, wishes to come clean, to have his 'sickness' attended to— 'I guess I'm a very sick guy'—and have his crime punished, he finds that his confession is rejected by an apathetic society, in fact one which was complicit with his crimes all along. It is finally revealed to him that, for all the atrocities he committed, he was *not* an outcast, not Stirner's 'never ceasing criminal' surrounded with 'the state's spy' but actually quite a normal person, a carrier of a universal disease. Hence the final monologue: 'But even after admitting this there is no catharsis. My punishment continues to elude me.'[158] This stands in diametrical opposition to the thrill of Handke's killer who finds his true self in the murderer within. The antidote to such psychologist reductionism would be to bear in mind the social and historical conditioning of the psyche, the fact that, as Easton Ellis reminds us, the psychopath in 'every one of us' is at the same time an *American* psycho (namely, a product of a given, capitalist society and culture, which, needless to say, can be Austrian, German, French or Italian just as well as American[159]).

At times, the convergence of the sociopolitical, on the one hand, with the cultural and psychological, on the other, is even more organic than can at first be suspected; Gregor Keuschnig's need for enemies, for instance, his recognition of their requisiteness in the quest for meaningful life and the constraint, in the lack of real enemies, to create them: does it not run parallel to the tendency to cherish the invigorating impact of wars and conflicts which was an indispensable ingredient in imperialist politics, and culture, for all of the past century. Suffice to recall Mussolini's words:

> Fascism does not, generally speaking, believes in the possibility or utility of perpetual peace. . . . War alone keys all human energies to their maximum tension. . . . Fascism carries this anti-pacifistic attitude into the life of the individual.[160]

Similar results are yielded when Mussolini's plainspoken assertion is juxtaposed with Zarathustra's lyrical exclamation: 'The spear which I throw at my enemies! How I thank my enemies that at last I can throw it!'[161] Likewise, the fear of the crowd displayed so vividly in *M*, the terrifying image of the uncurbed mob impressed on the bourgeois' retina, was barely an eccentric personal concern of Fritz Lang. As Western democracy went through its birth pangs, it was rather part of a general middle-class fright concerning the rise of the masses (In its acute form, this hysteria seems to have now been rather subdued—in part, likely through the realization that liberal democracy is far from entailing any such calamitous equality). Finally, the fact that in Tarantino's underworld one is not powerful because of having a gun, but rather one has a gun because of being powerful, is homologous to the official account of social inequalities under capitalism, assuring us that being rich or poor is not what determines our value, but simply the outward token of our immanent worth (or worthlessness). The repentant hit man's ethical conflict in *Pulp Fiction*, the affirmation of hierarchy within which he nonetheless attempts to insulate a measure of moral responsibility, can be seen as roughly demarcating the contours of the political discourse of the present-day democratic left, be it in American 'liberal' guise or in its European 'third-way' incarnation: for Jules as well as for the exponents of social democracy—who have either willingly admitted or resignedly digested the inevitability of domination and inequality—there remains merely the question of 'acting responsibly,' of 'taking care of the weak,' or, in Jules' words, of 'tryin' real hard to be shepherds.' In that regard, if something is to be learned from Tarantino and applied to politics, it is possibly that social-democratic resolutions to good, responsible domination are more capricious than reliable, and that, at length, every shepherd will lead his flock astray.

In the bourgeois psyche, as we have seen, social realities are assimilated, encrypted, assigned with objective status, and then gathered under such exchangeable titles as 'the human condition,' 'human nature,' 'authenticity,' or any other equivalent. This is undoubtedly not a neat ideological subterfuge aimed at ratifying social reality, but rather the spontaneous social overdetermination of the cultural, the moral and the psychological. Needless to say, nor is it the work of 'corrupt' or 'decadent' individual authors, suffering from personal pathologies; it is precisely this 'spontaneity' of the procedure, the fact that the social has been already imbibed in the collective 'reality of desire,' appropriated and fondly attached to by the subject, that makes it as culturally irresistible as it is politically effective: now that the subject has discovered his 'authenticity,' is truly convinced of its immediacy and completely unaware of the process by which he was interpellated, he will defend his authenticity ferociously against any meddling with his 'freedom.' This is the vicious circle of the Dionysian criminal, whose sense of authenticity increases in direct proportions to the success of the social interpellation. There is, in that respect, no obligation to choose between an external and an internal explanation of crime, either to pass the blame onto social conditions or to 'stir up the kernel of our desire,' as Žižek once posited[162]; at times, it is precisely by turning the gaze inwards that we sharply perceive society. For that reason, in trying to emerge safely out of the labyrinth of politics, our best guide may yet turn out to be our desire.

Epilogue: A Hero of Our Time

In following the trail of the Nietzschean hero of popular culture my intention was not to illuminate some obscure, if fascinating, territories at the edges of our cultural map. I have assumed, on the contrary, that he would serve as a good enough guide into the very heart of Western civilization. An unlikely guide, perhaps, as he seldom travels on the main road and prefers exotic or subterranean paths, and inasmuch as he often professes to be the firmest antagonist of our contemporary society and presents himself as an absolutely exceptional specimen, at times a rebel or an outcast, even someone who has transcended our society altogether, to reach a higher level of being. Yet for all the claim of overcoming humanity, it seemed to me that the Nietzschean hero could tell us more about our society than about its critics, more about the readily available human-all-too-human and less about a putative overman of the future. Like Lermontov's Pechorin, he would be best understood as representative of his age: 'A Hero of Our Time, gentlemen, is indeed a portrait, but not of a single individual; it is a portrait composed of all the vices of our generation in the fullness of their development.'[1] No doubt, the Nietzschean hero cannot be said to be a portrait of contemporary man in any *realistic sense*, not even psychologically so. Still— as Freud, one of Nietzsche's most famous 'disciples' taught us—daydreams, as well as nightmares, though not a 'correct' reflection of reality, can nonetheless provide us with invaluable insights into the dreamer's psyche. The attempt to juxtapose the social metaphors embodied in the Roarks, the Lecters and the Bonds with social and historical reality, was hence meant to enhance our understanding of both fantasy and society.

The suggestive power of Nietzscheanism and the high attractiveness of the 'solutions' it puts on offer, has a lot to do with the way it attempts to define, *both* enhance *and* restrict our sense of pleasure, greatly increasing certain appetites and desires while, simultaneously, struggling to delimit our scope of imagining those alternatives which it deems unwelcome and dangerous. This is what turns popular Nietzscheanism into such a perplexing mix of strategies, at the same time offensive and defensive, stimulating and containing, encouraging and punishing, dazzlingly radical and grimly conservative, willing to change all, so that all stays the same. For, as was argued, the social metaphor of the Nietzschean hero is ultimately a vindication of social reality. Of the arguments advanced in this study, this might prove the toughest to accept; for it is one thing to point up the existence of a Nietzschean undercurrent in our culture, and even to sample its waters and suggest they are not always crystal clear; yet it is quite another thing to claim that such is, in truth, the very mainstream. This realization, in turn, implies that the only appropriate critical confrontation with Nietzsche's legacy is such that comes to grips with its centrality. In social, cultural and ideological terms, Nietzsche is not now, and I think has never truly been, an outsider to our civilization, neither its 'iconoclastically constructive' critic, nor its 'nihilistically destructive' one; for better or for worse, our civilization is fundamentally—rather than coincidentally, tangentially or arbitrarily—Nietzschean. In that respect, all attempts to fortify liberalism against Nietzscheanism, even at their most genuine and incisive, are to a degree deceptive and inadequate, since there is, in fact, no external adversary to fortify oneself against, and no invader who might be driven outside the city walls.

If Nietzscheanism permeates our culture 'high' and 'low,' this is not due to some failure of liberalism, but rather because Nietzscheanism pertains to the very logic of liberalism, understood in terms of the 'grand economy' and its vicissitudes. In that sense, liberalism is bound to annex with, if not boil down into, some form or other of Nietzscheanism, whether explicit or implicit, vehement or moderate, crude or sophisticated, 'rightist' or 'leftist,' 'Republican' or 'Democratic,' 'Tory' or 'Labourite,' bold or soft-spoken, 'fascist' or 'democratic,' Adornian or Straussian, hedonistic or sadistic, *Bond*ian or *Lecter*ian—to think of just some of the virtually inexhaustible guises under which Nietzscheanism can make its presence felt. Indeed, one of the major conquests of Nietzscheanism is attested to by the fact that so many critiques of Nietzsche reveal themselves, under ideological scrutiny, as profoundly Nietzschean, whether knowingly denying their nature or being sincerely oblivious to it (or, as in most cases, as navigating somewhere in between the extremes of cynicism and obliviousness). To be sure, only rarely can one find examples of a thoroughly and consciously spurious 'anti-Nietzscheanism,' which, as has been argued in relation to neo-Straussianism, can consist in a mindful division between an overt anti-Nietzscheanism, designed to placate the masses, and a covert, conspiratorial Nietzscheanism, for the intellectual and political elect. Yet, however extreme such neo-Straussian strategy appears, it reflects a dialectic between an exoteric Nietzsche-critique and eso-teric Nietzsche-partisanship, which is hardly exceptional. Popular heroes can vividly bear out the fundamental, if schizophrenic, Nietzschean condition of our culture. We have seen, for example, how it does not crucially matter whether a popular hero, like Hannibal Lecter, explicitly espouses Nietz-scheanism, or, like James Bond, advocates an agenda that is explicitly *anti*-Nietzschean. Ian Fleming's secret agent, while surely not a fully conscious practitioner of covert Nietzscheanism, is *de facto* defending the same anti-democratic elite as does his unabashedly Nietzschean counterpart, Thomas Harris's cannibal-aristocrat. For, if 007 regularly defeats such evil, Nietz-schean psychopaths of Dr Lecter's ilk, he does so only after carefully rewrit-ing their menace as a plebeian-revolutionary one, thereby defending the op-erations of clean, responsible and *truly* elitist Nietzscheanism.

The fact that so much of Nietzsche scholarship is finally blind to the in-dispensability of exploitation in Nietzsche's theory mirrors the way the ex-ploitative premise *of our own society* has become largely invisible. The *ideo-logical* triumph of Nietzscheanism runs parallel to the *practical* triumph of the grand economy. This is a phenomenon that Geoff Waite has grasped with characteristic lucidity: 'We *look at* the "crazy" stuff in the corpus of this dead man. We *read* it, may even *interpret* or *deconstruct* it. But we don't ever *see* it completely—*especially* when we *think* we do. Part of this mechanism is confirmed repeatedly by almost everything produced by workers in the Nietzsche Industry. The really crazy stuff does not register, does not com-pute.'[2] Among the 'crazy stuff' Waite has in mind is Nietzsche's espousal of slavery, euthanasia, breeding; and he explains this failure of vision in terms of the distinctive structure of the Nietzschean text, the blind-spots which it forcefully generates, the tension between the exoteric messages and the es-oteric goals, the suggestive mastery of Nietzsche's rhetoric.[3] All these are vi-tal insights; yet they ought to be complemented, I feel, with the elementary realization that our inability to perceive the craziness in Nietzsche is con-nected with the fact that we do not compute 'the crazy stuff' in our social reality, that the iniquities in our social order have become commonsense to us, self-evident, inevitable and hence, also, incomputable. Indeed, in an era where the principle that 'there is no alternative' to the market economy has been globally accepted, sweeping forcefully across (and aside) old bound-aries between 'right' and 'left,' *ought* we really be shocked by Nietzsche's as-sertion that '"Exploitation" does not pertain to a corrupt or imperfect or primitive society: it pertains to the essence of the living thing as a funda-mental organic function, it is a consequence of the intrinsic will to power which is precisely the will to life'?[4] More than any outrageous raving, this statement sounds like the commonsensical stuff of our daily lives; and if, in fact, it *is* crazy, then the basic sanity of our socioeconomic system needs to be severely questioned.

All this is not to say that the modern world is what it is because of Nietz-scheanism and that we are all participants, willing or reluctant, in a colossal experiment conceived of in the mind of an exceedingly ambitious philosopher with the uncanny genius to put his schemes somehow into practice. Surely, like all would-be philosopher-kings, Nietzsche was deluding himself when he wrote the following to his sister:

> I have, quite literally speaking, the future of mankind in the palm of my hand
> . . . I play with a burden that would have crushed every mortal. For that which
> I have to do is *appalling* in every sense of the word: I do not challenge individuals, I challenge mankind as a whole with my terrible charge [Anklage]; whatever the decision taken, *for* me or *against* me, in any case an inexpressibly great fate [Verhängniß] attaches itself to my name.[5]

Nietzsche, in this case as in others like it,[6] clearly exaggerated the power of his ideas to dictate the course of historical events. Yet, surely, it would be no less misguided to accept Thomas Mann's opposing notion of Nietzsche's philosophy as the most sensitive seismograph, its needle registering the movements of the febrile spirit of the 'fascist epoch of the West.'[7] This would be to underestimate the role of Nietzsche, who liked to think of himself as dynamite, by ascribing him a mere passive part. If not omnipotent as its originator imagined, Nietzscheanism is certainly one of the most important ideological forces of the last century. And ideologies are not just receptive, registering machines; at times, they can *induce* earthquakes. While not constitutive of modernity in the sense of some *causa prima*, it would be difficult to think of modernity *without* Nietzscheanism at its ideological core, recruiting, directing, transforming, motivating, and, not least—detonating. In a passage from *On the Genealogy of Morality*, Nietzsche spoke about the slave revolt in morality as a 'huge and incalculably disastrous initiative,' adding that such revolt 'has only been lost sight of because—it was victorious.'[8] Would not such characterization of the slave morality that he abhorred apply today, mutatis mutandis, to describe the effects of *Nietzsche's* own ideological *counter*-revolt? With that suggestion, I bring to a close a study that endeavored to show how the popular ideology of Nietzscheanism and the reality of capitalist modernity make each other mutually invisible.

Endnotes

INTRODUCTION

1. Stanley Rosen, *The Ancient and the Moderns: Rethinking Modernity* (Indiana: St. Augustine's Press, 2002), 189.

2. Joseph Campbell, *The Hero with a Thousand Faces* (Princeton: Princeton Univ. Press, 1968), 38.

3. Fredric Jameson, *The Political Unconscious*: *Narrative as a Socially Symbolic Act* (Ithaca, New York: Cornell University Press, 1981).

4. Jaroslav Hašek, *The Good Soldier Švejk* (London: Penguin Books, 1973), 20.

5. Spike Lee, interviewed in *When We Were Kings*, dir. Leon Gast, USA, DAS Films Ltd; David Sonenberg Production; PolyGram Filmed Entertainment, 1996.

6. Muhammad Ali, in *When We Were Kings*.

7. Hašek, *The Good*, 1.

8. For a discussion of the conservative American popular hero, with references to Ayn Rand, see Jack W. Sattel, 'Heroes on the Right,' *Journal of Popular Culture* 11 (1977): 110–25.

9. Nietzsche, *GS*, 318.

10. Nietzsche, *WTP*, 503–4.

11. Cf. Fritz Stern, *The Politics of Cultural Despair: a Study in the Rise of the Germanic Ideology* (Berkeley, Los Angeles, London: University of California Press, 1961), 30, 128.

12. Eric Bentley, *A Century of Hero-Worship* (Boston: Beacon Press, 1957), 4 (the quotation dates from 1945).

13. Northrop Frye, *Anatomy of Criticism* (London: Penguin, 1990).

14. In that respect I find far too sanguine such constructions of Nietzsche's notion of heroism which celebrate it as (existentially) subversive and iconoclastic as Antonia Birnbaum's *Nietzsche. Les àventures de l'héroïsme* (Paris: Éditions Payot & Rivages, 2000).

15. Jerry Palmer, *Thrillers: Genesis and Structure of a Popular Genre* (London: Edward Arnold, 1978).

16. Nietzsche, *UD*, 111.

17. Nietzsche, *BGEB*, 57

18. Fredrick Appel, *Nietzsche Contra Democracy* (Ithaca and London: Cornell University Press, 1999); 'Nietzsche's Natural Hierarchy', *International Studies in Philosophy* xxix/3, (1997), 49–62.

19. Malcolm Bull, 'Where is the Anti-Nietzsche?' *New Left Review* 3, June (2000) 121–45.

20. Daniel Conway, *Nietzsche & the Political* (London, New York: Routledge, 1997).

21. Robert C. Holub, *Friedrich Nietzsche* (New York: Twayne Publishing, 1995).

22. Domenico Losurdo, *Nietzsche, il ribelle aristocratico* (Torino: Bollati Boringhieri, 2004).

23. Urs Marti, *Der grosse Pöbel und Sklavenaufstand* (Stuttgart-Weimar: Verlag J. B. Metzler: 1993); 'Der Plebejer in der Revolte. Ein Beitrag zur Genealogie des "höheren Menschen"' *Nietzsche Studien* 18 (1989): 550–71.

24. Renate Reschke, 'Die Angst vor dem Chaos. Friedrich Nietzsches Plebiszit gegen die Masse' *Nietzsche Studien* 16 (1987): 353–81.

25. Marc Sautet, *Nietzsche et la Commune* (Paris: éditions Le Sycomore, 1981).

26. Bernhard H. F. Taureck, *Nietzsches Alternativen zum Nihilismus* (Hamburg: Junius Verlag, 1991); *Nietzsche und der Faschismus—Ein Politikum* (Leipzig: Reclam Verlag, 2000).

27. Irving M. Zeitlin, *Nietzsche—A Re-examination* (Cornwall: Polity Press, 1994).

28. Geoff Waite, *Nietzsche's Corps/e. Aesthetics, Politics, Prophecy, or, the Spectacular Technoculture of Everyday Life* (Durham & London: Duke University Press, 1996).

29. Terry Eagleton, *The Ideology of the Aesthetic* (Oxford: Blackwell, 1990).

30. Jameson, *The Political*, especially chapters 4, 5; *Fables of Aggression–Wyndham Lewis, the Modernist as Fascist* (Berkeley: University of California Press, 1979).

31. John Carey, *The Intellectuals and the Masses. Pride and Prejudice among the Literary Intelligentsia, 1880–1939* (London: Faber and Faber, 1992).

32. Kaufmann's major study was *Nietzsche–Philosopher, Psychologist, Antichrist* (Princeton, New Jersey: Princeton University Press, 1974). To this should be added his many translations of Nietzsche to English, accompanied by extensive commentary. Among the many influential studies taking their cue from Kaufmann are: Bernd Magnus, *Nietzsche's Existential Imperative* (Bloomington, Ind.: Indiana University Press, 1978); Arthur Danto, *Nietzsche as Philosopher* (Columbia University Press, 1980); Richard Schacht, *Nietzsche* (London: Routledge & Kegan Paul, 1983); and Alexander Nehamas, *Nietzsche: Life As Literature* (Cambridge: Harvard University Press, 1985).

33. *Harry Potter and the Sorcerer's Stone*, dir. Chris Columbus, USA, Warner Bros., 2001.

CHAPTER 1: NIETZSCHE, THE POPULAR AND THE 'GRAND ECONOMY'

1. *Spider-Man*, dir. Sam Raimi. Columbia TriStar Films, 2002.

2. Don Lipper, 'Dispatches from "Andromeda"—The Nietzscheans,' *Space.com*, 06 .05.2000. http://www.space.com/sciencefiction/tv/andromeda_nietzscheans_000505 .html.

3. Jacques Derrida, 'Interpreting Signatures (Nietzsche/Heidegger): Two Questions,' *Philosophy and Literature*, 10: 246–62.

4. Alan White, *Within Nietzsche's Labyrinth* (New York and London: Routledge, 1990), 11.

5. Steven E. Aschheim, *The Nietzsche Legacy in Germany 1890–1990* (University of California Press, 1994), 3.

6. Aschheim, *The Nietzsche Legacy*, 7.

7. Aschheim, *The Nietzsche Legacy*, 4–5 (emphasis added).

8. Aschheim, *The Nietzsche Legacy*, 3–4.

9. Aschheim, *The Nietzsche Legacy*, 5.

10. Aschheim, *The Nietzsche Legacy*, 7–8.

11. Aschheim, *The Nietzsche Legacy*, 11.

12. Aschheim, *The Nietzsche Legacy*, 279.

13. Georg Lukács, *The Destruction of Reason* (London: The Merlin Press, 1962), 319.

14. H. G. Wells, *When The Sleeper Wakes* (London: Everyman, 1995), 4 (from the preface to the 1921 edition).

15. John Carey, *The Intellectuals and the Masses. Pride and Prejudice among the Literary Intelligentsia, 1880–1939* (London: Faber and Faber, 1992), 134–39.

16. Carey, *The Intellectuals*, 134–39.

17. Peter Gay, *Pleasure Wars. The Bourgeois Experience: Victoria to Freud, Volume 5* (New York, London: W. W. Norton, 1998), 215.

18. Albert S. Lindemann, *Esau's Tears: Modern Anti-Semitism and the Rise of the Jews* (Cambridge: Cambridge University Press, 1997), 162.

19. Wilhelm Röpke, *Civitas Humana* (Erlenbach, Zürich, 1946), 188.

20. F. A. Hayek, quoted in Reinhard Kühnl, *Liberalismus als Form bürgerlicher Herrshcaft–Von der Befreiung des Menschen zur Freiheit des Marktes* (Heilbronn: Distel Verlag, 1999), 119. For an analysis suggesting the primacy of economic class considerations over political rights even within the proto-liberalism of Hobbes and, particularly, of Locke, see C. B. Macpherson's pathbreaking study, *The Political Theory of Possessive Individualism: Hobbes to Locke* (Oxford: Clarendon Press, 1962).

21. Nietzsche, *GK*, 178.

22. Nietzsche, *GK*, 178–79.

23. Terry Eagleton, *The Ideology of the Aesthetic* (Oxford: Blackwell, 1990), 259.

24. Karl Marx and Friedrich Engels, *The Communist Manifesto* (London: Penguin, 1967), 97.

25. Nietzsche, *BGE*, 87.

26. Nietzsche, *BGE*, 45.

27. Nietzsche, *BGE*, 77.

28. Nietzsche, *WTP*, 77.

29. Nietzsche, *BGE*, 194.

30. A famous twentieth-century disciple of Nietzsche, Oswald Spengler, made this prosaic aspect of the will to power explicit when speaking about the Nordic people's 'instinct for power and property, for property as power.' In Oswald Spengler, *Jahre der Entscheidung. Deutschland und die Weltgeschichtliche Entwicklung* (München: DTV, 1980), 183.

31. Nietzsche, *WTP*, 461–62.

32. Nietzsche, *KSA* 2, 681–82.

33. Keith Ansell-Pearson, *An Introduction to Nietzsche as Political Thinker—The Perfect Nihilist* (Cambridge: Cambridge University Press, 1994), 91.

34. After all, Nietzsche's later writings will revert to a militant refutation of all concessions to labour. In *Twilight of the Idols*, for example, Nietzsche again attacks the 'stupidity,' 'the most irresponsible thoughtlessness' of the masters, yet now not on account of excessive exploitation, but on the very reverse charge of *excessive leniency*: for allowing the worker to serve in the military, form unions and vote, thereby undermining his servility: 'But what does one *want*?—to ask it again. If one wills an end, one must also will the means to it: if one wants slaves, one is a fool if one educates them to be masters' (*TI*, 106). It is a catch-22 predicament: the stick drives the worker to rebel out of misery, while the carrot yields the same effect, this time by indulging the worker's impudence. A combination of the two emerges as the solution, yet attaining the ideal ratio remains exasperatingly illusive.

35. Jacob Golomb, *Nietzsche's Psychology of Power* (Jerusalem: The Magnes Press, 1987), 135.

36. Ansell-Pearson, *An Introduction*, 91. See also the comparable, yet shorter discussion of the same passage by Manfred Riedel in his *Nietzsche in Weimar—ein deutsches Drama* (Reclam Leipzig, 2000), 55–56.

37. Nietzsche, *WTP*, 57.

38. Nietzsche, *WTP*, 164.

39. Nietzsche, *WTP*, 142.

40. Nietzsche, *WTP*, 129 (italics added).

41. Nietzsche, *WTP*, 155 (italics added).

42. Thomas Mann, 'Nietzsches Philosophie im Lichte Unserer Erfahrung,' in *Gesammelte Werke in Dreizehn Bänden*, vol. IX (Frankfurt am Main: Fischer, 1974), 695–96.

43. Nietzsche, *WTP*, 130.

44. Nietzsche, *WTP*, 166 (italics added).

45. Nietzsche, *HUMB*, 381–82.

46. Nietzsche, *WTP*, 130.

47. F. A. Hayek, *The Fatal Conceit—The Errors of Socialism* (Chicago: The University of Chicago Press, 1988), 118–19.

48. Ellen Meiksins Wood, *Democracy against Capitalism—Renewing Historical Materialism* (Cambridge: Cambridge University Press, 1995), 13.

49. Nietzsche, *GS*, 73.

50. Nietzsche, *WTP*, 7.

51. In Spengler we find a surprisingly more realistic evaluation of modernity. Spengler could affirm, with obvious approval, the hardened, brutal nature of 'west

European civilization.' 'And where,' he asked, 'could be found, among high Faustian humankind, from the crusades to the World War, that "slave morality," that soft renunciation, that *Caritas* of the nurse?' And he emphatically answered: 'Nietzsche's "slave morality" is a mirage. *His master morality is a reality.'* In Oswald Spengler, *Der Untergang des Abendlandes. Umrisse einer Morphologie der Weltgeschichte* (München: DTV, 1999), 445–46.

52. Cf. Nietzsche, *Z*, 121; *TI*, 104–5.

53. Cf. Nietzsche, *TI*, 103; *WTP*, 148.

54. Nietzsche, *WTP*, 78.

55. Nietzsche, *BT*, 11

56. Nietzsche, *BT*, 79.

57. Robert C. Holub, 'The Elisabeth Legend: The Cleansing of Nietzsche and the Sullying of His Sister,' in *Nietzsche, Godfather of Fascism? On the Uses and Abuses of a Philosophy*, ed. Jacob Golomb, Robert S. Wistrich (Princeton, New Jersey: Princeton University Press, 2002), 219.

58. Peter Sloterdijk, *Die Verachtung der Massen—Versuch über Kulturkampfe in der modernen Gesellschaft* (Frankfurt am Main: Suhrkamp, 2000), 27.

59. Yirmiyahu Yovel, *Spinoza and Other Heretics* (Tel Aviv: Poalim, 1988), 406–7.

60. Yovel forgets that historical fascism was backed by the bulk of the Italian and German social, economic, political, and cultural elites, endorsed—as far as the latter is concerned—by some of the artistic and philosophical 'luminaries' of the age, such as Jünger, Benn, Marinetti, d'Annunzio, Pirandello, Hamsun, Céline, Pound, W. Lewis, and many others. Or would he accept that a Nietzschean *and* a Nazi, like Heidegger, was just a 'small intellectual worker,' his susceptible, overinflated ego whipped into Dionysian frenzy? Secondly, he does not mention that Mussolini and Hitler faced stern resistance precisely from common, vulgar, working-class people, who realized all too well what sort of 'empowerment' they are going to get from these 'egalitarian' and 'horizontally-minded' leaders.

61. Thomas S. Hibbs, *Shows About Nothing: Nihilism in Popular Culture from* The Exorcist *to* Seinfeld (Dallas: Spence Publishing Company, 1999).

62. Paul Zweig, *The Adventurer* (London: Basic Books, 1974).

63. As further discussed in chapter 5.

64. Geoff Waite, *Nietzsche's Corps/e. Aesthetics, Politics, Prophecy, or, the Spectacular Technoculture of Everyday Life* (Durham & London: Duke University Press, 1996), 14.

65. Nietzsche, *EH*, 97.

66. Nietzsche, *SE*, 193.

67. Nietzsche, *SE*, 194.

68. Hence the fundamental fallacy in the frequent attempt to prove that Nietzsche was no rightist by pointing at the myriad of leftist Nietzscheans. That great many in the broadly defined 'Left' have taken to the unabashed patron of slavery, should pose a great *question* rather than sneak past us as an *answer*. If anything, one should think, it ought to problematize the leftism of those Nietzscheans, rather than somehow authenticate *Nietzsche's* leftism.

69. Waite, *Nietzsche's Corps/e*, 223.

70. Nietzsche, *KSB* 6, 327.

71. Jack London, *The Iron Heel* (Edinburgh: Rebel Inc., 1999), 7.

CHAPTER 2: HOW TO TAME A BULLDOG:
THE SOCIAL MISSION OF THE NIETZSCHEAN HERO

1. Karl Marx, *The Revolutions of 1848: Political Writings Volume I* (Harmondsworth: Penguin, 1993), 190.

2. David Harvey, *The Limits To Capital* (London, New York: Verso, 1999), 19.

3. C. B. Macpherson, 'Introduction' in Thomas Hobbes, *Leviathan* (Harmondsworth: Penguin, 1968), 52.

4. Macpherson, 'Introduction', 58, italics added.

5. Macpherson, 'Introduction', 58–59.

6. Alain Renaut, *The Era of the Individual* (Princeton, New Jersey: Princeton University Press, 1999), 31. Renaut's account expands into a comprehensive and valuable theory of modern individualism, including, as we shall shortly see, Nietzsche's take on the matter.

7. Renaut, *The Era*, 34.

8. Bertolt Brecht, 'Leben des Galilei', *Ausgewählte Werke in sechs Bänden*, Band 2 (Frankfurt am Main: Suhrkamp Verlag, 1997), 11–12.

9. Compare Anatol Schneider's distinction between the old, Enlightenment concept of individualism which was egalitarian and a younger sense of individualism, developing in the nineteenth century, which emphasized personal distinction. See his *Nietzscheanismus- Zur Geschichte eines Begriffs* (Würzburg: Königshausen und Neumann, 1997), 12.

10. Ralph Waldo Emerson, 'Self-Reliance', in *The Complete Essays and Other Writings* (New York: The Modern Library, 1940), 148.

11. Emerson, 'Self-Reliance', 149.

12. Emerson, 'Self-Reliance', 149.

13. Emerson himself was an important transitional figure in that regard, fluctuating between passages such as the one just quoted and others, of a quite different tone, where human equality, at least spiritual equality, is emphasized. A good example is the famous essay, *The Over-Soul*, which seeks to underline a transcendental soul uniting all men.

14. Nietzsche, *WTP*, 410–11.

15. Nietzsche, *TI*, 56.

16. Nietzsche, *WTP*, 162.

17. Renaut, *The Era*, 137.

18. Renaut, *The Era*, 137.

19. Renaut, *The Era*, 137.

20. Nietzsche, *BGE*, 204.

21. Nietzsche, *WTP*, 476.

22. Nietzsche, *WTP*, 475, italics added.

23. Nietzsche, *WTP*, 473–74.

24. Nietzsche, *Z*, 120–22.

25. Nietzsche, *BT*, 111.

26. Eric Bentley, *A Century of Hero-Worship* (Boston: Beacon Press, 1957), 78.

27. Marx, *The Revolutions*, 130.

28. Marx, *The Revolutions*, 133.

29. Nietzsche, *TI*, 108.

30. As much was acknowledged by Nietzsche, who wrote: 'In the face of such threatening storms, who dares to appeal with any confidence to our pale and exhausted religions, the very foundations of which have degenerated into scholarly religions? Myth, the necessary prerequisite of every religion, is already paralyzed everywhere, and even in this domain the optimistic spirit, which we have just designated as the germ of destruction in our society, has attained the mastery.' *BT*, 111.

31. This also holds true in regard to Nietzsche's critique of Spencer, who was at all times disparaged, but not for encouraging competition and exploitation. Rather Spencer was chastised for failing to bolster exploitation properly, for being a 'decadent, nihilist, moralist,' and so forth.

32. Nietzsche, *WTP*, 412.

33. Nietzsche, *WTP*, 398.

34. Nietzsche, *WTP*, 398.

35. Nietzsche, *GS*, 107.

36. Nietzsche, *GS*, 107–8.

37. Eric Bentley's formulation of this attempt at ennobling of the capitalist—of the 'practical man'—is also worth citing: 'In [Schopenhauer's] hierarchy of spirits, the artist and the philosopher are in the first rank; in the second is the *savant*, in the third the practical man, in the fourth the proletarian, in the fifth and last the savage. Nietzsche's endeavor was not so much to elevate the practical man to the first rank as to merge Schopenhauer's first three ranks into one superhuman being.' Bentley, *A Century*, 93.

38. Cf. Ayn Rand as quoted by Leonard Peikoff in the 'Afterword,' *The Fountainhead* (New York: Signet, 1993), 696.

39. Ayn Rand, *The Fountainhead* (New York: Signet, 1993), 91–92.

40. Rand, *The Fountainhead*, 92.

41. Rand, *The Fountainhead*, 133.

42. Rand, *The Fountainhead*, 134.

43. Nietzsche, *WTP*, 498.

44. This distinction is what Lukács usefully defined as 'direct and indirect apologetics of capitalism.' See: Georg Lukács, *The Destruction of Reason* (London: The Merlin Press, 1962), 354.

45. Nietzsche, *BT* Preface ('Attempt at a Self-criticism,' 1886), 22.

46. Cf. Raymond Geuss, 'Introduction,' to *The Birth of Tragedy and Other Writings*, ed. Raymond Geuss (Cambridge: Cambridge University Press, 1999), xxiii.

47. Geuss, 'Introduction,' xxiv.

48. Geuss, 'Introduction,' xxiv–xxv.

49. Nietzsche, *KSA* 9, 426

50. Tommaso Marinetti, as quoted by James Joll, *Europe since 1870: An International History* (London: Penguin, 1973), 127.

51. Vilfredo Pareto, as quoted by James Joll, *Europe since 1870: An International History* (London: Penguin, 1973), 130–31.

52. Cf. the critical synopsis in Reinhard Kühnl, *Liberalismus als Form bürgerlicher Herrshcaft–Von der Befreiung des Menschen zur Freiheit des Marktes* (Heilbronn: Distel Verlag, 1999), 65. The quintessential neo-liberal statement is F. A. Hayek's critique

of socialism in *The Road to Serfdom* (Chicago: The University of Chicago Press, 1994).

53. John Stuart Mill, 'Considerations on Representative Government,' in *On Liberty and Other Essays* (Oxford: Oxford University Press), 294–95.

54. Here, as elsewhere, Rand's exaggerated zeal, her *over*-commitment to the cause, as well as her habitual lack of tact, throw a rather ludicrous light, but not necessarily *falsifying* one, upon classical liberal tenets. As Slavoj Žižek observed: 'Rand fits into the line of "overconformist" authors who undermine the ruling ideological edifice by their very excessive identification with it' (Slavoj Žižek, 'Four Discourses, Four Subjects,' in *Cogito and the Unconscious*, Slavoj Žižek, ed., Durham, North Carolina: Duke University Press, 1998, 101).

55. Mill, *Considerations*, 300.

56. John Stuart Mill, 'On Liberty,' *On Liberty and Other Essays* (Oxford: Oxford University Press), 72–73.

57. John Stuart Mill, 'Chapters on Socialism,' in *Principles of Political Economy* (Oxford: Oxford University Press, 1998), 382.

58. Mill, *On Liberty*, 71.

59. Nietzsche, *WTP*, 399.

60. This mediating role has also been important in the transition from early liberal anti-imperialism to a rather more expansive stance: 'With his entire theory, Mill has been the most important intellectual figure in transforming English liberalism from a dominantly anti-imperialist theory to a very sophisticated defense of an expanding British Empire' (in Eileen P. Sullivan, 'Liberalism and Imperialism: J. S. Mill's Defense of the British Empire,' *Journal of the History of Ideas* 44, 4, 1983, 617).

61. Mill, *On Liberty*, 80.

62. Ishay Landa, 'Nietzsche, the Chinese Worker's Friend,' *New Left Review* 236 (1999): 3–23.

63. Nietzsche, *D*, 127.

64. Nietzsche, *GS*, 99.

65. Carey, *The Intellectuals*, 201.

66. Mill, *On Liberty*, 72.

67. G. M. Mara, S. L. Dovi, 'Mill, Nietzsche, and the Identity of Postmodern Liberalism,' *The Journal of Politics* 57, a (1995), 2.

68. Mara, Dovi, 'Mill, Nietzsche,' 4.

69. Consider, in addition to Mara and Dovi, the following view: 'If Nietzsche criticized liberalism, he could be regarded, from a certain viewpoint, . . . as an internal critic, whose activity ultimately strengthens that which he appears to attack' (Gal Gerson, *Liberalism: Texts, Contexts, Critiques*, Tel Aviv: The Open University, 2002, 194–95. Hebrew in the original, my translation). Also, in *Nietzsche and the Origin of Virtue* (London, New York: Routledge, 1991) Lester H. Hunt argues that '"Homer's contest" suggests the interesting possibility of a Nietzschean liberalism' (65) and that 'Nietzsche's model is an instance of . . . the liberal conception of order' (63). Mark Warren, for his part, contended that Nietzsche 'cannot be said to be a critic of liberal democracy in any comprehensive sense, even though commentators often construe him in this way. The scope of his criticism should be viewed as being limited to those aspects in which Christian and liberal democratic culture are in fact

continuous' in *Nietzsche and Political Thought* (Cambridge, Massachusetts, London: The MIT Press, 1991), 214. The most notable current proponent of Nietzsche as a liberal-bourgeois is probably Richard Rorty, who has endorsed a position he described as 'postmodernist bourgeois liberalism,' very much inspired by a Nietzschean sense of 'liberal ironism' (See his 'Postmodernist Bourgeois Liberalism,' in *Objectivity, Relativism and Truth: Philosophical Papers, Volume 1*, Cambridge: Cambridge University Press, 1991, 197–202).

70. In many ways, Nazi rhetoric echoed and emulated the emphasis of the liberal tradition on individual excellence, continually bidding to defend the European individual against the Asian masses. 'Marxism,' Hitler avows 'presents itself as the perfection of the Jew's attempt to exclude the pre-eminence of personality in all fields of human life and replace it by the numbers of the mass' In Adolf Hitler, *Mein Kampf* (Boston, New York: Houghton Mifflin Company, 1999), 447. As John Carey had forcefully argued, expressed by Hitler's genocidal plans was quite centrally the anxiety felt by the elites vis-à-vis mass power. Carey shows how schemes of mass killings were harbored in some of the most refined and capable literary minds of the epoch leading to the Second World War (1880–1939). The bitter historical truth which his iconoclastic book exposes is the fact that contempt for common human life, the life of persons who are '*ex termini*' less individual than others, was not the exclusive feature of a demented, far-right extremism, but rather the very *norm* in Western, high culture: 'the tragedy of *Mein Kampf* is that it was not, in many respects, a deviant work but one firmly rooted in European intellectual orthodoxy' (See, Carey, *The Intellectuals*, 208).

71. Giuseppe Tomasi di Lampedusa, *The Leopard* (London: Everyman's Library, 1991), 33.

72. Cf. Ayn Rand, *The Romantic Manifesto. A Philosophy of Literature* (New York: Signet), 1971.

73. As Slavoj Žižek did in *Four Discourses*, 101.

74. Cf. Philip Gordon's perceptive essay on Ayn Rand's heroes and their ideological service to capitalism: 'The Extroflective Hero: A Look at Ayn Rand,' *Journal of Popular Culture* 10, (1976-77), 701–10.

75. Harvey, *Limits*, 34.

76. Žižek, *Four Discourses*, 100.

77. Allan Bloom, *The Closing of the American Mind* (New York: Simon and Schuster, 1987), 62.

78. Cf. Nietzsche, *WTP*, 17, 316–18.

79. Hibbs, *Shows*, 38.

80. Hibbs, *Shows*, 35.

81. Hibbs, *Shows*, 41.

82. Hibbs, *Shows*, 43.

83. Hibbs, *Shows*, 156.

84. Hibbs, *Shows*, 159.

85. Hibbs, *Shows*, 177.

86. Hibbs, *Shows*, 182.

87. Hibbs, *Shows*, 38.

88. Allan Bloom, 'How Nietzsche Conquered America,' *The Wilson Quarterly* (Summer 1987): 80–93.

89. Hibbs, *Shows*, 19–20; *The Lion King*, dir Rob Minkoff, Roger Allers, Walt Disney Studios, 1994.

90. Nietzsche, *KSA* 11, 102.

91. In a series of lucid studies, the Canadian political scientist Shadia B. Drury has outed the closet Nietzscheanism, so to speak, of Leo Strauss himself and of his influential and well-placed followers, notable among them Allan Bloom. As Drury persuasively contends, the Straussians regard themselves as a basically Nietzschean elite whose covert mission is twofold: on the one hand, esoterically, they seek to attain a position of political power by influencing the ruling elite and often enough personally entering its ranks, where they endorse militantly elitist and expansionist policies, at home and abroad (see, *Leo Strauss And The American Right*, New York: St. Martin's Press, 1999. Drury's critique was first formulated in her *The Political ideas of Leo Strauss*, New York: St. Martin's Press, 1988). Complementarily, they seek to exercise a hegemonic influence over the broad masses: 'Strauss and Bloom are enemies of liberty more than democracy. Democracy makes it possible for supermen to manipulate the people. The difficulty is how to get the masses to consent to values that subvert hard-won liberal rights and freedoms. The ingenious solution is to use democracy itself to defeat liberalism. The idea is to turn the people against liberty and equal rights' (Shadia B. Drury, *Gurus of the Right*, http://www.uregina.ca/arts/CRC/gurus3.html).

92. Hibbs, *Shows*, 18.

93. Geoff Waite, *Nietzsche's Corps/e. Aesthetics, Politics, Prophecy, or, the Spectacular Technoculture of Everyday Life* (Durham & London: Duke University Press, 1996), 159.

94. *Ice Age*, dir. Chris Wedge, Carlos Saldanha, Fox Movies, 2002.

95. *Ice Age*.

CHAPTER 3: POPULAR NIETZSCHEANISM: AESTHETICS FOR EVERYONE AND NO ONE

1. See John Storey, *Cultural Theory and Popular Culture: A Reader* (Athens: The University of Georgia Press, 1998), 429. Already in the mid-1960s Umberto Eco has offered a similar division between 'apocalittici'—pessimistic critics of mass culture— and 'integrati'—critics who have made their peace with it. See his *Apocalittici e integrati* (Milano: Bompiani, 1964).

2. The terms do in fact sometimes appear coupled together, as when John Storey speaks about 'pessimistic elitism,' in his *Inventing Popular Culture—From Folklore to Globalization* (Oxford: Blackwell Publishing, 2003), 59.

3. Graeme Turner, *British Cultural Studies: An Introduction*, Second Edition (London and New York: Routledge, 1996), 205. Among those mentioned as possibly lenient towards capitalist hegemony are such critics as John Fiske, Janice Radway, Ien Ang and David Buckingham.

4. For a very useful and comprehensive discussion of British Cultural Studies, see Turner, *British*.

5. See John Carey, ed., *The Faber Book of Utopias* (London, Boston: Faber & Faber, 2000).

6. Dwight Macdonald, 'A Theory of Mass Culture,' in B. Rosenberg and D. White eds. *Mass Culture: The Popular Arts in America* (New York: Macmillan, 1957), 61.

7. Macdonald, 'A Theory,' 62.

8. Dominic Strinati, *Introduction to Theories of Popular Culture* (London, New York: Routledge, 1995), 16–17. For a useful critique of the very term 'mass culture' as an elitist shibboleth, see Alan Swingewood's classic *The Myth of Mass Culture* (Atlantic Highlands, N.J.: Humanities Press, 1977).

9. Terry Lovell, *Pictures of Reality: Aesthetics, Politics and Pleasure* (London: BFI Publishing, 1980), 58.

10. Lovell, *Pictures*, 59.

11. Cf. Lovell, *Pictures*, 61.

12. Lovell, *Pictures*, 62–63.

13. This reading of *The Smurfs* I initially derived from the internet article by J. Marc Schmidt *Socio-Political Themes in The Smurfs* (1998): http://www.geocities .com/Hollywood/Cinema/3117/sociosmurf2.htm.

14. Peyo, *Le Schtroumpf Financier* (Bruxelles: Editions du Lombard, 1999).

15. Piotr Emptypockets, *The Smurfs: A Communist Threat in Saturday Morning Cartoons*, http://twyla.reallyrules.com/scb.html.

16. Pierre Bourdieu, *Distinction: A Social Critique of the Judgement of Taste* (London: Routledge, 2002), 3.

17. Bourdieu, *Distinction*, 6.

18. The extent to which Bourdieu's take on Kant's position is indeed correct is debatable; yet it certainly reflects the tradition emanating from Kant's original formulations. It is in that sense, of relating to a certain aesthetic heritage, and not necessarily to Kant himself, that I abide by the term 'Kantian' in what follows. Moreover, as we shall see, *Nietzsche's* understanding of Kant's aesthetics was essentially the same as Bourdieu's, thus enabling a 'dialogue' between their perspectives.

19. Ortega y Gasset as quoted in Bourdieu, *Distinction*, 31.

20. Bourdieu, *Distinction*, 4.

21. Bourdieu, *Distinction*, 16.

22. Bourdieu, *Distinction*, 9.

23. As Jameson himself has shown in his excellent discussion of Wyndham Lewis, 'the modernist as fascist' in his *Fables of Aggression—Wyndham Lewis, the Modernist as Fascist* (Berkeley: University of California Press, 1979).

24. Karl Marx, *The Revolutions of 1848: Political Writings Volume I* (Harmondsworth: Penguin, 1993), 133.

25. T. Adorno and M. Horkheimer, *Dialectic of Enlightenment* (London: New York. Verso, 1999), 124.

26. Bourdieu, *Distinction*, 511–12.

27. Bourdieu, *Distinction*, 4.

28. Bourdieu, *Distinction*, 4–5.

29. Fredric Jameson, 'Reification and Utopia in Mass Culture,' in F. Jameson, *Signatures of the Visible* (New York, London: Routledge, 1992), 12.

30. Earlier in the same text, Jameson expressed an explicit adherence to 'traditional aesthetic philosophy (in particular . . . Kant),' which defined art as an activity which 'has no practical purpose or end in the "real world" of business or politics or

concrete human praxis generally. This traditional definition surely holds for all art that works as such,' Jameson, *Reification*, 10–11.

31. Macdonald, *A Theory*, 68.

32. Raymond Chandler, *The Simple Art of Murder* (New York: Vintage, 1998), 10.

33. Jameson, *Reification*, 9.

34. Jameson, *Reification*, 14.

35. Bourdieu, *Distinction*, 6.

36. As Tony Bennett rightly observed, 'the members of subordinate classes never encounter or are oppressed by a dominant ideology in some pure or class essentialist form; bourgeois ideology is encountered only in the compromised forms it must take in order to provide some accommodation for opposing class values' in Tony Bennett, Colin Mercer and Janet Woollacott, eds. *Popular Culture and Social Relations* (Milton Keynes: Open University Press, 1986), xv.

37. Fredric Jameson, *The Political Unconscious: Narrative as a Socially Symbolic Act* (Ithaca, New York: Cornell University Press, 1981), 19.

38. As Chirinos, a commoner girl in Cervantes' play *El Retablo de las Maravillas*, observes: 'The pine tree bears acorns; the pear-tree, pears; the vine, grapes; the honorable man, honor, being capable of yielding nothing else' in Miguel de Cervantes, *Teatro Completo*, ed. F. Sevilla Arroyo and A. Rey Hazzas (Barcelona: Planeta, 1987), 800.

39. Anon, 'Lazarillo de Tormes,' *Two Spanish Picaresque Novels* (London: Penguin, 1969), 78.

40. Cf. Pierre Bourdieu, *Sur la télévision: suivi de L'emprise du journalisme* (Paris: Raisons d'agir éditions, 1996).

41. As Stuart Hall claimed, in relation to Adorno's position, 'Ultimately, the notion of the people as a purely passive, outline force is a deeply unsocialist perspective.' In 'Notes on Deconstructing "the Popular,"' John Storey (ed.), *Cultural Theory and Popular Culture: A Reader*, 2nd ed. (Hemel Hempstead: Prentice Hall, 1998), 446.

42. Hall, *Notes*, 452.

43. Peter Sloterdijk, *Die Verachtung der Massen—Versuch über Kulturkampfe in der modernen Gesellschaft* (Frankfurt am Main: Suhrkamp, 2000), 57.

44. Nietzsche, *GK*, 179.

45. Nietzsche, *BGE*, 186–87.

46. Nietzsche, *GEN*, 78.

47. Nietzsche, *GEN*, 78–79.

48. Nietzsche, *GEN*, 80.

49. Karl Marx and Friedrich Engels, *The Communist Manifesto* (London: Penguin, 1967), 94.

50. Nietzsche, *BGEB*, 152.

51. D. G. Williamson, *Bismarck and Germany 1862–1890* (London, New York: Longman, 1998), 64.

52. Nietzsche, *TI*, 106

53. Nietzsche, *ST*, 9.

54. Nietzsche, *ST*, 10.

55. Nietzsche, *ST*, 10.

56. Nietzsche, *ST*, 33.

57. Nietzsche, *ST*, 30.

58. Nietzsche, *ST*, 29.

59. Nietzsche, *TI*, 101–2.

60. Nietzsche, *TI*, 102–3.

61. Nietzsche, *TI*, 103.

62. Nietzsche, *TI*, 104–5.

63. Nietzsche, *Z*, 121.

64. Nietzsche, *WTP*, 386.

65. Bismarck, as quoted as quoted by James Joll, *Europe since 1870: An International History* (London: Penguin, 1973), 91.

66. Nietzsche, *GEN*, 81.

67. The very rigid demarcation line drawn between popular and high culture is not coincidentally a product of the nineteenth century and even more so of the twentieth, the very era when mass consumption is consolidated. This is the time when the foothold gained by the masses is stronger than ever, and with it grows proportionately the need for a distinctive counter-identity. Cf. Paul DiMaggio, 'Cultural Entrepreneurship in Nineteenth-Century Boston,' *Media Cult. Soc.* 4:33–50 (1982): 303–21.

68. Bourdieu, *Distinction*, 5.

69. Mark Twain, *The Adventures of Huckleberry Finn* (Harmondsworth: Penguin, 1994), 12–13.

70. Nietzsche, *GEN*, 12–13.

71. Nietzsche, *GEN*, 36.

72. Nietzsche, *GEN*, 14–15.

73. Nietzsche, *TI*, 33.

74. Nietzsche, *BGE*, 185.

75. Nietzsche, *BGE*, 185.

76. Malcolm Bull, 'Where is the Anti-Nietzsche?' *New Left Review* 3, June (2000), 130.

77. Bull, *Anti-Nietzsche*, 127.

78. Nietzsche, *BGE*, 87.

79. Nietzsche, *WTP*, 458.

80. Nietzsche, *WTP*, 143.

81. Nietzsche, *TI*, 99.

82. Nietzsche, *TI*, 99–100.

83. Nietzsche, *Z*, 72.

84. Nietzsche, *Z*, 98.

85. Nietzsche, *A*, 164–65.

86. Nietzsche, *A*, 128.

87. Nietzsche, *Z*, 224.

88. Nietzsche, *EH*, 51–52. I have changed Hollingdale's translation of *Vernichtung* from 'destruction' to 'extermination.'

89. Gustave Flaubert, *Œuvres Complètes. Correspondence. Nouvelle Édition Augmentée: Deuxième Série 1847–1852* (Paris: Louis Conard, Libraire-Éditeur, 1926), 415.

90. Cf. Annemarie Etter, 'Nietzsche und das Gesetzbuch des Manu,' *Nietzsche Studien* 16, (1987), 340-52.

91. Nietzsche, *TI*, 68.

92. Nietzsche, *KSA* 2, 682.

93. Jack London, 'How I Became a Socialist,' in *The Portable Jack London*, ed. Earle Labor, (New York: Penguin, 1994), 458–59.

94. London, *How I Became*, 459.

95. London, *How I Became*, 460.

96. London, *How I Became*, 458.

97. London, *How I Became*, 461.

98. Jack London, *The Sea-Wolf* (Oxford, New York: Oxford University Press, 1992), 90.

99. Gerd Hurm, 'Of Wolves and Lambs: Jack London's and Nietzsche's Discourses of Nature,' *Nietzsche in American Literature and Thought*, ed. Manfred Pütz (Columbia: Camden House, 1995), 127.

100. Hurm, *Wolves*, 121.

101. Compare Patrick Bridgewater's assessment: 'rationally [London] may have been increasingly an advocate of the Socialism so detested by Nietzsche, but aesthetically he was totally captivated by the Superman-idea.' In *Nietzsche in Anglosaxony* (Leicester: Leicester University Press, 1972), 164.

CHAPTER 4: REALISM, ROMANTICISM, BYRONISM: THE GENEALOGY OF THE NIETZSCHEAN HERO

1. Northrop Frye, *Anatomy of Criticism* (London: Penguin, 1990), 33–35.

2. Frye, *Anatomy*.

3. Frye, *Anatomy*, 34.

4. E. R. Burroughs, *Tarzan of the Apes* (New York: Signet, 1990), 122.

5. Frye, *Anatomy*, 348.

6. Frye, *Anatomy*, 16.

7. Frye, *Anatomy*, 17. Italics added.

8. Frye, to be sure, was no Marxist literary critic. He seems, on the one hand, to have been aware of the need for a socially and historically oriented critical methodology—of the kind which Marxist literary analysis attempts to provide—as the only means for furnishing literary criticism with 'total coherence' and rescuing it from the arbitrariness of taste, but, on the other hand, was equally committed to the task of refuting precisely this, politically unacceptable, option. Recognizing this contradictory stance, the fundamental duality of his thought, we begin to understand how Frye could have become the champion of the great adversaries of Marxist criticism, the New Critics and their motto of 'the literary study of literature,' while crucially contributing to the making of *The Political Unconscious*, one of the major Marxist tracts in literary theory of the second half of the twentieth century. Jameson, for his part, was wholly aware of this self-refuting, double movement in Frye: see his comments in *The Political*, 70–71.

9. Frye, *Anatomy*, 34.

10. Paul Zweig, *The Adventurer* (London: Basic Books, 1974), vii.

11. Zweig, *The Adventurer*, 12–13.

12. Zweig, *The Adventurer*, 12.

13. Zweig, *The Adventurer*, 221–22.

14. Zweig, *The Adventurer*, 205.

15. Cf. Javier Salazar Rincón, *El Mundo Social del 'Quijote'* (Madrid: Editorial Gredos, 1986), especially 228–71.

16. Honoré de Balzac, *Eugénie Grandet* (Harmondsworth: Penguin, 1955), 154.

17. Daniel Defoe, *Robinson Crusoe* (Harmondsworth: Penguin Popular Classics, 1994), 8–10.

18. Defoe, *Robinson Crusoe*, 70. Italics added.

19. Defoe, *Robinson Crusoe*, 74. Italics added.

20. Zweig, *The Adventurer*, 113.

21. Zweig, *The Adventurer*, 115.

22. Which the bourgeoisie, according to Marx, initially aspired to be in order to legitimate its hegemonic claims vis-à-vis the privileged nobility. See, for example, 'Zur Kritik der Hegelschen Rechtsphilosophie, Einleitung.'

23. Zweig, *The Adventurer*, viii.

24. Zweig, *The Adventurer*, 3–4.

25. Zweig, *The Adventurer*, 4.

26. Nietzsche, *BTB*, 69.

27. Nietzsche, *BTB*, 64.

28. Nietzsche, *BTB*, 55, my italics.

29. Nietzsche, *BTB*, 56, my italics.

30. Nietzsche, *BTB*, 37.

31. Nietzsche, *BTB*, 37.

32. Nietzsche, *BTB*, 73.

33. Nietzsche, *BTB*, 84.

34. Nietzsche, *BTB*, 91.

35. Nietzsche, *BTB*, 115.

36. Nietzsche, obviously, was not alone in questioning realism aesthetically and socially, though Paul Zweig was right in assigning him a major role. Given the social nature of the problem—i.e. mass society—we find a social response to it cutting across national and cultural boundaries. France experienced a vigorous and passionate denial of realistic narrative, reaching its peak in the influential work of such symbolists and proto-surrealists as Baudelaire, Rimbaud and Lautréamont. They all, quite independently of Nietzsche, sought to move beyond good and evil, and all of them found realism standing in their way. A comparable contemporary trend, in English literature, was expressed, among others, by A. C. Swinburne, Walter Pater and James Thomson. For an overview of these authors' 'Dionysian' facets, see Robert D. Stock's erudite study, *The Flutes of Dionysus: Daemonic Enthrallment in Literature* (Lincoln and London: University of Nebraska Press, 1989), 296–304.

37. Frye, *Anatomy*, 59.

38. Frye, *Anatomy*, 60.

39. As programmatically expressed in her *The Romantic Manifesto: A Philosophy of Literature* (New York: Signet).

40. Frye, *Anatomy*, 60.

41. Lord Byron, *Selected Poems*, Canto III, XLV (Harmondsworth: Penguin, 1996), 429.

42. Byron, *Selected Poems*, 477.

43. Byron, *Selected Poems*, 483.

44. Byron, *Selected Poems*, 481.

45. Byron, *Selected Poems*, 496–97.

46. Mikhail Lermontov, *A Hero of Our Time* (London: Everyman, 1992), 116–17.

47. Nietzsche, *WTP*, 403.

48. Lermontov, *A Hero*, 126–27.

49. Nietzsche, *WTP*, 498.

50. On Nietzsche's opinion of Lermontov and of *A Hero of Our Time* we know something, if very little, from a letter (October 31, 1879) that contains the following comment: 'Meine Mutter . . . hat mir Lermontoff vorgelesen; ein mir sehr fremder Zustand, die westeuropäische Blasirtheit, ist allerliebst beschrieben, mit russischer Naivetät und halbwüchsiger Weltweltenweisheit—nicht wahr?' (*KSA* 5, 460). This was written at the height of Nietzsche's moderate, human-all-too-human phase and addressed to Paul Rée, an important agent in bringing this phase about; which may explain the slightly condescending, if amused, tone of Nietzsche's assessment. The Nietzsche of *The Will to Power*, as the above quotations suggest, might have found reason to take *A Hero of Our Time* more seriously. Perhaps he did. Yet I would not go as far as conjecture, on the basis of such scanty evidence, that Lermontov actually *influenced* Nietzsche's later writings. The similarities in outlook and rhetoric, whatever their origin, are at any rate noticeable.

51. Cf. Lukács' evaluation of literary Byronism in *The Historical Novel* (Lincoln, London: University of Nebraska Press, 1983), 33–34.

52. Byron, *Selected Poems*, 487.

53. Byron, *The Collected Poems of Lord Byron* (Hertfordshire: Wordsworth Poetry Library, 1994), 99.

54. Nietzsche, *WTP*, 469. We have also noted above (in the discussion of *David Strauss, the Confessor and the Writer*), how Nietzsche, criticizing the philistinism of his time, explicitly sanctioned the conservative quenching of the French revolution.

55. Byron, *Don Juan* (Harmondsworth: Penguin, 1973), 355.

56. Byron, *Don Juan*, 353.

57. Nietzsche, *Z*, 74.

58. Byron, *Don Juan*, 355.

59. Nietzsche, *WTP*, 42.

60. Robert Southey as quoted in R. W. Harris, *Romanticism and the Social Order 1780–1830* (London: Blandford Press, 1969), 279–80.

61. Lermontov, *A Hero*, 15–16.

62. Nietzsche, *Z*, 41–42.

63. It is nonetheless interesting, in this context, to recall Marx's conjecture, as summarized by his daughter Eleanor and Edward Aveling, that Byron would have eventually abandoned his radicalism, had he lived longer: 'As Marx . . . was wont to say: "The real difference between Byron and Shelley is this: those who understand them and love them rejoice that Byron died at thirty-six, because if he had lived he would have become a reactionary *bourgeois*; they grieve that Shelley died at twenty-nine, because he was essentially a revolutionist, and he would always have been one of the advanced guard of Socialism."' In 'Shelley and Socialism,' (1888), http://www.marxists.org/archive/eleanor-marx/1888/04/shelley-socialism.htm.

64. Byron, *Selected Poems*, 477.

65. Byron, *Selected Poems*, 500.

66. Stock, *The Flutes*, 253, my italics.

67. For a discussion of the 'superfluous man' in Russian literature with references to Pechorin, see Jehanne M. Gheith, 'The Superfluous Man and the Necessary Woman: A "Re-Vision,"' *Russian Review* 55, 2 (1996): 226–44.

68. Ian Fleming, *From Russia with Love* (London: Hodder and Stoughton, 1988), 87.

69. See, for Pechorin's chronic boredom, Lermontov, *A Hero*, 47–49.

70. Fleming, *From Russia*, 78.

71. Ian Fleming, *The Man with the Golden Gun* (London: Hodder and Stoughton, 1989), 13.

72. For Nietzsche's views on Czarist Russia, see the relevant discussion in chapter 3.

73. Vladimir Nabokov, 'Translator's Foreword,' in Lermontov, *A Hero*, 10.

74. Nabokov, *Translator's Foreword*, 11.

75. Nabokov, *Translator's Foreword*, 11.

76. Nabokov, *Translator's Foreword*, 10.

77. Nicos Poulantzas, *Political Power and Social Classes* (London, New York: Verso, 1987), 207.

78. Jerry Palmer, *Thrillers: Genesis and Structure of a Popular Genre* (London: Edward Arnold, 1978), 154.

79. Palmer, *Thrillers*, 117.

80. Palmer, *Thrillers*, 120.

81. Palmer, *Thrillers*, 121.

82. Palmer, *Thrillers*, 121–22.

83. Palmer, *Thrillers*, 122.

84. Palmer, *Thrillers*, 120.

85. As a matter of fact, one of Palmer's main examples of the competitive individual hero of the modern thriller is precisely James Bond, yet his analysis does not register the specifically Nietzschean side of this character.

86. Fredric Jameson, *The Cultural Turn: Selected Writings on the Postmodern 1983–1998* (London, New York: Verso, 1998), 18.

87. Jules Verne, *Twenty Thousand Leagues under the Sea* (London: Everyman's Library, 1996), 66–68.

88. Ian Fleming, *Dr No* (London: Hodder and Stoughton, 1988), 124–26.

89. Verne, *Twenty*, 38.

90. Fleming, *Dr No*, 127.

91. Verne, *Twenty*, 270.

92. Fleming, *Dr No*, 126.

93. Verne, *Twenty*, 49–50.

94. Fleming, *Dr No*, 131–32.

95. Verne, *Twenty*, 183.

96. Fleming, *Dr No*, 127.

97. Fleming, *Dr No*, 134.

98. Arthur Conan Doyle, *The Lost World & Other Stories* (Hertfordshire: Wordsworth, 1995), 1–2.

99. Conan Doyle, *The Lost World*, 3.

100. Conan Doyle, *The Lost World*, 4.

101. Conan Doyle, *The Lost World*, 5.

102. Conan Doyle, *The Lost World*, 109.

103. This reading of the story is opposed to that offered by Paul Zweig. Appreciating no irony or skepticism in the tale, Zweig saw it rather as an outright manifestation of Nietzschean adventurism: 'Where in the modern world must we look, then, to witness the Nietzschean confrontation which Conan Doyle's romantic hero mused about in *The Lost World*?' (Zweig, *Adventurer*, 225).

104. Interestingly, John Carey singled Conan Doyle out as one of those exceptional British turn-of-the-century intellectuals who did not share the disdain of the elite towards the rising masses. On the contrary, Conan Doyle was said to support the cause of 'the common man,' for example by positively depicting, in his Sherlock Holmes stories, such 'vulgar' characters as clerks or athletes. See, John Carey, *The Intellectuals and the Masses. Pride and Prejudice among the Literary Intelligentsia, 1880–1939* (London: Faber and Faber, 1992), 8–9, 16, 64.

105. Conan Doyle, *The Lost World*, 166.

CHAPTER 5: THE BOURGEOIS RENAISSANCE OF ARISTOCRATIC HEROISM

1. Nietzsche, *A*, 189–90.

2. Nietzsche, *GS*, 211.

3. Nietzsche, *GEN*, 94.

4. Nietzsche, *GEN*, 81.

5. Nietzsche, *GS*, 169.

6. Nietzsche, *HUM*, 146.

7. E. R. Burroughs, *Tarzan and the Jewels of Opar*, http://www-2.cs.cmu.edu/People/rgs/tar5-2.html.

8. Burroughs, *Tarzan and the Jewels of Opar*.

9. E. R. Burroughs *Tarzan of the Apes* (New York: Signet, 1990), 95.

10. Burroughs *Tarzan of the Apes*, 95–96.

11. Burroughs *Tarzan of the Apes*, 195.

12. Nietzsche, *GEN*, 25.

13. Nietzsche, *GEN*, 24–25.

14. Burroughs, *Jewels of Opar*.

15. Nietzsche, *GEN*, 27.

16. José Ortega y Gasset, *The Revolt of the Masses* (New York: W. W. Norton, 1952), 71–72.

17. Ortega y Gasset, *The Revolt*, 72.

18. Burroughs, *Tarzan of the Apes*, 136–37.

19. Burroughs, *Tarzan of the Apes*, 138.

20. José Ortega y Gasset, *Meditations on Hunting* (New York: Charles Scribner's Sons, 1972), 141.

21. Ortega y Gasset, *Meditations*, 98.

22. Stephan Malinowski, *Vom König zum Führer. Deutscher Adel und National-sozialismus* (Frankfurt am Main: Fischer, 2004), 62.

23. Malinowski, *König*, 69.

24. Malinowski, *König*, 68.

25. Burroughs, *The Return*, 26–27.

26. Burroughs, *The Return*, 32.

27. Nietzsche, *GEN*, 25.

28. Nietzsche, *WTP*, 73.

29. Nietzsche, *WTP*, 32–33.

30. E. R. Burroughs, *Tarzan and the Golden Lion*, internet: http://gutenberg.net .au/0100271.txt.

31. Burroughs, *Tarzan of the Apes*, 95–96.

32. Burroughs, *The Jewels of Opar*, internet: http://www-2.cs.cmu.edu/People/rgs/ tar5-2.html.

33. Two discussions of the unsolvable conflict between Nietzscheanism and Rousseuvianism are Keith Ansell-Pearson's *Nietzsche Contra Rousseau. A Study of Nietzsche's Moral and Political Thought*, Cambridge: Cambridge University Press, 1991, and Eric Blondel's, 'Nietzsche Contra Rousseau: Goethe Versus Catilina?' *History of European Ideas* 11 (1989): 675–83.

34. Nietzsche, *WTP*, 72.

35. Nietzsche, *WTP*, 58.

36. Nietzsche, *WTP*, 61–62.

37. Nietzsche, *WTP*, 73.

38. Nietzsche, *WTP*, 74.

39. Nietzsche, *WTP*, 75.

40. Cf. Demosthenes Savramis, 'Der moderne Mensch zwischen Tarzan und Superman,' in *Comics und Religion—Eine interdisziplinäre Diskussion*, ed. Jutta Wermke (Munich: Wilhelm Fink Verlag, 1976): 110–120. For a discussion of the further development of the Tarzan myth in comics, see Thomas A. Pendleton's, 'Tarzan of the Papers,' *Journal of Popular Culture* 12, (1978–1979): 691–701. F. X. Blisard, however, advances the opposite argument that it was the Hollywood version of Tarzan which established the popular hero as an icon of white supremacy, against the original stories' intent. See, his 'Tarzan versus Tarzan, or, Will the Real Ape-Man Please Stand Up and be Counted? Investigations in American Mythology,' in *The Nubian News. Advocate for the African/Latino Community. Validating the Nubian Perspective*, 2000. Internet source: http://www.nubiannews.com/archive/2000/feb00/tarzan1.htm

41. Burroughs, *Tarzan of the Apes*, 277–78.

42. Burroughs, *Tarzan of the Apes*, 288.

43. E. R. Burroughs, *The Return of Tarzan* (New York: Ballantine Books, 1972), 34.

44. Burroughs, *The Return* of Tarzan, 24–25.

45. See, for example, Eric Cheyfitz, *The Poetics of Imperialism: Translation and Colonization from The Tempest to Tarzan* (University of Pennsylvania Press, 1997); Betsy L. Nies, *Eugenic Fantasies : Racial Ideology in the Literature and Popular Culture of the 1920s* (London: Routledge, 2002), 37–39; John F. Kasson, *Houdini, Tarzan, and the Perfect Man: The White Male Body and the Challenge of Modernity in America* (New York: Hill & Wang, 2002).

46. Cf. Shlomo Sand, *Film as History: Imagining and Screening the Twentieth Century* (Tel Aviv: Am Oved, 2002), 304–5.

47. *Tarzan Escapes*, dir. John Farrow, William Wellman, USA, Warner Studios, 1936.

48. John Carey, *The Intellectuals and the Masses. Pride and Prejudice among the Literary Intelligentsia, 1880–1939* (London: Faber and Faber, 1992), 71.

49. Nietzsche, *GS*, 108.

50. Ian Fleming, *From Russia with Love* (London: Hodder and Stoughton, 1988), 80–81.

51. My discussion of Bond focuses almost exclusively on the figure emerging from Ian Fleming's original stories, whose Nietzscheanism is far more overt than in the many subsequent films. For an interesting discussion of Bond as a protean figure, evolving and transforming through different media adaptations and throughout historical periods, see Tony Bennett, 'The Bond Phenomenon: Theorising a Popular Hero,' *Southern Review* 16, 2, July, (1983): 195–225.

52. Cf. The sub-section 'good living' in Hans Christoph Buch's fine analysis of Bond's ideology 'James Bond oder der Kleinbürger in Waffen,' in *Der Kriminalroman I. Zur Theorie und Geschichte einer Gattung*, ed. Jochen Vogt (Munich: Wilhelm Fink Verlag, 1971), 237–41.

53. Nietzsche, *Z*, 296.

54. Nietzsche, *WTP*, 23.

55. Nietzsche, *WTP*, 41.

56. Nietzsche, *WTP*, 75.

57. Anthony Burgess, 'The James Bond Novels: An Introduction,' in Ian Fleming, *Casino Royale* (London: Hodder and Stoughton, 1988), 6.

58. Nietzsche, *WTP*, 41.

59. Ian Fleming, *Goldfinger* (London: Hodder and Stoughton, 1989), 22.

60. Nietzsche, *HC*, 194. For a discussion of the particular brand of 'Nietzschean liberalism' of *Homer on Competition*, see Lester H. Hunt, *Nietzsche and the Origin of Virtue* (London, New York: Routledge, 1991), 59–65.

61. Nietzsche, *HC*, 187.

62. Nietzsche, *HC*, 187.

63. Nietzsche, *HC*, 189–90.

64. Nietzsche, *HC*, 192.

65. Nietzsche, *GK*, 178–79.

66. Nietzsche, *HC*, 190.

67. Nietzsche, *HC*, 192.

68. For the connection between Nietzsche's thought and sports, though without taking into consideration the ideological import, see the following essays, published in *International Studies in Philosophy* XXX/3, 1998: Larwence J. Hatab, 'The Drama of Agonistic Embodiment: Nietzschean Reflections on the Meaning of Sports,' 97–107; Steven G. Crowell, 'Sport as Spectacle and as Play: Nietzschean Reflections,' 109–22; Richard Schacht, 'Nietzsche and Sport,' 123–30.

69. Nietzsche, *HC*, 192.

70. Nietzsche, *HC*, 188.

71. Ian Fleming, *Casino Royale* (London: Hodder and Stoughton, 1988), 83–84.

72. Ian Fleming, *Moonraker* (London: Hodder & Stoughton, 1989), 58–59.

73. Fleming, *Moonraker*, 189.

74. Nietzsche, *GK*, 178–79.

75. Nietzsche, *Z*, 138.

76. John Calvin, *Institutes of the Christian Religion*, McNeil, Battles ed. (Philadelphia: Westminster), 926.

77. Fleming, *The Man*, 94–95.

78. Fleming, *From Russia*, 78.

79. Fleming, *You only Live Twice* (London: Hodder and Stoughton, 1988), 23.

80. Nietzsche, *Z*, 74.

81. Nietzsche, *Z*, 54.

82. Nietzsche, *GS*, 270.

83. Nietzsche, *TI*, 31.

84. Ian Fleming, *Thunderball* (London: Hodder and Stoughton, 1989), 147–48.

85. Nietzsche, *WTP*, 385.

86. Fleming, *Thunderball*, 21.

87. Fleming, *Thunderball*, 27.

88. Fleming, *Thunderball*, 37.

89. Fleming, *Thunderball*, 37.

90. Fleming, *From Russia*, 78.

91. Fleming, *The Man*, 26.

92. Burgess, 'The James Bond Novels,' 6.

93. Burgess, 'The James Bond Novels,' 6.

94. Burgess, 'The James Bond Novels,' 6.

95. Nietzsche, *KSA* 9, 468.

96. Ian Fleming, *Live and Let Die* (London: Hodder & Stoughton, 1988), 170–71.

97. Nietzsche, *TI*, 75.

98. Fleming, *Moonraker*, 15.

99. Fleming, *Moonraker*, 61–62.

100. Fleming, *Moonraker*, 24.

101. Fleming, *Moonraker*, 25.

102. Fleming, *Moonraker*, 32.

103. Fleming, *Moonraker*, 18.

104. Fleming, *Dr No*, 131.

105. Fleming, *Dr No*, 130.

106. Fleming, *Dr No*, 132.

107. Fleming, *Dr No*, 132.

108. Fleming, *Dr No*, 148.

109. Fleming, *Dr No*, 134.

110. Fleming, *The Man*, 41.

111. Fleming, *Live and Let Die*, 225.

112. Fleming, *Moonraker*, 40.

113. Fleming, *Live and Let Die*, 75.

114. Fleming, *Live and Let Die*, 217–18.

115. Fleming, *From Russia*, 53.

116. Fleming, *From Russia*, 54.

117. Fleming, *From Russia*, 110.

118. Feroz Ahmad *The Making of Modern Turkey* (London and New York: Rout-ledge, 1993), 179.

119. Ahmad, *Modern Turkey*, 183.

120. Norman Mailer, *The Naked and the Dead* (London: Flamingo, 1993), 329.

121. Mailer, *The Naked*, 423.

122. Mailer, *The Naked*, 568.

123. Robert Solotaroff, *Down Mailer's Way* (Urbana: University of Illinois Press, 1974), 16. See also Patrick Paul Christle's incisive discussion of *The Naked and the Dead* in his doctoral dissertation *The Beleaguered Individual: A Study of Twentieth-Century American War Novels,* dissertation (The University of Tennessee, Knoxville 2001), http://www.drchristle.com/title.html.

124. Mailer, *The Naked*, 327.

125. Fleming, *You Only Live Twice*, 171.

126. Fleming, *You Only Live Twice*, 171.

127. Fleming, *You Only Live Twice*, 154.

128. Fleming, *You Only Live Twice*, 173–74.

129. Fleming, *You Only Live Twice*, 153.

130. Fleming, *You Only Live Twice*, 43.

131. Fleming, *You Only Live Twice*, 43.

132. Fleming, *You Only Live Twice*, 59.

133. Fleming, *You Only Live Twice*, 59.

134. Fleming, *You Only Live Twice*, 60.

135. Fleming, *You Only Live Twice*, 60.

136. Fleming, *You Only Live Twice*, 76–77.

137.   Fleming, *You Only Live Twice*, 78.

138. An illuminating indication of the right-wing—indeed, quasi-fascist—Nietzscheanism underlying Fleming's narrative is obtained when Tiger Tanaka's views are compared with those of one of the most significant Nietzscheans of the first half of the twentieth century, Oswald Spengler (who was highly influential in the English-speaking world, inspiring such intellectuals as Northrop Frye and Arnold Toynbee). Writing in the 1930s, Spengler's analysis of Japanese, American and English societies is remarkably similar to that of Bond's Japanese friend. Regarding America, Spengler, too, highlights with concern the rebellious nature of the many 'not 100 percent Americans,' the recent immigrants, and asks: 'But how many inhabitants of this country innerly do not belong at all to this ruling Anglo-Saxon type? Leaving the blacks out of it, in the twenty years preceding the war only few Germans, English and Scandinavians have immigrated, as compared to 15 millions Poles, Russians, Czechs, Balkan Slavs, Eastern Jews, Greeks, minor Asians, Spaniards and Italians.' Japan Spengler assesses positively, when exalting 'the old, proud, honorable and brave ruling class of the Samurai,' but he must affirm with consternation the fact that this land has been 'poisoned with the democratic-Marxist forms of the white nations.' And finally, with regards to England, the German vitalist points out the general weakening symbolized by the demise of the British Empire, chastises the decaying British elites—young people educated at Eton and Oxford, who now no longer heed the appeal of 'England expects everyman to do his duty'—and laments the simultaneous rise of the 'masses' (which, he insists are the descendants of the inferior 'original population'). To be sure, unlike Tanaka, Spengler's analysis does

not leave any room for a putative revival of the English elites, whose decadence he deems irreversible (all quotations are from Oswald Spengler, *Jahre der Entscheidung. Deutschland und die Weltgeschichtliche Entwicklung*, München: DTV, 1980, 76–86).

139. Gina Macdonald, *James Clavell: A Critical Companion* (Westport: Greenwood Publishing Group, 1996), 2.

140. James Clavell, *King Rat* (New York: Dell Books, 1982), 8. Italics in the original.

141. There are vastly conflicting versions regarding the true extent of the misery in Changi. Without actually claiming to have accurately described his stay in the camp—the author dutifully clarified in an introductory note that the story is fictional—Clavell nonetheless made the most of an autobiographical 'truth-claim.' Thus, for example, in a 1975 interview Clavell spoke of Changi as 'a school for survivors' endowing him with 'an awareness of life others lack' and implying that he barely survived the camp: 'I feel very fortunate to be alive.' (as quoted in Macdonald, *Clavell*, 2–3). G. Macdonald, in the only book known to me that deals exclusively with Clavell's work, could thus affirm 'the biographical nature' of *King Rat*, and further suggest that 'Clavell's horrifying Changi experiences' endowed him with 'newly acquired values' which he 'defended . . . throughout his life: the value of the individual, . . . and the importance of free enterprise and capitalist venture' (Macdonald, *Clavell*, 3). Underpinning such truth-claim are Macdonald's data of the staggering death-toll in Changi: '140,000 out of 150,000 inmates died—that is, only 10,000, or one in every fifteen, survived' (Macdonald, *Clavell*, 3). This, however, collides frontally with the data provided by the historian Kevin Blackburn in an intriguing and amply documented essay according to which 'atrocities did not occur at Changi. Out of the 87,000 POWs who passed through the camp, only 850 died' (Kevin Blackburn, 'Commemorating and Commodifying the Prisoner of War Experience in South-East Asia: The Creation of Changi Prison Museum,' *Journal of the Australian War Memorial*, 33, 2000, http://www.awm.gov.au/journal/j33/blackburn .htm). More strikingly still, Blackburn goes on to suggest that Changi's historically unfounded reputation as a 'chamber of horrors' and 'the most notorious camp in Asia' is in no small measure *a product* of Clavell's immensely popular fiction. He thus speaks of an 'image of Changi, largely deriving from *King Rat*, as a place where only the fittest men survived.' My discussion, at any rate, will focus on the ideological aspects of Clavell's novel rather than its historiographic reliability.

142. Clavell, *King Rat*, 12.

143. Clavell, *King Rat*, 13.

144. Clavell, *King Rat*, 67.

145. 'Second' refers not to the date of publication but to the chronological order of the respective epochs in which the stories take place. For convenience, there follows a list of the five novels of the 'Asian Saga' (in brackets are added the dates of publication): *Shōgun*, 1600 (1975), *Tai-Pan*, 1841 (1966), *Gai Jin*, 1862 (1993), *King Rat*, 1945 (1962), *Noble House*, 1963 (1981).

146. Clavell, *King Rat*, 27.

147. Clavell, *King Rat*, 57.

148. James Clavell, *Shōgun* (London: Hodder and Stoughton, 1975), 46.

149. Clavell, *King Rat*, 40.

150. Clavell, *King Rat*, 57.

151. Clavell, *King Rat*, 111.
152. Nietzsche, *GS*, 102–3.
153. Clavell, *King Rat*, 350.
154. Clavell, *Shōgun*, 22.
155. Clavell, *King Rat*, 78.
156. Clavell, *King Rat*, 82–83.
157. Nietzsche, *TI*, 59.
158. Clavell, *King Rat*, 292.
159. Clavell, *King Rat*, 284–85.
160. Clavell, *King Rat*, 285.
161. Clavell, *King Rat*, 294.
162. Clavell, *King Rat*, 98.
163. Clavell, *King Rat*, 352. Italicized in the original.
164. Clavell, *King Rat*, 323.
165. Clavell, *King Rat*, 337.
166. See chapters 4 and 5 of Fredric Jameson, *The Political Unconscious: Narrative as a Socially Symbolic Act* (Ithaca, New York: Cornell University Press, 1981).
167. Jameson, *The Political*, 268.
168. Jameson, *The Political*, 201. A comprehensive discussion of the historical uses of *ressentiment* as derived from Nietzsche and elaborated in the work of such important European thinkers as Max Scheler or Max Weber is Wolfgang Conrad's *Ressentiment in der Klassengesellschaft—Zur Diskussion um einen Aspekt religiösen Bewußtseins* (Göttingen: Verlag Otto Schwartz, 1974), 8–36 especially. On Conrad's negotiation of Nietzschean themes, see George Butte, 'What Silenus Knew: Conrad's Uneasy Debt to Nietzsche,' in *Joseph Conrad: Critical Assessments*, vol. IV, ed. K. Carabine (Mountfield: Helm Information, 1992): 271–83.
169. Quoted in Jocelyn Baines, *Joseph Conrad: A Critical Biography* (London: Weidenfeld and Nicholson, 1967), 80–81.
170. Joseph Conrad, *The Nigger of the 'Narcissus'* (London: Everyman, 1997), 18–19. All emphases added.
171. Conrad, *The Nigger*, 18.
172. Conrad, *The Nigger*, 8.
173. Conrad, *The Nigger*, 29.
174. Conrad, *The Nigger*, 100–101.
175. Cf. Michael Greaney's commentary on the novel, in *Conrad, Language, and Narrative* (Cambridge: Cambridge University Press, 2002), 12–13.
176. Conrad, *The Nigger*, 102–3.
177. Nietzsche, *WTP*, 34.
178. Conrad, *The Nigger*, 104.
179. Conrad, *The Nigger*, 95.
180. It is in this light that we must appreciate the purportedly 'anti-colonialist' critique of Conrad's later masterpiece, *Heart of Darkness*, for what it really is: an existential justification of colonialism with all its brutality. This great story, to be sure, can be read *against* Conrad's own existential musings, since its ideological purpose was conveyed far more indirectly than in other works, notably *The Nigger of The 'Narcissus,'* but also *The Secret Agent* and *Under Western Eyes*. For all their differences, both Kurtz and Singleton are authentic men, who have realized the inevitability of

exploitation, suffering and death. That Kurtz was consumed and overwhelmed by such insight while Singleton endures it like a 'stone caryatid' is of little consequence in that respect.

181. Conrad, *The Nigger*, 96.

182. Conrad, *The Nigger*, 124.

183. Conrad, *The Nigger*, 125.

184. Conrad, *The Nigger*, 127.

185. Jameson, *The Political*, 202.

186. Ayn Rand, *The Fountainhead* (New York: Signet, 1993), 697.

187. Rand, *The Fountainhead*, 296.

188. Conrad, *The Nigger*, 79.

189. Rand, *The Fountainhead*, 699.

190. Rand, *The Fountainhead*, 700.

191. Jameson, *The Political*, 202.

192. Nietzsche, *Z*, 123.

193. See the section 'Nietzsche and the Critique of Religion as Resentment,' in his *Suspicion and Faith: The Religious Uses of Modern Atheism* (New York: Fordham University Press, 1998).

194. Nietzsche, *Z*, 121–22.

195. Nietzsche, *Z*, 124.

196. Nietzsche, *Z*, 123.

197. Rand, *The Fountainhead*, 389.

198. Rand, *The Fountainhead*, 263.

199. Rand, *The Fountainhead*, 302.

200. Rand, *The Fountainhead*, 699.

201. Conrad, *The Nigger*, 8.

CHAPTER 6: 'THE JOY OF THE KNIFE': NIETZSCHEAN GLORIFICATION OF CRIME

1. Ernest Mandel, *Delightful Murder: Social History of the Crime Story* (Minneapolis: University of Minnesota Press, 1984), 1.

2. The term 'social bandit' is Eric Hobsbawm's (see his *Bandits*, New York: The New Press, 2000).

3. Nietzsche, *TI*, 110.

4. Nietzsche, *TI*, 110.

5. Although there is no conclusive evidence that Nietzsche actually read Stirner, 'The degree to which Nietzsche is anticipated by Stirner both in ideas and in prose style can hardly be a coincidence.' (Irving M. Zeitlin, *Nietzsche: A Reexamination*, Cornwall: Polity Press, 1994,113). As Zeitlin argues, Nietzsche most probably had avoided mentioning Stirner, fearing, with justice, that this might substantially weaken his solicitous claim to originality. For more information and a useful discussion of Marx and Engels' famous criticism of Stirner in *The German Ideology*, and its implications concerning Nietzsche, see Zeitlin, *Nietzsche*, 113–26.

6. Max Stirner, *The Ego and Its Own*, edited by David Leopold (Cambridge: Cambridge University Press, 1995), 170.

7. Fredric Jameson, *The Political Unconscious: Narrative as a Socially Symbolic Act* (Ithaca, New York: Cornell University Press, 1981), 153–54.

8. Stirner, *The Ego*, 259.

9. Stirner, *The Ego*, 240.

10. Cf. Karl Löwith's verdict on Stirner as 'absolutizing bourgeois egoism,' in his classic study of German philosophy, *Von Hegel zu Nietzsche: Der revolutionäre Bruch im Denken des neunzehnten Jahrhunderts* (Hamburg: Meiner, 1995), 269.

11. Stirner, *The Ego*, 235.

12. Some critics, for example Lawrence S. Stepelevich, have contended that Stirner did not believe in the ego as such but only in *his* ego, but this could hardly be squared with Stirner's insistence on speaking on part of the egoist as such and on prescribing his actions and morals. In fact, even conceding such an interpretation and assuming that Stirner merely directed this injunction at himself, this would still have meant an erection of a fixed idée against *Stirner's* unique self, which again is the greatest of 'iniquities.' See, Stepelevich, 'Max Stirner as Hegelian' *Journal of the History of Ideas* 4 (1985): 597–617.

13. Nietzsche, *TI*, 56.

14. Nietzsche, *Z*, 75.

15. Nietzsche, *WTP*, 412.

16. Stirner, *The Ego*, 178.

17. Stirner, *The Ego*, 179.

18. Stirner, *The Ego*, 181.

19. Nietzsche, *WTP*, 403.

20. Cf. Stirner, *The Ego* 181, 256.

21. Nietzsche, *TI*, 110

22. Nietzsche, *WTP*, 391–93.

23. Nietzsche, *WTP*, 391–93.

24. Nietzsche, *Z*, 65–66.

25. Nietzsche, *Z*, 65–66.

26. Nietzsche, *Z*, 61.

27. Urs Marti, 'Der Plebejer in der Revolte. Ein Beitrag zur Genealogie des "höheren Menschen"' *Nietzsche Studien* 18 (1989), 566. Nietzsche stated his admiration of Prado and Chambige in a correspondence with August Strindberg (7/12/1988) and Jacob Burckhardt (6/1/1889).

28. Nietzsche, *WTP*, 392.

29. Stirner, *The Ego*, 229.

30. Stirner, *The Ego*, 180–81.

31. Nietzsche, *TI*, 111.

32. Nietzsche, *WTP*, 392.

33. Nietzsche, *WTP*, 417.

34. Nietzsche, *WTP*, 391.

35. Nietzsche, *WTP*, 394.

36. Nietzsche, *BGE*, 52.

37. Charles Dickens, *Great Expectations* (Harmondsworth: Penguin, 1996), 346.

38. See, Mike Maguire, ed. *The Oxford Handbook of Criminology* (Oxford: Oxford press, 2002), 12, 155.

39. Honoré de Balzac, *Lost Illusions* (Harmondsworth: Penguin, 1971), 647.

40. Balzac, *Lost Illusions*, 641.

41. Antonio Gramsci, *Selections from Cultural Writings* (Cambridge, Massachusetts: Harvard University Press, 1991), 355–9. See also Geoff Waite, *Nietzsche's Corps/e. Aesthetics, Politics, Prophecy, or, the Spectacular Technoculture of Everyday Life* (Durham & London: Duke University Press, 1996), 345–6.

42. Honoré de Balzac, *A Harlot High and Low* (Harmondsworth: Penguin, 1970), 358.

43. Balzac, *A Harlot*, 434.

44. Balzac, *A Harlot*, 514.

45. Balzac, *Lost Illusions*, 644.

46. Balzac, *Lost Illusions*, 650.

47. Balzac, *Lost Illusions*, 648–49.

48. Balzac, *Lost Illusions*, 649.

49. Balzac, *Lost Illusions*, 647.

50. Balzac, *A Harlot*, 185–86.

51. Balzac, *A Harlot*, 161–62.

52. Balzac, *A Harlot*, 337.

53. Balzac, *A Harlot*, 425.

54. Honoré de Balzac, *Old Goriot* (Harmondsworth: Penguin, 1959), 223.

55. See *WTP*, 34, where Nietzsche writes: 'One has to respect fatality—that fatality that says to the weak: perish!' or Nietzsche, *A*, 128.

56. Honoré de Balzac, *The Wild Ass's Skin* (Harmondsworth: Penguin, 1977), 255.

57. Balzac, *A Harlot*, 502.

58. Balzac, *A Harlot*, 502.

59. Balzac, *A Harlot*, 443.

60. Balzac, *A Harlot*, 443.

61. Balzac, *A Harlot*, 460.

62. Balzac, *A Harlot*, 443.

63. Martha Grace Duncan, *Romantic Outlaws, Beloved Prisons: The Unconscious Meaning of Crime and Punishment* (New York: New York University Press, 1996), 57.

64. Duncan, *Romantic Outlaws*, 193

65. Duncan, *Romantic Outlaws*, 192.

66. Duncan, *Romantic Outlaws*, 5.

67. Charles Bukowski, *Ham on Rye* (Edinburgh: Rebel Inc., 2000), 91.

68. See Ward Churchill, Jim Vander Wall, *Agents of Repression. The FBI's Secret Wars Against the Black Panther Party and the American Indian Movement* (Boston, MA: South End Press, 1990), 5.

69. Duncan, *Romantic Outlaws*, 54.

70. Duncan, *Romantic Outlaws*, 54.

71. Duncan, *Romantic Outlaws*, 55.

72. The source of all quotations from the protocol is: Douglas Linder, UMKC School of Law-Famous American Trials, http://www.law.umkc.edu/faculty/projects/ftrials/leoploeb/leopold.htm.

73. Nietzsche, *BGE*, 97.

74. *M—Eine Stadt sucht einen Mörder*, dir. Fritz Lang, Germany, Nero Film AG, 1931. See, for a discussion of the film's groundbreaking role in the serial killer genre, Anton Kaes, *M* (London: bfi, 2000). Lang's avid interest in Nietzsche is well known, and so is the fact that some of the major protagonists of his early 'German' films have been molded after Nietzsche's *Übermensch*, for example Freder in *Metropolis*, or even more notably, the character of the enigmatic master criminal Dr. Mabuse. I have chosen to discuss the usually overlooked Nietzschean thematic of *M*, whose protagonist, though by no means super human, nonetheless evinces attributes of Dionysian crime, possibly to a greater extent than the more extravagant Mabuse. For more information on Lang's idiosyncratic Nietzscheanism, see: Patrick McGilligan, *Fritz Lang: The Nature of the Beast* (London: Faber & Faber, 1997); Tom Gunning, *The Films of Fritz Lang. Allegories of Vision and Modernity* (London: BFI publishing, 2000), 123, 175, 288; and Kluas Kreimeier, *Die Ufa—Story: Geschichte eines Filmkonzerns* (München: Carl Hanser, 1992), 105.

75. Fritz Lang, *Why I Am Interested in Murder* (1947), as quoted in: Lotte H. Eisner, *Fritz Lang* (New York: DaCapo Press, 1976), 111.

76. All *M* quotations are from the film's subtitles (translator unspecified), with some minor alterations.

77. Fritz Lang, as quoted in Eisner, *Fritz Lang*, 112. Eisner likewise commented: 'The criminal has brutally outraged a well-established code of society. First we are "horrified and disgusted," we are concerned about the "sanctity of human life"; it is a matter of the "self-preservation of society." Then follows a typical Lang idea, expressed again and again in his films: we begin to feel something like sympathy in the strict sense of the word' (111–12).

78. See Philip L. Simpson, *Psycho-Paths: Tracking the Serial Killer Through Contemporary American Film and Fiction* (Southern Illinois University Press, 2000), 213–14.

79. Simpson, *Psycho-Paths*, 77.

80. Simpson, *Psycho-Paths*, 24.

81. Thomas S. Hibbs, *Shows About Nothing: Nihilism in Popular Culture from* The Exorcist *to* Seinfeld (Dallas: Spence Publishing Company, 1999), 80.

82. Simpson, *Psycho-Paths*, 95.

83. Cf. Jeffrey Niesel, 'The Horror of Everyday Life: Taxidermy, aesthetics, and consumption in horror films,' *Interrogating Popular Culture: Deviance, Justice, and Social Order*, ed. Sean A. Anderson, Gregory J. Howard (New York: Harrow & Heston, 1998), 31. See also, Hibbs, *Shows*, 79.

84. Gilles Deleuze, 'Coldness and Cruelty,' in *Masochism* (New York: Zone Books, 1991), 37.

85. Deleuze, *Coldness*, 29.

86. The significance of male self-mastery as a token of sexual-social distinction was highlighted by Bourdieu, as well: 'men are, ex officio, on the side of culture whereas women (like the working class) are cast on the side of nature. Women are therefore less imperatively required to censor and repress "natural" feelings as the aesthetic disposition demands (. . . the refusal of nature, or rather the refusal to surrender to nature, which is the mark of dominant groups—which start with *self*-control—is the basis of the aesthetic disposition).' (Pierre Bourdieu, *Distinction: A Social Critique of the Judgement of Taste*, London: Routledge, 2002, 40).

87. Deleuze, *Coldness*, 39.

88. Nietzsche, *Z*, 93.

89. Nietzsche, *Z*, 244–45.

90. Cf. Nietzsche, *CW*, 161.

91. See, Deleuze, *Coldness*, 95–96. Compare, also, Jones Irwin's essay 'The Cruelty Beyond Cruelty: Deleuze and the Concept of Masochism,' *Perspectives on Evil and Human Wickedness* 1, No. 1 (2002): 51–60, where it is argued that Masoch offers a very different evaluation of suffering to that of Nietzsche.

92. One commentator even praised Lecter for 'showing us . . . that gender has no bearing on competence, worth, or humanity. This is a lesson other males in the film—and others in real life—have yet to learn,' in Greg Garrett, 'Objecting to Objectification: Re-viewing the Feminine in *The Silence of the Lambs*,' *Journal of Popular Culture* 27, 4, Spring 1994, 10.

93. *Manhunter*, dir. Michael Mann, USA, de Laurentiis Entertainment Group, 1986.

94. Nietzsche, *WTP*, 503.

95. Originally in Nietzsche *KSA* 9, 207. The translation is Geoff Waite's, from *Nietzsche's Corps/e*, 301. He uses this quotation in the context of an interesting discussion of Nietzsche's 'male fantasy' and 'misogyny' (see 301–3).

96. Thomas Harris, *Red Dragon* (London: Harrow Books, 1993), 201.

97. Nietzsche, *TI*, 33.

98. Nietzsche, *BGE*, 209.

99. Nietzsche, *KSA* 11, 89. Consider also page 137 in the same volume, as well as Geoff Waite's discussion of the way Nietzsche linked vivisection and euthanasia, in *Nietzsche's Corps/e*, 296–97.

100. Nietzsche, *GEN*, 47.

101. Nietzsche, *GK*, 179.

102. Nietzsche, *GS*, 255. Walter Kaufmann, in a footnote, characteristically interpreted this as referring to the way Nietzsche's philosophical development has pained his family—mother and sister—and the Wagners. However, as the immediately preceding quotation from *The Greek State* shows, this 'inflicting of suffering' was by no means restricted by Nietzsche to personal relationships; rather, it was intended from the very start as a general social principle, concerning not only the family but also the *famulus* (i.e., the slave).

103. Edgar R. Burroughs, *The Beasts of Tarzan*, http://www-2.cs.cmu.edu/People/rgs/tar3-8.html.

104. Ayn Rand, *The Fountainhead* (New York: Signet, 1993), 217.

105. Rand, *The Fountainhead*, 272.

106. See E. Ann Kaplan's 'Is the Gaze Male?' in *Feminism and Film*, ed. E. Ann Kaplan (Oxford: Oxford University Press, 2000): 119–38, for a feminist critique of the social/psychoanalytic structure of female sexuality in which women are conditioned to experience pleasure from a position of submission. Interestingly, for Kaplan, a possible alternative to the male-sadist construction of sexual roles is the concept of 'mothering' based on equality, which dovetails nicely with our discussion of Deleuze's contrast between sadism and the 'law of the father' and masochism, dominated by the mother and eliminating the father.

107. Ian Fleming, *On Her Majesty's Secret Service* (London: Penguin Books, 2002), 38. See also, on Bond's sexism and sadism, Christoph Buch, 'James Bond oder der

Kleinbürger in Waffen,' in *Der Kriminalroman I. Zur Theorie und Geschichte einer Gattung*, ed. Jochen Vogt (Munich: Wilhelm Fink Verlag, 1971), 233–37 and 241–43, respectively.

108. Fleming, *Her Majesty*, 52.

109. Ian Fleming, *From Russia with Love* (London: Hodder and Stoughton, 1988), 111.

110. Fleming, *From Russia*, 112.

111. Nietzsche, *BGE*, 166–67.

112. Fleming, *From Russia*, 110.

113. Primo Levi, 'Useless Violence,' in *The Drowned and the Saved* (London: Abacus, 1991): 84–85.

114. See Deleuze, *Coldness*, 69–70.

115. Leo Strauss, *On Tyranny*, ed. V. Gourevitch, M. S. Roth (Chicago and London: The University of Chicago Press, 2000), 90.

116. Strauss, *On Tyranny*, 91.

117. Cf. Joe Sanders, 'At the Frontiers of the Fantastic: Thomas Harris's *The Silence of the Lambs*,' *New York Review of Science Fiction* 39, Nov. 1991, 5.

118. Simpson, *Psycho-Paths*, 95.

119. John Carey, *The Intellectuals and the Masses. Pride and Prejudice among the Literary Intelligentsia, 1880–1939* (London: Faber and Faber, 1992), 4.

120. The motif of the serial killer as a fundamentally Christian avenger of social depravity finds its most succinct expression in the 1995 film *Seven* (dir. David Fincher, USA, New Line Cinema), in which the killer symbolically inflicts punishment on the seven deadly sins, thus pointing at the corruption of modern society (as lucidly analyzed by Hibbs, *Shows*, 90–101 and by Simpson, *Psycho-Paths*, 194–202). The film may have influenced the writing of *Hannibal*, which advances a parallel conception of the criminal as an unlikely social 'reformer.'

121. Thomas Harris, *Hannibal* (New York: Dell Publishing, 2000), 523.

122. Harris, *Hannibal*, 542.

123. Predictably, even such cultural anti-capitalism suffices to stir the furious indignation of America's ultraist right, whose delegates rush to denounce such films as *Hannibal* as a sadist-communist attack on traditional American values. See, for example, William Norman Grigg's 'In Sade's Shadow,' *The New American* 17, no. 8, April 9, 2001 (http://www.thenewamerican.com/tna/2001/04-09-2001/vo17no08_sade.htm), where it is claimed, among other things, that the Marquis de Sade is 'Communism's little-acknowledged founding father.'

124. All *Pulp Fiction* quotations are from the script by Quentin Tarantino, http://www.godamongdirectors.com/scripts/pulp.shtml.

125. Hibbs, *Shows*, 134–35.

126. Norman Mailer, *The Naked and the Dead* (London: Flamingo, 1993), 91.

127. Nietzsche, *BGE*, 218.

128. Stone, to be sure, acknowledged a Nietzschean side to his film, remarking in an interview that 'It's really about the idea of a superman and the need to control all life and attain true wisdom' (Oliver Stone as quoted in David Williams, 'Analyzing Oliver Stone,' *Film Threat 18*, October 1994, 54.)

129. For a review of *Natural Born Killers* underscoring, as well as praising, the Nietzschean creative authenticity of the film's protagonists, see Heidi Nelson Hoch-

enedel, 'Natural Born Killers: Beyond Good and Evil,' http://www.geocities.com/ Hollywood/2682/heidi1.htm. Hochenedel, however, relates this Nietzschean message to Oliver Stone, the director, without referring to Tarantino.

130. Quentin Tarantino, *Natural Born Killers*, script: http://www.godamongdirectors .com/scripts/killers.shtml.

131. Nietzsche, *Z*, 41–42.

132. Cf. Richard Tithecott's critique of the subgenre's essential failure to deal with the social conditioning of violence, in his *Of Men and Monsters: Jeffrey Dahmer and the Construction of the Serial Killer* (Madison: University of Wisconsin Press, 1997), 7–12.

133. Simpson, *Psych-Paths*, 53.

134. Amy Taubin, 'Killing Men,' *Sight and Sound*, 1.1, May 1992, 16.

135. Bret Easton Ellis, *American Psycho* (London: Picador, 2000), 392.

136. Easton Ellis, *American Psycho*, 378.

137. For an insightful analysis of the novel's critique of capitalist consumerism see Chris Mcmahon, 'Postmodern Evil: Overconsumption in Bret Easton Ellis' *American Psycho*,' *Perspectives on Evil and Human Wickedness* 1, no. 1 (2002): 61–79. ·

138. In Simpson's reading the novel poignantly satirizes cultural elitism: 'Bateman and his peers have artistic pretensions, but only in the self-flattering sense that "art" somehow stands at a critical distance from common culture and thus can only be appreciated by those such as themselves, possessed of sensitivity and refined intellect' (*Psycho-Paths*, 152).

139. Nietzsche, *Z*, 298.

140. Cf. Nietzsche, *WTP*, 17, 316–18. On the concept of nihilism in Nietzsche see, for example, Alan White, 'Nietzschean Nihilism: A Typology,' *International Studies in Philosophy* 14, 2, (1987): 29–44. For a positive reading of Nietzschean nihilism as providing the pluralist affirmation of a post-modern world, see Gianni Vattimo, *The End of Modernity: Nihilism and Hermeneutics in Post-modern Culture* (Cambridge: Polity Press, 1988).

141. Easton Ellis, *American Psycho*, 377.

142. Easton Ellis, *American Psycho*, 394.

143. *American Psycho*, dir. Mary Harron, USA-Canada, 2000.

144. Easton Ellis, *American Psycho*, 375.

145. Easton Ellis, *American Psycho*, 373.

146. Easton Ellis, *American Psycho*, 378.

147. Easton Ellis, *American Psycho*, 378–79.

148. Easton Ellis, *American Psycho*, 282.

149. Peter Handke, *Die Stunde der wahren Empfindung* (Frankfurt am Main: Suhrkamp, 1999), 7.

150. Handke, *Die Stunde*, 16.

151. Handke, *Die Stunde*, 167.

152. Handke, *Die Stunde*, 133.

153. Handke, *Die Stunde*, 166.

154. Handke, *Die Stunde*, 44–45.

155. Handke's vision of crime compares interestingly with that of another important Austrian author, though of an earlier period, Arthur Schnitzler, who, in his short story *The Murderer* (1910), told of a bourgeois male eliminating his devoted,

low-class lover, to clear the path for a high-class marriage. He, too, feels consequentially torn apart, the deed conflicting with his sense of bourgeois respectability: 'Yes, the man who . . . with wanton delight had embraced the lover he was planning to dispatch an hour later, seemed to be completely different from the man who was now drinking his tea, surrounded by familiar walls, in a tranquil, comfortable, bourgeois setting.' And he, too, then recognizes himself, triumphantly, in the killer: 'Yet later on, as he got out of bath and caught his thin, naked reflection in the mirror, he suddenly became aware that it was he himself who had done the inconceivable. He saw his eyes shine with an hard sparkle and felt himself worthier than ever to press the waiting bride to his heart.' (Arthur Schnitzler, 'Der Mörder,' *Erzählungen*, Düsseldorf, Zürich: Artemis & Winkler, 2000, 348). Unlike Handke, however, Schnitzler was by no means content to construe this as a discovery of one's 'authenticity,' taking place in a psycho-existential vacuum. On the contrary, he weaves a social satire targeting the remorseless ambition of the bourgeois protagonist who he is eventually dismissed by his 'gütburgerliche' lover with the same brutal iciness he transitorily prided himself of, and dies thinking of the true lover he has killed.

156. Slavoj Žižek, *Looking Awry—An Introduction to Jacques Lacan through Popular Culture* (London: October Books, 1992), 16–17.

157. Ernst Jünger, *Der Kampf als inneres Erlebnis* (Berlin 1922), 38.

158. Another noteworthy effort at subverting the dominant narrative is Jon Turteltaub's film *Instinct* (1999), which is something of a rejoinder to *The Silence of the Lambs*, even featuring Anthony Hopkins in the psychopath's role. Hopkins plays an anthropologist who returns from a research of wild gorillas in Africa as an irascible aggressor. As the title initially seems to suggest, the prolonged absence from civilization has unleashed the protagonist's murderous drives, his 'instinct.' Yet, as we gradually learn, the very opposite is true: the peaceful animals have taught the scientist a lesson in benignity, which was brutally interrupted by an intruding hunting mission, slaughtering the gorillas. Rousseau is vindicated against Nietzsche, as true, *gentle* instinct is contrasted with the beastliness of culture.

159. Interestingly, however, Hollywood's overwhelming concern with serial killers appears to have produced, outside of America, an identification of American culture and politics as such with this killing-obsession. This has lead, in the context of opposition to a perceived American-controlled 'globalization,' to a refutation of serial killing as an alien, neo-imperialist, typically American phenomenon. A salient example of such trend is the French film *Six-Pack* (2000, directed by Alain Berberian, and based on the novel of the same name by Jean-Hugues Oppel) where the Parisian police is chasing an American serial killer, who is, moreover, a high functionary in the American embassy. Whatever the political merit and use of such view of serial killing as a detrimental American export to be rejected along with McDonald's burgers, it should not allow us to forget the markedly *European* origins of the aesthetics of murder, a tradition in which France, precisely, has figured prominently and consistently, represented by such notables as Sade, Lautréamont, Gide and Genet, to name but a few. There is hence a profound historical irony in the fact that the American disciple has learnt so well from his European master and appropriated the killer so thoroughly as to create in the latter a sense of estrangement from his own cultural tradition.

160. Benito Mussolini, 'Fascism: Doctrine and Institutions,' *Modern European Civilization*, Num. 133–34, 468–69.

161. Nietzsche, Z, 108.

162. Slavoj Žižek, 'The Spectre of Ideology,' *Mapping Ideology*, ed. Slavoj Žižek (London-New York 1994), 6.

EPILOGUE: A HERO OF OUR TIME

1. Mikhail Lermontov, *A Hero of Our Time* (London: Everyman, 1992), 15–16.

2. Geoff Waite, *Nietzsche's Corps/e. Aesthetics, Politics, Prophecy, or, the Spectacular Technoculture of Everyday Life* (Durham & London: Duke University Press, 1996), 355.

3. See, Waite, *Nietzsche's Corps/e*, especially, 291–93, 352–56.

4. Nietzsche, *BGE*, 194.

5. Nietzsche, *KSB* 8, 473–74.

6. As when, on a similar note, he wrote to Malwida von Meysenbug in 1884: 'I wish to force mankind to decisions that will determine its whole future, and it may so happen that at some point whole millennia will make their most solemn vows in my name.' (*KSB* 6, 510).

7. Thomas Mann, 'Nietzsches Philosophie im Lichte Unserer Erfahrung,' in *Gesammelte Werke in Dreizehn Bänden*, vol. IX (Frankfurt am Main: Fischer, 1974), 702.

8. Nietzsche, *GEN*, 19.

Bibliography

1. NIETZSCHE, FRIEDRICH

(References to the abbreviated titles of Nietzsche's works as they are cited throughout the study.)

German Editions:

KSA   *Sämtliche Werke: Kritische Studienausgabe in 15 Einzelbänden*. Herausgegeben von Giorgio Colli und Mazzino Montinari, Berlin, New York: Walter de Gruyter, 1988.

KGB   *Kritische Gesamtausgabe des Briefwechsels*, herusgegeben von Giorgio Colli und Mazzino Montinari, Berlin, New Zork: Walter de Gruyter, 1975.

KSB   *Sämtliche Briefe: Kritische Studienausgabe in 8 Bänden*. Herausgegeben von Giorgio Colli und Mazzino Montinari, Berlin, New York: Walter de Gruyter, 1986.

English Translations

A   'The Anti-Christ,' published with *TI* (see below).

BT   'The Birth of Tragedy,' in *The Birth of Tragedy and The Case of Wagner*, trans. Walter Kaufmann, New York: Vintage, 1967.

BTB   *The Birth of Tragedy and Other Writings*, ed. Raymond Geuss, trans. Ronald Speirs, Cambridge: Cambridge University Press, 2000.

BGE   *Beyond Good and Evil*, trans. R. J. Hollingdale, Harmondsworth: Penguin, 1990.

BGEB   *Beyond Good and Evil*, trans. Marion Faber, Oxford: Oxford University Press, 1998.

CW   'The Case of Wagner,' in *The Birth of Tragedy and The Case of Wagner*, trans. Walter Kaufmann, New York: Vintage, 1967.

D   *Daybreak: Thoughts on the Prejudices of Morality*, trans. R. J. Hollingdale, Cambridge: Cambridge University Press, 1982.

EH   *Ecce Homo*, trans. R. J. Hollingdale, Harmondsworth: Penguin, 1992.

GEN   *On the Genealogy of Morality*, trans. Carol Diethe, Cambridge: Cambridge University Press, 1994.

GK   'The Greek State,' included in *On the Genealogy of Morality*, trans. Carol Diethe, Cambridge: Cambridge University Press, 1994, pp. 176–86.

GS   *The Gay Science*, trans. Walter Kaufmann, New York: Vintage, 1974.

HC   'Homer on Competition,' included *On the Genealogy of Morality*, trans. Carol Diethe, Cambridge: Cambridge University Press, 1994, pp. 187–94.

HUM   *Human, All Too Human*, trans. Marion Faber, London: Penguin, 1984.

HUMB   *Human, All Too Human: A Book for Free Spirits*, trans. R. J. Hollingdale, Cambridge: Cambridge University Press, 1986.

RWB   'Richard Wagner in Bayreuth,' the fourth of Nietzsche's *Untimely Meditations*, trans. R. J. Hollingdale, Cambridge: Cambridge University Press, 1997, pp. 195–54.

SE   'Schopenhauer as Educator,' the third of Nietzsche's *Untimely Meditations*, trans. R. J. Hollingdale, Cambridge: Cambridge University Press, 1997, pp. 127–94.

ST   'David Strauss, the Confessor and the Writer,' the first of Nietzsche's *Untimely Meditations*, trans. R. J. Hollingdale, Cambridge: Cambridge University Press, 1997, pp. 1–55.

TI   'Twilight of the Idols,' published together with *A* (see above) in *Twilight of the Idols and the Anti-Christ*, trans. R. J. Hollingdale, Harmondsworth: Penguin, 1990.

UD   'On the Uses and Disadvantages of History for Life,' the second of Nietzsche's *Untimely Meditations*, trans. R. J. Hollingdale, Cambridge: Cambridge University Press, 1997, pp. 59–123.

WTP   *The Will to Power*, trans. Walter Kaufmann and R. J. Hollingdale, New York: Vintage, 1968.

Z   *Thus Spoke Zarathustra*, trans. R. J. Hollingdale, Harmondsworth: Penguin, 1969.

2. OTHER SOURCES

Adorno, T., and M. Horkheimer, *Dialectic of Enlightenment*. London, New York: Verso, 1999.

Ahmad, Feroz. *The Making of Modern Turkey*. London and New York: Routledge, 1993.

Ang, Ien. 'Feminist Desire and Female Pleasure.' *Camera Obscura* 16, 1988: 179–90.

Anon. 'Lazarillo de Tormes.' *Two Spanish Picaresque Novels*. London: Penguin, 1969.

Ansell-Pearson, Keith. *Nietzsche Contra Rousseau. A Study of Nietzsche's Moral and Political Thought*. Cambridge: Cambridge University Press, 1991.

———. *An Introduction to Nietzsche as Political Thinker: The Perfect Nihilist*. Cambridge: Cambridge University Press, 1994.

Appel, Fredrick. 'Nietzsche's Natural Hierarchy.' *International Studies in Philosophy* Xxix/3, 1997: 49–62.

———. *Nietzsche Contra Democracy*. Ithaca and London: Cornell University Press, 1999.

Aschheim, Steven E. *The Nietzsche Legacy in Germany 1890–1990*. University of California Press, 1994.

Baines, Jocelyn. *Joseph Conrad: A Critical Biography*. London: Weidenfeld and Nicholson, 1967.

Balzac, Honoré de. *Eugénie Grandet*. Harmondsworth: Penguin, 1955.

———. *Old Goriot*. Harmondsworth: Penguin, 1959.

———. *A Harlot High and Low*. Harmondsworth: Penguin, 1970.

———. *Lost Illusions*. Harmondsworth: Penguin, 1971.

———. *The Wild Ass's Skin*. Harmondsworth: Penguin, 1977.

Bennett, Tony. 'The Bond Phenomenon: Theorising a Popular Hero.' *Southern Review* 16, no. 2, July, 1983: 195–225.

Bennett, Tony, Colin Mercer, and Janet Woollacott, eds. *Popular Culture and Social Relations*. Milton Keynes: Open University Press, 1986.

Bentley, Eric. *A Century of Hero-Worship*. Boston: Beacon Press, 1957.

Birnbaum, Antonia. *Nietzsche: Les aventures de l'héroïsme*. Paris: Éditions Payot & Rivages, 2000.

Blackburn, Kevin. 'Commemorating and Commodifying the Prisoner of War Experience in South-East Asia: The Creation of Changi Prison Museum.' *Journal of the Australian War Memorial*, 33, 2000, http://www.awm.gov.au/journal/j33/blackburn.htm.

Blisard, F. X. 'Tarzan versus Tarzan, or, Will the Real Ape-Man Please Stand Up and be Counted? Investigations in American Mythology.' In *The Nubian News. Advocate for the African/Latino Community. Validating the Nubian Perspective*, 2000, http://www.nubiannews.com/archive/2000/feb00/tarzan1.htm.

Blondel, Eric. 'Nietzsche Contra Rousseau: Goethe Versus Catilina?' *History of European Ideas* 11, 1989: 675–83.

Bloom, Allan. 'How Nietzsche Conquered America.' *The Wilson Quarterly*, Summer 1987: 80–93.

———. *The Closing of the American Mind*. New York: Simon and Schuster, 1987.

Bourdieu, Pierre. *Sur la télévision: Suivi de L'emprise du journalisme*. Paris: Raisons d'agir éditions, 1996.

———. *Distinction: A Social Critique of the Judgement of Taste*. London: Routledge, 2002.

Brecht, Bertolt. 'Leben des Galilei.' Pp. 7–109 in *Ausgewählte Werke in sechs Bänden*, Band 2, Frankfurt am Main: Suhrkamp Verlag, 1997.

Bridgewater, Patrick. *Nietzsche in Anglosaxony*. Leicester: Leicester University Press, 1972.

Buch, Hans Christoph. 'James Bond oder der Kleinbürger in Waffen.' Pp. 227–49. in *Der Kriminalroman I. Zur Theorie und Geschichte einer Gattung*, edited by Jochen Vogt, München: Wilhelm Fink Verlag, 1971.

Bukowski, Charles. *Ham on Rye*. Edinburgh: Rebel Inc., 2000.

Bull, Malcolm. 'Where is the Anti-Nietzsche?' *New Left Review* 3, June 2000:121–45.

Burgess, Anthony. 'The James Bond Novels: An Introduction.' 1987. Pp. 1 6 in Ian Fleming, *Casino Royale*. Lonodn: Hodder & Stoughton, 1988.

Burroughs, Edgar R. *Tarzan and the Golden Lion*, http://gutenberg.net.au/ebooks01/0100271.txt.

———. *Tarzan and the Jewels of Opar*, http://www.wwu.edu/~stephan/Tarzan/tarzan05.html.

———. *The Return of Tarzan*. New York: Ballantine Books, 1972.

———. *Tarzan of the Apes*. New York: Signet, 1990.

———. *The Beasts of Tarzan*, http://www.wwu.edu/~stephan/Tarzan/tarzan03.html.

Butte, George. 'What Silenus Knew: Conrad's Uneasy Debt to Nietzsche.' Pp. 271–83 in *Joseph Conrad: Critical Assessments*, vol. IV, edited by K. Carabine, Mountfield: Helm Information, 1992.

Byron. *Don Juan*. Harmondsworth: Penguin, 1973.

———. *The Collected Poems of Lord Byron*. Hertfordshire: Wordsworth Poetry Library, 1994.

———. *Selected Poems*. Harmondsworth: Penguin, 1996.

Calvin, John. *Institutes of the Christian Religion*. McNeil, Battles ed. Philadelphia: Westminster, 1960.

Campbell, Joseph. *The Hero with a Thousand Faces*. Princeton: Princeton Univ. Press, 1968.

Carey, John. *The Intellectuals and the Masses. Pride and Prejudice among the Literary Intelligentsia, 1880–1939*, London: Faber and Faber, 1992.

———, ed. *The Faber Book of Utopias*. London, Boston: Faber & Faber, 2000.

Cervantes, Miguel de. *Teatro Completo*. Edited by F. Sevilla Arroyo and A. Rey Hazzas, Barcelona: Planeta, 1987.

Chandler, Raymond. *The Simple Art of Murder*. New York: Vintage, 1998.

Cheyfitz, Eric. *The Poetics of Imperialism: Translation and Colonization from* The Tempest *to* Tarzan. University of Pennsylvania Press, 1997.

Christle, Patrick Paul. *The Beleaguered Individual: A Study of Twentieth-Century American War Novels*. Dissertation, the University of Tennessee, Knoxville 2001, http://www.drchristle.com/title.html.

Churchil, Ward, and Jim Vander Wall. *Agents of Repression: The FBI's Secret Wars Against the Black Panther Party and the American Indian Movement*. Boston, MA: South End Press, 1990.

Clavell, James. *Shōgun*. London: Hodder and Stoughton, 1975.

———. *King Rat*. New York: Dell Books, 1982.

Conan Doyle, Arthur. *The Lost World & Other Stories*. Hertfordshire: Wordsworth, 1995.

Conrad, Joseph. *The Nigger of the 'Narcissus.'* London: Everyman, 1997.

Conrad, Wolfgang. *Ressentiment in der Klassengesellschaft–Zur Diskussion um einen Aspekt religiösen Bewusstseins*. Göttingen: Verlag Otto Schwartz, 1974.

Conway, Daniel W. *Nietzsche & the Political*. London, New York: Routledge, 1997.

Crowell, Steven G. 'Sport as Spectacle and as Play: Nietzschean Reflections.' *International Studies in Philosophy* XXX/3, 1998: 109–22.

Danto, Arthur. *Nietzsche as Philosopher*. New York: Columbia University Press, 1980.

Defoe, Daniel. *Robinson Crusoe*. Harmondsworth: Penguin Popular Classics, 1994.

Deleuze, Gilles. 'Coldness and Cruelty.' Pp. 7–138 in *Masochism*, Gilles Deleuze, New York: Zone Books, 1991.

Derrida, Jacques. 'Interpreting Signatures (Nietzsche/Heidegger): Two Questions.' *Philosophy and Literature*, 10: 246–62.

Dickens, Charles. *Great Expectations*. Harmondsworth: Penguin, 1996.

Diethe, Carol. *Historical Dictionary of Nietzscheanism*. Lanham, Md. & London: The Scarecrow Press, Inc., 1999.

DiMaggio, Paul. 'Cultural Entrepreneurship in Nineteenth-Century Boston,' *Media Cult. Soc.* 1982, 4:33–50, 303–21.

Drury, Shadia B. *Gurus of the Right*, http://www.uregina.ca/arts/CRC/gurus3.html.

———. *The Political ideas of Leo Strauss*. New York: St. Martin's Press, 1988.

———. *Leo Strauss And The American Right*. New York: St. Martin's Press, 1999.

Duncan, Martha Grace. *Romantic Outlaws, Beloved Prisons: The Unconscious Meaning of Crime and Punishment*. New York: New York University Press, 1996.

Eagleton, Terry. *The Ideology of the Aesthetic*. Oxford: Blackwell, 1990.

Easton Ellis, Bret. *American Psycho*. London: Picador, 2000.

Eco, Umberto. *Apocalittici e integrati*. Milano: Bompiani, 1964.

Eisner, Lotte H. *Fritz Lang*. New York: DaCapo Press, 1976.

Emerson, Ralph Waldo. 'Self-Reliance.' Pp. 145–69 in *The Complete essays and Other Writings*, New York: The Modern Library, 1940.

Emptypockets, Piotr. *The Smurfs: A Communist Threat in Saturday Morning Cartoons*, http://twyla.reallyrules.com/scb.html.

Etter, Annemarie. 'Nietzsche und das Gesetzbuch des Manu.' *Nietzsche Studien*, 1987, 16: 340–52.

Flaubert, Gustave. *Œuvres Complètes : Correspondence: Nouvelle Édition Augmentée. Deuxième Série (1847–1852)*. Paris: Louis Conard, Libraire-Éditeur, 1926.

Fleming, Ian. *Casino Royale*. London: Hodder and Stoughton, 1988.

———. *Dr No*. London: Hodder and Stoughton, 1988.

———. *From Russia with Love*. London: Hodder and Stoughton, 1988.

———. *Live and Let Die*. London: Hodder & Stoughton, 1988.

———. *Thunderball*. London: Hodder and Stoughton, 1988.

———. *You only Live Twice*. London: Hodder and Stoughton, 1988.

———. *Goldfinger*. London: Hodder and Stoughton, 1989.

———. *Moonraker*. London: Hodder & Stoughton, 1989.

———. *The Man with the Golden Gun*. London: Hodder and Stoughton, 1989.

———. *On Her Majesty's Secret Service*. London: Penguin Books, 2002.

Frye, Northrop. *Anatomy of Criticism*. London: Penguin, 1990.

Garrett, Greg. 'Objecting to Objectification: Re-viewing the Feminine in *The Silence of the Lambs*.' *Journal of Popular Culture* 27, 4, Spring 1994: 1–12.

Gay, Peter. *Pleasure Wars. The Bourgeois Experience: Victoria to Freud, Volume 5*. New York, London: W. W. Norton, 1998.

Gerson, Gal. *Liberalism: Texts, Contexts, Critiques*. (Hebrew) Tel Aviv: The Open University, 2002.

Geuss, Raymond. 'Introduction' Pp. vii–xxx in Friedrich Nietzsche, *The Birth of Tragedy and Other Writings*, edited by Raymond Geuss, Cambridge: Cambridge University Press, 1999.

Gheith, Jehanne M. 'The Superfluous Man and the Necessary Woman: A "Re-Vision."' *Russian Review* 55, 2, 1996: 226–44.

Golomb, Jacob. *Nietzsche's Psychology of Power*. (Hebrew) Jerusalem: The Magnes Press, 1987.

Gordon, Philip. 'The Extroflective Hero: A Look at Ayn Rand.' *Journal of Popular Culture* 10, 1976–1977: 701–10.

Gramsci, Antonio. *Selections from Cultural Writings*. Cambridge, Massachusetts: Harvard University Press, 1991.

Greaney, Michael. *Conrad, Language, and Narrative*. Cambridge: Cambridge University Press, 2002.

Grigg, William Norman. 'In Sade's Shadow.' *The New American* 17, no. 8, April 9, 2001, http://www.thenewamerican.com/tna/2001/04-09-2001/vo17no08_sade.htm.

Gunning, Tom. *The Films of Fritz Lang. Allegories of Vision and Modernity*. London: BFI Publishing, 2000.

Hall, Stuart. 'Notes on Deconstructing "the Popular."' Pp. 442–53 in *Cultural Theory and Popular Culture: A Reader*, edited by John Storey, Hemel Hempstead: Prentice Hall, 1998.

Handke, Peter. *Die Stunde der wahren Empfindung*. Frankfurt am Main: Suhrkamp, 1999.

Harris, R. W. *Romanticism and the Social Order 1780–1830*. London: Blandford Press, 1969.

Harris, Thomas. *Red Dragon*. London: Harrow Books, 1993.

———. *Hannibal*. New York: Dell Publishing, 2000.

Harvey, David. *The Limits To Capital*. London, New York: Verso, 1999.

Hašek, Jaroslav. *The Good Soldier Švejk*. London: Penguin Books, 1973.

Hatab, Lawrence J. 'The Drama of Agonistic Embodiment: Nietzschean Reflections on the Meaning of Sports.' *International Studies in Philosophy* XXX/3, 1998: 97–107.

Hayek, F. A. *The Fatal Conceit—The Errors of Socialism*. Chicago: The University of Chicago Press, 1988.

———. *The Road to Serfdom*. Chicago: The University of Chicago Press, 1994.

Hibbs, Thomas S. *Shows About Nothing: Nihilism in Popular Culture from* The Exorcist *to* Seinfeld. Dallas: Spence Publishing Company, 1999.

Hitler, Adolf. *Mein Kampf*. Boston, New York: Houghton Mifflin Company, 1999.

Hobsbawm, Eric. *Bandits*. New York: The New Press, 2000.

Hochenedel, Heidi Nelson. 'Natural Born Killers: Beyond Good and Evil,' http://www.geocities.com/Hollywood/2682/heidi1.htm.

Holub, Robert C. *Friedrich Nietzsche*. New York: Twayne Publishing, 1995.

———. 'The Elisabeth Legend: The Cleansing of Nietzsche and the Sullying of His Sister.' Pp. 215–34 in *Nietzsche, Godfather of Fascism? On the Uses and Abuses of a Philosophy*, edited by. Jacob Golomb and Robert S. Wistrich, Princeton, New Jersey: Princeton University Press, 2002.

Hunt, Lester H. *Nietzsche and the Origin of Virtue*. London, New York: Routledge, 1991.

Hurm, Gerd. 'Of Wolves and Lambs: Jack London's and Nietzsche's Discourses of Nature.' Pp. 115–38 in *Nietzsche in American Literature and Thought*, edited by Manfred Pütz, Columbia: Camden house, 1995.

Irwin, Jones. 'The Cruelty Beyond Cruelty: Deleuze and the Concept of Masochism.' *Perspectives on Evil and Human Wickedness* 1, no. 1, 2002, pp. 51–60.

Jameson, Fredric. *Fables of Aggression: Wyndham Lewis, the Modernist as Fascist.* Berkeley: University of California Press, 1979.

———. The Political Unconscious: Narrative as a Socially Symbolic Act. Ithaca, New York: Cornell University Press, 1981.

———. 'Reification and Utopia in Mass Culture.' Pp. 9–34 in F. Jameson, *Signatures of the Visible,* New York, London: Routledge, 1992.

———. *The Cultural Turn: Selected Writings on the Postmodern, 1983–1998.* London, New York: Verso, 1998.

Joll, James. *Europe since 1870: An International History.* London: Penguin, 1973.

Kaes, Anton. *M.* London: BFI, 2000.

Kaplan, E. Ann. 'Is the Gaze Male?' Pp. 119–38 in *Feminism and Film,* edited by E. Ann Kaplan, Oxford: Oxford University Press, 2000.

Kasson, John F. *Houdini, Tarzan, and the Perfect Man: The White Male Body and the Challenge of Modernity in America.* New York: Hill & Wang, 2002.

Kaufmann, Walter. *Nietzsche—Philosopher, Psychologist, Antichrist.* Princeton, New Jersey: Princeton University Press, 1974.

Kreimeier, Klaus. *Die Ufa—Story: Geschichte eines Filmkonzern.* München: Carl Hanser, 1992.

Kühnl, Reinhard. *Liberalismus als Form bürgerlicher Herrshcaft—Von der Befreiung des Menschen zur Freiheit des Marktes.* Heilbronn: Distel Verlag, 1999.

Lampedusa, Giuseppe Tomasi di. *The Leopard.* London: Everyman's Library, 1991.

Lampert, Laurence. *Leo Strauss and Nietzsche.* Chicago: University of Chicago Press, 1996.

Landa, Ishay. 'Nietzsche, the Chinese Worker's Friend.' *New Left Review* 236, 1999: 3–23.

Lermontov, Mikhail. *A Hero of Our Time.* London: Everyman's Library, 1992.

Levi, Primo. 'Useless Violence.' Pp. 84–85 in *The Drowned and the Saved,* London: Abacus, 1991.

Lindemann, Albert S. *Esau's Tears: Modern Anti-Semitism and the Rise of the Jews.* Cambridge: Cambridge University Press, 1997.

Lipper, Don. 'Dispatches from "Andromeda"—The Nietzscheans.' *Space.com,* 06.05.2000, http://www.space.com/sciencefiction/tv/andromeda_nietzscheans_000505.html.

London, Jack. *The Sea-Wolf.* Oxford, New York: Oxford University Press, 1992.

———. 'How I Became a Socialist.' Pp. 458–61 in *The Portable Jack London,* edited by Earle Labor, New York: Penguin, 1994.

———. *The Iron Heel.* Edinburgh: Rebel Inc., 1999.

Losurdo, Domenico. *Nietzsche, il ribelle aristocratico.* Torino: Bollati Boringhieri, 2004.

Lovell, Terry. *Pictures of Reality: Aesthetics, Politics and Pleasure.* London: BFI, 1980.

Löwith, Karl. *Von Hegel zu Nietzsche: Der revolutionäre Bruch im Denken des neunzehnten Jahrhunderts.* Hamburg: Meiner 1995.

Lukács, Georg. *The Destruction of Reason.* London: The Merlin Press, 1962.

———. *The Historical Novel,* Lincoln, London: University of Nebraska Press, 1983.

Macdonald, Dwight. 'A Theory of Mass Culture.' Pp. 59–73 in *Mass Culture: The Popular Arts in America*, edited by B. Rosenberg and D. White. New York: Macmillan, 1957.

Macdonald, Gina. *James Clavell: A Critical Companion*. Westport: Greenwood Publishing Group, 1996.

Macpherson, C. B. *The Political Theory of Possessive Individualism: Hobbes to Locke*. Oxford: Clarendon Press, 1962.

———. 'Introduction.' Pp. 9–64 in *Leviathan*, Thomas Hobbes, Harmondsworth: Penguin, 1968.

Magnus, Bernd. *Nietzsche's Existential Imperative*. Bloomington, Indiana: Indiana University Press, 1978.

Maguire, Mike, ed. *The Oxford Handbook of Criminology*. Oxford: Oxford press, 2002.

Mailer, Norman. *The Naked and the Dead*. London: Flamingo, 1993.

Malinowski, Stephan. *Vom König zum Führer: Deutscher Adel und Nationalsozialismus*. Frankfurt am Main: Fischer, 2004.

Mandel, Ernest. *Delightful Murder: Social History of the Crime Story*. Minneapolis: University of Minnesota Press, 1984.

Mann, Thomas. 'Nietzsches Philosophie im Lichte Unserer Erfahrung.' Pp. 675–712 in *Gesammelte Werke in Dreizehn Bänden*, vol. IX, Frankfurt am Main: Fischer, 1974.

Mara, G. M., and Dovi, S. L. 'Mill, Nietzsche, and the Identity of Postmodern Liberalism.' *The Journal of Politics* 57, a, 1995: 1–23.

Marx, Karl, and Engels, Friedrich. *The Communist Manifesto*. London: Penguin, 1967.

Marx, Karl. *The Revolutions of 1848. Political Writings Volume I*. Harmondsworth: Penguin, 1993.

———. *Capital-Volume 3*. Harmondsworth: Penguin, 1991.

Marx-Aveling, Edward and Eleanor. 'Shelley and Socialism.' 1888, http://www.marxists.org/archive/eleanor-marx/1888/04/shelley-socialism.htm.

Marti, Urs. 'Der Plebejer in der Revolte. Ein Beitrag zur Genealogie des "höheren Menschen."' *Nietzsche Studien* 18, 1989: 550–571.

———. *Der grosse Pöbel und Sklavenaufstand*. Stuttgart-Weimar: Verlag J.B. Metzler: 1993.

McGilligan, Patrick. *Fritz Lang: The Nature of the Beast*, London: Faber & Faber, 1997.

Mcmahon, Chris. 'Postmodern Evil: Overconsumption in Bret Easton Ellis' *American Psycho*.' *Perspectives on Evil and Human Wickedness* 1, no. 1, 2002: 61–79.

Meiksins Wood, Ellen. *Democracy against Capitalism—Renewing Historical Materialism*. Cambridge: Cambridge University Press, 1995.

Mill, John Stuart. *On Liberty and Other Essays*. Oxford: Oxford University Press, 1998.

———. *Principles of Political Economy*. Oxford: Oxford University Press, 1998.

Nabokov, Vladimir. 'Translator's Foreword,' 1958. Pp. 1–13 in *A Hero of our Time*, M. Lermontov, London: Everyman's Library, 1992.

Nehamas, Alexander. *Nietzsche: Life As Literature*. Cambridge, Massachusetts: Harvard University Press, 1985.

Nies. Betsy L. *Eugenic Fantasies: Racial Ideology in the Literature and Popular Culture of the 1920s*. London: Routledge, 2002.

Niesel, Jeffrey. 'The Horror of Everyday Life: Taxidermy, Aesthetics, and Consumption in Horror Films.' Pp.16–31 in *Interrogating Popular Culture: Deviance, Justice, and Social Order*, edited by Sean A. Anderson, Gregory J. Howard, New York: Harrow & Heston, 1998.

Ortega y Gasset, José. *The Revolt of the Masses*. New York: W. W. Norton, 1952.

———. *Meditations on Hunting*. New York: Charles Scribner's Sons, 1972.

Palmer, Jerry. *Thrillers: Genesis and Structure of a Popular Genre*. London: Edward Arnold, 1978.

Peikoff, Leonard. 'Afterword.' Pp. 696–704 in *The Fountainhead*, Ayn Rand, New York: Signet, 1993.

Pendleton, Thomas A. 'Tarzan of the Papers.' *Journal of Popular Culture* 12, 1978–1979: 691–701.

Peyo. *Le Schtroumpf Financier*. Bruxelles: Editions du Lombard, 1999.

Poulantzas, Nicos. *Political Power and Social Classes*. London, New York: Verso, 1987.

Rand, Ayn. *The Romantic Manifesto: A Philosophy of Literature*. New York: Signet, 1971.

———. *The Fountainhead*. New York: Signet, 1993.

Renaut, Alain. *The Era of the Individual*. Princeton, New Jersey: Princeton University Press, 1999.

Reschke, Renate. 'Die Angst vor dem Chaos. Friedrich Nietzsches Plebiszit gegen die Masse.' *Nietzsche Studien* 16, 1987: 353–81.

Riedel, Manfred. *Nietzsche in Weimar—Ein deutsches Drama*. Reclam Leipzig, 2000.

Rincón, Javier Salazar. *El Mundo Social del 'Quijote'* Madrid: Editorial Gredos, 1986.

Röpke, Wilhelm. *Civitas Humana*. Erlenbach, Zürich, 1946.

Rorty, Richard. 'Postmodernist Bourgeois Liberalism.' Pp. 197–202 in *Objectivity, relativism and Truth: Philosophical Papers, Volume 1*, Cambridge: Cambridge University Press, 1991.

Rosen, Stanley. *The Ancient and the Moderns: Rethinking Modernity*. Indiana: St. Augustine's Press, 2002.

Sand, Shlomo. *Film as History—Imagining and Screening the Twentieth Century*. (Hebrew) Tel Aviv: Am Oved, 2002.

Sanders, Joe. 'At the Frontiers of the Fantastic: Thomas Harris's *The Silence of the Lambs*,' *New York Review of Science Fiction* 39, Nov. 1991: 1–6.

Sattel, Jack W. 'Heroes on the Right.' *Journal of Popular Culture* 11, 1977: 110–25.

Sautet, Marc. *Nietzsche et la Commune*. Paris: éditions Le Sycomore, 1981.

Savramis, Demosthenes. 'Der moderne Mensch zwischen Tarzan und Superman.' Pp. 110–20 in *Comics und Religion—Eine interdisziplinäre Diskussion*, edited by Jutta Wermke, Munich: Wilhelm Fink Verlag, 1976.

Schacht, Richard. *Nietzsche*. London: Routledge & Kegan Paul, 1983.

———. 'Nietzsche and Sport.' *International Studies in Philosophy* XXX/3, 1998: 123–30.

Schmidt, J. Marc. *Socio-Political Themes in The Smurfs* (1998), http://www.geocities .com/Hollywood/Cinema/3117/sociosmurf2.htm.

Schneider, Anatol. *Nietzscheanismus—Zur Geschichte eines Begriffs*. Würzburg: Königshausen und Neumann, 1997.

Schnitzler, Arthur. *Erzählungen*. Düsseldorf, Zürich: Artemis & Winkler, 2000.

Simpson, Philip L. *Psycho Paths: Tracking the Serial Killer through Contemporary American Film and Fiction*. Southern Illinois University Press, 2000.

Sloterdijk Peter. *Die Verachtung der Massen—Versuch über Kulturkampfe in der modernen Gesellschaft*. Frankfurt am Main: Suhrkamp, 2000.

Solomon, Robert C. and Higgins Kathleen, M. *What Nietzsche Really Said*. New York: Schocken Books, 2000.

Solotaroff, Robert. *Down Mailer's Way*. Urbana: University of Illinois Press, 1974.

Spengler, Oswald. *Jahre der Entscheidung. Deutschland und die Weltgeschichtliche Entwicklung*. München: DTV, 1980.

———. *Der Untergang des Abendlandes. Umrisse einer Morphologie der Weltgeschichte*. München: DTV, 1999.

Stepelevich, Lawrence S. 'Max Stirner as Hegelian.' *Journal of the History of Ideas* 4, 1985: 597–617.

Stirner, Max. *The Ego and Its Own*. Cambridge: Cambridge University Press, 1995.

Stock, Robert D. *The Flutes of Dionysus: Daemonic Enthrallment in Literature*. Lincoln and London: University of Nebraska Press, 1989.

Storey, John, ed. *Cultural Theory and Popular Culture: A Reader*. Athens: The University of Georgia Press, 1998.

———. *Inventing Popular Culture*: *From Folklore to Globalization*. Oxford: Blackwell Publishing, 2003.

Strauss, Leo. *On Tyranny*. Chicago and London: The University of Chicago Press, 2000.

Strinati, Dominic. *Introduction to Theories of Popular Culture*. London, New York: Routledge, 1995.

Sullivan, Eileen P. 'Liberalism and Imperialism: J. S. Mill's Defense of the British Empire.' *Journal of the History of Ideas* 44, 4, 1983: 599–617.

Tarantino, Quentin. *Natural Born Killers*. Script, http://www.godamongdirectors.com/scripts/killers.shtml.

———. *Pulp Fiction*. Script, Internet source: http://www.godamongdirectors.com/scripts/pulp.shtml.

Taubin, Amy. 'Killing Men.' *Sight and Sound* 1.1, May 1992: 14–19.

Taureck, Bernhard H. F. *Nietzsches Alternativen zum Nihilismus*. Hamburg: Junius Verlag, 1991.

———. *Nietzsche und der Faschismus–Ein Politikum*. Leipzig: Reclam Verlag, 2000.

Tithecott, Richard. *Of Men and Monsters*: *Jeffrey Dahmer and the Construction of the Serial Killer*. Madison: University of Wisconsin Press, 1997.

Turner, Graeme. *British Cultural Studies: An Introduction*. Second Edition, London and New York: Routledge, 1996.

Twain, Mark. *The Adventures of Huckleberry Finn*. Harmondsworth: Penguin, 1994.

Vattimo, Gianni. *The End of Modernity: Nihilism and Hermeneutics in Post-modern Culture*. Cambridge: Polity Press, 1988.

Verne, Jules. *Twenty Thousand Leagues under the Sea*. London: Everyman's Library, 1996.

Waite, Geoff. *Nietzsche's Corps/e. Aesthetics, Politics, Prophecy, or, the Spectacular Technoculture of Everyday Life*. Durham & London: Duke University Press, 1996.

Warren, Mark., *Nietzsche and Political Thought*. Cambridge, Massachusetts, London: The MIT Press, 1991.

Wells, Herbert George. *When The Sleeper Wakes*. London: Everyman, 1995.

Westphal, Merold. *Suspicion and Faith: The Religious Uses of Modern Atheism*. New York: Fordham University Press, 1998.

White, Alan. 'Nietzschean Nihilism: A Typology.' *International Studies in Philosophy* 14 2, 1987: 29–44.

———. *Within Nietzsche's Labyrinth*. New York and London: Routledge, 1990.

Williams, David. 'Analyzing Oliver Stone.' *Film Threat* 18, October 1994: 52–55.

Williamson, D. G. *Bismarck and Germany 1862–1890*. London, New York: Longman, 1998.

Yovel, Yirmiyahu. *Spinoza and Other Heretics*. (Hebrew) Tel Aviv: Poalim, 1988.

Zeitlin, Irving M. *Nietzsche: A Re-examination*. Cornwall: Polity Press, 1994.

Žižek, Slavoj. *Looking Awry: An Introduction to Jacques Lacan through Popular Culture*, London : October Books, 1992.

———, ed. *Mapping Ideology*, London, New York: Verso, 1994.

———.'Four Discourses, Four Subjects.' Pp. 74–116 in *Cogito and the Unconscious*, edited by Slavoj Žižek, Durham, North Carolina: Duke University Press, 1998.

Zweig, Paul. *The Adventurer*. London: Basic Books, 1974.

3. FILMS (LISTED ALPHABETICALLY BY TITLES)

American Psycho. Dir. Mary Harron, USA-Canada, 2000.

Harry Potter and the Sorcerer's Stone. Dir. Chris Columbus, USA, Warner Bros., 2001.

Ice Age. Dir. Chris Wedge, Carlos Saldanha, USA, Fox Movies, 2002.

Instinct. Dir. Jon Turteltaub, USA, Spyglass Entertainment, Touchstone Pictures, 1999.

M—Eine Stadt sucht einen Mörder. Dir. Fritz Lang, Germany, Nero Film AG, 1931.

Manhunter. Dir. Michael Mann, USA, de Laurentiis Entertainment Group, 1986.

Phenomenon. Dir. Jon Turteltaub, USA, Touchstone Pictures, 1996.

Seven. Dir. David Fincher, USA, New Line Cinema, 1995.

Six-Pack. Dir. Alain Berberian, France, Chrysalide, Alain Sarde, TF1, 2000.

Spider-Man. Dir. Sam Raimi, USA, Columbia TriStar Films, 2002.

Tarzan Escapes. Dir. John Farrow, William Wellman, USA, Warner Studios, 1936.

The Lion King. Dir. Rob Minkoff, Roger Allers, USA, Walt Disney Studios, 1994.

The Silence of the Lambs. Dir. John Demme, USA, Orion, 1991.

When We Were Kings. Dir. Leon Gast, USA, DAS Films Ltd; David Sonenberg Production; PolyGram Filmed Entertainment, 1996.

Index

About the Author

Ishay Landa is a Minerva Fellow at the Technische Universität in Braunschweig, Germany. For several years, he taught history at the Ben-Gurion University, Beer Sheva, Israel, where he obtained his Ph.D. in 2004. He received a number of fellowships, among them from the DAAD (German Academic Exchange Service). His research interests span from history and philosophy to *Ideologiekritik* and pop culture, and he has published essays, for example, on Karl Marx and Friedrich Nietzsche, Martin Heidegger, Fredric Jameson, J. R. R. Tolkien, James Bond, and Mr. Bean. His current postdoctoral research deals with fascism in Europe from 1920 to 1945, its ideology and practice, and the conflicting ways it has been represented since the end of the Second World War.